Lecture Notes in Computer Science 1655
Edited by G. Goos, J. Hartmanis and J. van Leeuwen

Springer
Berlin
Heidelberg
New York
Barcelona
Hong Kong
London
Milan
Paris
Singapore
Tokyo

Seong-Whan Lee   Yasuaki Nakano (Eds.)

Document Analysis Systems: Theory and Practice

Third IAPR Workshop, DAS'98
Nagano, Japan, November 4-6, 1998
Selected Papers

Series Editors

Gerhard Goos, Karlsruhe University, Germany
Juris Hartmanis, Cornell University, NY, USA
Jan van Leeuwen, Utrecht University, The Netherlands

Volume Editors

Seong-Whan Lee
Korea University, Center for Artificial Vision Research
Anam-dong, Seongbuk-ku, 136-701 Seoul, Korea
E-mail: swlee@image.korea.ac.kr

Yasuaki Nakano
Shinshu University, Department of Information Engineering
500 Wakasato, 380-8553 Nagano, Japan
E-mail: nakano@cs.shinshu-u.ac.jp

Cataloging-in-Publication data applied for

Die Deutsche Bibliothek - CIP-Einheitsaufnahme

Document analysis systems : theory and practice ; third IAPR workshop ; selected papers / DAS '98, Nagano, Japan, November 4 - 6, 1998. Seong-Whan Lee ; Yasuaki Nakano (ed.). - Berlin ; Heidelberg ; New York ; Barcelona ; Hong Kong ; London ; Milan ; Paris ; Singapore ; Tokyo : Springer, 1999
(Lecture notes in computer science ; Vol. 1655)
ISBN 3-540-66507-2

CR Subject Classification (1998): I.7.5, I.5, I.4, I.7

ISSN 0302-9743
ISBN 3-540-66507-2 Springer-Verlag Berlin Heidelberg New York

Typesetting: Camera-ready by author
SPIN: 10704062 06/3142 – 5 4 3 2 1 0 Printed on acid-free paper

Preface

Recently, there has been an increased interest in the research and development of techniques for components of complete document analysis systems. In recognition of this trend, a series of workshops on Document Analysis Systems commenced in 1994, under the leadership of Henry Baird. The first workshop, held in Kaiserslautern, Germany, in October, 1994, was chaired by Andreas Dengel and Larry Spitz. The second workshop on Document Analysis Systems was held in Malvern, PA, USA, in October, 1996, chaired by Jonathan J. Hull and Suzanne Liebowitz Taylor. The DAS workshop has been one of the most prestigious technical meetings, bringing together a large number of scientists and engineers from all over the world to express their innovative ideas and report on their latest achievements in the area of document analysis systems.

The papers in this special book edition were rigorously selected from the Third IAPR Workshop on Document Analysis Systems (DAS'98), held in Nagano, Japan, on 4 - 6 November 1998. It is worth mentioning that the papers were chosen for their original and substantial contributions to the workshop theme and this special book edition. From among the 53 papers that were presented by authors from 11 countries at the DAS'98 after critical reviews by at least three experts, we carefully selected 29 papers for this special book edition. Most of the contributions in this edition have been expanded or extensively revised to include helpful discussions, suggestions, or comments made during the workshop. The papers deal with a wide range of research on document analysis systems, such as design principles, theoretical analysis, implementation techniques, and experimental results.

In keeping with the main topics of document analysis systems research, the papers contributed to this special book edition are organized into five sections:

Part I: Document Image Compression and Retrieval

Part II : Document Structure Analysis

Part III: Handwriting Recognition

Part IV: Document Image Analysis

Part V: Document Analysis System

This book is primarily addressed to researchers involved in document analysis systems who wish to increase their knowledge and expertise regarding these topics. It furthermore aims at the audience of those scientists who work in the various disciplines represented in the sections of the book. We would like to express our sincere appreciation to all the contributors and reviewers; this special edition would have not been publishable without them. The reviewers contributed generous amounts of time in the review process. They include H.S. Baird (Xerox Palo Alto Research Center, USA), A. Belaïd (UMR LORIA, France), H. Bunke (University of Bern, Switzerland), Y. Choi (Sookmyung Women's University, Korea), A. Dengel (German Research Center for AI, Germany), D. Doermann (University of Maryland, USA), T. Ejima (Kyushu Institute of Technology, Japan), H. Fujisawa (Central Research Labaratory, Hitachi, Ltd., Japan), J.J. Hull (Ricoh California Research Center, USA), Y. Ishitani (Toshiba Corporation, Japan), J. Kanai (Panasonic Information and Networking Technologies Laboratory, USA), G. Kim (Sogang University, Korea), J. Kim (Yonsei University, Korea), S.H. Kim (Chonnam National University, Korea), F. Kimura (Mie University, Japan), S.-W. Lee (Korea University, Korea), Y. Lee (Yonsei University, Korea), G. Maderlechner (Siemens AG, Germany), Y. Nakano (Shinshu University, Japan), H. Nishida (Ricoh, Japan), A.L. Spitz (Document Recognition Technologies, USA), C.Y. Suen (Concordia University, Canada), M. Suzuki (Kyushu University, Japan), Y.Y. Tang (Hong Kong

Baptist University, Hong Kong), and K. Yamamoto (Gifu University, Japan).

Finally, we would also like to acknowledge all authors and participants of the workshop who facilitated the communication between investigators and created an insightful and stimulating environment. Our appreciation also goes to A. Hofmann, Editor at Springer-Verlag for his patience and help in guiding us through this task. We hope that this book will promote further research in document analysis systems.

August 1999 Seong-Whan Lee and Yasuaki Nakano

Table of Contents

Measuring the Robustness of Character Shape Coding

A. Lawrence Spitz and Paul Marks

Document Recognition Technologies, Inc.
459 Hamilton Avenue, Suite 204
Palo Alto, California 94301, USA
{spitz,marks}@docrec.com

Earlier claims of great robustness for the character shape coding process have been largely unsupported. We provide quantitative measures of the sensitivity of the character shape coding process to the text input, production values and image quality and to the complexity of the destination character shape codes. Using this evaluation tool we can tune the character shape coding process in a systematic way and also develop new versions of the shape codes appropriately adapted to particular applications.

1 Introduction

The process of generating Character Shape Codes (CSCs) encodes only the grossest features of character image size and placement, while ignoring the high spatial frequency features that Optical Character Recognition (OCR) relies upon [1][2]. Because character shape coding is a lossy transform resulting in an ambiguous representation of the characters in the document, it is important that robustness be maintained at as high a level as possible lest the representation become meaningless. The robustness required varies with the particular application, but whether that application is word spotting, language identification, information retrieval or support for word recognition, tolerance for a range of production values and types of noise present in document images is quite important.

Reliance only on gross features of characters reduces the susceptibility to significant noise, distortion and low resolution. In enhancing the representation, we must balance the desired increased specificity (reduced ambiguity) of new character shape code versions with the change in susceptibility to font variabilities and image defects.

We measure robustness by synthesizing text images with particular characteristics and subsequently analyzing these images.

Synthesis involves several steps. We describe some statistics of frequent words and of letter juxtaposition in English and the construction of ground truth appropriate for measuring character shape code accuracy in Section 2. In Section 3, we describe the generation of text images based on this truth information and on typesetting font, face and size variations. Section 4 describes differing forms of degradation based on the types of noise commonly found in document images.

Likewise, image analysis has several aspects. Multiple versions of CSCs are briefly described in Section 5. We compare the character shape coded output to the truth data that have been appropriately transformed into CSCs in Section 6, and show how noise affects performance in Section 7 and the effects relevant to Character Shape Coding in Section 8.

In Section 9 we draw conclusions from the current study and lay out some of the outstanding problems that deserve attention in future work in Section 10.

2 Synthesis

Text image synthesis has two components, signal and noise. The signal is that part of the text image that is under the control of the producer and is the result of the combination of character content and production values. Noise is the degradation of the signal and, in this study, is modeled by inputs to a document image defect model.

We measure the performance of character shape coding under a large number of varying, largely independent, conditions. The variables are shown in Table 1.

Table 1: Variables over which we measured character shape coding accuracy.

Variable	Number of values	Variable	Number of values	Variable	Number of values
Font	17	Spacing	15	Blur	4
Face	3 (nominal)	Resolution	3	Threshold	9
Point size	11	Skew	7	Sensitivity	9

Testing all possible combinations would result in the generation of more than 50 million images and thus make a full analysis impossible. We examine each variable while holding the others constant at an arbitrary, but sub-optimal, level. In other words, we investigate the degradation due to the change of one variable when there is already some degradation from other influences. Thus it is the shape of the curve of degradation that is important rather than the absolute values of accuracy as a function of the variable.

2.1 Ground Truth

The truth file starts out with the English sentence "The quick brown fox jumps over the lazy dog" which contains all the letters of the alphabet. The rest of the truth is based on the analysis of a training corpus of 650,000 words. The truth contains the 63 highest frequency words that together comprise 35% of the words in the corpus while retaining capitalization. That is, **the** and **The** are considered separate words.

The 69 most frequent non blank-containing bigrams and the 90 most frequent trigrams follow. These n-grams represent 72% and 36% of the characters respectively. A text image of the truth file is shown in Figure 1.

3 Production Values

We had a high level of control over the typesetting of the test images.

3.1 Fonts

The fonts studied are shown in Figure 2 and named in Table 3. Proportionally spaced, mono-spaced, serif, sans-serif and script-like fonts are included.

3.2 Faces

There are three faces (Roman, Bold, Italic) represented for most fonts. However, not all fonts are present in all faces, and there are combinations of faces such as BoldOblique which are found only in a small number of fonts.

The quick brown fox jumps over the lazy dog
the and of to a in that I is was for it you with on as be The have
at are by had this not said he we her all they from about an but she
will were or his would so has up out And But which who there their
been me one them do my if can when over people other
th he in er an re on at nd en es or ar te ou it to al ha st ng ti ed
nt ve is as le co se of ne me ll ea ra de ri ro li hi ic io ma om ca
be ce el la il ut ta ch ur ho no pe us un ec ly fo wa si rs et pr ad
the and ing ion ent tio hat her for tha ter ati ver ere ate all you res
ill thi ers com are was wit con eve rea ith out men ear his est hin ons
pro one our ave ive ted nce ove rat ess int ome ica sta oun tin ine not
ant art oul man igh ide ist ste per but ght der hav ect ort cou pre she
tra nte uld ain str wer und ust ell cal era ice hey oth nde ore ind ure

Fig. 1: Text image of the truth file set in 10 pt Times Roman rendered at 300 dpi.

The quick brown fox jumps over the lazy dog
The quick brown fox jumps over the lazy dog
The quick brown fox jumps over the lazy dog
The quick brown fox jumps over the lazy dog
The quick brown fox jumps over the lazy dog
The quick brown fox jumps over the lazy dog
The quick brown fox jumps over the lazy dog
The quick brown fox jumps over the lazy dog
The quick brown fox jumps over the lazy dog
The quick brown fox jumps over the lazy dog
The quick brown fox jumps over the lazy dog
The quick brown fox jumps over the lazy dog
The quick brown fox jumps over the lazy dog
The quick brown fox jumps over the lazy dog
The quick brown fox jumps over the lazy dog
`The quick brown fox jumps over the lazy dog`
The quick brown fox jumps over the lazy dog
The quick brown fox jumps over the lazy dog
The quick brown fox jumps over the lazy dog
The quick brown fox jumps over the lazy dog
The quick brown fox jumps over the lazy dog
The quick brown fox jumps over the lazy dog
The quick brown fox jumps over the lazy dog
The quick brown fox jumps over the lazy dog
The quick brown fox jumps over the lazy dog
The quick brown fox jumps over the lazy dog
The quick brown fox jumps over the lazy dog
The quick brown fox jumps over the lazy dog
The quick brown fox jumps over the lazy dog
The quick brown fox jumps over the lazy dog
The quick brown fox jumps over the lazy dog
The quick brown fox jumps over the lazy dog
The quick brown fox jumps over the lazy dog
The quick brown fox jumps over the lazy dog
The quick brown fox jumps over the lazy dog
The quick brown fox jumps over the lazy dog
The quick brown fox jumps over the lazy dog
The quick brown fox jumps over the lazy dog
The quick brown fox jumps over the lazy dog
The quick brown fox jumps over the lazy dog
The quick brown fox jumps over the lazy dog
The quick brown fox jumps over the lazy dog
The quick brown fox jumps over the lazy dog
The quick brown fox jumps over the lazy dog
The quick brown fox jumps over the lazy dog
The quick brown fox jumps over the lazy dog
The quick brown fox jumps over the lazy dog

Fig. 2: "The quick brown fox jumps over the lazy dog" rendered into 47 font/face combinations.

3.3 Point size

We varied the type size from 2 pt to 12 pt in 1 pt steps.

3.4 Horizontal Spacing

On proportionally spaced fonts we start with the designed pair kerning value and add or subtract space to encourage or discourage the touching of character pairs.

On Courier (the only mono-spaced font in our study) we started with the default character pitch and added and subtracted inter-character space from that value.

3.5 Image Generation

The transformation from the ASCII truth information to an image file is a two step process. First the Aladdin Enterprises `gslp.ps` program, functionally similar to the Adobe UNIX program `enscript`, but modified to give user control over horizontal spacing, is run to produce a PostScript output file. then the PostScript file is rendered into a TIFF bitmap at 300 spi by the Aladdin `gs` (GhostScript) program.

The resultant TIFF images are cropped to within one pixel of the data on all four sides.

4 Image Degradation

We use the Baird image defect model to add different types and degrees of degradation to the synthesized images. Note that we apply the degradation to page images rather than character images as Baird does in his examples. See [5] for a more complete discussion of the types of degradation performed.

The effects of varying several variables are shown in Figures 3 - 7. Threshold and sensitivity are two variables that are not independent. Decreasing threshold and increasing sensitivity both make the image darker.

4.1 Sensitivity

The quick brown fox jumps over the lazy dog

Fig. 3: Increasing the sensitivity behaves much like the reduction of threshold and results in additive noise.

4.2 Threshold

The quick brown fox jumps over the lazy dog

The quick brown fox jumps over the lazy dog

Fig. 4: The effects of low threshold resulting in additive noise and of high threshold resulting in character image degradation.

4.3 Skew

Skew is a common document image defect. Traditional OCRs often recognize individual characters without regard for their positions with respect to the neighboring characters. Character shape coding, on the other hand, is wholly dependent on the knowledge of the baseline and x-line positions in the text line and thus potentially more vulnerable to skew-induced errors than OCR would be. Determining these fiducial lines is a process which must be either tolerant of skew or rely on upstream skew detection and correction. In our implementation we detect and correct skew before attempting to perform character shape coding.

The quick brown fox jumps over the lazy dog

The quick brown fox jumps over the lazy dog

Fig. 5: Image skew of -4 and +2 degrees.

4.4 Blur

The quick brown fox jumps over the lazy dog

Fig. 6: Blur can cause otherwise separate characters to touch.

4.5 Resolution

The quick brown fox jumps over the lazy dog
The quick brown fox jumps over the lazy dog
The quick brown fox jumps over the lazy dog

Fig. 7: Re-sampling the basic image at 300, 200 and 100 spi.

5 Character Shape Coding

Character shape coding ($V_{0\text{-}2}$) has been discussed in a number of previous publications [1][2]. In this paper we will add three new versions, two of which (V_3 and V_5) take advantage of the presence of one or more vertical stems in some ascender characters. V_3 lumps all x-height characters together, providing great robustness in poor images. These coding methods are outlined in Table 2.

Table 2: Character shape coding schemes for alphabetic characters.

<table>
<tr><th>Characters</th><th>V_0</th><th>V_1</th><th>V_2</th><th>V_3</th><th>V_4</th><th>V_5</th></tr>
<tr><td>amorsuvxwz</td><td rowspan="4">x</td><td rowspan="2">x</td><td>x</td><td rowspan="4">x</td><td rowspan="2">x</td><td rowspan="2">x</td></tr>
<tr><td>n</td><td>n</td></tr>
<tr><td>c</td><td colspan="2" rowspan="2">e</td><td colspan="2">c</td></tr>
<tr><td>e</td><td colspan="2">e</td></tr>
<tr><td>ACGIOQSTUVWXYZflt</td><td colspan="3" rowspan="6">A</td><td>A</td><td rowspan="6">A</td><td>A</td></tr>
<tr><td>HMN</td><td>N</td><td>N</td></tr>
<tr><td>bhkL</td><td>b</td><td>b</td></tr>
<tr><td>BDEKR</td><td>E</td><td>E</td></tr>
<tr><td>PF</td><td>P</td><td>P</td></tr>
<tr><td>dJ</td><td>d</td><td>d</td></tr>
<tr><td>j</td><td colspan="6">j</td></tr>
<tr><td>i</td><td colspan="6">i</td></tr>
<tr><td>gpqy</td><td colspan="6">g</td></tr>
</table>

However, space restrictions dictate that in this paper we restrict the results of analysis to V_0 (the most basic version) and V_5 (the most complex) except in the instance of overall performance on various fonts and point size.

6 Analysis

The large number of variables, each of which can take on a large number of values, and the multidimensional nature leads to an overwhelming amount of data and considerable difficulty in isolating the effects of individual variables. In order to work around this complexity, we have adopted a method that might be characterized as serial one dimensional analysis which is analogous to a ridge following algorithm.

We ran initial tests on varying point size on three proportional (one serif, one serif italic and one san-serif) fonts and one mono-spaced. After that we held point size constant and varied only the font.

Since, in this paper, we are only concerned with the accuracy of the character shape coding process, not in the accuracy of determining word shape tokens, for instance, we remove blank characters from both the encoded truth and from the test data. Doing so loses information about incorrectly interpolated spaces and missed spaces, but makes the remaining analysis much easier.

The two strings are compared using the Wagner-Fischer algorithm [6]. We collect information on the insertions, deletions and substitutions between the encoded truth and the output of the character shape coder.

7 Overall Results

7.1 Production Values

In Table 3 we show the accuracy of CSC V_0 through V_5 on all 47 fonts. It is interesting to note that V_5 accuracy, though in general less than V_0 accuracy, approaches it for some fonts. This is a good illustration of how the selection of an appropriate CSC version can enhance the shape coding process. Also note that the inappropriateness of V_5 CSCs for italic fonts is obvious.

Column by column comparisons can yield significant insights. For example, comparing V_3 to V_2 shows the degradation in performance due to the difficulty in detecting the southward concavity that allows us to distinguish a "**n**" from other x-height characters. Likewise V_1 compared to V_0 shows the difficulty of detecting eastward concavity and V_5 and V_3 demonstrate the reliable detachability of the crossbar in an "**e**".

Figures 8 and 9 show the effects of varying the synthesis of the images. We start by selecting a single font and varying the point size. As can be readily seen, above 6 pt, the character shape coding process is very accurate. At 10 pt, it is essentially perfect.

Table 3: Character shape coding accuracy as a function of font, sorted by accuracy on V_0 coding

Font/Face	Accuracy (%)					
	v_0	v_1	v_2	v_3	v_4	v_5
Textbook-Bold	100.0	100.0	100.0	100.0	100.0	100.0
NewCenturySchlbk-Roman	100.0	100.0	100.0	100.0	100.0	100.0
Antiqua	100.0	100.0	100.0	100.0	100.0	100.0
Palatino-Roman	100.0	100.0	100.0	99.8	100.0	99.8
Antiqua-Bold	100.0	100.0	100.0	99.8	100.0	99.8
NewCenturySchlbk-Bold	100.0	100.0	99.8	99.8	100.0	99.8
Textbook	100.0	100.0	97.8	99.8	100.0	99.8
Magazine	100.0	100.0	97.8	99.8	100.0	99.8
Helvetica	100.0	100.0	97.8	93.2	100.0	93.2
Handbook	100.0	100.0	97.8	100.0	100.0	100.0
Courier	100.0	100.0	100.0	89.0	100.0	100.0
Magazine-Italic	100.0	97.3	97.3	89.9	100.0	89.9
Handbook-Italic	100.0	83.2	83.2	88.7	100.0	88.7
AvantGarde-Book	99.8	99.8	99.8	92.9	99.8	92.9
Palatino-Bold	99.7	99.7	99.7	99.5	99.7	99.5
Helvetica-Oblique	99.7	99.7	99.7	88.2	99.7	88.2
Helvetica-Narrow-Bold	99.7	99.7	99.7	92.5	99.7	92.5
Helvetica-Narrow	99.7	99.7	97.5	92.6	99.7	92.6
Helvetica-BoldOblique	99.7	99.7	99.7	90.9	99.7	87.9
Helvetica-Bold	99.7	99.7	99.7	99.2	99.7	99.2
AvantGarde-DemiOblique	99.7	99.7	99.7	91.0	99.7	91.0
AvantGarde-BookOblique	99.7	99.7	99.7	88.4	99.7	88.4
Magazine-Bold	99.5	99.5	99.5	99.2	99.5	99.2
Helvetica-Narrow-Oblique	99.5	99.5	99.5	88.1	99.5	88.1
Handbook-Bold	99.5	99.5	99.4	99.1	99.5	99.1
College-Bold	99.5	99.5	92.9	99.2	99.5	99.2
College	99.5	99.7	92.9	99.4	99.7	99.4
Times-Bold	99.4	99.2	92.5	99.1	99.2	98.9
Helvetica-Narrow-BoldOblique	99.4	99.4	99.4	90.6	99.4	87.6
Bookman-Light	99.2	99.2	99.1	99.1	99.2	99.1
AvantGarde-Demi	98.9	98.9	98.9	97.8	98.9	97.8
NewCenturySchlbk-Italic	98.7	84.6	84.6	87.3	96.1	84.7
NewCenturySchlbk-BoldItalic	98.7	84.6	84.6	87.4	96.1	84.7
Antiqua-Italic	98.7	98.7	98.7	87.3	98.7	87.3
Palatino-Italic	98.6	84.9	85.1	87.1	98.6	87.1
Palatino-BoldItalic	98.4	98.4	98.4	87.1	98.4	87.1
Lazurski	98.4	95.8	95.6	98.1	95.8	95.8
Times-Roman	98.3	98.3	98.1	97.8	98.3	97.8
Times-BoldItalic	98.3	84.1	84.1	86.8	98.3	86.8
Bookman-DemiItalic	97.6	97.6	97.6	90.4	97.6	90.4
College-Italic	95.6	95.6	88.8	84.1	95.6	84.1
Textbook-Italic	95.4	92.8	92.9	83.6	95.4	84.0
Bookman-Demi	95.3	95.3	88.5	94.3	95.3	94.2
Bookman-LightItalic	94.8	95.3	95.1	86.9	91.7	82.5
ZapfChancery-MediumItalic	94.5	90.7	84.4	83.0	90.7	79.7
Advertisement	91.4	91.2	84.4	84.3	91.0	84.1
Times-Italic	89.5	72.6	72.6	78.6	89.5	78.3

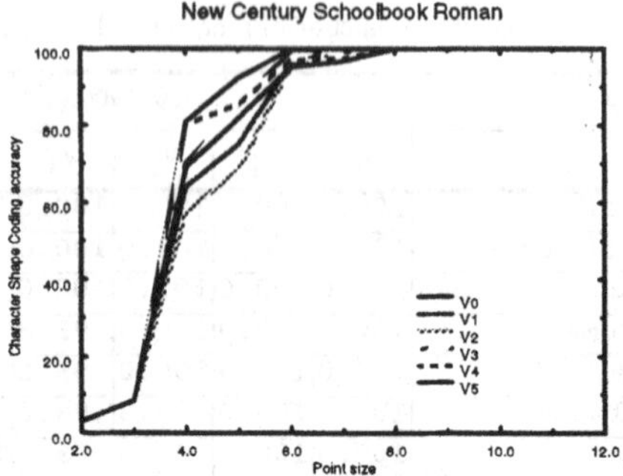

Fig. 8: Effect of point size on character shape coding accuracy.

Referring back to Figure 2, note that the first font shown, `Advertisement`, is designed without descenders, and contains many glyphs comprising multiple connected components where the canonical form has only one (**g,h,n,m,r,u,w**). Clearly this font is inappropriate for shape coding, but as its name indicates, it was not designed for general purpose running text. It is included here to demonstrate the contrast to more traditional fonts.

Varying the horizontal spacing between characters reveals the susceptibility of the font to the generation of unintended ligatures between character pairs. Note that Courier is extremely robust in the face of tight spacing.

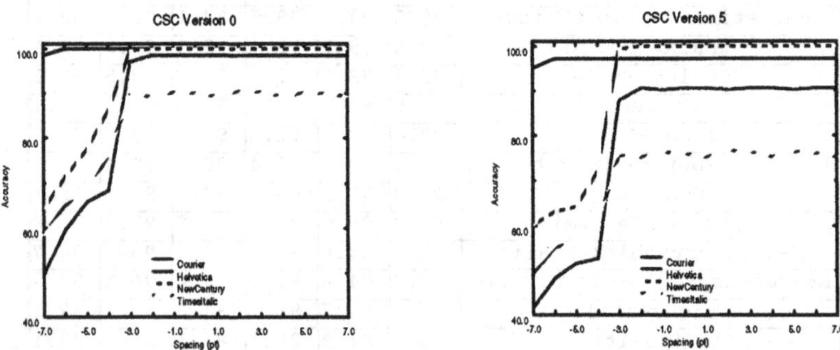

Fig. 9: Spacing (kerning in proportionally spaced fonts) is only important below the threshold where characters start to touch one another.

7.2 Effect of Noise

Figures 10 through 13 demonstrate the effects of adding different types of noise to the signal.

Note that the two CSC versions demonstrate approximately the same response to additive noise induced by a low threshold, while they exhibit different behaviors when a high threshold induces rough or broken characters.

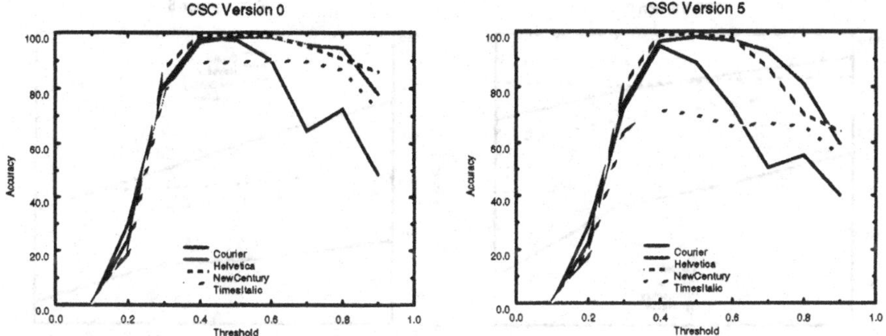

Fig. 10: The effect of varying the threshold on four fonts and two CSC versions

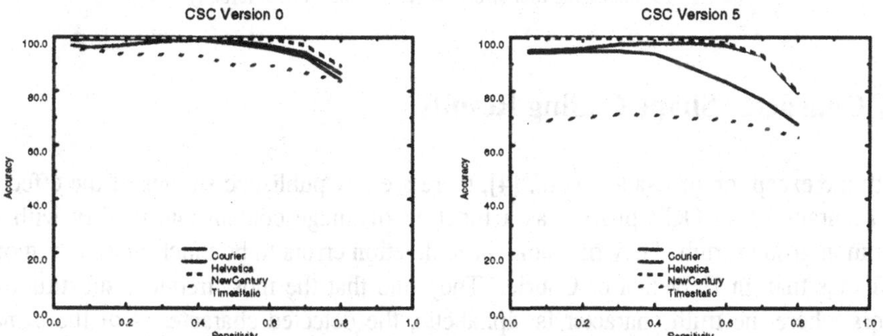

Fig. 11: The effect of varying the sensitivity on four fonts and two CSC versions

The effect of skew on the character shape coding process is minimal, due largely to the skew (and warp) detection and correction incorporated into the process of CSC generation [3].

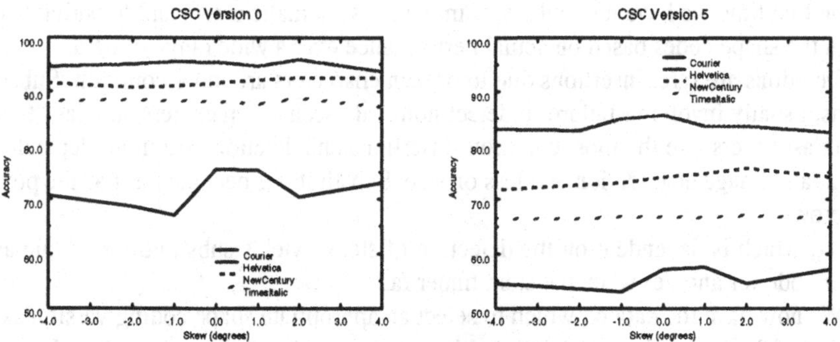

Fig. 12: Skew does not affect accuracy very much.

Courier is much less tolerant of blur than New Century Schoolbook.

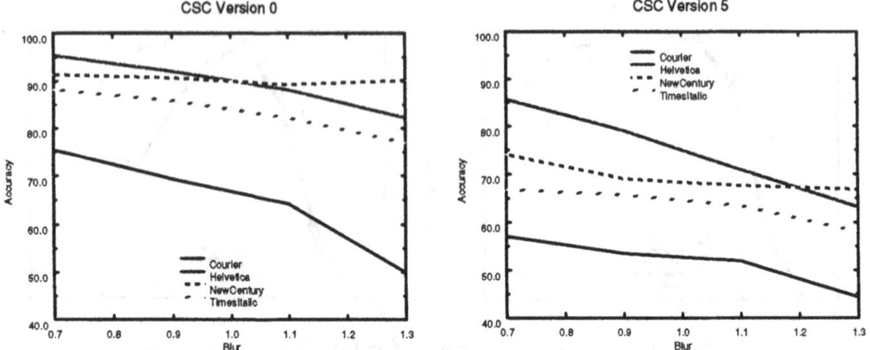

Fig. 13: Increasing blur affects different fonts very differently.

8 Character Shape Coding Results

With the exception of Esakov, *et al.* [4], there are few published studies of the effects on accuracy of an OCR process as a function of image content and quality with a common ground truth. They find non-space deletion errors to be much more common in Times than in Helvetica or Courier. They find that the most frequent substitution errors where the truth character is alphabetic, the detected character is of the same broad shape code class as the truth, i.e. ascenders yield ascenders, x-height yields x-height. An important exception is "**r**" detected as "**t**" for Times. "**e**" is frequently detected as "**c**" for both Times and Courier. For some versions of our shape coding process, this would constitute an error, for others "**e**" and "**c**" map to the same class.

Some characters are more or less susceptible to shape coding errors than others. For the first time we have the tools to examine the systematic errors and to perhaps re-design the shape codes based on actual performance over a wide range of data.

Deletions are rare. Insertions due to broken characters are more common. Substitutions, usually involving failure to detect nominal ascender characters such as "**t**" as having ascenders, are the most common. Insertions and deletions are more dependent on font and image degradation and less on size. Substitutions become rarer as the point size grows.

V_5, which is dependent on the detection of stems, yields substitutions of one ascender code for another when the stem finder fails.

We now have the data on which to select an appropriate shape coding version as a function of the font and generalizations about image quality. It is obvious that V_5 is inappropriate for italic (or oblique) fonts because of the lack of vertical stems. Should it become necessary to process large amounts of italic text, a CSC version could be developed to detect the slanted stems.

9 Conclusions

Developing these techniques for evaluation of character shape coding performance has been a useful exercise in supporting the application of this technology to various classes of problems. In addition, the results of this evaluation have been fed back into the character shape coding process in order to find bugs and to suggest ways of extending the shape coding process.

In the process we have developed three new versions of the CSC set and started to develop guidelines for the application of particular versions for particular applications. The most obvious example of this is the development of a CSC version tuned to Courier. This version is suitable for application to typewritten corpora where Courier is the dominant font.

Recognizing the difficulty of assessing commercial character recognizers, we would like to encourage the study of real OCRs and their sensitivity to font and image quality variables.

Of the four fonts studied in depth, New Century Schoolbook Roman is the most robust in terms of tolerance to changes in production values and image degradation.

10 Future Work

None of the high frequency words, bigrams or trigrams used in this study contains a "`ff`", "`fi`" or "`fl`" character sequence. In our training corpus these character sequences only occurred in 1.3% of the words. However when these sequences do occur and when many proportionally spaced fonts are in use, these character pairs are set as ligatures resulting in a single CSC being generated for two characters of ground truth. Without modification, our current analysis would count this as a deletion error. A more thorough analysis should account for the low frequency occurrence.

The truth on which we tested contains very few capital letters. It contains no punctuation or characters needed to represent languages other than English (e.g.: ä, ô, ñ, ø, å, ß, ç). In order to evaluate text in the languages that use these characters, representative truth files must be developed and images based on this truth must be analyzed.

In this study we ignored the presence or absence of inter-word spaces in the interest of testing only character shape coding accuracy. In the future we will address the problem of word shape token accuracy which will rely on accurate detection of spaces.

Acknowledgments

We appreciate the assistance of Henry Baird in ensuring that our implementation of the image defect model is functionally equivalent to his published model. L. Peter Deutsch modified GhostScript to give us full control over kerning. Daniel Lopresti found a substantive error in an earlier version of this paper and made other useful suggestions.

References

1. A. L. Spitz, "Generalized line, word and character finding", *Progress in Image Analysis and Processing III*. S. Impedovo (ed.), pp. 377-383, World Scientific, (1993).
2. A. L. Spitz, "Text characterization by connected component transformation", *Proc. SPIE*, San Jose, CA, pp. 97-105, (1994).
3. A.L. Spitz, "Analysis of compressed document images for dominant skew, multiple skew and logotype detection", *Comp. Vision Image Understanding*, 70, 3, pp. 321-334, (1998).
4. J. Esakov, D.P. Lopresti & J.S. Sandberg, "Classification and distribution of optical character recognition errors", Proc. SPIE, San Jose, CA, pp. 204-216, (1994).
5. H. S. Baird, "Document image defect models", H.S. Baird, H. Bunke, and K. Yamamoto, eds., *Structured Document Analysis*. New York, Springer-Verlag, pp. 546-556, (1992).
6. R. A. Wagner & M. J. Fischer, "The String-to-String Correction Problem", *J. Assoc. Computing Machinery*, 21,1, pp. 168-173, (1974).

Group 4 Compressed Document Matching

Dar-Shyang Lee and Jonathan J. Hull

Ricoh California Research Center
2882 Sand Hill Road, Suite 115
Menlo Park, CA 94025
{dsl,hull}@crc.ricoh.com

Abstract. Numerous approaches, including textual, structural and featural, for detecting duplicate documents have been investigated. Considering document images are usually stored and transmitted in compressed forms, it is advantageous to perform document matching directly on the compressed data. A two-stage process for matching Group 4 compressed document images is presented. In the coarse matching stage, ranked hypotheses are generated based on compression bit profile correlations. These candidates are further evaluated using a feature set similar to the pass codes. Multiple descriptors based on local arrangement of the feature points are constructed for efficient indexing into the database. Performance of the algorithm on the UW database is discussed.

1 Introduction

As electronic document images become prevalent, efficient retrieval methods become increasingly more important. A common solution is to perform OCR followed by a text based search. Recently, alternatives to the text-based approach have been developed by extracting features directly from images, with the goal of achieving efficiency and robustness over OCR. An example of such a feature is word length. Using sequences of word lengths in documents as indexes, Hull identifies similar documents by comparing the number of hits in each image generated by the query [4]. Spitz maps alphabetic characters to a small set of character shape codes (CSC) which can be used to compile search keys for ASCII text retrieval [10]. CSC's can also be obtained from text images based on the relative positions of connected components to baselines and x-height lines, as used by Spitz for word spotting in document images [9]. Doermann, et. al. extend the application of CSC's to document duplicate detection by constructing multiple indexes using short sequences of CSC's extracted from the first line of text of sufficient length [2]. All of these methods are inherently text-line based. Line, word or even character segmentation need to be performed. The duplicate detection mechanism in DocBrowse is based on horizontal projection profiles [1]. The distance between wavelet coefficient vectors of the profiles represents document similarity. It is noted that this method out-performs the text-based approach on degraded documents and documents with small amounts of text.

Since the majority of document images in databases are stored in compressed formats, it is advantageous to perform document matching on compressed files. Not only does this eliminate the need for decompression and recompression, the reduced memory requirement makes commercialization more feasible. Matching compressed files of course presents additional challenges. For CCITT Group 4 compressed files, *pass codes* have been shown to contain critical information in identifying similar documents. In Hull's work, pass codes extracted from a small text region are used with the Hausdorff distance metric to correctly identify 92.5% of duplicate documents [3]. However, calculation of the Hausdorff distance is computationally intensive and the number of distance calculations scales linearly with the size of database. The computational cost can be reduced by measuring global similarities of pass code distributions. It has been shown that the number of pass codes inside the cells of a fixed grid can effectively retrieve visually similar documents, and can be used as a preprocessing step for the Hausdorff measure [5].

In this paper, we present a two-stage algorithm for duplicate detection of Group 4 (G4) compressed documents. The first stage performs coarse matching based on document profile correlation. Global statistics such as line spacing and text height are used to confine the search space. If multiple candidates are generated, a set of *endpoint* features is extracted from the query document for detailed matching. Similar to the pass codes, the endpoint features contain sufficient information for various levels of processing, including page skew and orientation estimation. In addition, endpoint features are stable, symmetric and easily computable from Group 4 compressed files.

The rest of the paper is organized as follows. Details of the coarse matching processing, including profile extraction, global statistics calculation and feature robustness are discussed in Section 2. Section 3 describes the detailed matching procedure which includes endpoint feature extraction and generation of local descriptors. Section 4 discusses experimental results and suggests further improvements, followed by conclusions in Section 5.

2 Coarse Matching

The coarse matching process retrieves documents based on their profile similarities. Although a horizontal profile does not always contain sufficient information to uniquely identify a document, it is reasonable to assume that duplicate documents should have similar profiles. First, the *compression bit profile* is computed from the G4 compressed query image. Spectral analysis techniques are then applied on the bit profile to generate robust global statistics for database indexing. The precomputed bit profiles of the selected candidates are correlated against the profile of the query image to produce a set of ranked hypotheses. Further processing may be avoided if a highly confident match is found by correlation. Figure 1 summarizes the coarse matching process.

The deterministic nature of G4 encoding leads to the expectation that the same image pattern will produce a similar compression ratio regardless of its location. In general, halftones require the most number of bits for encoding; texts require fewer bits, and background even fewer. For images which are text-dominant and oriented horizontally, the bit profiles should show peaks and valleys corresponding to text lines. For a set of point sizes commonly occurring in documents, the compression ratio for

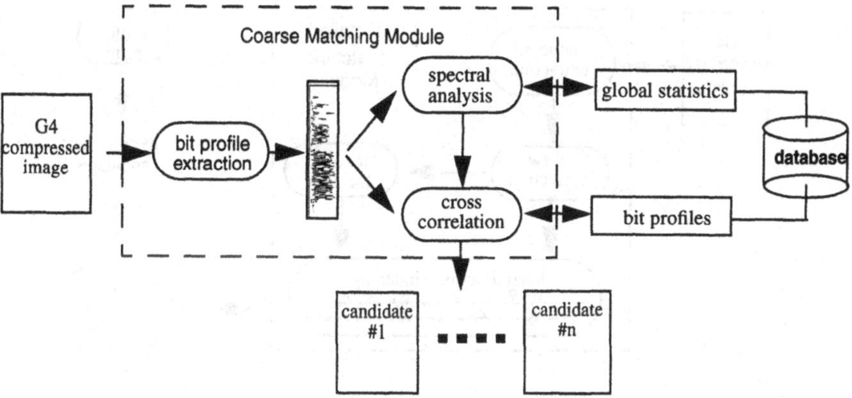

Figure 1: An overview of the coarse matching algorithm. Spectral analysis is first performed on the bit profile to get global statistics for indexing. Profile cross correlations against the selected set of images are used for hypothesis generation.

full page-width text lines is quite consistent, making them distinguishable from halftones, despite the fact that their ink densities may be similar. In contrast to the horizontal projection of ink density, the bit profile shows where the information really is. Large black regions often encountered at edges of photocopied documents will have almost no effect on the bit profile, whereas large peaks will be produced in an ink density profile. In fact, the bit profile will not look much different if the page is in reverse video. Obviously, this would be a serious disadvantage if large black regions carry significant meanings as in, for example, tables and forms.

Cross correlation is used to measure similarities between profiles. Global characteristics of profiles can be used to reduce the number of distance calculations. The periodic nature of bit profiles suggests spectral properties will be more useful than statistical moments. Intuitively, the dominant line spacing, the number of text lines and the location of text provide a good first-level characterization of a document. The dominant line spacing can be directly calculated from the highest peak in the power spectrum density. Although spectral analysis does not provide a quantitative measure of the number of text lines, the energy under the peak frequency is a good indication of the amount of text on the page. To estimate the location of the text lines, we apply a bandpass filter, centered at the dominant line spacing frequency, to the profile. The filtered signal will have large amplitude at text locations. Sections of the profile which are linear in phase correspond well to text blocks. We use the centroid of this text energy profile and the width of the 90% energy span as an estimation for text location and concentration. These two numbers, along with peak frequency and total text energy, are used to define a search window in the space of database images.

3 Detailed Matching

Since visually different documents can have similar compression profiles, a second

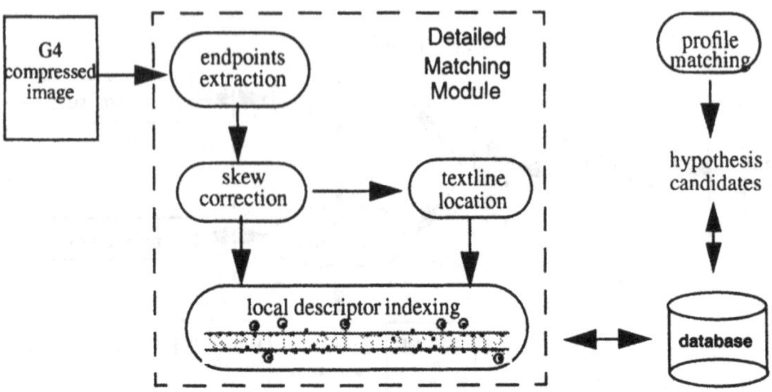

Figure 2: Summary of the detailed matching process. Skew corrected endpoint features in the ascender and descender regions are used for document indexing.

stage process may be necessary to resolve any ambiguities. To obtain more information, a set of *endpoint features* similar to pass codes is extracted from the G4 image. After feature analysis, a subset of these features are identified as markers. Descriptors based on the positions of these markers are generated for document indexing. Cross validation is carried out against document candidates provided by the coarse matching procedure. This process is illustrated in Figure 2.

3.1 Endpoint Extraction

In the Group 4 compression format [6], each scan line is encoded with respect to the line above. The starting points for two consecutive runs, referred to as *changing elements,* on both lines are identified at any time with respect to the current encoding point, a_0. Based on the relative positions among these *changing elements*, one of three possible modes, *horizontal*, *vertical* or *pass* mode, is selected for encoding. After encoding, a_0 is moved forward and the process is repeated. The process is reversed during decoding. Therefore, the *mode* information is decoded first, but positions of the changing elements are also maintained at all times.

It has been noticed that pass codes occur at locations corresponding to "bottoms of strokes" (*white pass*) or "bottoms of holes" (*black pass*). For Roman alphabets, these feature points occur at the end of a downward vertical stroke or the bottom of a curved stroke. The alignment of these pass codes near baselines and the structural information they carry make them very useful in a variety of tasks such as skew estimation[8] and text matching [3]. Equally important is the fact that they can be extracted easily from a G4 compressed file.

While pass codes are very informative, they have some drawbacks. First of all, they are unstable in the sense that while all *white pass* codes correspond to *bottoms of strokes*, not all *bottoms of strokes* will be represented by pass codes. As a result of the context-dependent nature of G4 encoding *modes*, identical local patterns of changing elements can be encoded as a pass code or part of a horizontal mode. Another limitation of pass codes is that they are asymmetric. While the bottom of a stroke or a hole is captured, there is no information about the top of the stroke or hole. For example, the bottom of a "d" often contains two pass codes, one white and one black, while no feature point on the top of the character is captured.

Based on these observations, we propose extraction of *endpoint* features directly from the changing elements. There are two sets of endpoints: *up* and *down* endpoints. *Down* endpoints are bottoms of strokes, the same as what white pass codes capture. However, they are extracted by directly comparing the positions of changing elements, eliminating the possibility of obscurity by horizontal encoding. All bottoms of strokes are *down* endpoints and vice versa. The tops of strokes are similarly extracted as *up* endpoints. Since endpoints are detected based on relative positions of changing elements, they are as easy to calculate as pass codes. Figure 3 shows an image segment and its corresponding endpoints. It is apparent that *down* endpoints align at the baseline while *up* endpoints align at the x-height line. This allows for information such as text height, page orientation and ascenders to be extracted. The symmetric nature of the *up* and *down* endpoints is also beneficial in dealing with inverted pages. If the page is inverted, the endpoints for the correctly oriented page can be obtained by switching the *up* and *down* endpoints followed by a simple coordinate remapping. There is no need for rescanning the compressed document.

3.2 Document Indexing

Following feature extraction, we convert the two dimensional endpoint information to a one dimensional representation for efficient indexing. Several simple steps are involved in this process. First, page skew is estimated and corrected using a process similar to that described by Spitz [8]. The smoothed horizontal projection profiles for the skew corrected *up* and *down* endpoints, which will be referred to as *U* profile and *D* profile, are used to locate text lines. Since x-height lines must be above their corresponding base lines, the *D* profile must lag behind the *U* profile. We calculate the maximum correlation between the U profile and D profile within an offset constrained by the dominant line spacing, which is obtained from spectral analysis of the profiles. In the correlated profile, wherever a local maximum in the *U* profile matches up with a local maximum in the *D* profile, separated by a distance equal to text height, there is a good possibility that a text line is located.

Given a set of text line locations, the endpoints within each textline zone are extracted. Since we also have the x-height line and baseline location, we can define the ascender and descender zones. With well-defined reference lines, there are several possibilities to encode endpoints as sequences. We observed that endpoints occurring inside the x-height zone are more susceptible to noise due to touching, fragmentation, serifs and font style variations. Therefore, endpoints in the middle zones are ignored. Only up endpoints above the x-height line and down endpoints below the baseline are used as markers. We use sequences of quantized distances between consecutive markers as descriptors. Negative values are used for distances between down endpoint markers to distinguish them from those of up endpoint markers. The left-most endpoint in each text line region is used as a reference point. To maintain the two dimensional structure, descriptors across text lines are concatenated, separated by a 0. Hence, a string of positive and negative values will be generated for given lines of text, as shown

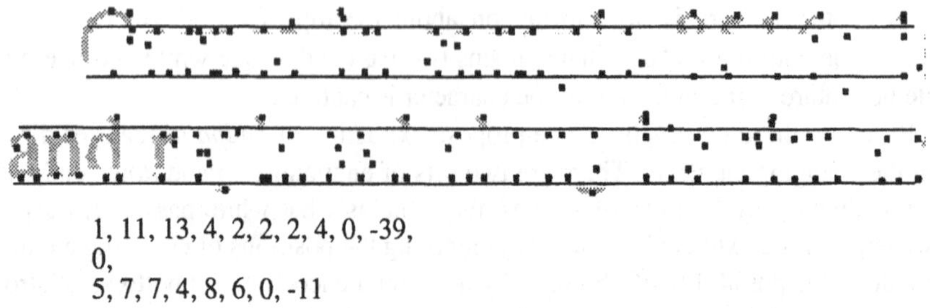

Figure 3: An example of endpoints within a two text line region. Endpoints in the ascender and descender zones are used as markers for index generation.

at the bottom of Figure 3. Alternatively, marker distances in the ascender and descender zones can be interleaved in strictly left to right order. However, similar performances are observed.

Each document in the database is reverse indexed by sequences of n consecutive distances. Similarly, k sequences of n consecutive distances are formed during a test query. The weight for each descriptor is inversely proportional to the number of documents it indexes. Suppose n is 5 in the example of Figure 3, then k=15 sequences S_1=(1, 11, 13, 4, 2), S_2=(11, 13, 4, 2, 2), S_3=(13, 4, 2, 2, 2) ... S_{15}=(4, 8, 6, 0, -11) will be generated. Each of the k sequences, S_i, contributes a score of $1/(k*m_i)$ to every one of the m_i documents that S_i indexes. Documents that receive scores greater than a threshold are returned. Clearly, large n values will produce fewer, more unique descriptors. However, longer sequences are also more susceptible to disruption by noise.

4 Results and Discussions

Experiments are conducted on a set of 979 document images from the University of Washington (UW) database [7]. Of the 979 images, 292 images (146 pairs) have a matching counterpart. Each of the 292 images is used as a query for retrieving its counterpart from the remaining 978 images. The coarse and detailed matching procedures were tested independently as well as in combination. Results on each experiment will be presented.

In our implementation of the coarse matching algorithm, the original bit profile obtained at the vertical image resolution is down sampled by averaging to 36 dpi. Thus we produce 396 bytes (11 inch x 36 dpi x 8 bits) of data for a typical 8.5"x11" page. Cross correlation of the bit profiles produced 86.0% correct on top choice, and 95.2% correct on top 20 choices. Using the global statistics for indexing, the average number of candidates for cross correlation calculation is reduced by 90% without any loss in the recall rate. The Discrete Fourier Transforms of the bit profiles for images in the database are precomputed and stored, so cross correlation can be calculated by a vector product. Therefore, each image query involves extracting the bit profile, filtering by global statistics, followed by approximately 100 vector products of dimension 396.

In the detailed matching experiment, endpoints were extracted from a 1.5 by 1 inch region from the first body of text in the image using the ground truth information. The text line location algorithm was then applied to detect endpoints in the ascender and descender zone. Although some of those regions contained non-text portions of the image, we relied on the line location algorithm to eliminate any feature points not belonging to textlines. Once the ascender and descender zones were defined, a sequence of distances between endpoint markers was generated for each patch. Taking every 3, 4, and 5 consecutive distances as an index, multiple descriptors were constructed for a database query. Using the weighting scheme described above, 92.5% of the duplicates are correctly detected. This performance is comparable to the computationally intensive Hausdorff distance based method [3]. In addition, the indexing approach has much greater scalability than the distance based strategy.

In the combined test, we return the result of the coarse match if the correlation score of the top choice is greater than 0.85 and the difference between the top and second choice score is more than 0.03. Otherwise, the top twenty choices are passed on for detailed matching. As a result, 70% of the images are accepted after coarse matching, and only 30% of the images require detailed matching. The overall correct rate for the system is 93.8%. Therefore, coarse matching by profile correlation not only improves execution efficiency but also eliminates candidates which otherwise would be confused by detailed matching alone. Clearly, different results will be achieved by modifying the decision rule. We have not taken into account the problem of false alarm in our performance analysis. The effectiveness of the combination rule is contingent upon the assumption that we expect exactly one duplicate for each query. Lacking such restrictions, as in most practical cases, the detailed matching should always be invoked to improve the reliability of detection.

Since realistic timing of our prototype, which consists of research code written in C, Perl and Splus, is difficult, we provide a speed analysis based on hypothetical situation of a single query into a database containing one million documents. At 8 minutes per 978 images for optimized C code running on a 70MHz Sparc20 [3], one million Hausdorff distance calculation would require one week of CPU time. For the proposed method, assuming the same 90% reduction is achieved by global statistics of document profile, correlation on 100,000 images is required, which would take approximately 2 seconds on the Sparc20. Adding on the time required for endpoints extraction, skew correction and indexing for the query mage, we estimate the overall time to be around 5 seconds, roughly 5 orders of magnitude improvement in speed.

We analyzed the errors made by both stages of the system and found few surprises. Excluding errors introduced by scale differences and non-linear distortions, which can not be handled by the proposed method, the most common errors resulted from skewed images and misaligned columns. Page rotation has the effect of locally averaging horizontal projection profiles, making the peaks and valleys less prominent. Without any estimate or correction for page rotation, the coarse matching algorithm has no correction for document skew. Although text line location, based on horizontal profiles of skew corrected feature points, is skew tolerant, it has difficulty handling multicolumn pages. Non-colinear columns can lead to aliasing and incorrect line spacing estimation and text line location.

Several improvements, which are subject to further research, are possible. The skew corrected endpoint projection profile, which is used for text line location, displays similar characteristics to the bit profile, and it can be used for coarse matching. However, endpoint profiles are spiky and the results are sensitive to the smoothing parameters. To improve the robustness of text line location in documents with non-colinear columns, one solution is to use a vertical projection profile for column segmentation. Another solution is to perform text line location within vertical slices of the document, and use only the high confidence results in hope of avoiding column boundaries. Obviously, such analysis is still vulnerable to documents with complex layouts. Moreover, spurious feature points occurring beyond text line boundaries can generate false descriptors. Some measures for detecting the horizontal extent of text lines should be provided. Since the feature points have been skew corrected and the positions of the x-height lines and baselines are known, finding the ends to such line segments should be relatively trivial. Furthermore, the regions for descriptor generation should be automatically determined. In our experiment, we used ground truth information for identifying corresponding text regions in document images. This registration process should be replaced by an automatic region selection scheme. Generating descriptors for every located text line will increase the database size and reduce precision. Some criteria for identifying candidate regions should be investigated. One possibility is to base the selection on local feature point densities.

5 Conclusions

We described a two-stage process for detecting duplicate documents in Group 4 compressed images. Coarse matching generates ranked hypotheses based on profile similarities. Global statistics obtained from spectral analysis of profiles can be used to confine the search space. If no high confidence match is found, multiple candidates are further evaluated by a detailed matching process utilizing a set of endpoint features directly computable from the Group 4 decompression scheme. Descriptors based on sequences of distances between endpoint markers provide efficient indexing to the database. Experiments on the UW database showed 93.8% correct rate in detecting duplicates.

References

1. V. Chalana, A. Bruce, and T. Nguyen, "Duplicate document detection in DocBrowse", SPIE Conference on Document Recognition V, pp. 169-178, 1998.
2. D. Doermann, H. Li, O. Kia and K. Kilic, "The Detection of Duplicates in Document Image Databases", Technical Report CS-TR-3739, University of Maryland, 1997.
3. J. J. Hull, "Document Matching on CCITT Group 4 Compressed Images", SPIE Conference on Document Recognition IV, pages 82-87, 1997.
4. J. J. Hull, "Document image matching and retrieval with multiple distortion-invariant descriptors", Proceedings of DAS, pages 383-400, 1994.

5. J. J. Hull, “Document image similarity and equivalence detection”, International Journal on Document Analysis and Recognition, Vol. 1, No. 1, pp.37-42, 1998..
6. R. Hunter, A. H. Robinson,” International Digital Facsimile Coding Standards,” Proceedings of the IEEE, Vol. 68, No. 7, pp. 854-867, 1980.
7. I. T. Phillips, S. Chen, R. M. Haralick, “CD-ROM document database standard”, Proceedings of the 2nd ICDAR, pp. 478-483, 1993.
8. A. L. Spitz, “Skew determination in CCITT group 4 compressed document images,” Proceedings of SDAIR, pp. 11-25, 1992.
9. A. L. Spitz, “Using character shape codes for word spotting in document images”, Shape, Structure and Pattern Recognition, pages 382-389. World Scientific, 1995.
10. A. L. Spitz, “Using character shape coding for information retrieval”, Proceedings of the 4th ICDAR, pp. 974-978, 1997.

Restoration of Decorative Headline Images for Document Retrieval

Tomio Amano

IBM Research, Tokyo Research Laboratory, 1623-14, Shimotsuruma, Yamato-shi, Kanagawa-ken 242, Japan

Abstract. This paper describes a method for restoring decorative character images in headlines of newspapers and magazines. Although headlines contain useful keywords for document retrieval, conventional OCRs cannot always recognize them because the characters are often printed in reverse and with various background textures. We made filters that generate multiple candidate images by changing a small number of simple parameters (namely, by setting a threshold for stroke-width filtering and reversing black and white), so that one of the candidates contains a "normal" image whose characters are printed in black on a white background. If all the candidate images are recognized and an index is created, the keywords in headlines are expected to be retrieved without manual keyword entry and verification processes. In an experiment that we conducted, about 90% of characters in headline images segmented from newspapers were restored in the sense that one of the restored candidate images contained correct character images.

1 Introduction

Entry of existing paper documents is still an obstacle to the widespread adoption of electronic document management systems. Various efforts have been made to improve the accuracy of document layout analysis and character recognition. Recently, the focus has shifted to a different approach based on the functions required by applications. For example, Chen et al. [1] proposed a system for summarizing documents on the basis of images instead of coded text, which can eliminate the workload of verifying and correcting for OCR results. Senda et al.[2] investigated a retrieval scheme, related to document query by keyword, that uses multiple candidates of character segmentation and recognition results. These studies showed that the complete results of document analysis are not always necessary to meet an application's requirements.

In this paper, we investigate a method for restoring decorative headline images that follows the multiple candidate approach. Headlines in newspapers and magazines contain useful keywords for retrieval. However, conventional OCRs cannot recognize the characters, because headlines are often printed in reverse and with background textures. To deal with such decorative images, a preprocess that restores "normal images[3, 4, 5] and recognition algorithm that is not affected by the decorations [6] have been proposed. We think the former is superior in that it can be easily incorporated into existing systems. Our purpose is to make the preprocess approach more robust and flexible by using the multiple candidates. To generate the candidate images, we have developed a stroke-width filter whose the results are independent of the accuracy of the preceding layout analysis process and any heuristics. The behavior of the filter is defined by a small number of parameters. We generated candidate images from 50 actual newspaper headlines, varying the parameters, and recognized them by using OCR software, to confirm that they include proper images.

The rest of this paper is organized as follows: Section 2 describes an document retrieval system, and the required properties of an image-restoring method. Section 3 explains the mechanism of our stroke-width filter. Experimental results for 50 headline images are given in section 4. In section 5, we discuss the validity of the approach and possible future enhancements.

2 Image restoration for document retrieval

Figure 1 shows the assumed process flow of keyword registration using multiple candidates. First, layout analysis is applied to an input image and headline areas are segmented. For each headline image, multiple candidates (including the original image) for restored images are generated. Every candidate image is processed by a conventional OCR subsystem, and all the recognition results are used to make an index. A query word will be matched with the index. The registration tasks are performed without any manual processes for verifying and correcting the OCR results, and consequently the cost of document registration is reduced.

In view of the automated flow, the restoration method should work independently of fluctuations in the results of the preceding layout analysis. Some prior restoring algorithm normalize the image with respect to the font width or height, or extract features from the image to examine the properties of the background. The results will vary according to variations in the input, whether or not neighboring headline areas are segmented separately. If two headlines with different font sizes and different background textures are segmented as a single area (strict separation is sometimes difficult), the restoration process fails. To generate candidates for a restored image, we adopted a simple and stable algorithm rather than an intelligent and autonomous one.

3 Generating candidate images for restoration

Figure 2 shows example of decorative character images. Character strokes are represented by black lines on white, white lines on black, or outlines. The background texture is not always uniform: Sometimes only part of the background is textured, the texture changes gradually. To deal with such variations, two filtering processes based on morphological operations are used in combination with black-and-white reversal.

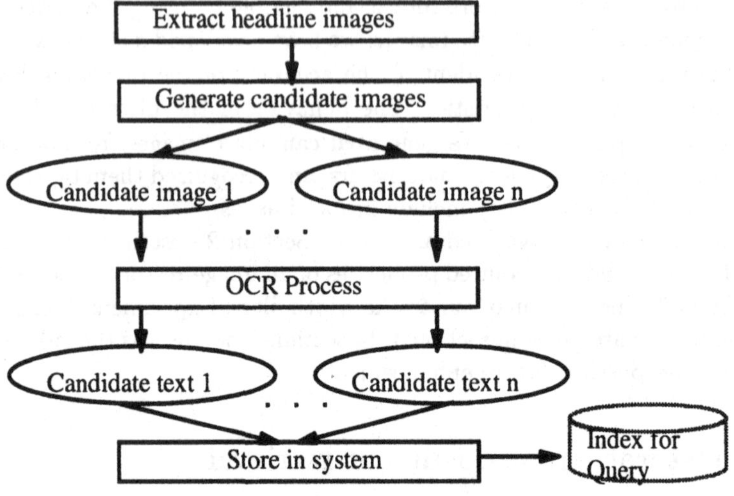

Fig. 1. Registration of headlines for information retrieval.

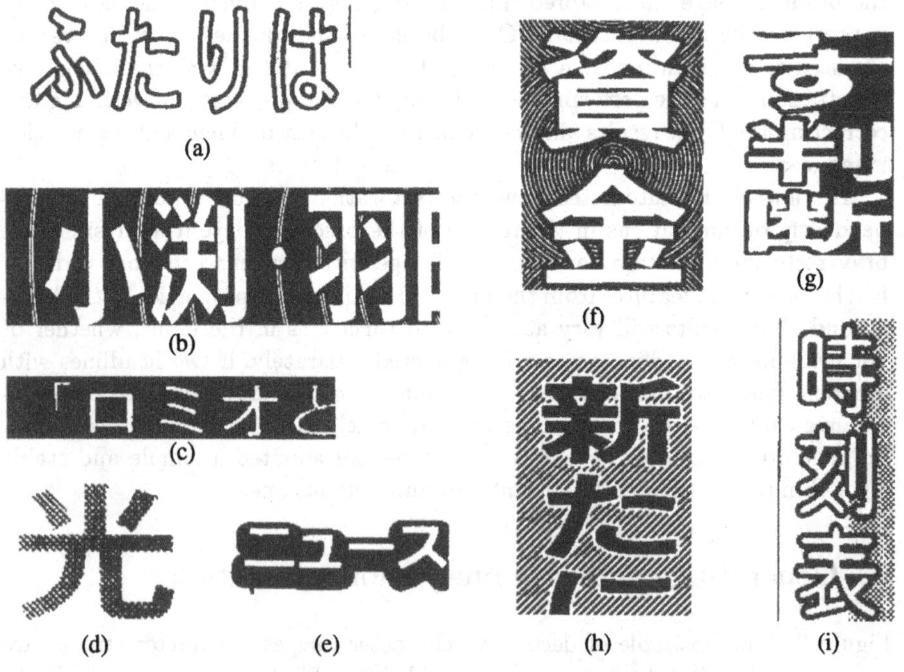

Fig. 2. Examples of decorative headline images.

1. Stroke-width filtering
2. Blurring by means of a closing operation

Since the widths of character strokes are greater than those of lines in background texture, a stroke-width filter can extract foreground character images if an appropriate range of stroke widths is given. Blurring is effective for recovering cases in which character strokes are painted with texture e.g., Figure 2(d)).

3.1 Stroke-width filters

To describe the structure of the filters, let us define some primitive operators and procedures. Opening operators O_n^h and O_n^v erase horizontal and vertical black runs when the lengths are less than a threshold value n. Closing operators C_n^h and C_n^v replace horizontal and vertical white runs with black runs when their lengths are less than a threshold value n. Let I be an original image; $O_n^h(I)$ means an opened image. Pixel-wise operators $\vee, \wedge, and \oplus$ are used to represent OR, AND, and exclusive OR, respectively. Using this notation, selection operators that extract black runs whose lengths are within a specified minimum value m and maximum value n are defined.

$$S_{m-n}^h(I) \equiv O_m^h(I) \oplus O_{n+1}^h(I) \tag{1}$$

$$S_{m-n}^v(I) \equiv O_m^v(I) \oplus O_{n+1}^v(I) \tag{2}$$

Two relaxation procedures $RP_1(S, D)$ and $RP_2(S, D)$ are used to investigate the connectivity of black runs between a source image S and a destination image D. If a run in S is judged to belong to D, the run is moved to D from S. The pseudo-code of the procedures is shown in Figures 3.

A stroke-width filter is constructed on the basis of the operators and the procedures according to following three steps (Figure 5 shows intermediate results).

Step 1: Three intermediate images, – a candidate for the characters, C, a candidate for the background, B, and unclassified image, U – are generated from the original input image I. First, C is generated by extracting horizontal and black runs by minimum and maximum values of the width, m and n, which are given as parameters.

$$C \leftarrow S_{m-n}^h(I) \vee S_{m-n}^v(I) \tag{3}$$

The difference between I and C is set to U.

$$U \leftarrow I \oplus C \tag{4}$$

A background image is generated as areas which both the widths and heights are greater than the maximum stroke width n.

$$B \leftarrow O_{n+1}^h(U) \wedge O_{n+1}^v(U) \tag{5}$$

Step 2: Relaxation procedures $RP_1(U, C)$ and, $RP_1(B, C)$ are used to recover runs that step 1 failed to extract as parts of foreground characters. Each black run in U and B is moved to C if it is connected to more than a threshold number of pixels in C.

```
Relaxation process RP1(S, D)
{
 Perform the following processes until no run is moved {
  Raster-scan S for each observed run Rs {
   Investigate the preceding and next scan lines of Rs in D.
    Count the number of pixels (N) connected to Rs.
    If the corresponding area of the next line is filled
    with pixels belonging to S, the following scan line
    is investigated instead.
   if ((Rs is horizontally connected to D
   and N ≥length of Rs + 1)/2 ) or N ≥ length of Rs ) {
    Move Rs from S to D.
   }
  }
 }
}

Relaxation process RP2(S, D)
{
 Perform the following processes until no run is moved {
  Raster-scan S for each observed run Rs {
   Investigate the preceding and next scan lines of Rs in D.
    Count the number of pixels (N) connected to Rs.
   if ((Rs is horizontally connected to D
   and N ≥(length of Rs + 1)/2 ) or N ≥ length of Rs ) {
    Move Rs from S to D.
   }
  }
 }
 Perform same the same processes the changing main scanning direction {
  :
 }
}
```

Fig. 3. Pseudo-code for the relaxation procedures

Step 3: In contrast to step 2, the following procedures are used to screen out surplus runs in C:

$$RP_2(C, B) \tag{6}$$

$$RP_2(U, B) \tag{7}$$

$$B \leftarrow O_m^h(O_m^v(B)) \tag{8}$$

$$RP_2(C, B) \tag{9}$$

Figure 4 shows examples of the restoration of stroke-width filtering for several conditions of black-and-white reversal and ranges of stroke width.

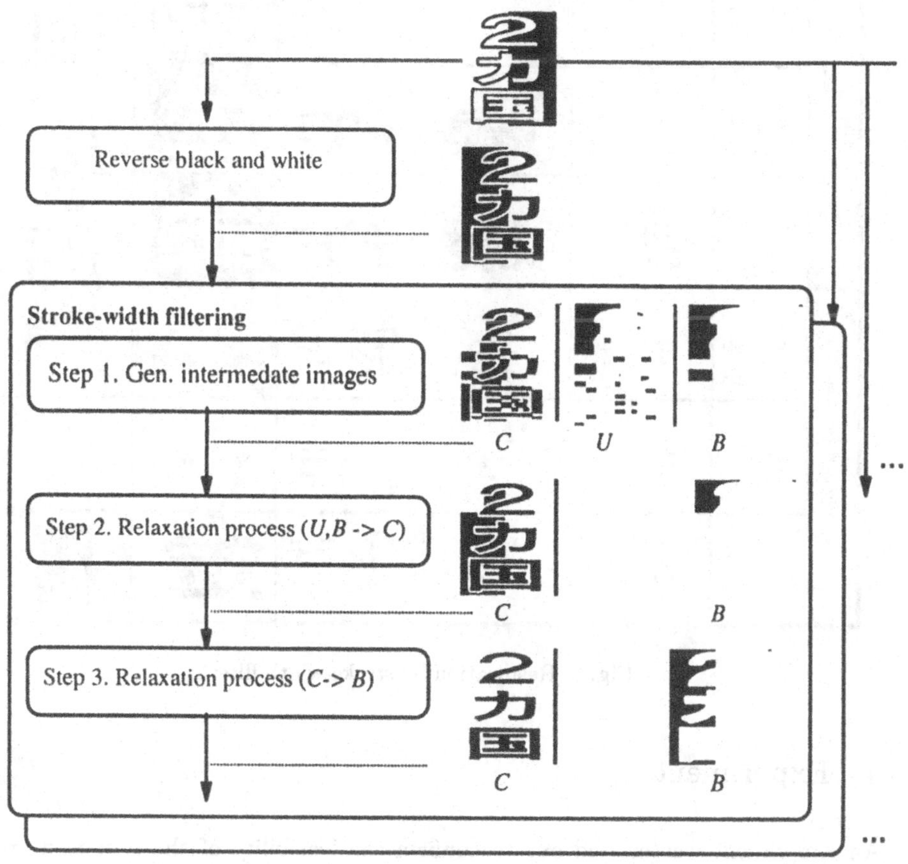

Fig. 4. Examples of restoration of decorative character images

3.2 Blurring

Blurring consists of consecutive closing and opening operations.

$$C \leftarrow O_4^v(O_4^h(C_4^v(C_4^h(I)))) \tag{10}$$

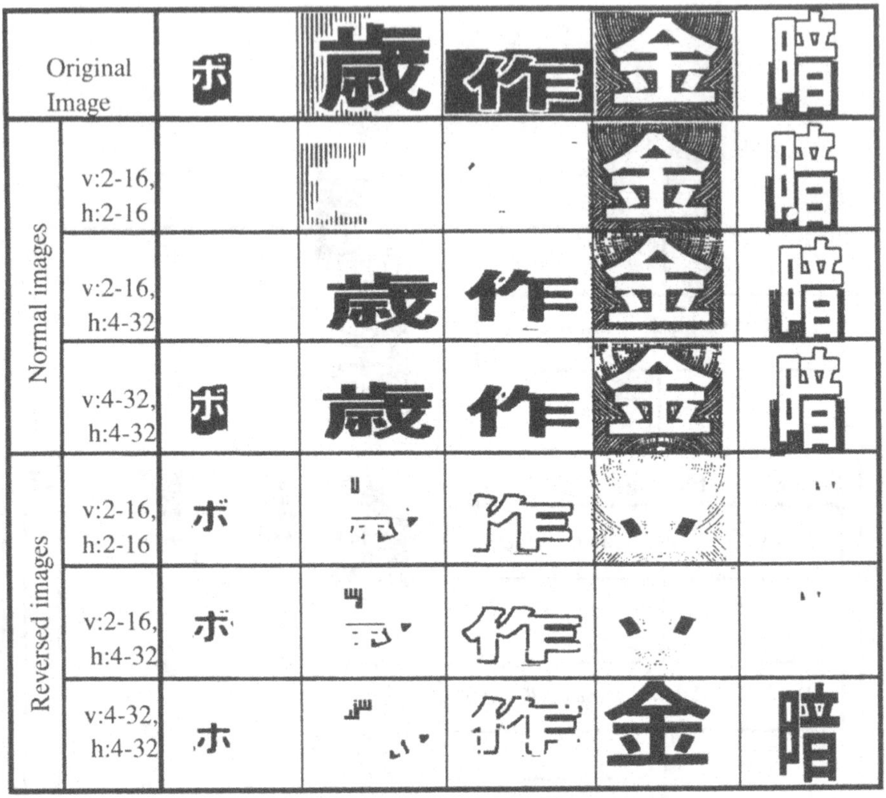

Fig. 5. Restoration by stroke-width filtering

4 Experiments

An experiment was carried out to confirm the feasibility of the proposed approach. Plural newspapers were scanned in 200 dpi resolution, and 50 headline images were manually segmented. All the images contained various decorations, and consequently could not be recognized by conventional OCRs. Using stroke-width filtering and blurring, we generated 12 candidate images (2 (normal or black-and-white reversed)$\times$ (5 (stroke width variations) + 1 (blurring))) from each headline image. We tried five stroke width parameters: 2-16 pixels; 4-32 pixels; 8-64 pixels for both of horizontal and vertical strokes, 2-16 pixels for horizontal strokes and 4-32 pixels for vertical strokes, and 4-32 pixels for horizontal strokes and 8-64 pixels for vertical strokes. The last two combinations were added to take account of the fact that some fonts have thinner horizontal than vertical strokes.

Although some noise and lost pixels were observed, a properly restored (black characters on white background) image was included among the candidates for 46 of the images. For more quantitative evaluation, the restored images were recognized by an OCR software product obtainable at stores. We calculated the recognition accuracy, selecting the candidate images that showed the best results. The restoration accuracy for 526 characters was 85%. Of 79 errors, 28 were caused by the OCR software itself. We expect that 90% (475/526) of decorative characters can be restored and used to make indexes for document retrieval.

Table 1 shows the distribution of parameters that gave the best results for each headline image. It shows that various decorative patterns are covered by multiple parameter sets.

Table 1. Parameters giving the best candidate images

Parameters	Stroke-width filtering										Blurring	
(Vertical and horizontal	2-16		4-32		4-32		8-64		8-64		4	
stroke widths)	2-16		2-26		4-32		4-32		8-64		4	
(Reverse/Normal)	R	N	R	N	R	N	R	N	R	N	R	N
Number	7	2	10	12	9	2	1	1	0	1	0	2

The 51 restoration errors are divided into two groups: 17 cases caused by partial noises or lost strokes, and 34 cases in which restoration failed for the overall image. Figure 6 shows examples of the second group. Figure 6(a) shows an unexpected decoration style in which character strokes are represented by outline and texture. In Figures 6(b) and 6(c), relaxation procedures did not work well for changes of background texture. A proper candidate could not be generated for the case shown in Figure 6(d), owing to the use of unsuitable blurring parameters (only one combination of blurring parameters was used in the experiment).

5 Conclusion

A method of restoring decorative headline images for document retrieval has been studied. To take account of fluctuation in the results of the preceding layout analysis, multiple candidate images are generated without parameter estimation and size normalization. In experiment using 50 actual headline images, stroke-width filtering and blurring generated candidates that could be recognized by conventional OCRs for 90% of decorative characters.

Assuming an automated method of document registration, it is more practical to use multiple candidates than a single restored image, because the decorations of headlines are arbitrarily designed by publishers. Our experiment shows that a simple stroke-width filter with a small number of parameter sets can cover various types of texture and font sizes. Even if unexpected decorations appear, the only extra work required is to create additional filters that can deal with the decorations.

In the proposed approach, the OCR and retrieval engine have to process more data because multiple images are passed to an OCR. However, most headlines

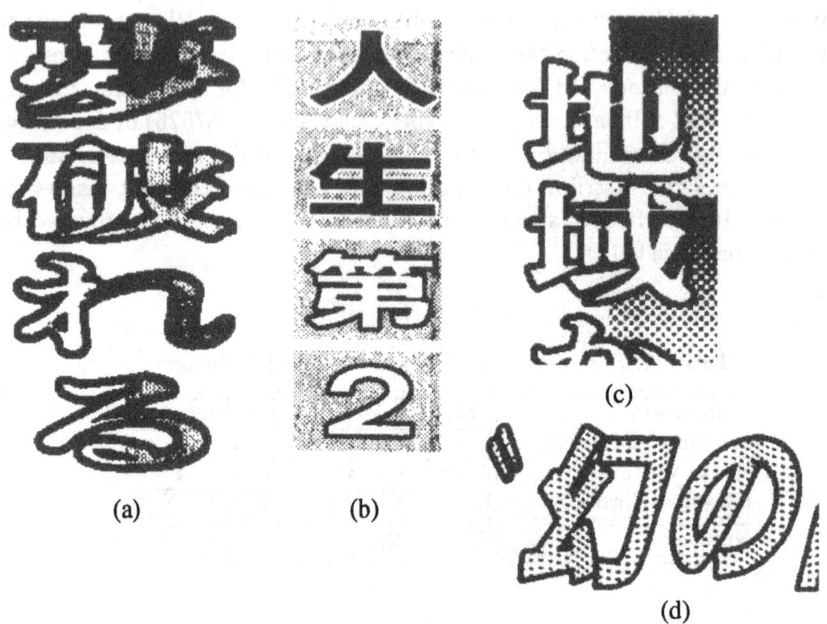

Fig. 6. Examples of restoration failures

contain only about 20 characters at most. Even if 100 times more data are produced, the increase in the number of characters to be recognized will be less than 2000, which is about the number of characters on a single page of an average document. We think this is a tolerable price to pay for the advantage of being to able to retrieve headline text.

In this paper, we proposed a multiple-candidate approach to headline text retrieval, and described a mechanism for generating candidate images. We are planning to verify the approach within an automated flow (from layout analysis to character recognition process). Since the relaxation processes are performance bottlenecks of our approach, and they sometimes cause restoration failures, we also plan to enhance relaxation algorithms used in stroke-width filtering.

References

1. Chen, R. and Bloomberg, S.: Extraction of Indicative Summary Sentences from Imaged Documents, ICDAR'97, pp. 227–232 (1997).
2. Senda, S. Minoh, M. and Ikeda, K.: Document Image Retrieval System Using Character Candidates Generated by Character Recognition Process, ICDAR '93, pp. 541–546, (1993).
3. Liang, S. Ahmadi, M. and Shridhar, M.: A Morphological Approach to Text String Extraction from Regular Periodic Overlapping Text/Background images, *CVGIP:Graphical Models and Image Processing*, Vol. 56, No. 5, pp. 402–413 (1994).

4. Lin, C. Takai, M. and Narita, S: Decorative Character Restoration by Image Processing, *Technical report of IEICE* (in Japanese) PRU94-12 (1994).
5. Takebe H, Katsuyama Y, and Naoi S.: Character String Extraction from Newspaper Headlines with a Background Design by Recognizing a Combination of Connected Components, *Proceeding of the 1998 Information and Systems Society Conference of IEICE* (in Japanese) D-12-22 (1998).
6. Sawaki, M and Hagita, N.: Recognition of Degraded Machine-Printed Characters Using a Complementary Similarity Measure and Error-Correction Learning, *Trans. IEICE*, Vol. E79-D, No. 5, pp. 491–497 (1996).

Document Image Analysis Using a New Compression Algorithm

Shulan Deng[1], Shahram Latifi, and Junichi Kanai[2]

[1] Department of Electrical and Computer Engineering, University of Nevada Las Vegas, Las Vegas, NV 89154-4026, {deng, latifi}@ee.unlv.edu

[2] Panasonic Information and Networking Technologies Laboratory, PINTL, 2 Research Way, Princeton, NJ 08540, USA, kanaij@research.panasonic.com

Abstract. By proper exploitation of the structural characteristics existing in a compressed document, it is possible to speed up certain image processing operations. Alternatively, one can derive a compression scheme which would lend itself to an efficient manipulation of documents without compromising the compression factor. Here, a run-based compression technique is discussed for binary documents. The technique, in addition to achieving bit rates comparable to other compression schemes, preserves document features which are useful for analysis and manipulation of data. Algorithms are proposed to perform vertical run extraction, and similar operations in the compressed domain. These algorithms are implemented in software. Experimental results indicate that fast analysis of electronic data is possible if data is coded according to the proposed scheme.

1 Introduction

In a large scale document conversion operation, paper documents are scanned, the quality of the scanning process is assured, and the document images are analyzed. Document images are usually compressed before being archived and analyzed. Traditional document analysis systems decompress page images completely before analyzing them. Systems that extract useful information in the compressed domain result in significant computational savings.

In the CCITT (newly renamed as ITU) Group 4 domain, Spitz [10] adapted the Baird's alignment technique to look for the pass modes, which are heavily populated at the fiducial point position of data, for detecting skew. Maa [6] observed that bars and space of barcodes are upright and should be perfectly aligned. Hence barcodes can be identified by finding the vertical mode codewords in the compressed domain. Recently Hull [5] compared the locations of pass modes contained in two bounding boxes for possible match while addressing the problem of document image matching.

In this paper, we will modify coding rules of the Group 4 and then derive a new coding scheme called Modified G4 or MG4, which gives us the flexibility for storage and processing. In our vision, such an algorithm is useful as an internal compression method of a document processing system. A filter is used to convert the compressed data into one of the standard formats, such as CCITT G4, to maintain compatibility with other systems. This paper is organized as follows: an introduction of MG4 is presented in Section 2. Section 3 analyzes the MG4's performance and presents the experimental results. Based on the MG4 scheme, some algorithms for extraction of vertical runs, connected component extraction, and skew detection are proposed and results are given in Section 4. Section 5 concludes the paper.

2 Modified Group 4 (MG4)

The Group 4 [3] encoding is a two-dimensional coding, in which each coding line is coded with respect to the previous line, "reference line". Since scan lines in a document file are highly correlated, we can take advantage of this characteristic to explore pixel level structures within several adjacent lines. The coding scheme for the Group 4 includes three coding modes: pass mode, vertical mode, and horizontal mode. These modes are defined by relationship among five changing picture elements. In Group 4, an object of interest cannot be easily discriminated from the background in compressed domain. It is also difficult to perform other image analysis in this domain. To overcome this deficiency, a modified Group 4 coding scheme (MG4) is proposed.

We regard the image as black objects on a white background, which is the case for most applications. This new coding scheme is designed based on the following three considerations:

- To encode the data based on runs for fast processing
- To keep the original structure in the compressed domain as much as possible
- To reduce two-dimensional redundancy to improve compression

The scheme is based on the notions of reference run and coding run. Let b_1, b_2 denote the coordinates of the endpoints of the run in the reference line and a_1, a_2 denote the coordinates of the endpoints of the run on the coding line. If the intervals $[b_1, b_2)$ and $[a_1, a_2)$ have overlapping projections, i.e., the following inequalities hold:

$$a_1 \leq b2 \quad and \quad b1 \leq a2 \tag{1}$$

then we call $b_1 b_2$ and $a_1 a_2$ the reference run and the coding run, respectively. A coding run is the run to be currently encoded. If a coding run has more than one reference run, then for simplicity, the leftmost reference run is chosen to encode the coding run. We define three modes for MG4 coding scheme: new vertical mode, new pass mode, and new horizontal mode.

2.1 Vertical Mode in MG4

The definition of vertical mode in Group 4 is extended here. In the MG4, if a coding run has a corresponding reference run, then the coding run can be represented by vertical mode. In other words, this mode occurs when the run on reference line has overlapping pixels with the coding run, i.e., satisfy Ineq. 1. In this mode we have two parameters with sign to encode; these are represented as $V(a_1b_1, b_2a_2)$ (see Fig. 1).

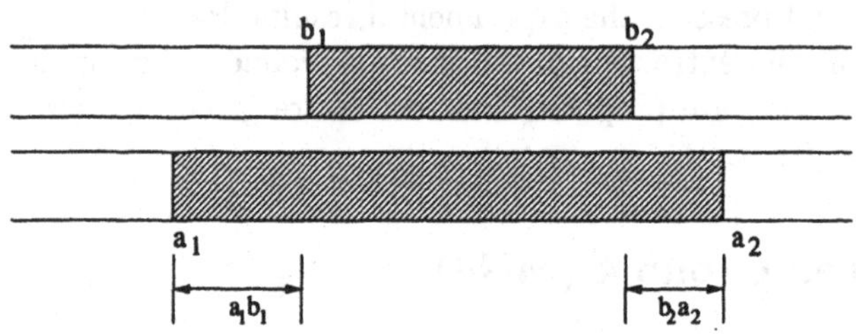

Fig. 1. MG4: Vertical mode

2.2 Pass Mode in MG4

New pass mode can be denoted as $P(n)$, where n is a non-negative integer. When n is 0, the coding run uses the same reference run as the last coding run (see Fig. 2). When n is nonzero, the case in Fig. 3 occurs. In this case, n records the number of runs skipped on reference line, then a vertical mode can be employed to encode the coding run.

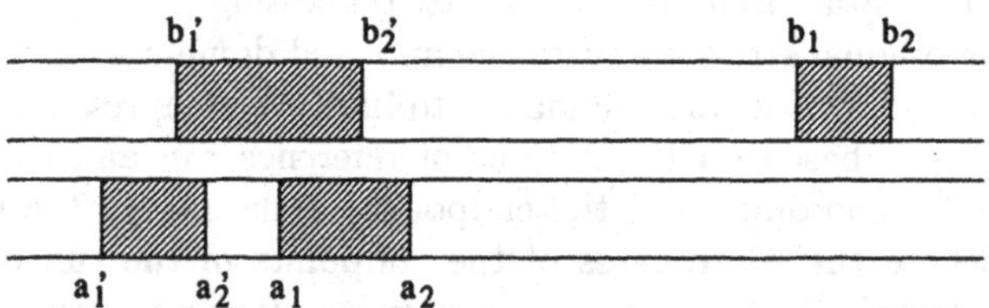

Fig. 2. MG4: New pass mode P(0)

Suppose the two runs $a'_1a'_2, a_1a_2$ in Fig. 2 are to be encoded. Since the run $b'_1b'_2$ satisfies the Inequality 1, it is the reference run of the coding run $a'_1a'_2$. So the $V(a'_1b'_1, -a'_2b'_2)$ is used to encode $a'_1a'_2$. Then next coding run is a_1a_2. It is seen that $b'_1b'_2$ still satisfies the Inequality 1 and is the reference run of a_1a_2. The modes $P(0), V(-b'_1a_1, b'_2a_2)$ are the representation of a_1a_2 in the compressed domain. For the same reason, we encode the case of Fig. 3 as $V(a'_1b'_1, -a'_2b'_2), P(2), V(a_1b_1, -a_2b_2)$. Because of the pass mode, two dimensional correlation can be utilized to maximum extent while compressing an image. So the pass mode implies compression efficiency and structure information.

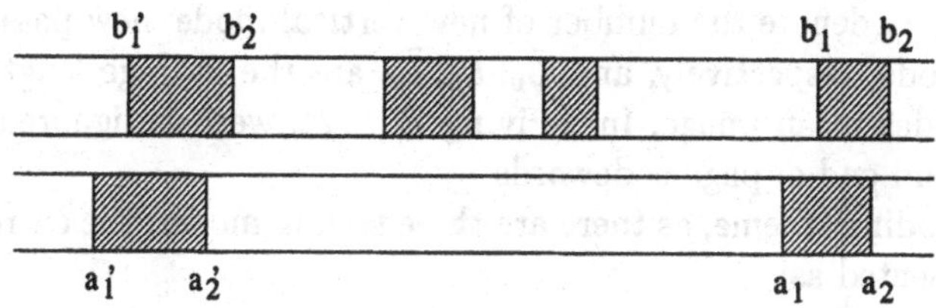

Fig. 3. MG4: New pass mode P(2)

2.3 Horizontal Mode in MG4

This mode occurs when a reference run cannot be found for the coding run. It represents a situation that the run just above the coding run on reference line is a white run. Obviously it implies the beginning of local characteristic region or connected component. The white run and black run are coded as $H(a_2'a_1, a_1a_2)$ (see Fig. 4).

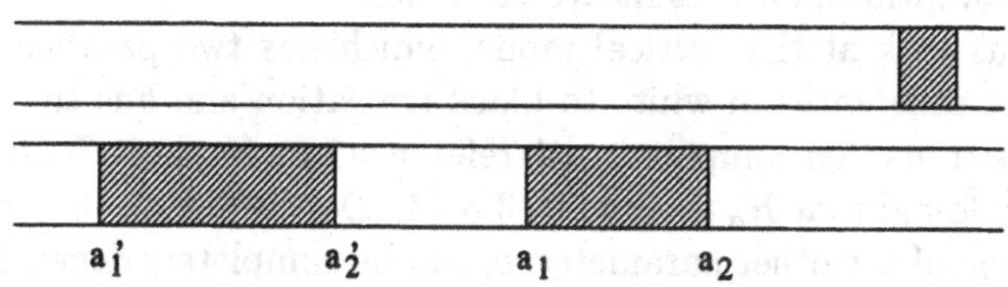

Fig. 4. MG4: New horizontal mode

The MG4 code is based on the modified Huffman scheme. Every mode's code has two parts: a flag indicating the mode, and a value or two values representing the length of the black run or white run. These values are taken from the white-run and black-run code tables of one dimensional coding.

3 Performance Analysis

MG4 is a statistical type coding in which highly probable symbols will get short codes. In this section, we will derive an estimation for the compression ratio that the MG4 yields, and present experimental results.

3.1 Compression Ratio Estimation

Compression ratio for MG4 is given by:

$$CF \approx \frac{Total\ Number\ of\ Pixels\ in\ Image}{n_v\bar{L}_v + n_p\bar{L}_p + n_h\bar{L}_h} \tag{2}$$

where n_v, n_p, n_h denote the number of new vertical mode, new pass mode, new horizontal mode, respectively, and $\bar{L}_v, \bar{L}_p, \bar{L}_h$ are the average lengths of corresponding modes in an image. In deriving Eq. (2), we have ignored the size of end-of-line, and end-of-page codewords

In MG4 coding scheme, as there are three coding modes, the entropy of MG4 can be represented as:

$$H_{MG4} = \sum_{i=1}^{3} P_i H_i \tag{3}$$

where P_1, P_2, P_3, denote these three modes' probabilities, and H_1, H_2, H_3 correspond to their entropies.

Starting with different ideas, we apply the approach used by Huang [4] to analyze the performance of MG4. It is noted that our model used is different from Huang's Predictive Differential Quantizing (PDQ). In the PDQ, the quantities Δ' (changes in white-to-black transition locations) and Δ'' (changes in the black runlengths) are transmitted, together with the New start and Merge messages indicating the start and the end of a black area. On the other hand, in our model, the three modes of vertical mode, pass mode, and horizontal mode are used. Because of the similarity of MG4 and PDQ, the derivations will be identical under our assumptions, and result are cited here.

First let us look at the vertical mode, which has two parameters a and b, where a is the differences in white to black transition and b is the difference in black to white transition compared with reference run. Suppose H_a is the entropy of a, then it is found that H_a is equal to 3.5 [4]. Depending on the type of image, the distribution of the other parameter, b, can be completely dependent on the a or completely independent of a. And the the entropy of b, H_b, satisfies: $0 \leq H_b \leq 2H_a$. To simplify the analysis, assuming that H_a=H_b. Also, suppose the number of pass mode and horizontal mode is much smaller than the number of vertical mode, and the number of vertical mode is approximately equal to the number of runs. Then according to Eq. (2) and the above assumptions, compression ratio can be roughly estimated as: $CF = (Average\ \ Run\ \ length)/3.5$.

3.2 Experimental Results

This new coding scheme is based on the international A4 paper-size standard. In this experiment, we chose CCITT1-CCITT8, the *de facto* standard test images, as test files each digitized at 200 dpi and converted into binary image with the size of 513229 bytes. The new coding scheme is implemented in software on a SGI O2 workstation under Unix environment. Experimental results shows the actual average occurrence probability of the three modes: 86% (vertical), 9% (pass) and 5% (horizontal). We can see that the vertical mode occurs with a much higher probability than the other modes. It is found that MG4 achieves high compression which is close to Group 4. On the average, compression ratio is about 17:1.

From the experiment, we found that the average run-length is 45.532 pixels. According to above CF formula, the compression factor is equal to 13. We assume H_a=H_b while deriving the formula. In fact, in the test image set, the H_b is less than H_a because of the correlation between a and b, so it should not be surprising that the estimated compression factor is smaller than the experimental results.

4 Document Analysis

An image analysis system realizes the objective of understanding document by using different algorithms or techniques in different stages of analysis. In the following subsections, we will discuss several subsystems of document analysis which can operate directly in MG4 domain: vertical run extracting systems, connected component extraction, and skew detection.

4.1 Extraction of Vertical Runs

Extraction of vertical runs from compressed image data is useful for operations such as rotation, and smearing [11]. Shima et al. [9] present a method of converting horizontal runs into vertical runs while rotation of the binary image based on coordinates of data for the start and the end of the run is executed. Yet, in this method, every black pixel is accessed in order to extract the vertical run, which increases computational complexity.

We notice that the beginning and ending points of each vertical run can be also detected while a MG4 compressed data is symbol decoded. The characteristics of MG4 are utilized to speed up the procedure of vertical run extraction by examining the modes encountered . As mentioned before, in vertical mode, if a_1 is to the left of b1, it will be the beginning of vertical runs; if a_1 is to the right of b1, it will be the ending of vertical runs. $V(0,0)$ can be ignored. For the pass mode ($n > 0$), the reference runs skipped are the end of vertical runs. And a horizontal mode always indicates the beginning of vertical runs. If the reference line above the coding run is black, the gap between the coding runs indicates the ending of vertical runs.

In Fig. 5, six typical relative positions of two runs on adjacent lines are shown. Figure 5.A presents three cases of detecting the beginning of vertical run, in which the starting position of the run on coding line is located to the left of that of the run on the reference line. The black thick line stands for the areas of vertical run's beginning. In every case of Fig. 5.B, the starting position of the run on coding line is located to the right of that of the run on the reference line and the ending points of the vertical run are marked by black thick lines. X' in Fig. 5 is the relocated starting point for next comparison.

Obviously, for the beginning of every vertical run, there always exist corresponding end points. We can easily get them and more importantly, get this information efficiently. For the document image with high resolution, whose average length of black runs is relatively large, the improvement in speed will be significant because the algorithm operates directly on the rundata.

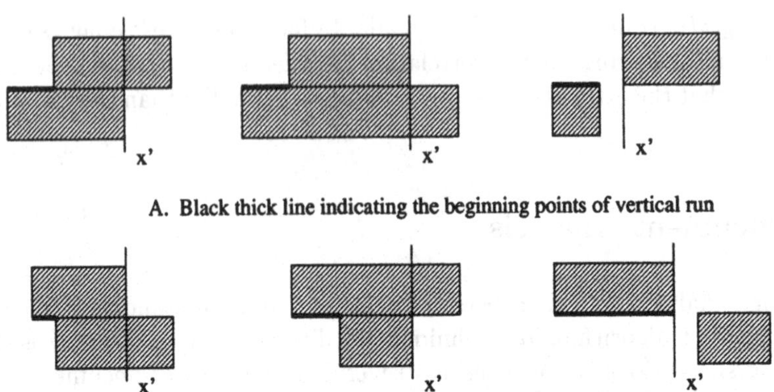
x'
x'
x'
A. Black thick line indicating the beginning points of vertical run
x'
x'
x'
B. Black thick line indicating the ending points of vertical run

Fig. 5. Finding the beginning point and ending point of vertical run

4.2 Connected Component Extraction Analysis

An important part of the image analysis is to decompose the image into entities (object, region, and blob). Connected components are extracted and used in a number of ways, such as calculating the number of objects, object matching and analysis of components. In traditional methods, the extraction of components is often done by using 2×2 [2] or 3×3 window to scan the image for contour detecting, making it time-consuming. MG4 is actually a differential coding scheme which keeps the information about the object's contour. Because of this characteristic, we can organize useful information in compression domain to do the component extraction easily.

We must mention that Pavlidis [8] extends the result of a hybrid vectorization algorithm and describes a thinning method (LAG) to operate directly on the run length encoding of bilevel image. There are some similarities between our algorithm and Pavlidis' because both methods are proposed to process run data. However, our analysis and algorithm are based on MG4, a new coding scheme designed for easy processing in compressed domain. Therefore, our algorithms are essentially different. In MG4, the horizontal mode often indicates the starting point of a component. Sometimes there are several horizontal modes for a single connected component which eventually are connected by a pass mode with nonzero parameter. When the vertical mode is encountered, the current run is part of a component. If a pass mode with parameter 0 occurs, next run coded by vertical mode is also connected with the component.

Extraction of connected components can be performed using steps below (see Fig. 6):

1. The information of two adjacent scan lines is always renewed and kept after finishing the processing of every scan line.

2. The horizontal code is searched in the compressed domain. If a horizontal code whose black run represents the beginning of a component is found, then a database is generated for the new component.
3. According to the particular property of each mode, parts of component on subsequent lines are extracted and saved into corresponding databases.
4. The ending of a component is indicated by the horizontal mode's white run or a pass mode with non-zero parameter on the next line.
5. The databases which belong to the same component are merged to form a single database by checking whether current coding run has other reference runs. Then this database contains information of a connected component.

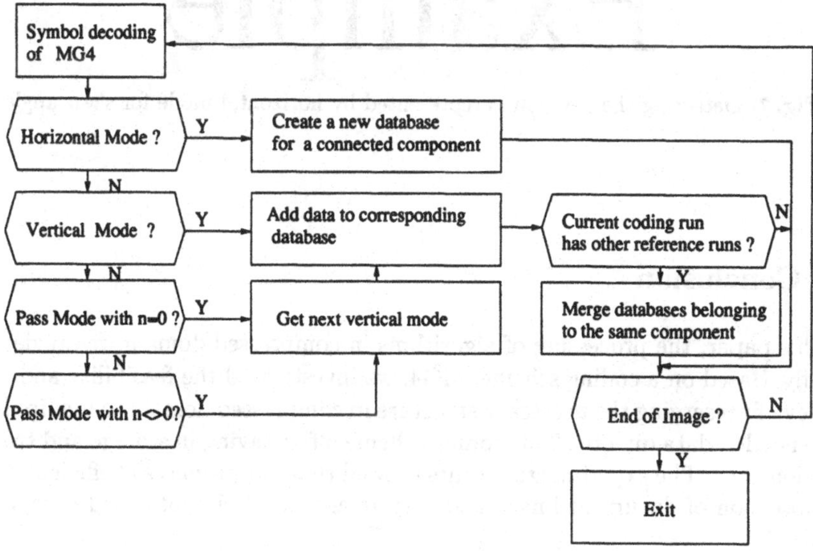

Fig. 6. MG4: Flow Chart of Connected Component Extraction

In our experiments, the complexity of algorithms is approximately of the order of the number of run length code segments. Also, components are extracted without decompressing the image. As a result, the processing speed is much faster than that in special domain.

4.3 Skew Detection

Skew detection is not a new topic. Many algorithms have been studied. Most of them was done in the spatial domain [1, 7]. As we mentioned before, Spitz found the skew angle by detecting the occurrence of pass mode in the Group 4 domain. It turns out that in MG4 domain we have the same convenience to detect the skew angle as in the Group 4 domain. The principle is that the horizontal mode often distributed at the top point of every character. Figure 7 illustrates the distribution of horizontal mode in a document image. Thus, many of these points are on or near the x-height line of a text-line. We measure the slope of extracted text lines according to the distribution of horizontal run to determine the skew angle. Combining the alignment-measure approach with locating the maximum techniques, we detect the skew angle in MG4 domain. Experiments show that the accuracy and the speed for estimating skew angle is comparable with that in Group 4 domain.

Fig. 7. Detecting the key points represented by horizontal mode for skew angle

5 Conclusion

In this paper, the processing of algorithms in compressed domain was reviewed briefly. Based on a coding scheme, MG4, we investigated the feasibility and efficiency of preserving the necessary structure in compressed domain to manipulate the encoded data directly. This coding scheme offers saving in storage and transmission time. The experimental results showed that our promises of efficient data compression of document image and easy image processing of coded data were realized.

Acknowledgment

This work was supported by NSF Research Grant IRI-9616206 and by NASA Research Grant NAG5-3994. Kanai worked on this project when he was research scientist at the Information Science Research Institute, University of Nevada, Las Vegas.

References

1. H. S. Baird: Proc. of SPSE Symp. on Hybrid Imaging Sys. Rochester, N.Y. **78** (1987) 21–24
2. N.Bartneck: Computing. **42** (1989) 17–34
3. CCITT Recommendation T.6, Facsimile Coding Schemes and Control Functions for Group IV Facsimile Apparatus, In Terminal Equipment and Protocols for the Telematic Services, Vol. VII, Fascicle VII.3, Geneva 1989

4. T. Huang: IEEE Transactions on Communication.
5. J. J. Hull and J. F. Cullen: Proc. Of 4th Intern. Conf. on Document Analy. and Recogn., Ulm, Germany. (1997) 308–312
6. C. Maa: Graphical Models and Image Processing. **56** 1994 352–356
7. Y. Nakano, Y. Shima, H. Fujisawa et al., Proc. of Intern. Conf. on Patt. Recogn. 1990 687–689
8. T. Pavlidis: Graphical Models and Image Processing. **35** 1986 111-127
9. Y. Shima, S. Kashioka, and J. Higashino: Systems and Computers in Japan. **20** 1989 91–102
10. A. L. Spitz: Proc. of the 1st Symp. on Document Analy. and Inform. Retri. 1992 11–25
11. F.M. Wahl, K.Y. Wong, and R.G. Casey: Computer Graphics and Image Processing. **20** 1982 375-390

A General Approach to Quality Evaluation of Document Segmentation Results

Michael Thulke[1], Volker Märgner[1], and Andreas Dengel[2]

[1] Institute for Communications Technology, Braunschweig Technical University, Schleinitzstraße 22, D-38092 Braunschweig, Germany
maergner@ifn.ing.tu-bs.de

[2] German Research Center for Artificial Intelligence (DFKI), Erwin-Schrödinger-Straße, D-67663 Kaiserslautern, Germany
dengel@dfki.uni-kl.de

Abstract. In order to increase the performance of document analysis systems a detailed quality evaluation of the achieved results is required. By focussing on segmentation algorithms, we point out that the results produced by the module under consideration should be evaluated directly; we will show that the text-based evaluation method which is often used in the document analysis domain does not accomplish the purpose of a detailed quality evaluation. Therefore, we propose a general evaluation approach for the comparison of segmentation results which is based on the segments directly. This approach is able to handle both algorithms that produce complete segmentations (partition) and algorithms that only extract objects of interest (extraction). Classes of errors are defined in a systematic way, and frequencies for each class can be computed. The evaluation approach is applicable to segmentation or extraction algorithms in a wide range. We have chosen the character segmentation task as an example in order to demonstrate the applicability of our evaluation approach, and we suggest to apply our approach to other segmentation tasks.

1 Introduction

Quality evaluation (or benchmarking) is gaining in importance because of several reasons: the increasing quality of document analysis systems during the last few years has made it more and more difficult to achieve a further increase in quality.[1,2] Moreover, the complexity of the systems has increased; the effect is that modifications within one module — even if just one parameter is modified — may often lead to an unpredictable behaviour towards other modules. The increasing amount of ready-to-use algorithms and the exploitation of new application fields for document analysis are making it rather difficult to find a suitable configuration. In conclusion, both, a detailed qualitative and a detailed quantitative failure analysis are needed for further improvement.

When making an evaluation, there may exist two different objectives:

- Benchmarking for the user. In this case, only the final results (e. g. the ASCII text from an OCR system or a set of categories from a document categorization system) are of interest - there is no motivation to look at internal details.
- Benchmarking for the system developer. Here, a detailed failure analysis is necessary. This requires to focus not only on final results, but on intermediate results, i.e. on the output of the specific module. The module's output must be accessible and needs to be compared with the corresponding ground truth. Our focus is lying on this objective.

There are several possibilities to evaluate a module (we will discuss them later). The way we do it is empirical, not analytical. That means we are using the results which the module produces for evaluation. The module under consideration is a black box — we do not want to perform an algorithmic analysis. The module's results are compared with ideal results (ground truth).

In this paper, the modules under consideration are segmentation modules of document analysis systems. The module's output as well as the ground truth are segments. That means, they are of a geometrical, not of a symbolic kind. Thus, the evaluation is made on the basis of segments.

The paper is tructured as follows: in the next section we examine the problem of segmentation in document analysis systems. Section 3 discusses other evaluation approaches which can be used to benchmark segmentation modules. Section 4 shows the disadvantages of text-based evaluation in the case of focussing on a detailed failure analysis. In section 5 we propose our general approach to the evaluation of segmentation results. This approach was successfully taken to character segmentation. The application to character segmentation is subject of section 6. We finish with a conclusion.

2 Segmentation Modules in Document Analysis Systems

In a document analysis system where image areas have to be segmented several tasks have to be carried out.

Consider the layout analysis task. After deskewing each document page, the layout has to be analysed. This task, also denoted as *zoning*, consists primarily of segmenting the image into text blocks and non-text blocks, and is followed by the determination of a reading order for text blocks. There is a broad spectrum of approaches to the layout analysis problem. Early work was done by Wahl et al.[3] Later a survey paper was written by Haralick.[4]

The extraction of regions-of-interest, e.g. the address block location in a mail-sorting task, can be considered as a special case of the segmentation task. The difference lies only in the fact that, in address block location, it is known that exactly one segment has to be found.

The way from text blocks to isolated characters involves several segmentation steps: the text lines have to be isolated, followed by a segmentation of each line into words and characters. These segmentation tasks have in common that the segmentation primarily goes on in one direction: line segmentation[1] from top to bottom, word and character segmentation from left to right — in contrast to the layout analysis task, where, in general, no total ordering of the segments exists. Nevertheless, in each case the segments are two-dimensional objects. For line, word and character segmentation, there is a number of papers proposing a wide range of solutions. The main emphasis lies on character segmentation, which is not surprising, because this seems to be the most crucial topic. For a survey of character segmentation methods, see e.g. Casey and Lecolinet.[5]

3 Other Contributions to the Segmentation Evaluation Task

There are several approaches to the evaluation of segmentation results or, more generally, to the evaluation of pattern analysis tasks. Figure 1 gives a classification scheme of the different approaches.

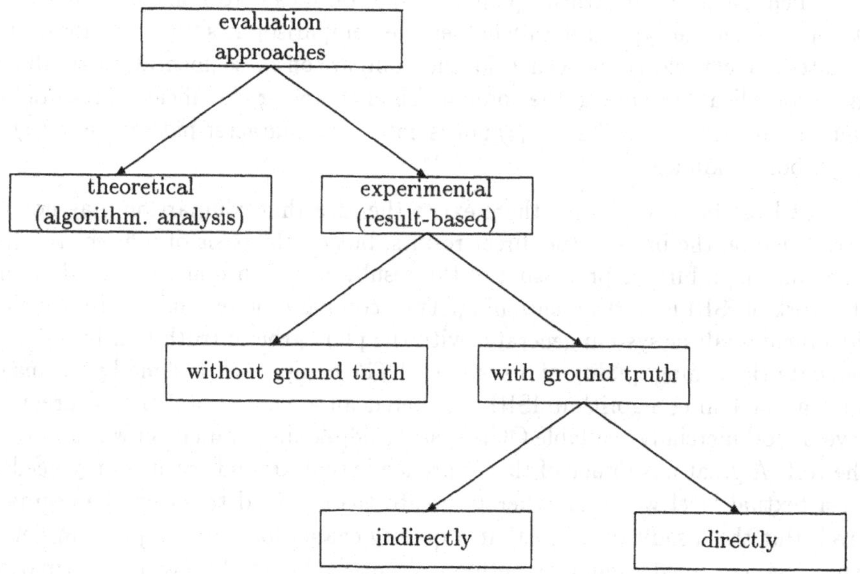

Fig. 1. Classification of evaluation approaches

First we can distinguish between a theoretical analysis and an experimental approach. In the theoretical approach, the algorithm will be analysed in order to

[1] By line segmentation we mean the segmentation *into* lines; in the same way, we say character segmentation when we mean the segmentation *into* characters.

derive its behaviour. The input data are assumed to be composed of ideal data degraded by noise. Input data degradation is propagated analytically throughout the algorithm. E.g., Haralick proposed an approach that uses covariance propagation.[6] —Approaches like this one are mainly used in the domain of low-level computer vision algorithms; edge detection would be an example for this. This approach would hardly be applicable since segmentation modules from the document analysis domain do not belong to the class of analyzable low-level algorithms.

On the contrary, experimental evaluation considers a module that should be characterized as a black box. The evaluation is based on the results only. This approach is much more pragmatic and is independent of the underlying algorithm.

It is possible to implement some *on-line measures* which can be used to evaluate a specific aspect of quality. On-line means that the system itself can calculate the measure of assessing the quality of its results. Ground truth is not necessary. But when making a detailed and comprehensive quality evaluation, this methodology cannot be sufficient.

When using ground truth, quality evaluation means to make a comparison. It depends on the type of data whether the comparison is simple or more complicated. It can easily be seen that the comparison of segmentation results is more complicated than e.g. the comparison of character classification results because segmentation results are *(i)* not isolated like character patterns nor *(ii)* of a symbolical kind.

Not least because of this, there exists the idea that comparison may not be performed on the basis of the direct results, but on the basis of indirect results. That means, a further processing of the results has been done. In this domain, the work of ISRI is worth mentioning. They compare the textual results which a document analysis system generates with the plain ground truth text in order to evaluate the zoning quality of a system.[7] The comparison is done by means of a string-matching algorithm. ISRI conducted an annual test of the accuracy of several commercially available OCR systems.[8] Zoning evaluation was a part of the test. A great advantage of this approach is that ground truth is only needed on a textual level which is easier to create than ground truth on the segment level. But the disadvantage is, that a quality evaluation which reports in detail what has happened cannot be perfomed. This is due to the loss of information that occurs when the segments are converted to a stream of character symbols.

This disadvantage does not exist when an evaluation s made on the basis of direct results, say, of the segment data itself. When this approach is used, the segmentations have to be compared. Several authors have worked on this approach, both from the document analysis community and from the computer vision community, in general. Yanikoglu and Vincent used this approach to evaluate zoning results.[9] Chen has worked on segmentation algorithms and developed a segmentation comparison procedure to evaluate their performance.[10] Hoover et al. developed a procedure for segmentation comparison of range images; [11] but their method of comparing segmentations can be transferred to the document analysis domain without problems.

Beside the question how to perform the evaluation there is the task to provide test data. There are two extremes: the collection of real data and, since this is often a very laborious task, the generation of synthetic data. For several years, the document analysis community was using synthetic images including image degradation models. First work on this topic was done by Baird.[12]

It can be stated that hardly any efforts were taken to carry out evaluation on the character segmentation level. We mentioned before that character segmentation is a very crucial topic. Moreover, it was reported that the majority of errors is due to incorrect segmentation rather than incorrect character recognition. This is true for constrained handwriting as well as for printed text.[14, 15]

4 Evaluation on the Textual Level and Its Disadvantages

Evaluation on textual results will have several disadvantages in view of assessing the quality of a (character) segmentation module. Consider the character recognition task of a text field that usually consists of several characters. The system's output text string is compared with the ground truth string; usually a string-matching algorithm using the Levenshtein distance, a well-known method based on the dynamic programming principle, is used. When having applied this matching procedure, four different classes (of errors) may occur: *(i)* a character is *correctly* recognized; *(ii)* a character is incorrectly recognized *(substitution)*; *(iii)* a character is incorrectly *inserted*; *(iv)* a character is incorrectly *deleted.* Criticism of the text-based evaluation approach is summarized in the following three points:

1. *The text-based approach is not able to distinguish between segmentation and recognition errors.*
   Interference between segmentation errors and recognition errors is possible. Figure 2 gives an example where an erroneous segmentation has been classified as a substitution error which creates the impression that there has been a recognition error.

ground truth text: 57; *detected text:* 37
⇒ *errors made: 1 × substitution.*

Fig. 2. Example of confusion regarding recognition and segmentation error

2. *The classes of errors are not suited to the problem.*
   Consider the class *insertion*. Even when the text result has an insertion it is not clear what really caused it. The cause for an insertion effect may be an erroneous interpretation of a noise-like object as a character image. But an insertion might also be caused by an erroneous splitting operation. When making a text-based evaluation, one cannot decide which specific type of segmentation error has occurred.
3. *The match which is detected cannot be guaranteed to be the correct one.*
   Figure 3 shows a part of a document image, the ground truth text and the detected text. The character 'w' was splitted up into two fragments; these fragments were classified as 'v' and 'i'. The character 'i' was misclassified as a 'l'. The ground truth text 'i' was brought into match with the character 'i' in the output string; this alignment is wrong because the underlying image parts are disjoint.
   The goal of the string-matching algorithm is to find the alignment referring to the minimum transformation cost; but this alignment is only useful for describing the effort that a subsequent system has to perform in order to achieve correct results. Therefore, the alignment only describes the error's effect but not the error itself, a fact which becomes obvious especially when looking at the errors the segmentation module can cause.

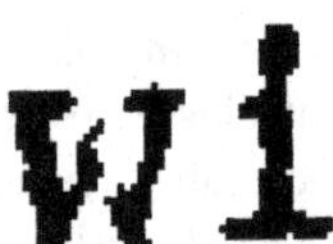

ground truth text: `wi`*; detected text:* `vil`
⇒ *errors made: 1 × substitution, 1 × insertion.*

Fig. 3. Example of an incorrect match owing to lack of geometrical knowledge

5 An Approach to the Evaluation of Segmentation Results

In the following section we are presenting a general approach to the evaluation of segmentation algorithms. Our approach is based on geometrical data and can be considered as a framework from which concrete evaluation methods can be derived for use in a specific domain.

In the great majority of cases, a segmentation becomes — to be precise — an extraction (or detection or isolation), because only some objects present in the area to be analyzed are objects of interest and others not. As a consequence, our approach can handle pure segmentation algorithms as well as extraction algorithms.

5.1 Problem Definition

Let I be the set of indices from the area to be segmented, e.g. $I = [0, X) \times [0, Y)$ in a two-dimensional image with dimensions $X \times Y$ (or a part of it)[2]. We now define a *segment* $u_i \subset I$ as an arbitrary non-empty, partial set of I. A *segmentation* is now a partitioning of I into a set of segments, that is *(i)* $I = \bigcup_i u_i$ and *(ii)* $u_i \cap u_j = \emptyset$ for all i, j $(i \neq j)$.

There are two types of segments: segments which denote objects-to-detect and a segment consisting of the remaining area. The first we call hereinafter *segments of interest* and the latter we call *noise segment.* As we will see below, these types of segments will be handled differently.

When making an evaluation, we have a ground truth segmentation $G = G_{obj} \cup \{g_{noise}\}$ with $G_{obj} = \{g_1, \ldots, g_M\}$ and the segmentation detected from the system $S = S_{obj} \cup \{s_{noise}\}$ with $S_{obj} = \{s_1, \ldots, s_N\}$ where g_i resp. s_j denote the segments of interest.

The first step when to compare two segmentations is to achieve relationships between a single segment from G and a single segment from S.

Let $|\cdot|$ denote the number of elements of a set; we define an *overlap function* $G \times S \rightarrow \mathcal{N}_0, (g, s) \mapsto |g \cap s|$ which counts the number of pixels common to $g \in G$ and $s \in S$. Given two segmentations G and S, the values of this function can be displayed in a two-dimensional table; there exist the marginal conditions $|g| = \sum_{s \in S} |g \cap s|$, $|s| = \sum_{g \in G} |g \cap s|$ and $|I| = \sum_{g \in G} \sum_{s \in S} |g \cap s|$. The following evaluation methods are based on this overlap function.

5.2 Elementary Classes of Errors

When the errors where a specific segment is participated should be classified, the following elementary classes of errors can be found intuitively:
(i) Several segments were merged together (hereinafter called *merge*);
(ii) a segment was split in several fragments (*split*);
(iii) a segment was completely ignored (*miss*);
(iv) a segment was detected where no segment should be (*false*);
(v) parts of a segment are missing (*partial miss*);
(vi) noise was added to a segment (*partial false*).
The overlapping function described above may be used to derive these types of errors. According to the classes of errors introduced above, we define the following sets of segments:
(i) For the class *merge*: A detected segment belongs to the class *merge* if and only if it overlaps with at least two ground truth segments-of-interest. Or, more formally:

$$S_{Merge} := \{s \in S_{obj} | \bigvee_{g^{(1)}, g^{(2)} \in G_{obj}, g^{(1)} \neq g^{(2)}} |g^{(1)} \cap s| > 0 \wedge |g^{(2)} \cap s| > 0\}.$$

[2] Note that we use only the indices of the pixels, not the pixel values themselves.

Having defined this, one can define the set of the *ground truth* segments which participated:

$$G_{Merge} := \{g \in G_{obj} | \bigvee_{s \in S_{Merge}} |g \cap s| > 0\}.$$

Note that one ground truth segment can participate in merge errors from several (detected) segments.
(ii) In the same way, two sets denote the segments which participate on split errors:

$$G_{Split} := \{g \in G_{obj} | \bigvee_{s^{(1)}, s^{(2)} \in S_{obj}, s^{(1)} \neq s^{(2)}} |g \cap s^{(1)}| > 0 \wedge |g \cap s^{(2)}| > 0\},$$

$$S_{Split} := \{s \in S_{obj} | \bigvee_{g \in G_{Split}} |g \cap s| > 0\}.$$

(iii) The set of segments which have been completely missed is defined as

$$G_{Miss} := \{g \in G_{obj} | \neg \bigvee_{s \in S_{obj}} |g \cap s| > 0\}.$$

(iv) Analogously we define

$$S_{False} := \{s \in S_{obj} | \neg \bigvee_{g \in G_{obj}} |g \cap s| > 0\}.$$

The last two classes of errors, *(v)* and *(vi)*, are defined as follows:

$$G_{PartialMiss} := \left\{g \in G_{obj} \middle| |g \cap s_{noise}| > 0 \wedge \bigvee_{s \in S_{obj}} |g \cap s| > 0\right\},$$

$$S_{PartialMiss} := \{s \in S_{obj} | \bigvee_{g \in G_{PartialMiss}} |g \cap s| > 0\},$$

$$S_{PartialFalse} := \left\{s \in S_{obj} \middle| |g_{noise} \cap s| > 0 \wedge \bigvee_{g \in G_{obj}} |g \cap s| > 0\right\},$$

$$G_{PartialFalse} := \{g \in G_{obj} | \bigvee_{s \in S_{PartialFalse}} |g \cap s| > 0\}.$$

Having defined these classes of errors, it is obvious to use the number of segments belonging to a set as an error metric. For example, with $M_{Split} = |G_{Split}|$ we can use the absolute frequency M_{Split} or the relative frequency M_{Split}/M as an error metric.

The use of these classes of errors gives a good impression how often a specific type of segmentation error occurs. But it is important to note that these classes of errors are not disjoint. For example, a ground truth segment may be a member of the split class and may be a member of the merge class simultaneously. Therefore, a unique classification into disjoint classes is not possible.

There is a second limitation when using these elementary classes of errors. In some applications, there may be an interest which segments are involved in a concrete segmentation error (this will be demonstrated in section 6.2). Questions like that cannot be handled by this evaluation approach.

In the next section, we propose an approach which overcome these limitations.

5.3 Generation and Classifications of Regions

We define for two arbitrary segments a and b the relation $a \sim b$ if and only if $|a \cap b| > 0$.[3] So $a \sim b$ means that segments a and b overlap significantly. Since the segments within G do not overlap, a and b cannot be both from G. The same is true for segments within S. Let $a \simeq b$ be an equivalence relation induced by $\sim$. The equivalence relation is transitive; as a consequence, $a \simeq b$ is valid if there exists a sequence of segments $u_1, \ldots, u_n$ with $a \sim u_1 \land u_1 \sim u_2 \land \ldots \land u_n \sim b$. According to the $\simeq$ relation we construct the equivalence classes in $G_{obj} \cup S_{obj}$, hereinafter called *regions*. Each region r contains segments from G_{obj} and/or segments from S_{obj}.

The next step is to check for each region r_k whether it overlaps with g_{noise} (that means, noise has been misclassified as an object or as part of an object) and/or whether it overlaps with s_{noise} (object or part of it has been misclassified as noise). More formally, we define the predicates $G_{noise}(k) :\iff |g_{noise} \cap \bigcup_{u \in r_k} u| > 0$ and $S_{noise}(k) :\iff |s_{noise} \cap \bigcup_{u \in r_k} u| > 0$.

We define — for the sake of completeness — $g_{noise} \cap s_{noise}$ being an additional region if it is non-empty. Thereby we obtain that the set of regions is a partitioning of I.

Classification of Regions

We characterize the quality of the segmentation by the quality of its regions. Therefore, we classify each region.

Let $g_{obj}^{(k)}$ be the number of ground truth segments-of-interest of a region r_k and $s_{obj}^{(k)}$ the number of detected segments-of-interest. The following constraints are a consequence of the region building mechanism:

(i) Since the segmentations G and S cover each the whole area of I, each region must at least contain parts from G and parts from S.

(ii) A region which consists only of noise on the ground truth side does not have the capability to combine detected segments. The same holds for a region which consists only of noise on the detected side.

Furthermore, we group the possible values for $g_{obj}^{(k)}$ and $s_{obj}^{(k)}$ into the categories $\{0, 1, >1\}$. Together with taking the above-mentioned constraints into account, this leads to 19 disjoint classes of errors, as shown in table 1.

[3] Alternatively one can define $|a \cap b| > \delta$ where $\delta \geq 0$ is a small fixed threshold value.

	$g_{obj}^{(k)}$	$G_{noise}(k)$	$s_{obj}^{(k)}$	$S_{noise}(k)$	class name
1	0	true	0	true	*noise*
2	0	true	1	false	*false*
3	1	false	0	true	*miss*
4	1	false	1	false	*correct*
5	1	false	1	true	*correct incl. object as noise*
6	1	false	>1	false	*split*
7	1	false	>1	true	*split incl. object as noise*
8	1	true	1	false	*correct incl. noise as object*
9	1	true	1	true	*correct incl. object as noise and noise as object*
10	1	true	>1	false	*split incl. noise as object*
11	1	true	>1	true	*split incl. object as noise and noise as object*
12	>1	false	1	false	*merge*
13	>1	false	1	true	*merge incl. object as noise*
14	>1	false	>1	false	*merge+split*
15	>1	false	>1	true	*merge+split incl. object as noise*
16	>1	true	1	false	*merge incl. noise as object*
17	>1	true	1	true	*merge incl. object as noise and noise as object*
18	>1	true	>1	false	*merge+split incl. noise as object*
19	>1	true	>1	true	*merge+split incl. object as noise and noise as object*

Table 1. Classes of errors

Applying this classification scheme to concrete segmentation results, relative frequencies can be computed for each class. Because there are 17 classes where ground truth segments-of-interest are involved, we are able to compute 17 frequencies of ground truth segments-of-interest w. r. t. the total number of ground truth segments-of-interest. In the same way 17 frequencies of detected segments-of-interest w. r. t. the total number of detected segments-of-interest can be computed. Note that the classification scheme is completely symmetrical regarding ground truth and detected segmentation.

By using these measures, it exists a duality: There are e. g. two measures for the merge class, one from the ground truth side and one from the detected side. In order to avoid this duality, the number of regions belonging to each of the 19 classes can alternatively be used. Using this way, we obtain 19 frequencies. A single quality measure — although it is very problematic to characterize such a complex task by one value — can be obtained by computing a weighted sum over the class frequencies. Figure 4 illustrates the basic evaluation approach.

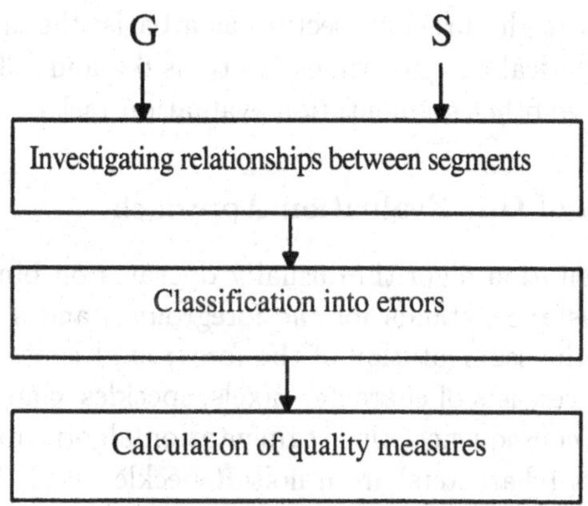

Fig. 4. Overview of the basic evaluation approach

5.4 Derivation of Concrete Evaluation Methods

It depends on the individual *evaluation* task whether it is necessary for an evaluation to compute all these values in detail. Moreover it depends on the individual *segmentation* task whether each class of error can occur. Often it is possible to simplify this evaluation approach by uniting some classes of errors.

Consider the example of a noise-free segmentation evaluation. In this case there does not exist either ground truth noise or detected noise. As a consequence, only classes with $\neg G_{noise}(k) \wedge \neg S_{noise}(k)$ can occur. This leads to a simple segmentation evaluation scheme with 4 possible classes when using the region-based approach, as shown in table 2 (the region index k is omitted for purposes of readability).

	g_{obj}	s_{obj}	**class name**
1	1	1	*correct*
2	1	>1	*split*
3	>1	1	*merge*
4	>1	>1	*merge+split*

Table 2. Reduced classification scheme

6 Application to Character Segmentation

In this section we report on the evaluation of a character segmentation module. Our focus lies on the evaluation method itself, neither on the segmentation algorithm nor on the results of the evaluation. We use the segmentation evaluation approach presented in the previous section as a basis; the approach will be extended by some practical considerations (sections 6.2 and 6.3); these extensions are also applicable to other segmentation evaluation tasks.

6.1 Application of Our Evaluation Approach

A character segmentation algorithm usually operates on binary images, where a value of 1, for instance, stands for the foreground, and a value of 0, for the background. Only the segmentation of the foreground is of interest; in particular, the foreground consists of character pixels, speckles, character or field boxes on forms etc. As a consequence, this segmentation algorithm has to distinguish segments-of-interest (characters) from noise (speckles etc.). For evaluating this task, the generation of ground truth is necessary. Therefore, we make the following decisions:

1. The set of indices from the area to be segmented *(I)* contains only the indices of foreground pixels.
2. All non-character foreground objects are declared as noise.
3. Each single character image is exactly one segment-of-interest.

Having made these decisions, the segmentation evaluation framework is applicable.

We used text line images taken from about 400 address blocks printed in various fonts. For each text line, the results of the character segmentation module are organized in a segment hypothesis graph as shown in figure 5.

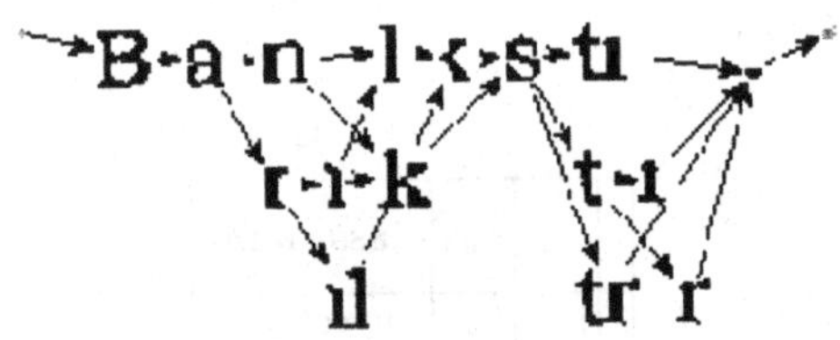

Fig. 5. Segment hypothesis graph

This data structure is very popular when to represent character segmentation results. Each path through the graph represents one possible segmentation. Furthermore, the character classification results (including classifier confidences) may be attached to each segment node.

Ground truth was created half-automatically. In a first step, the best path was selected from the hypothesis graph by using a criterion based on the confidences of the character classification results of each segment. This segmentation was suggested in order to be checked or corrected manually by means of our interactive graphical tool INSEGD (*Interactive Segmentation of Documents*).[16]

When doing the evaluation, we generated all possible paths throughout the hypothesis graph and compared them with the ground truth segmentation. For each comparison, we calculated a weighted sum over the class frequencies of the segmentation errors occurred. We chose the path with the best score.

The evaluation tool SEGEVAL implements the approach described in the previous section. Figure 3 gives an exemplary output for the region-based evaluation approach.

		G		S		#Regions
1 : 1	[Correct]:	97.973%	(18657)	98.464%	(18657)	18657
1 :(1+noise)	:	0.467%	(89)	0.470%	(89)	89
(1+noise): 1	:	0.000%	(0)	0.000%	(0)	0
(1+noise):(1+noise)	:	0.000%	(0)	0.000%	(0)	0
M : 1	[Merge] :	0.924%	(176)	0.464%	(88)	88
M :(1+noise)	:	0.021%	(4)	0.011%	(2)	2
(M+noise): 1	:	0.000%	(0)	0.000%	(0)	0
(M+noise):(1+noise)	:	0.000%	(0)	0.000%	(0)	0
1 : M	[Split] :	0.152%	(29)	0.306%	(58)	29
1 :(M+noise)	:	0.005%	(1)	0.011%	(2)	1
(1+noise): M	:	0.000%	(0)	0.000%	(0)	0
(1+noise):(M+noise)	:	0.000%	(0)	0.000%	(0)	0
M : M	[M+S] :	0.179%	(34)	0.195%	(37)	17
M :(M+noise)	:	0.000%	(0)	0.000%	(0)	0
(M+noise): M	:	0.000%	(0)	0.000%	(0)	0
(M+noise):(M+noise)	:	0.000%	(0)	0.000%	(0)	0
noise : 1	[False] :	-	-	0.079%	(15)	15
1 : noise	[Miss] :	0.278%	(53)	-	-	53
Total	:		(19043)		(18948)	

Table 3. Exemplary output of the segmentation evaluation tool

6.2 Inclusion of Segment Attributes

Besides the ground truth generation on the segment level, we generated textual reference data, too. So each ground truth segment is attributed by its character class. Therefore, it is possible to select a specific class of segmentation error and to make a further distinction by using the character classes involved. Consider, for example, the class merge. By using the region-based approach, it was possible to detect which sequences of characters were the favourites for a merge. Therefore, it was possible to discover in a quantitative manner that most frequently the letter combinations '`tr`', '`ri`' and '`rf`' lead to a merge.

6.3 Evaluation of Hypothesis Generation

Here, the goal is to assess the quality of the hypothesis graph. The ideal case would be a graph that contains only one path being the correct one. Since the segments are of a geometrical nature, it is possible to count the number of hypotheses a over a specific pixel (x, y) or over a specific ground truth segment g. For example, it could be stated that the average number of hypotheses $(\bar{a}(g_i))$ over uppercase ground truth segments is lower than the average number over lower case segments.

It should be noticed that $\bar{a}(x, y)$ is an *on-line measure* and, therefore, it can be used to detect image areas where the segmentation is unsafe.

7 Conclusion

Recently it has been recognized that the character segmentation task is a very critical one within the list of tasks of a document analysis system. Now as before, too little effort is made to deal with the thorny subject of performance evaluation, especially for the segmentation domain.

First, we pointed out that text-based evaluation of segmentational tasks has several disadvantages, e. g. it only describes the effect of the errors made and not the errors itself. Therefore, it is not sufficient for a detailed error analysis.

Secondly, we proposed a general approach to the evaluation of segmentation or extraction algorithms. In this approach, we introduced elementary classes of segmentation errors that are obvious. Furthermore we developed a segmentation evaluation approach which provides disjoint classes of errors. Since the evaluation is based on the segments directly, it is applicable to segmentation algorithms in a wide range and not restricted to a specific domain.

We demonstrated the applicability of our approach by means of a practical example for the character segmentation task. Besides the application to character segmentation as presented here, we also have applied our evaluation approach to the zoning task. Finally, we want to suggest the use in other segmentation tasks, within and without the document analysis domain.

References

1. T. Pavlidis: *Problems in the Recognition of Poorly Printed Text*, Proc. Symposium on Document Analysis and Information Retrieval, Las Vegas 1992, pp. 162–173
2. M. D. Garris: *Method and Evaluation of Character Stroke Preservation on Hand-print Recognition*, National Institute of Standards and Technology (NIST) Technical Report NISTIR 5687, July 1995; published in: SPIE, Document Recognition III, pp. 321–332, San Jose, January 1996
3. F. M. Wahl, K. Y. Wong, R. G. Casey: *Block Segmentation and Text Extraction in Mixed Text/Image Documents*, Computer Graphics and Image Processing, Vol. 20, 1982, pp. 375–390
4. R. M. Haralick: *Document Image Understanding: Geometric and Logical Layout*, CVPR, Seattle, USA, June 1994
5. R. G. Casey, E. Lecolinet: *A Survey of Methods and Strategies in Character Segmentation*, IEEE Transactions on Pattern Analysis and Machine Intelligence, July 1996, pp. 690–706

6. R. M. Haralick: *Propagating Covariance in Computer Vision*, Workshop on Performance Characteristics of Vision Algorithms, Robin College, Cambridge, UK, April 1996
7. J. Kanai, S. V. Rice, T. A. Nartker, G. Nagy: *Automated Evaluation of OCR Zoning*, IEEE Transactions on Pattern Analysis and Machine Intelligence, Vol. 17, No. 1, Jan. 1995, pp. 86–90
8. S. V. Rice, F. R. Jenkins, T. A. Nartker: *The Fifth Annual Test of OCR Accuracy*, Information Science Research Institute, University of Nevada, Las Vegas, Technical Report ISRI TR-96-01, April 1996
9. B. A. Yanikoglu, L. Vincent: *Ground-truthing and Benchmarking Document Page Segmentation*, Proc. 3rd Intern. Conf. on Document Analysis and Recognition (ICDAR), Montréal, Canada, 1995, pp. 601–604
10. S. Chen, R. M. Haralick, I. T. Phillips: *Perfect Document Layout Ground Truth Generation Using DVI Files and Simultaneous Word Segmentation From Document Images*, Proc. Fourth Annual Symposium on Document Analysis and Information Retrieval, Las Vegas 1995, pp. 229–248
11. A. Hoover, G. Jean-Baptiste, X. Jiang, P. J. Flynn, H. Bunke, D. Goldgof, K. Bowyer, D. Eggert, A. Fitzgibbon, R. Fisher: *An Experimental Comparison of Range Image Segmentation Algorithms*, IEEE Transactions on Pattern Analysis and Machine Intelligence, July 1996, pp. 1–17
12. H. S. Baird: *Document Image Defect Models*, in: *Structured Document Image Analysis*, Springer, New York, 1992, pp. 546–556
13. M. Thulke: *Use of Geometrical Ground Truth for Quality Evaluation of Document Segmentation Algorithms*, in: W. Förstner (editor): Workshop *Performance Characteristics and Quality of Computer Vision Algorithms*, Braunschweig, Germany, September 1997
14. P. Stubberud, J. Kanai, V. Kalluri: *Adaptive Restoration of Text Images Containing Touching or Broken Characters*, Information Science Research Institute (ISRI) 1995 Annual Research Report, pp. 61–96
15. C. L. Wilson, J. Geist, M. D. Garris, R. Chellappa: *Design, Integration and Evaluation of Form-Based Handprint and OCR Systems*, NIST Internal Report 5932, December 1996
16. R. Bippus, V. Märgner: *Data Structures and Tools for Document Database Generation: An Experimental System*, Proc. Third Intern. Conf. on Document Analysis and Recognition (ICDAR), Montréal, Canada, 1995, pp. 711–714

This work is partly supported by the German Ministry of Education, Science and Research (BMBF) under the contract number 01IN503L/1.

Form Analysis by Neural Classification of Cells

Y. Belaïd and A. Belaïd

LORIA-CNRS
Campus scientifique B.P. 239
54506 Vandœuvre-lès-Nancy CEDEX France
E-mail: {ybelaid,abelaid}@loria.fr

Abstract. Our aim in this paper is to present a generic approach for linearly combining multi neural classifier for cell analysis of forms. This approach can be applied in a preprocessing step in order to highlight the different kind of information filled in the form and to determine the appropriate treatment. Features used for the classification are relative to the text orientation and to its character morphology. Eight classes are extracted among numeric, alphabetic, vertical, horizontal, capitals, etc. Classifiers are multi-layered perceptrons considering firstly global features and refining the classification at each step by looking for more precise features. The recognition rate of the classifiers for 3. 500 cells issued from 19 forms is about 91%.

1 Introduction

Form analysis becomes with the success of OCR/ICR techniques a very promising domain with different issues and applications. Several administrations and companies are today faced to a fast treatment of their forms in different domains such as order lecture, revenue form capture or multiple choice question paper analysis. Systems designed this last decade for form analysis are numerous and themes are varied. However, all of these systems are oriented towards a full form recognition without a real separation between the different phases. This makes difficult the reuse of systems and leads sometimes, for a new application, to the complete rewriting of the techniques. So, we have considered that for some classes of forms such as the tax forms, cells are the base of the form analysis and cell classification can constitute a generic part of a form analysis system.

Considering cell detection and extraction, the literature mentions mainly two approaches. The most common one deals with known forms and uses a detailed model for each class of forms [2–4, 8]. Although the systems are efficient on specific forms, they can be hardly applied to other kind of forms. In opposite, the systems, in the other approach, ignore any a priori knowledge on the form and base the analysis mainly on cell analysis [5, 6]. Although they are more general than the first ones and can be applied on a wide range of forms, their performance is limited because of their lack of knowledge.

Our aim in this paper is to propose an intermediate solution for unknown form analysis based on cell classification. Cells are first extracted from the form and classified according to different criteria based more on the content aspect than on its semantic interpretation.

The cell extraction and classification is a very important step in a form analysis process for several reasons:

- The information contained in the form is mainly located in the cells.
- The cell extraction allows to locate the information and to situate it according to the rows and columns. This leads to find at the same time the layout and the logical structure of the form (correspondence between rows and columns, number of dimensions, etc.).
- The exam of the content of each cell can help to the content classification, first by separating cells containing the information from empty ones, second, by analyzing the type of content (text, digits, etc.) in order to apply on it the adequate treatment.
- At last, the cell extraction and content classification can help to the preclassification of forms with a modest investigation.

The outline of this paper is as follows. After a brief description of the approach used for the cell location in section 2, we present in section 3 the different classes retained for the classification and give in section 4 the classification schema. Details dealing with the main classification steps will be then exposed in this section. So, we show the different features used for the different classes and the hierarchy of neural architectures. At last, before concluding, some experiments and results will be discussed in section 5.

2 Cell Extraction

As mentioned in [7] cell location and extraction is operated in three steps.

In the first step, lines are detected in the image by applying Hough Transform. This technique was used for its robustness and reliability. It transforms the following line problem in a counting point problem [1]. In order to avoid a multitude of line candidates, voting points are limited to only those belonging either to the contours or to the black or gray areas. A recursive cut of the polar parameter space of lines and a fusion of close cells allow to fast locate the accumulation areas.

In the second step, segments associated to the lines, are extracted from the image. The line following is operated by advantaging the closest black pixels of the Hough lines. The lines detected can be simple, double, continuous or discontinuous, contours of black and gray areas, or vertical alignments of parentheses.

The cells are located at the third step. They are represented by a graph which arcs are the horizontal and vertical segments and which nodes are the intersection points between horizontal and vertical lines. Cells are given by the research for minimum circuits of the graph.

This first part of the system has been tested with success on French tax forms as well as on tables. The line extraction takes about 30" per image.

3 Cell Classes

A detailed study of French tax forms leads us to define eight classes for cells described below:

- DIGI: it regroups the set of cells containing only digits. These digits generally correspond to amounts and can be preceded by the sign '+' or '-'.
- GRAY: it corresponds to gray areas which cannot be filled by any kind of data.
- HLET (for horizontal letters): all cells which text is horizontally aligned and which are constituted by alphanumeric chains containing lower-case letters and probably higher-case letters are affected to this class. They correspond essentially to form wordings.
- VLET (for vertical letters): it reassembles the same kind of cells within the class HLET but with text vertically aligned.
- HHCL (for horizontal higher-case letters): cells containing higher-case letters horizontally aligned and some digits or symbols such as parentheses are attributed to this class. These cells often correspond to wordings representing amounts.
- VHCL (for vertical higher-case letters): it corresponds to the class HHCL but considering only cells which text is vertically aligned.
- BLAC: it regroups cells in inverse video (with black foreground). These cells play a particular role in our forms.
- EMPT (for empty classes): this class regroups all the cells containing any data.

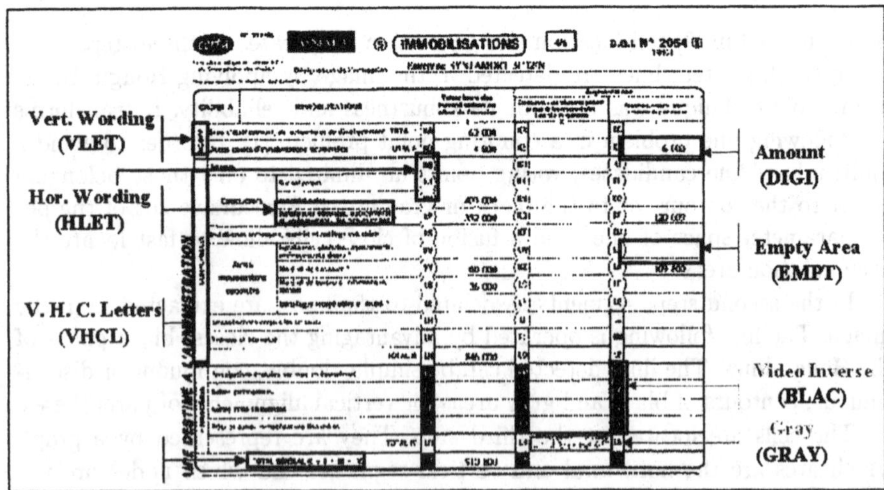

Fig. 1. *Example of Classes.*

The choice of these classes depends of course on our application but can be adapted on other kind of forms. Figure 1 gives an example of a form highlighting these different classes.

4 Analysis Phases

The analysis schema consists of three main phases (cf. fig. 2:

- In the first phase, cells are extracted by line searching, segment reconstruction and cycle delimitation within the graph of line crossings
- In the second phase, some features are extracted from the cells either globally on the hole data or more precisely on the different connected components within each cell
- In the third phase, these features are analyzed by a list of classifiers which decide for one belonging class among the eight classes defined below

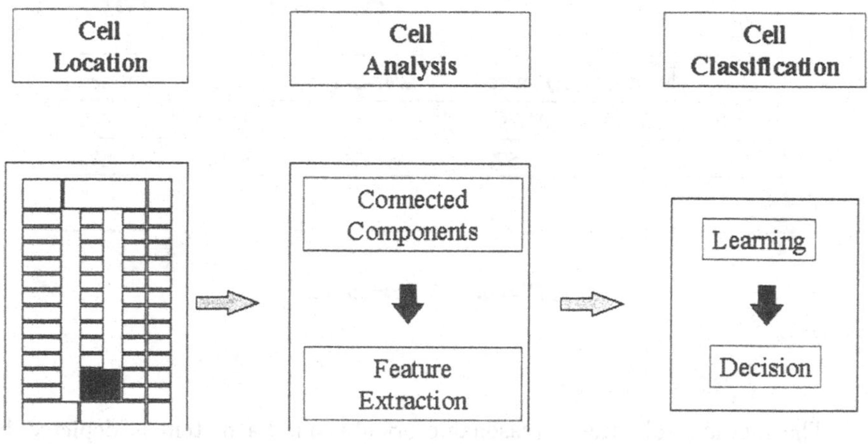

Fig. 2. *Analysis Phases.*

4.1 Cell Extraction

For line extraction, we used Hough transform on polar coordinates. Because of its slowness, the original method was improved by a filtering of voting points and a clever clustering of the accumulator cells in the Hough space (depending on line direction).

For filtering, only points belonging to contours vote. Thanks to this filtering, the system is not disturbed by the black strips and can detect accurately their contour. For thick lines, the two edges are merged.

The clustering in the polar coordinates is made up by a recursive cutting up algorithm.

Figure 3.a shows the hough straight line, the voting pixel and the current segment followed. Figure 3.b shows the line extraction by Hough. We can notice that lines made up by brackets and black strips are also found. Finally, Figure 3.c synthesises the different extraction rates, for well delimitation, under- and over-segmentation, and for omission.

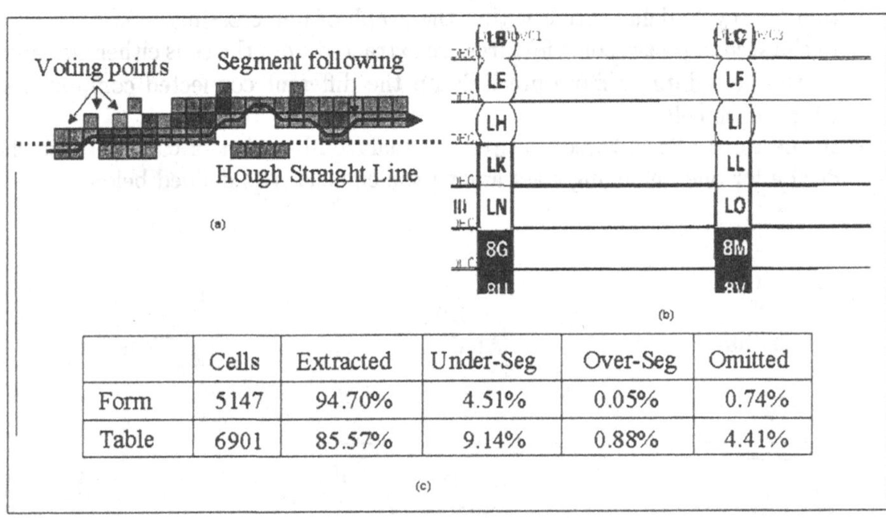

	Cells	Extracted	Under-Seg	Over-Seg	Omitted
Form	5147	94.70%	4.51%	0.05%	0.74%
Table	6901	85.57%	9.14%	0.88%	4.41%

Fig. 3. *Cell Extraction.*

The method tolerates a reasonable orientation. Each item is depicted by a box in a specific colour. Even though the method gives a very indifferent quality, it provides a good base for a global classification of the cells. Joined characters and overlapping characters with horizontal lines are usually disturbing the classification(cf. fig. 4.

4.2 Cell Classification

The cell classification schema can be divided into three steps as shown if fig. 5.

The classification is performed progressively in order to discard rapidly the obvious cases and to refine the others.

The role of the first step is to give a rapid decision on the simple cases such as GRAY, EMPT and BLAC and to separate the remaining classes into two main categories depending on the alignment: horizontal or vertical. Because of the ill quality of the image, this classification is operated globally on the cell images by using some numeric features.

	(Ne pas reporter le montant des centimes)*		Exercice N 1	Exercice N-1 2
PRODUITS EXCEPTIONNELS	Produits exceptionnels sur opérations de gestion	HA		
	Produits exceptionnels sur opérations en capital *	HB	219 800	
	Reprises sur provisions et transferts de charges	HC		
	Total des produits exceptionnels (7) (VII)	HD	219 800	
CHARGES EXCEPTIONNELLES	Charges exceptionnelles sur opérations de gestion	HE	5 416	
	Charges exceptionnelles sur opérations en capital *	HF	125 987	
	Dotations exceptionnelles aux amortissements et provisions	HG	5 200	
	Total des charges exceptionnelles (7) (VIII)	HH	136 603	
3 - RESULTAT EXCEPTIONNEL (VII - VIII)		HI	83 196	
Participation des salariés aux résultats de l'entreprise	(IX)	HJ		
Impôts sur les bénéfices *	(X)	HK		
	TOTAL DES PRODUITS (I + III + V + VII)	HL	3 336 905	
	TOTAL DES CHARGES (II + IV + VI + VIII + IX + X)	HM	3 273 685	
4 - BENEFICE OU PERTE (total des produits - total des charges)		HN	63 220	
		HO		

Fig. 4. *Cell Extraction.*

The objective of the second step is to refine the classification within both categories The classification is operated directly on the image of the CCs of the cell. Two specific neuronal nets are used at this level.

The third stage is used for some disturbing cases corresponding to cut characters such as the zero which seriously handicaps the straightforward classification of the digits. A specific classifier is used for a possible merging of cut digits.

4.3 Classification from CC Parameters

12 simple numerical parameters have been experimentally determined for the classification in the first step.

1. Number of connected components: this is related to the number of CCs after a merging step introduced because of the presence of numerous cut characters (cf. fig. 6). The merging is made within a cell, line by line. Two CCs are merged if they respect the following constraints:
   - they belong to the same text line,
   - they are consecutive in the line,
   - they are superposed (cf. fig. 7.a) or overlapped with an important intersection area (cf. fig. 7.b) or overlapped with a small intersection and where one of the CC is very small compared to the average size of the Cell's CCs studied.

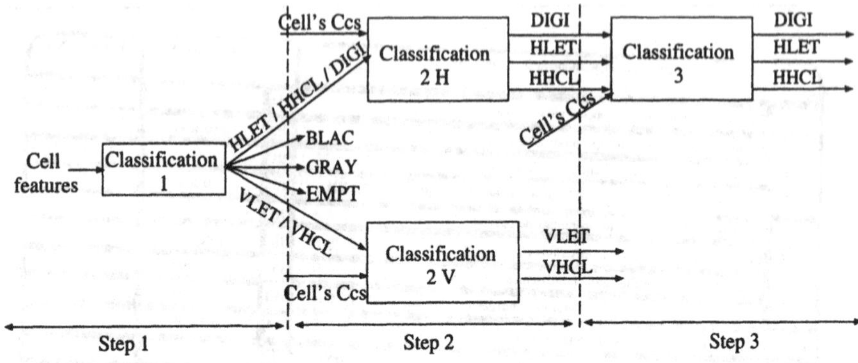

Fig. 5. *Cell Classification.*

Fig. 6. *Connected Components Before Merging.*

2. Text alignment: we have observed in the forms studied that the cells which are more wide than tall, contain text horizontally aligned. In opposite, when the cells are more tall then wide, the text can be aligned horizontally or vertically. An analysis of the text is then necessary in this case. Three cases are considered:
   - the number of horizontal CCs , i.e. those which the height is greater than the width,
   - the homogeneity of the height of the text lines,
   - the height of the greater CCs of each line.

   If the number of horizontal CCs is important, text lines are homogeneous and if there are CCs in each line which height is similar to the line height,

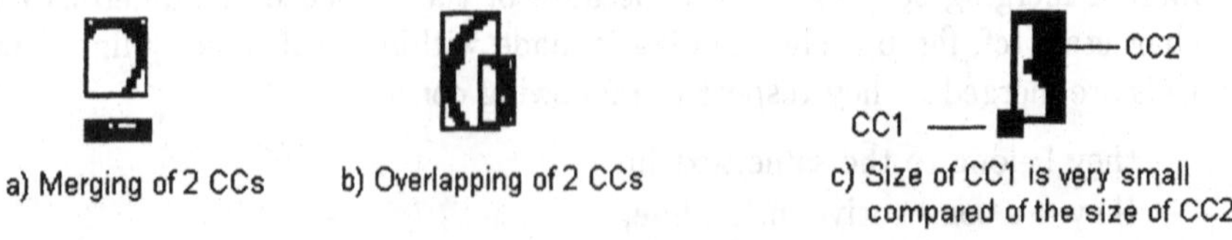

Fig. 7. *Different configurations of Connected Components.*

the text is considered as horizontally aligned. Otherwise, it is considered as vertically aligned.

3. Number of text lines: the text lines are detected by analyzing the histogram obtained by horizontal or vertical projection of the image.
   This analysis is performed in three steps:
   - In the first step, the black areas of the histogram are delimited. When the text is of a good quality and lines are not overlapped, each black area corresponds to a text line. To avoid to take into account the noise, only black areas are considered with a size experimentally fixed to 3 pixels for the height and 5 pixels for the width. It is important to combine the height and the width in order to avoid to consider as noise, lines containing only one character (cf. fig 8).

Fig. 8. *Example of a Line containing only one Character.*

   - In the second step, picks found are merged where they are close (separated with less than 3 pixels). In fact, in some cases, a line can be represented by two picks. This is the case for the line of 9 because the letter 'g' of the word 'outillage' is composed of two CCs.

Fig. 9. *Bad Segmented Characters.*

   - Lines previously found are examined in order to separate couples of consecutive lines connected by the down-strokes of the ones or the stems of the others (cf. fig 10). For this, each black area is analyzed so that picks separated by a valley which height is less than a threshold 's' which value has been fixed at 28% of the greatest height (cf. fig 11) are extracted. These picks are compared if they are neghbours. We begin by analyzing the picks having the deepest valleys. If the distance between a pair of picks is less than the sum of the width of the two picks, this probably indicates the presence of two close text lines. If the widths of these two potential lines are comparable, then two separated lines are considered. In the other cases, we merge the two picks which forms a single line. When all the picks have been treated by pairs, we compare the size of the lines obtained during this step. If their size is homogeneous, the lines are selected, else only lines extracted in the second step are preserved.

Fig. 10. *Very Close Text Lines.*

4. Number of classes of CC heights. It is obtained from the analysis of height histogram of the CCs.
   A pick is indicated by a high value of the histogram. The class searching is determined as follows:
   Begin
   Create a class with the biggest pick.
   Examine the others picks in a decreasing order.
   Let Pc be the current pick, search Pg a bigger pick than Pc and the closest of Pc.
   If Pc is enough close to Pg
   then Pc belongs to the same class than Pg
   else create a new class containing Pc.
   End
5. Number of CC width classes.
6. Number of width classes of the spaces between CCs.
7. Average number of black segments per line in a CC.
8. Average density of black pixels per CC.
9. Density of black pixels in a cell.
10. Average height of CCs.
11. Number of CCs deleted: this value is determined during the CC extraction step; it corresponds to the number of CCs assimilated to the noise.
12. Ratio between the number of CCs deleted and the total number of CCs.
    The choice of these 12 parameters results from a series of observations and tests realized on a database built up for this problem and from which we have verified the contribution of each one of these parameters in the classification process.

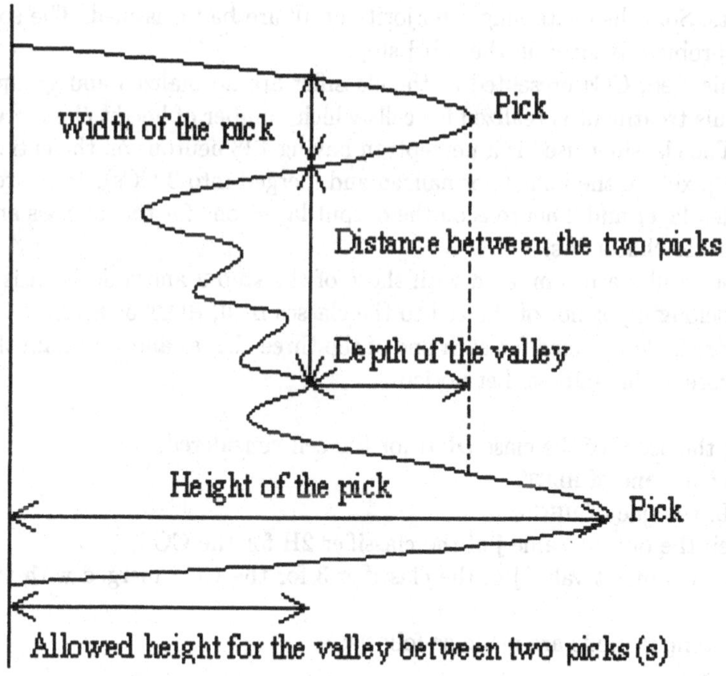

Fig. 11. *Example of two Consecutive Picks Used for Line Detection.*

The classifier uses a mono-layer perceptron with 12 neurons on the entry layer (for the 12 parameters) and 5 neurons on the exit layer (for the 5 classes retained).

4.4 Classification from Cell CCs

This phase including the steps 2 and 3 of the classification process, tends to classify cells containing text into three classes: DIGI, HLET and HHCL for cells with horizontal alignment or into two classes: VLET and VHCL for cells with vertical alignment. In the tax forms, there was not amounts vertically aligned. This explains the class difference in relation with the alignment.

In the second step, the entry data of the classifier is the size normalized image of a CC. The classifier retained is a perceptron with a hidden layer. It contains 64 neurons on the entry layer (the 64 pixels of the normalized image of a CC), 12 neurons on the hidden layer and 2 or 3 neurons on the output layer according to the alignment of the studied cell. A value is associated to each output. For every output, we compute the product of the values of each CC of the considered cell. The output having the higher product is attributed to the cell.

The results obtained at the end of this step are satisfactory except for the DIGI class. Errors come essentially from the '0' often bad segmented and cut in two parts. So, cells containing a majority of '0' are bad classified. The solution for this problem is given in the third step.

In this step, CCs presented to the classifier are normalized and grouped by pairs. This treatment is realized for cells which number of height class of CCs is 1 or 2. The classifier used is a perceptron having 128 neurons on the entry layer (the 128 pixels of the image normalized and merged into 2 CCs), 18 neurons on the hidden layer and 2 neurons on the output layer: one for the '0' class and one for the other characters.

These results are compared with those of the step 2 and a decision is taken for the belonging or not of the cell to the classes DIGI, HLET or HHCL.

A score is determined for each one of the three classes and we retain the one which score is the highest. Let notice

ScDIGI: the score of the class DIGI for the cell considered,
ScHLET: the one of HLET,
ScHHCL: the one of HHCL,
SjC2Hcci: the output value j of the classifier 2H for the CC i,
SjC3cci: the output value j of the classifier 3 for the CC i merged with the CC i+1.

The computations are made as follows:

Begin

```
ScDIGI, ScHLET, ScHHCL = 1

i = 1
For every CC i of the current cell do
    If S1C3cc i ¡ S2C3cc i then
    ScDIGI = ScDIGI * S1C2Hcci
    ScHLET = ScHLET * S2C2Hcci
    ScHHCL = ScHHCL * S3C2Hcci
    i = i +1
    Else
        ScDIGI = ScDIGI * S1C3cci
        ScHLET = ScHLET * S2C2Hcci * S2C2Hcci + 1
        ScHHCL = ScHHCL * S2C2Hcci * S2C2Hcci + 1
        i = i +2
    Endif
Endfor
```

End

5 Results and Discussion

The classification process was tested on 19 French tax forms belonging to the General Direction of French Revenue. The classification time for one form is about 1'45" on a SUN Ultra Spark station, model 140 MHz.

The results obtained are detailed in the table 1 and the classification rates are presented in table 2. A classification example of a form is given in 12. The color attributed to each cell indicates the class found (cf. fig 3). A classification error is materialized by the presence of a little square on the bottom left. It has the colour of the wanted class.

	DIGI	HLET	HHCL	VLET	VHCL	GRAY	BLAC	EMPT	Total Number of Cells
DIGI	638	9	6	0	0	0	0	0	653
HLET	5	587	233	0	0	4	0	0	829
HHCL	4	22	308	4	2	2	0	0	342
VLET	0	0	0	23	0	0	0	0	23
VHCL	0	0	0	0	72	0	0	0	72
GRAY	0	0	1	0	0	23	1	0	25
BLAC	0	0	0	0	0	0	72	0	72
EMPT	0	0	2	0	0	7	0	1479	1488

Table 1. *Form Classification Results.*

DIGI	HLET	HHCL	VLET	VHCL	GRAY	BLAC	EMPT	TOTAL
97.70%	70.81 %	90.06 %	100.00 %	100.00 %	92.00 %	100.00%	99.40%	91.38%

Table 2. *Classification Rates.*

We can remark that the scores are very good for the classes DIGI, VLET, VHCL, GRAY, BLAC and EMPT, but are less good for the classes HLET and HHCL. There are several reasons explaining the confusions:

- The bad quality of images can produce an over-segmentation (cf. fig. 11) or a under-segmentation (cf. fig. 12).
- Some characters have the same morphology in lower-case and higher-case and cannot be differentiated after normalization. It is the case of characters as 'c', 'o', 's', 'u', 'v', 'x' and 'z'.

Several solutions can be considered in order to resolve these problems:

- creation of a reject class for cells for which it is difficult to make a choice between the classes HLET and HHCL,
- fusion of the classes HLET and HHCL: this fusion gives a general classification rate equal to 98,32%,
- the consideration of the CC height before normalization.

DIGI	HLET	HHCL	VLET	VHCL	GRAY	BLAC	EMPTY
red	brown	orange	clear green	dark green	cyan	yellow	mauve

Table 3. *Colors of the eigh Cell Classes.*

6 Conclusion

This paper outlines a feasibility study for the classification of form cells into eight classes depending on the presence of information or not, on the text alignment: horizontal or vertical and the character modes higher-case or lower-case. Few systems have been developed in this sense. Most of the classification methods developed try to differentiate between text and non text areas. We used a perceptron for the classification. It is mono-layer for the first step which realizes a pre-classification by using numerical parameters. It contains one hidden layer for the steps 2 and 3 which analyze the text areas from normalized images of CCs. The results obtained are acceptable. Improvements and adaptations remain are possible. Acknowledgements: The authors wish to thank N. Pican for providing us with his implementation of the perceptron algorithm.

References

1. RISSE T., Hough Transform for Line Recognition : Complexity of E vidence Accumulation and Cluster Detection, Computer Vision, Graphics, and Image Processing, Vol. 46, 1989, pp. 327-345.
2. CASEY, FERGUSON D., MOHIUDDIN K. and WALACH E., Intelligent Form s Processing System, Machine Vision and Applications, Vol. 5, n 3, 1992, pp. 14 4-155.
3. ISHITANI Y., Model Matching Based on Association Graph for Form Image Understanding, in Proceedings of ICDAR'95 : 3rd International Conference o n Document Analysis and Recognition, Montral, Canada, 1995, pp. 287-292.
4. YUAN J., TANG Y. Y. and SUEN C. Y., Four Directional Adjacency G raphs (FDAG) and Their Application in Locating Fields in Forms, in Proceedings o f ICDAR'95 : 3rd International Conference on Document Analysis and Recognition, Montral, Canada, 1995, pp. 752-755.
5. HIRAYAMA Y., Analysing Form Images by Using Line-Shared-Adjacent Cell Relations, in Proceedings of ICPR'96 : 13th International Conference on Pa ttern Recognition, 1996, pp. 768-772.
6. SHIMOTSUJI S. and ASANO M., Form Identification based on Cell St ructure, in Proceedings of ICPR'96 : 13th International Conference on Pattern Re cognition, 1996, pp. 793-797.
7. TUROLLA E. BELAD Y. and BELAD A., Form item extraction based on line searching, in Graphics Recognition : Methods and Applications, Lecture Not es in Computer Science, Vol. 1072, 1996, pp. 69-79.
8. ARAI H. et ODAKA K., From Processing Based on Background Region Analysis, in Proceedings of ICDAR'97 : 4th International Conference on Document Analysis and Recognition, Ulm, Allemagne, Vol. 1, 1997, pp. 164-169.

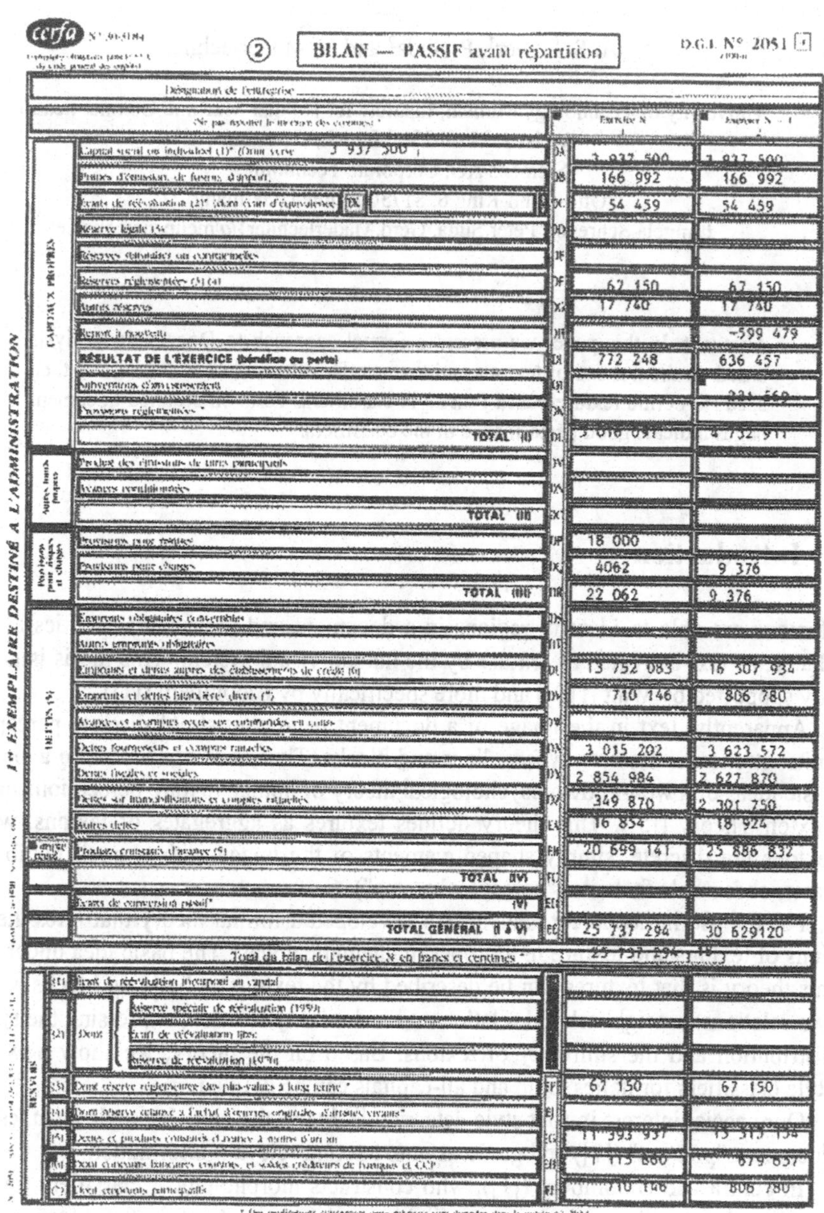

D.G.I. N° 2051

② **BILAN — PASSIF avant répartition**

1er EXEMPLAIRE DESTINÉ A L'ADMINISTRATION

Désignation de l'entreprise

	(Ne pas reporter le montant des centimes) *		Exercice N	Exercice N – 1
CAPITAUX PROPRES	Capital social ou individuel (1)* (Dont versé 3 937 500)	DA	3 937 500	3 937 500
	Primes d'émission, de fusion, d'apport	DB	166 992	166 992
	Ecarts de réévaluation (2)* (dont écart d'équivalence EK)	DC	54 459	54 459
	Réserve légale (3)	DD		
	Réserves statutaires ou contractuelles	DE		
	Réserves réglementées (3) (4)	DF	67 150	67 150
	Autres réserves	DG	17 740	17 740
	Report à nouveau	DH		–599 479
	RÉSULTAT DE L'EXERCICE (bénéfice ou perte)	DI	772 248	636 457
	Subventions d'investissement	DJ		231 569
	Provisions réglementées *	DK		
	TOTAL (I)	DL	5 016 091	4 732 911
Autres fonds propres	Produit des émissions de titres participatifs	DM		
	Avances conditionnées	DN		
	TOTAL (II)	DO		
Provisions pour risques et charges	Provisions pour risques	DP	18 000	
	Provisions pour charges	DQ	4062	9 376
	TOTAL (III)	DR	22 062	9 376
DETTES (5)	Emprunts obligataires convertibles	DS		
	Autres emprunts obligataires	DT		
	Emprunts et dettes auprès des établissements de crédit (6)	DU	13 752 083	16 507 934
	Emprunts et dettes financières divers (7)	DV	710 146	806 780
	Avances et acomptes reçus sur commandes en cours	DW		
	Dettes fournisseurs et comptes rattachés	DX	3 015 202	3 623 572
	Dettes fiscales et sociales	DY	2 854 984	2 627 870
	Dettes sur immobilisations et comptes rattachés	DZ	349 870	2 301 750
	Autres dettes	EA	16 854	18 924
Compte régul.	Produits constatés d'avance (5)	EB	20 699 141	25 886 832
	TOTAL (IV)	EC		
	Ecarts de conversion passif* (V)	ED		
	TOTAL GÉNÉRAL (I à V)	EE	25 737 294	30 629120
	Total du bilan de l'exercice N en francs et centimes *		25 737 294 , 10	
RENVOIS	(1) Ecart de réévaluation incorporé au capital			
	(2) Dont Réserve spéciale de réévaluation (1959)			
	Ecart de réévaluation libre			
	Réserve de réévaluation (1976)			
	(3) Dont réserve réglementée des plus-values à long terme *	EF	67 150	67 150
	(4) Dont réserve relative à l'achat d'oeuvres originales d'artistes vivants*	EJ		
	(5) Dettes et produits constatés d'avance à moins d'un an	EG	11 393 937	15 315 134
	(6) Dont concours bancaires courants, et soldes créditeurs de banques et CCP	EH	1 115 860	679 657
	(7) Dont emprunts participatifs	EI	710 146	806 780

* Des explications concernant cette rubrique sont données dans la notice n° 2032.

Fig. 12. *An Example of Form Classification.*

A Formal Approach to Textons and Its Application to Font Style Detection

A. Schreyer[1], P. Suda[2] and G. Maderlechner[2]

[1]University of Technology Munich, Institute for Human-Machine-Communication, Arcisstr. 21, 80290 Munich, Germany
[2]Siemens AG, Corporate Technology, Otto-Hahn-Ring 6, 81730 Munich, Germany
{Angela.Schreyer, Peter.Suda, Gerd.Maderlechner}@mchp.siemens.de

Abstract. In this paper we present a formal approach to Document Analysis based on the notions of textons and texture. This theoretical framework is then used to define texture-based font style classifiers. Tests on scanned document pages indicate good performance of the classifiers.

1 Introduction

Humans are able to identify regions in a document and their characteristics at first glance, as text is treated as texture by the human visual system. This thesis is generally supported by Watt ([10]) and more specifically by Bloomberg ([1]).

Apparently, text in the image of a document page consists of discrete perceptual units: strokes, characters, words, lines and blocks. Thus, it is reasonable to adopt the basic ideas of a well-known psychological theory of human texture perception: Julesz' Texton Theory ([5]). This theory defines textures as aggregates of textons, where textons are discrete, simply shaped elements of the image with a small number of basic, observable features ("perceptual atoms").

For the use in document analysis we developed a formal theory that fixes the notions of textons and texture in a proper mathematical way. The basic idea underlying this theory is that textures can be described by the textons as building blocks and by two relations: a neighborhood relation and a similarity relation, expressing the spatial distribution and the similarity of textons. Based on the theory, we show how font style classifiers for italics, bold and all-capitals can be defined.

Our special interest in font style detection is due to the fact, that style changes in a document "pop out" ([7]) and guide us in extracting relevant information.

In contrast to Bloomberg ([1]), who constructs morphological classifiers for texture-based font style analysis, we explicitly model elements of font style textures by textons. Automatic detection of italics, bold and all-capitals by explicit features is also described in[2]. The usefulness of font style detection for information retrieval is mentioned, but the paper's aim is improving OCR by previous font style analysis.

Not only the font style, but the predominant font of running text in an English document is identified in [6] using a database of function words in various fonts.

In [4] the term texton is used in a different meaning, namely for the logical components of text (characters, words, etc.) in a hierarchical manner.

The overall aim of our work is attention-based extraction of relevant information from documents by classifying typography and layout features. Doermann ([3]) also uses these features, in order to determine the role of document parts in the process of transferring information.

2 Formal Definition of Textons

Julesz defines textons to be discrete elements or objects with a set of observable features. This definition can be formalized in a simple way:

Definition 2.1: A *texton structure* TS is a 4-tuple $TS=(D,\Gamma,E,\Phi)$ with the properties

1. $D\in\mathbf{R}^2$ is a non-empty compact subset of $\mathbf{R}^2$.
2. Γ is a finite partition of D and for each $\gamma\in\Gamma$, γ is non-empty and compact.
3. $E=E_1\times\ldots\times E_n$ is a feature space.
4. $\Phi:\Gamma\rightarrow E$ is a function, assigning each γ from Γ a feature vector from E.

Remarks:

1. D is called the *domain,* and a pair $t=(\gamma, \Phi(\gamma))$ is called a *texton* in the texton structure TS. Given a texton $t=(\gamma, \Phi(\gamma))$, then $Dom(t)$ denotes the *carrier* γ and $Prop(t)$ the *feature vector* $\Phi(\gamma)$ of the texton t.
2. Given two textons s and t, then $Dom(s)\cap Dom(t)\neq\emptyset \Leftrightarrow s=t$. This models the assumption that textons are discrete objects.
3. Let $TEX_{D,\Gamma,E,\Phi}$ denote the set of all textons of a given texton structure $TS=(D,\Gamma,E,\Phi)$. If it is not misleading we write TEX instead of $TEX_{D,\Gamma,E,\Phi}$.
4. For n-dimensional texton structures we can replace $\mathbf{R}^2$ by $\mathbf{R}^n$. For discrete texton structures we take the integers $\mathbf{Z}$ instead of the reals $\mathbf{R}$.

For a formal definiton of texture we consider that Julesz defines textures as aggregates of similar textons of constant density. In our framework this means that textons have to be connected spatially and that they should have similar features. To model connectedness and similarity we introduce two relations:

Definition 2.2: Let $TS=(D,\Gamma,E,\Phi)$ be a texton structure and TEX the set of all textons. Then $N\subseteq TEX\times TEX$ is called a *neighborhood relation* in TEX, if

1. $\forall t\in TEX$: $(t, t)\in N$.
2. $\forall s, t\in TEX$: $(s, t)\in N\rightarrow(t, s)\in N$.

Definition 2.3: Let E be a feature space,then $\Sigma\subseteq E\times E$ is a *similarity relation*, if Σ is an equivalence relation.

Remarks:

1. Σ induces a partition of the feature space. Given two textons s and t, and a similarity relation Σ, then s and t have equivalent features in respect of Σ, if $(Prop(s), Prop(t))\in\Sigma$.

2. Each similarity relation Σ can be composed from component similarity relations $\Sigma_i \subseteq E_i \times E_i$. It is also evident that each similarity relation Σ induces component similarities $\Sigma_1, ..., \Sigma_n$.

Definition 2.4: Let $TS=(D,r,E,\Phi)$ be a texton structure, TEX the set of all textons, $N \subseteq TEX \times TEX$ a neighborhood relation and $\Sigma \subseteq E \times E$ a similarity relation. Then two textons s and t from TEX are *N-Σ-connected,* if there exists a chain $t_1, ..., t_n \in TEX$ such that:

1. $s = t_1$ and $t = t_n$.
2. $\forall i = 1, ..., n-1$: $(t_i, t_{i+1}) \in N$ and $(Prop(t_i), Prop(t_{i+1})) \in \Sigma$.

Remark:

N-Σ-connectedness is the key to the definition of textures, because the underlying idea is that textures consist of chains of similar textons. It is evident that if s is *N-Σ*-connected with t, then t is also *N-Σ*-connected with s.

Definition 2.5: Let $TS=(D,r,E,\Phi)$ be a texton structure, TEX the set of all textons, $N \subseteq TEX \times TEX$ a neighborhood relation and $\Sigma \subseteq E \times E$ a similarity relation. Then a set $T \subseteq TEX$ is a *N-Σ-texture*, if

1. $\forall s, t \in T$: s and t are *N-Σ*-connected,
2. $\forall s \notin T$: there is no $t \in T$ such that s and t are *N-Σ*-connected.

Remarks:

1. Textures are sets of maximally *N-Σ*-connected textons.
2. Let S and T be *N-Σ*-textures, then $S \cap T \neq \emptyset \Leftrightarrow S=T$. This means that textures do not share textons. In addition, for textures S and T with $S \neq T$ the sets $\bigcup_{s \in S} Dom(s)$ and $\bigcup_{t \in T} Dom(t)$ are disjoint.

Under the definition's viewpoint document segmentation means to find a hierarchical sequence of textures in the document, i.e. to establish *a texton hierarchy*. When performing a bottom-up analysis, this hierarchy is installed by the lemma:

Lemma 2.1: Let $TS=(D,r,E,\Phi)$ be a texton structure, TEX the set of all textons and $TEXTURES$ the set of all *N-Σ*-textures, that are formed by a neighborhood relation $N \subseteq TEX \times TEX$ and a similarity relation $\Sigma \subseteq E \times E$.

Furthermore, be $E^*=E^*_1 \times ... \times E^*_m$ a feature space, $\Delta: TEXTURES \rightarrow E^*$ and $\Theta: TEXTURES \rightarrow r^*$, where $r^*=\{\bigcup_{t \in T} Dom(t) : T \in TEXTURES\}$ and $\Theta(T)=\bigcup_{t \in T} Dom(t)$.

Then there exists a function $\Phi^*: r^* \rightarrow E^*$ such that the diagram Fig.1 commutes.

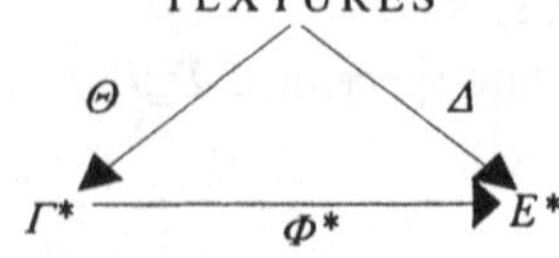

Fig. 1. $\Phi^*: \Gamma^* \rightarrow E^*$

Remarks:

1. As r^* is a finite partition of D, and Φ^* is a feature assignment according to Definition 2.1, $TS^*=(D,r^*,E^*,\Phi^*)$ is a texton structure.
2. The mapping Δ reflects that the features of a constructed texton at the new level are calculated from features of those textons used in construction.
3. As higher level textons are constructed from textures (= sets of lower level textons), there is a natural inclusion between the textons in a hierarchy. To denote that a lower level texton t contributed to the creation of a higher level texton s we write in the following $t \succ s$.
4. The theoretical framework also allows to assign statistical features to a higher level texton. For example, let $\Xi \subseteq E \times E$ be a similarity relation different from Σ. Then a feature $e \in E$ is dominant for a texture T in respect of Ξ, if
$\forall e' \in E$: $|\{t: (Prop(t), e) \in \Xi\}| \geq |\{s: (Prop(s), e') \in \Xi\}|$.
The feature e can be taken as a characterizing feature of the higher level texton. This is exactly what is done for font style detection with more elaborate statistical methods (Chapter 4).
5. So far, we were only concerned with one texton structure over a domain D and the construction of hierarchies. In practice, we have to deal with different interwoven texton structures simultaneously reflecting different textural aspects.

In general, document analysis uses rather simple features to characterize textons. Among them are size and position of a texton as follows:

Let r be a partition of D. Then we can define for each $\gamma \in r$:

$$TOP(\gamma) = \max\{y : (x,y) \in \gamma\}, \qquad BOT(\gamma) = \min\{y : (x,y) \in \gamma\}$$
$$LEFT(\gamma) = \min\{x : (x,y) \in \gamma\}, \qquad RIGHT(\gamma) = \max\{x : (x,y) \in \gamma\}$$
$$HEIGHT(\gamma) = TOP(\gamma) - BOT(\gamma) + 1, \qquad WIDTH(\gamma) = LEFT(\gamma) - RIGHT(\gamma) + 1$$

Subsequently, one can define a mapping $\Phi(\gamma)=(TOP(\gamma), BOT(\gamma), LEFT(\gamma), RIGHT(\gamma), HEIGHT(\gamma), WIDTH(\gamma))$, providing us with a basic feature vector. Apart from these basic geometric features, a texton may have additional features, e.g. area, orientation and, for higher level textons, the amount of lower level textons used for construction, etc..

3 Grouping and Texton Hierarchy

A short explanation of the grouping process is given, because in our approach the hierarchical grouping of strokes (s) to character textures, character to word textures, etc. is a prerequisite for font style detection. Steps upwards in the texton hierarchy are done, when we construct from a character texture the character texton c, from a word texture the word texton w, from a line texture the line texton l and from a block texture the block texton b, such that

$$s \succ c \succ w \succ l \succ b.$$

Although the texton theory is general enough to describe grouping on bit and run level, we start at the level of strokes. The carrier γ of a stroke is an area of 8-connected black runs, such that there is no split- or merge-run in the area. (split-/merge-run: at least two connected runs in the next/previous image line). The strokes are grouped to character textons by the strokes' geometric properties. The neighborhood relation N is the 8-connection relation between strokes. The similarity relation Σ considers width, height and orientation of a stroke.

On the basis of character textons the word textures can be found, for example with relations similar to the following:

Let $c1$, $c2$, $c3$ be character textons, then
$(c1, c2) \in N :\Leftrightarrow$
$RIGHT\_OF(c1, c2) \wedge \forall c3: DISTANCE(c1, c2) \leq DISTANCE(c1, c3) \wedge$
$DISTANCE(c1, c2) \leq \min\{HEIGHT(c1), HEIGHT(c2) \wedge$
$DISTANCE(c1, c2) < MAXDIST \wedge ...$
$(c1,c2) \in \Sigma :\Leftrightarrow |HEIGHT(c1)-HEIGHT(c2)| \leq \min\{HEIGHT(c1), HEIGHT(c2\} \cdot 0.67 \wedge$
$OVERLAP(c1, c2) > \min\{HEIGHT(c1), HEIGHT(c2)\} / 4 \wedge ....$

The distance is given by the difference between the left border of $c2$ and the right border of $c1$. $c2$ is right of $c1$, if the left border of $c2$ is right of the left border of $c1$ and $c1$ and $c2$ have an overlap in vertical direction.

Next, the word textons are grouped to lines by quite similar neighborhood and similarity relations.

During grouping, features of the newly established textons can be calculated, e.g. the word and line features geometrical borders, base line, top line, average character height, area, and the line feature line skew.

The most sophisticated grouping step is the investigation of block textures, as we get confronted with a multitude of different two-dimensional texture models that are based on the multitude of possible block layouts. The basic neighborhood relation N is given by the distance between two vertically adjacent lines. The basic similarity relation Σ is given by the average character height within a line.

In the following, we use *STROKES* to denote the set of all stroke textons, *CHARS* for the character textons, *WORDS* for the word textons, *LINES* for the line textons, and *BLOCKS* for the block textons in a document.

4 Font Style Detection

Based on the results of the grouping process a further texture analysis determines different font styles for the words in the document. The classification process gives a new feature for a word texton based on the features of the textons on lower levels. This new feature can be used with a new similarity relation in a more elaborate texture analysis to find pop outs on a higher level.

4.1 Italics Classification

Italics font style is characterized by the slant of the approximately vertical stroke textons in a word. The slant of a stroke as a stroke texton feature is given by the angle α between the vertical line and the connecting line of the top-most and bottom-most black run of the stroke (Fig. 2).

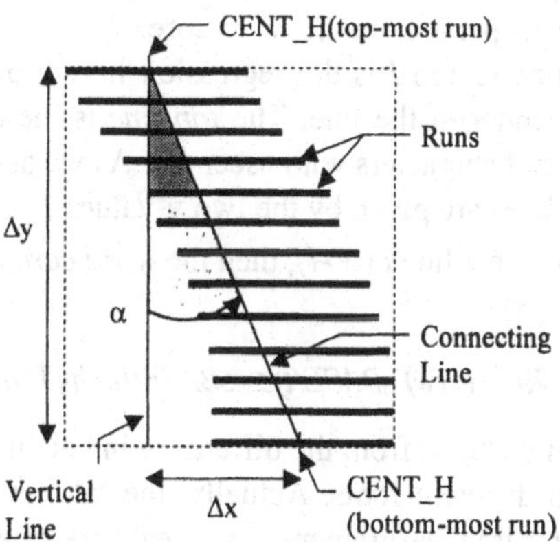

Fig. 2. Slant of a stroke

If $s \in STROKES$, then the slant of s is

$$SLANT(s) = \tan(\alpha) = \frac{CENT\_H(TOP\_MOST\_RUN(s)) - CENT\_H(BOTTOM\_MOST\_RUN(s)) + 1}{HEIGHT(s)}$$

where *CENT_H* denotes the middle of the according top-most and bottom-most run.

To derive a mean slant for a word texton $w \in WORDS$, we investigate the approximately vertical strokes, that contributed to the word texture:

$$A\_VERTICALS(w) = \{s : s \succ w \wedge HEIGHT(s) > WIDTH(s)\}$$

The mean slant of the word w is given by

$$MEAN\_SLANT(w) = \sum_{s \in A\_VERTICALS(w)} SLANT(s) / |A\_VERTICALS(w)|$$

and the mean slant of a text block b∈BLOCKS by

$$MEAN\_SLANT(b) = \sum_{w \in \{w : w \succ b \wedge w \in WORDS\}} MEAN\_SLANT(w) / |\{w : w \succ b \wedge w \in WORDS\}| .$$

With these features, the new feature *ITALICS*(*w*) for the word texton *w* is given:

Let *w* be a word texton and *b* the block texton with $w \succ b$, then

$$ITALICS(w) :\Leftrightarrow MEAN\_SLANT(w) > TH \vee MEAN\_SLANT(b) > TH.$$

According to Table 1, we have set the threshold $TH = 0.12 \approx \tan(7°)$.

Due to the statistical nature of the feature, word slants are only reliable for words that have a significant number of approximately vertical strokes. Experiments have shown nice classifier performance for words with more than three characters.

4.2 Bold Classification

A word in bold font style is characterized by its black intensity, which is caused by the number of black pixels per area in the word core.

The *base line* of a line texton l is the regression line through the bottoms of the characters without descender in the line. The *top line* is the regression line through the tops of the capitals and characters with ascender. As we assume the lines to be deskewed, the regression lines are given by the two y-values $TOP(l)$ and $BASE(l)$.

Given a word texton w in a line l ($w \succ l$), then the *word core* of w is given by:

$$WORD\_CORE(w)= \{(x,y): LEFT(w) \leq x \leq RIGHT(w) \wedge BASE(l) \leq y \leq BASE(l)+h \cdot (TOP(w)-BASE(l)+1)\},$$

with h=0.67. h has been deduced from the difference in height between lowercase and uppercase characters in different fonts. Actually, the ratio is 0.74 (Table 1), but we take a smaller ratio to ensure measurement in the real core area of the word.

Note, that the word core is not a texton. It is only a region in the basic domain D underlying the texton structure.

Given the word core for a word w in line l we can define the *black intensity of the word* w by:

$$BLACK\_INTENS(w)= |WORD\_CORE(w) \cap Dom(w)| / (\mathrm{h}(TOP(w)-BASE(l)+1) \cdot WIDTH(w)).$$

As this local intensity cannot determine bold font style, we investigate the intensity distribution across the document by setting up a histogram of the intensity values for the document. From this histogram we derive a threshold for classification.

Let $1 \leq i,j \leq N_{bin}$, then the histogram of black intensity values is given by

$$H(i) = |\{w: w \in WORDS \wedge i = \lfloor N_{bin} \cdot BLACK\_INTENS(w) \rfloor\}|$$

and the derived *threshold* by

$$TH = (\max\{i : \forall j : H(i) \geq H(j)\} + d) / N_{bin},$$

with N_{bin} =100 and d=8 set empirically.

We also define the *black intensities for blocks*. Let b be a block texton, then

$$BLACK\_INTENS(b)= \sum_{w \in \{w: w \succ b \wedge w \in WORDS\}} BLACK\_INTENS(w) / |\{w: w \succ b \wedge w \in WORDS\}|.$$

Thus, the new feature $BOLD(w)$ for the word texton w is given by:

Let w be a word texton and b the block texton with $w \succ b$, then

$$BOLD(w) :\Leftrightarrow BLACK\_INTENS(w) > TH \vee BLACK\_INTENS(b) > TH.$$

This classifier works nice for words with a reasonably sized word core, i.e. for words with more than 3 characters. For words with less characters we can extend the definition by using the direct predecessor *PRED(w)* and successor *SUC(w)*:

If w is a word with less than four characters, then

$$BOLD(w) :\Leftrightarrow BLACK\_INTENS(w) > TH \wedge$$
$$(BLACK\_INTENS(PRED(w)) > TH \vee BLACK\_INTENS(SUC(w)) > TH).$$

4.3 All-capitals Classification

All-capitals words are characterized by the heights of the contained characters. For statistic classification, the character heights are compared to an adaptive threshold that is calculated from the mean height of lines in a block.

The mean height of lines in a block b is given by

$$MEAN\_L\_HEIGHT(b) = \sum_{l \in \{l: l \succ b \wedge l \in LINES\}} (TOP(l) - BASE(l) + 1) \,/\, \left|\{l: l \succ b \wedge l \in LINES\}\right|.$$

Given a word w in line l of a block b then

$$ALL\_CAPIT(w) :\Leftrightarrow \forall c \in CHARS, c \succ w : (TOP(c) - BASE(l) + 1 > h \cdot MEAN\_L\_HEIGHT(b)).$$

Given a block b with character c in line l, then

$$ALL\_CAPIT(b) :\Leftrightarrow$$
$$\frac{\left|\{c : c \succ b \wedge TOP(c) - BASE(l) + 1 > h \cdot MEAN\_L\_HEIGHT(b) \wedge c \in CHARS\}\right|}{\left|\{c : c \succ b \wedge c \in CHARS\}\right|} > 0.67$$

Experiments on synthetic documents (Chapter 5.1) have yielded the ratio of 0.74 between the height of lowercase characters without ascender or descender and the height of capital characters. For robust all-capitals classification h=0.85 is chosen.

Essentially, the *ALL_CAPIT* classifier for blocks counts big characters. If more than 2/3 of a block's characters are big, the whole block is an *all-capitals* block.

We end up in the following classifier for the new feature *ALL_CAPITAL(w)*:

Let w be a word texton and b the block texton with $w \succ b$, then

$$ALL\_CAPITAL(w) :\Leftrightarrow ALL\_CAPIT(w) \vee ALL\_CAPIT(b).$$

The classifier does not treat words with less than three characters, because with these words there is ambiguity between words completely in all-capitals style and those that contain both capital characters and characters with ascender.

5 Tests and Results

5.1 Tests on Synthetic Documents

Synthetic documents were used to test features for font styles under standardized conditions. There were synthetic documents in four different typefaces and in 3 different font sizes each in italics and bold font style. All synthetic documents were printed on a laser printer at 600dpi and then scanned at 300dpi with fixed threshold.

Each synthetic document contains the alphabet once printed in lowercase and once in uppercase, and the numbers from 0 to 9. The characters are divided into groups of differing basic structure (present or lacking ascender and descender), so that the differently structured characters can be examined separately.

To investigate the threshold *TH* for italics classification, the average of the slants over the whole document was calculated for all synthetic documents, once in italic (A) and once in plain (B) font style (Table 1). A comparison suggests the value *TH*=0.12 at the lower bound of A as an appropriate threshold.

Table 1. Results for slant

Font	A	B
Arial, 8pt	0.13	0.02
Arial, 10pt	0.13	0.02
Arial, 12pt	0.11	0.02
Times New Roman, 8pt	0.17	0.01
Times New Roman, 10pt	0.19	0.01
Times New Roman, 12pt	0.19	0.01
Graphite Light, 8pt	0.19	0.11
Graphite Light, 10pt	0.25	0.12
Graphite Light, 12pt	0.19	0.11
Courier, 8pt	0.13	-0.01
Courier, 10pt	0.14	0.01
Courier, 12pt	0.14	0.02

Table 2 gives the results for the measurement of the ratio of character heights *A* = height(*lowercase without ascender and descender*)/height(*uppercase)*, that is used for defining the word core and classifying all-capitals. Its average is 0.74 for all font families and heights.

Table 2. Results for height ratio

Font	A
Arial, 8pt	0.76
Arial, 10pt	0.76
Arial, 12pt	0.75
Times New Roman, 8pt	0.72
Times New Roman, 10pt	0.72
Times New Roman, 12pt	0.70
Graphite Light, 8pt	0.67
Graphite Light, 10pt	0.73
Graphite Light, 12pt	0.65
Courier, 8pt	0.83
Courier, 10pt	0.77
Courier, 12pt	0.76

5.2 Tests on Scanned Document Pages

We tested our classifiers on document pages from the UW-III Document Image Database ([9]). We chose the 20 pages S000bin.tif to S00kbin.tif, that are scanned directly from original scientific papers at 300dpi. The text on every page (excluding graphics and formulas) was processed by the above classifiers (example: Fig. 3).

Table 3. Results for document pages S000bin.tif to S00kbin.tif

Font style	#(words in respective style)	#(correctly classified words in respective style	#(plain words)	#(falsely classified plain words)
Italics	378	350 (93%)	16338	19 (0.1%)
Bold	568	542 (95%)+11(all-capitals)	16148	9 (0.06%)
All-Capitals	94	89 (95%)	16622	24 (0.1%)+103(numerals)

Table 3 shows, how many words in the respective style were detected correctly and how many words in plain style were marked falsely as being printed in the respective font style. Note, that the bold classifier missed 11 bold words printed in all-capitals. With the present approach all-capitals are a problem, because the greater part of uppercase characters lies outside the defined word core. The all-capitals classifier also suffers from a structural problem, that is given by the fact that the height of numerals is almost the same as the height of uppercase characters.

6 Conclusion and Future Work

We presented a first step towards a texture-based approach to document analysis. We established a formal theory of texture, inspired by Julesz' Texton Theory, and transferred the psychological notion of textons to a mathematical one. Within our formal framework, the paper described classifiers for bold, italics and all-capitals font style. The classifiers can be implemented efficiently, because they use relatively simple features, that can be calculated partially during the preceding grouping process. The good performance of the classifiers on scanned documents showed the practical relevance of our approach.

At present, we are extending our theory, so that the detection of additional layout features in a document can be described consistently in the framework of textons. It is our aim to detect those layout features that would attract a human's attention at first glance, in order to enable attention-based extraction of relevant information from documents ([8]).

Fig. 3. Grouping and font style detection on s00mbin.tif (dark grey: bold, medium grey: italics, light grey: all-capitals)

References

1. D. S. Bloomberg: Multiresolution Morphological Approach to Document Image Analysis, Proc. ICDAR, Saint-Malo, 1991, pp. 963 – 971
2. B. B. Chaudhuri, U. Garain: Automatic Detection of Italic, Bold an All-Capital Words in Document Images, Proc. ICPR , Brisbane, 1998, pp. 610 – 612
3. D. Doermann, A. Rosenfeld, E. Revlin: The Function of Documents, Proc. ICDAR, Ulm, 1997, pp. 1077 - 108
4. D. Dori, D. Doermann, C. Shin, R. Haralick, I. Phillips, M. Buchmann, D. Ross: The Representation of Document Structure: A Generic Object-Process Analysis in P. S. P. Wang and H. Bunke (editors): Handbook on Optical Character Recognition and Document Image Analysis, 1996
5. B. Julesz, J. R. Bergen: Textons: The Fundamental Elements in Preattentive Vision and Perception of Textures, The Bell System Technical Journal, Vol. 62, No. 6, 1983, pp. 1619 - 1645
6. S. Khoubyari, J. J. Hull: Font and Function Word Identification in Document Recognition, Computer Vision and Image Understanding, Vol. 63, No. 1, 1996, pp. 66 - 74
7. T. S. Klitz, J. S. Mansfield, G. E. Legge: Font "Pop Out" in Text Images, OSA Annual Meeting Technical Digest, 23, 1992, pp. 170
8. A. Schreyer, P. Suda, G. Maderlechner: The Idea of Attention-Based Document Analysis, Proc. DAS, Nagano, 1998
9. UW-III English/Technical Document Image Database, CD-ROM, University of Washington, 1996
10. R. Watt: The Visual Analysis of Pages of Text in R. Sassoon: Computers and Typography, Intellect Books, Oxford, 1993, pp. 179 – 201

A Statistical Method for an Automatic Detection of Form Types

Saddok Kebairi[1], Bruno Taconet[1], Abderrazak Zahour[1], Said Ramdane[1]

[1]Laboratoire d'Informatique du Havre, Université du Havre,
Place Robert Schuman, 76610, Le Havre, France.
{kebairi, taconet, zahour, ramdane}@iut.univ-lehavre.fr

Abstract. In this paper, we present a method to classify forms by a statistical approach ; the physical structure may vary from one writer to another. An automatic form segmentation is performed to extract the physical structure which is described by the main rectangular block set. During the form learning phase, a block matching is made inside each class ; the number of occurrences of each block is counted, and statistical block attributes are computed. During the phase of identification, we solve the block instability by introducing a block penalty coefficient, which modifies the classical expression of Mahalanobis distance. A block penalty coefficient depends on the block occurrence probability. Experimental results, using the different form types, are given.

1 Introduction

An important problem in an automatic form reading system is the form type identification. As Doermann et al.[1] said, the form identification lies essentially on an appropriate choice of the information primitives extracted by the document segmentation. Several methods for matching forms structures have been reported in literature: for the construction of the model, Mao et al[2] use the attributes of the horizontal and vertical lines, of the junction points and the regions. However, there must be at least two horizontal lines in every form for reliable recognition and registration. The authors[3] used three types of line segment to represent a form. A fuzzy matching is used for the form recognition. Ishitani[4] presented a method that operates in a hierarchical way. At first, a line matching is constructed, which gives a compatibility graph. On this graph, the first clique is searched to identify the homogenous regions. The used compatibility criterion takes in account the similarities based on the intersection number in the lines. The author explains his choice by the robustness, insensibility to scale variation and noise distortion. Another approach[5] proposed a model based on detecting lines as basic items. A matching graph is proposed for an automatic localization and the extraction of the form field-in data.[6] Another model[7] is based on attributed relational graphs and the system performs form registration and location fields using algorithms based on the hypothesize-and-verify paradigm. The authors[8] described a system that locates form structures by matching horizontal and vertical lines between two forms. The approach is based on the A^*-searh-algorithm. The system proposed by Dubiel et al.[9] runs independently from any restriction on form layout and requires neither an identification number nor any prespecified line structure. The classification is done by searching counterparts of characteristic blocks of text lines of each reference pattern in filled form. The authors[10] described three classifiers which focus on form identification. For the first two, the information based on a pyramidal image decomposition is used by the k-Nearest-Neighbor and the Multilayer Perceptron. The third uses the information extracted from the form content as a tree structure.

This paper describes a system which allows to identify automatically different types of forms **without any sign of reference**. A method for the extraction of the main representative rectangular blocks of the physical structure document is presented. The required thresholds for this extraction are determined automatically and are adapted to the form type. In the phase of training, models are described by a vector of features that integrates elements of statistical nature (average, standard deviation). The difficulty lies in the fact that, for several samples of a given model, the obtained blocks are not necessarily stable. They can group together (phenomenon of the merging block) or divide in several blocks (phenomenon of the fragmentation block). Therefore, every model is going to appear according to several possible configurations of blocks. During the form learning phase, the probability of occurrence of every block is counted. During the phase of identification, we watch the blocks' instability while introducing a coefficient of penalty based on this probability of occurrence for every block. The decision of affecting a form to a class is taken by calculating a distance between the unknown form and the profile of matching of every model, if one exists. Recently,[11] we used the Mahalanobis distance which could not be used in the general case, because the vector of feature has a variable dimension. For this reason, we propose a modified expression of this distance. This modified distance is enriched by a balancing of the penalty affected to every block. The more rarely the concerned block appears, the more this penalty increases the distance. Thus the smallest distance calculated in this way, permits to affect to the unknown form the nearest class.

This paper is organized as follows: In section 2, we describe the general organization of our system. Section 3 presents the automatic form segmentation. Section 4 describes the learning mechanism. Section 5 describes the form type identification procedure. Experimental results and conclusion are presented in section 6.

2 General structure of our system

The general structure of our system is illustrated in figure 1. During the phase of learning, first of all we, define the filled items:[12] the professor localizes the rectangular zones of insertion of handwritten data, and enters the attributes of the support of the handwritten data (number and type of support: rectangular boxes, continuous or dotted reference lines, etc.). For this use, we have developed a graphical user interface (Figure 2). Secondly, a vectorial statistical model of every class is constructed automatically. This model takes into account the attributes of the main rectangular blocks which define the physical structure of the document.

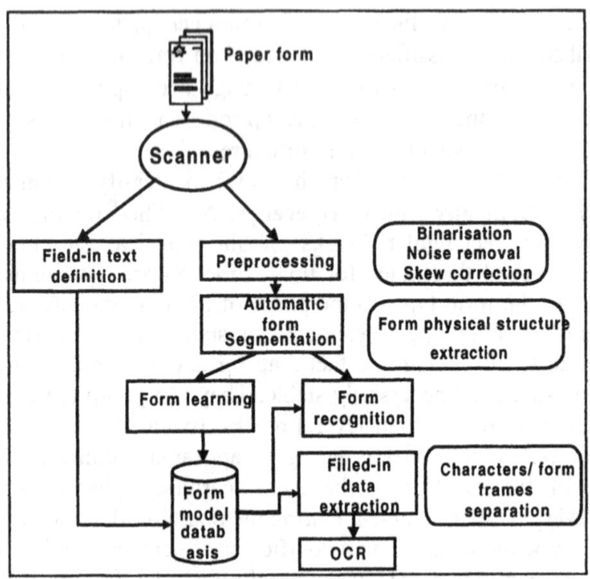

Fig. 1. General structure of our system

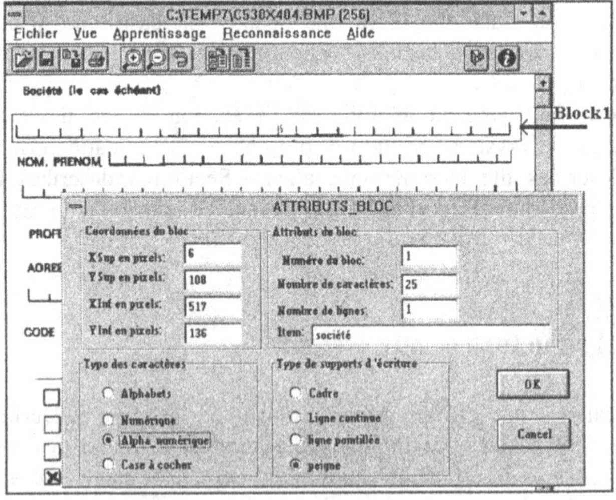

Fig. 2. Learning of the first block of a form

3 Form automatic segmentation

The process of the automatic segmentation into main rectangular blocks of text is described as follows: we begin by extracting all the white inscribed maximal rectangles by using the algorithm of rectangulation.[13,14] We construct the distribution of these white rectangles versus two variables ; length of horizontal side, length of vertical side (Figure 3). We are going to exploit this distribution in order to determine the two threshold rectangles: one is vertical, the other one is horizontal. A threshold rectangle is the minimum boundary of the text block. So, these threshold rectangles are adapted automatically to the type of the form. The exploitation of the distribution is made as following: we note that in the region around the origin (small x, small y) the peaks are very elevated and the density is very strong ; these rectangles represent the inter-character separators and inter- word separators. The horizontally lengthened rectangles (big x, small y) are few and represent the horizontal inter-block spaces. The vertically lengthened rectangles (small x, big y) are also few. They represent the inter-blocks and inter-columns. The aim is to retain only inter-block and inter-column separator rectangles. For this, we construct a separator line in the plane of the distribution, in two steps: first of all, we calculate the length average of the horizontal side (resp. vertical) m_h (resp. m_v) and the corresponding standard deviation s_h (resp. s_v), for all white horizontal rectangles (resp. vertical). The broken line whose sides are parallel to the axes and of abscissa $m_h+s_h/2$ (resp. ordinate $m_v+s_v/2$) forms the first separating line (Figure 5). Afterwards, we only keep the rectangles situated beyond this separating line. In the second step, we calculate the average m_{ch} (resp. m_{cv}) of the length (resp. of the width) of the remaining rectangles. The real separator line is the broken line, for which the sides are parallel to the axes and of abscissa m_{ch}(rep. of ordinate m_{cv}). The horizontal threshold rectangle (resp. vertical) is chosen as the nearest rectangle to the separating line in the authorized corresponding zone. Therefore, the set of the text separators is given by all white rectangles whose sizes are superior or equal to a threshold rectangle. Then, we construct the complement of the image of all the text separators. The minimal bounding rectangular blocks are then searched in the text blocks.

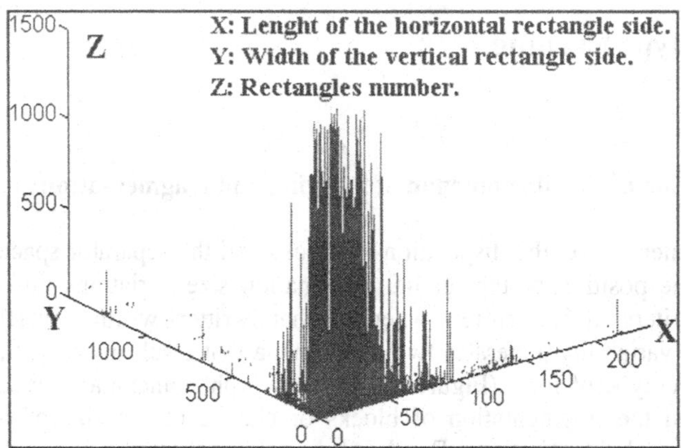

Fig. 3. White rectangles distribution

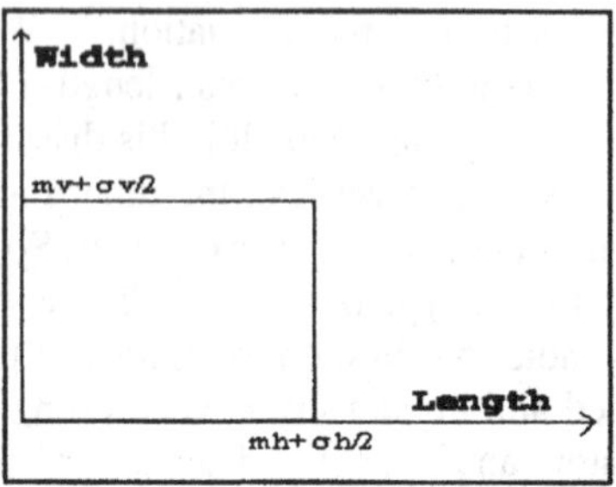

Fig. 4. First separator

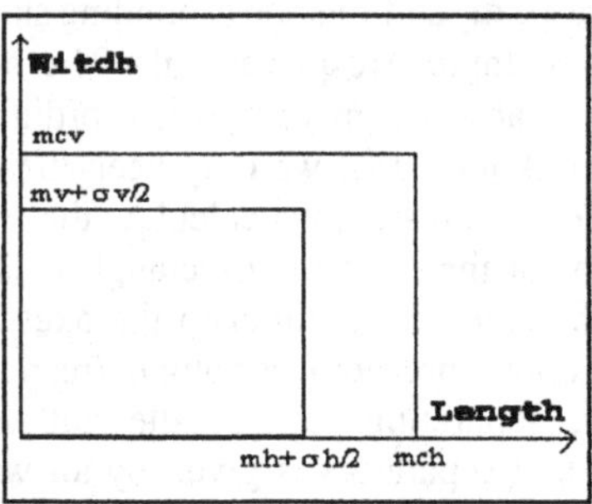

Fig. 5. Second separator

4 Form type learning

4.1 Detection of the phenomenon of merging and fragmentation

In the general case, the disposition of blocks and the separator spaces are variable owing to the position or the textual information size variations introduced by the different writers. It is manifest when the handwritten writing overflows the data fields. This variability generates two phenomena that result in several configurations for one same type of form (Figure 6). These two phenomena are given by either the merging and the fragmentation of blocks or change of the size of one or several blocks independently of others. For the clarity of exposing our approach, we limit the discussion to the case of having two forms of the same class. Be C a class of a type form and $F_1, F_2 \in C$; two filled-in forms of which physical structure is represented respectively by rectangular blocks set: $E1=\{b_{11},b_{12},...,b_{1n}\}$, $E_2=\{b_{21},b_{22},...,b_{2m}\}$ where b_{ik} represents a block of k label belonging to the F_i form , n and m designate respectively the finished block numbers of the F_1 and F_2 physical structure form. Every block $b_{ik} \in E_i$ is characterized by a vector V of attributes: V={x_{ik},y_{ik},l_{ik},h_{ik}} where x_{ik}, y_{ik} represent the rectangle center coordinates defining the block k $\in E_i$; l_{ik}, h_{ik} designate respectively the length and height of the block b_{ik}. The matching of blocks of F_1 with those of the F_2 form is made according to a criterion of Euclidean distance between their center position attributes:

$$d(b_{1k}, b_{2l}) = \left[(x_{1k} - x_{2l})^2 + (y_{1k} - y_{2l})^2\right]^{1/2} \quad (1)$$

where k=1,...n and l=1,...m. To a block $b_{1k} \in F_1$ corresponds a block $b_{2k'} \in F_2$ if the following condition is satisfied:

$$d(b_{1k}, b_{2k'}) = \min_{l}\left[(x_{1k} - x_{2l})^2 + (y_{1k} - y_{2l})^2\right]^{1/2} \quad (2)$$

An erroneous matching between blocks, could occur during a phenomenon of merging or fragmentation. Indeed a big block could be matched to several small corresponding blocks. In this case, there is a conflict, therefore, no bijective matching can be done. However, we must establish a correspondence between the big block of the picture of one sample and the small blocks of another one.

We are going to define the 8-neighborhood of a block, then we will associate to every block a vector of attributes that characterizes the relation with the 8 neighbors. We got inspiration from Allen's[15] and Walischewski's[16] works. Any block possesses 8 neighbors, the picture sides being sometimes considered as a neighbor's border, if needs be. A neighboring block can be in one of the eight directions given in Figure 7. Figure 8 shows the 13 positions of the horizontal side of the superior block.[13] Figure 9 and Figure 10 show the restriction to 9 and 4 positions that we made respectively. In the same way, the respective positions of the 7 other neighbors can be easily deducted.

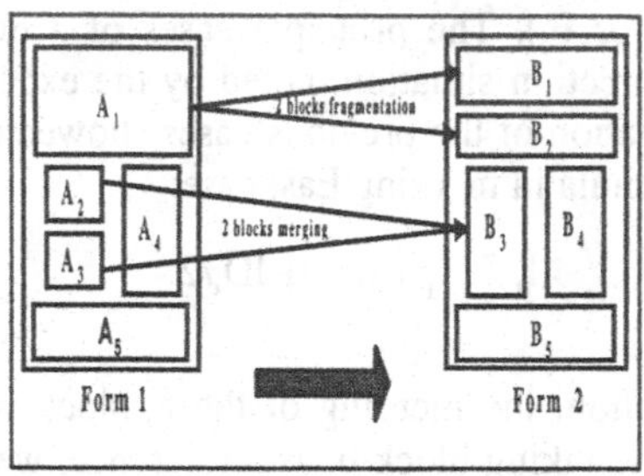

Fig. 6. Merging and fragmentation phenomena

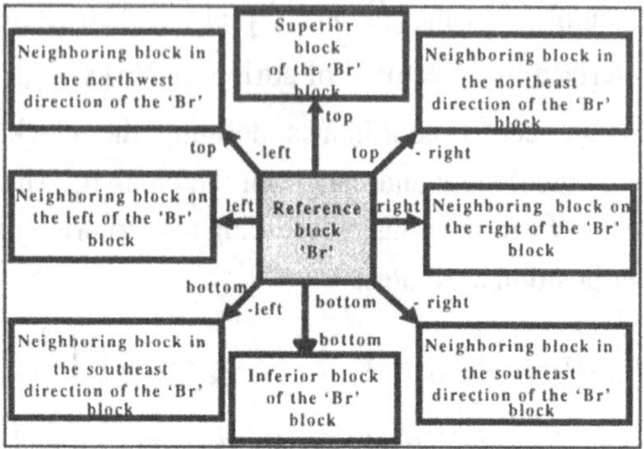

Fig. 7. 8-neighborhood of a block

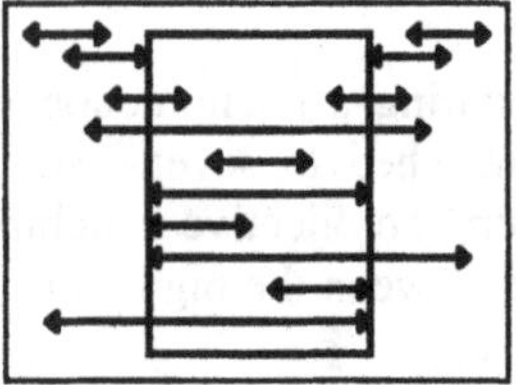

Fig. 8. The 13 relative positions the superior block[13]

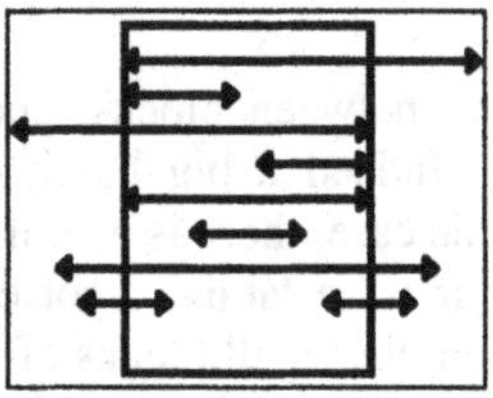

Fig. 9. The 9 relative positions of the inferior bloc

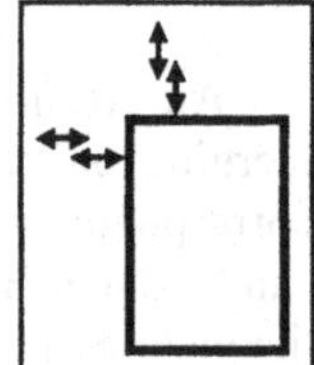

Fig. 10. The 4 relative positions of the Northwest block

The attributes of the vector are divided in two types (Figure 11): the first is the separator distances between a block and its 8 neighbors, and the second type is the heights respectively (lengths) of the neighboring blocks according to the vertical direction respectively (horizontal). Both types number twelve each. Let's investigate, the block merging of the block b_1 and its right neighbor b_2. After merging, b_1 and b_2 will be matched with the B block (Figure 12). Figure 13 illustrates attributes of a block in a F_i form (F_1 or F_2). The principal cases of a block elongation and of its neighbor in the right direction situation, noted by the experience, are represented by Figure 14. The investigation of the previous cases showed in Figure 14 enabled us to propose the general formula in merging East case:

$$l_2 \geq l_1 + dD_1 + lD_1/2 \tag{3}$$

In the slanting direction, the merging of the b_1 block will take place with the b_2 block (Figure 15). While taking block b_3 as a reference, we get the two conditions of merging respectively in the two directions East and North :

$$l_2 + dGB_2 > l_1 + dGB_1 + dDH_1 \quad \text{and} \quad l_2 \geq l_1 + dDH_1 + lDH_1/2 \tag{4}$$

and

$h_2 + dBG_2 > h_1 + dBG_1 + dHD_1$ and $(h_2 \geq h_1 + dHD_1 + hHD_1/2$

where the coefficient 1/2 comes from the fact that a block can not have a size change superior to 50% from a form to another. With the same reasoning, we can deduct the rules of merging of the b_1 block in the other directions. The determination of the fragmentation of a block b_1 of the form F_1 in several blocks in the form F_2, comes back to the detection of a merging in the opposite sense. Therefore the processing of the phenomenon «merging-fragmentation» comes back to applying the method of merging detection described before successively in both directions (of F_1 toward F_2 then, of F_2 toward F_1).

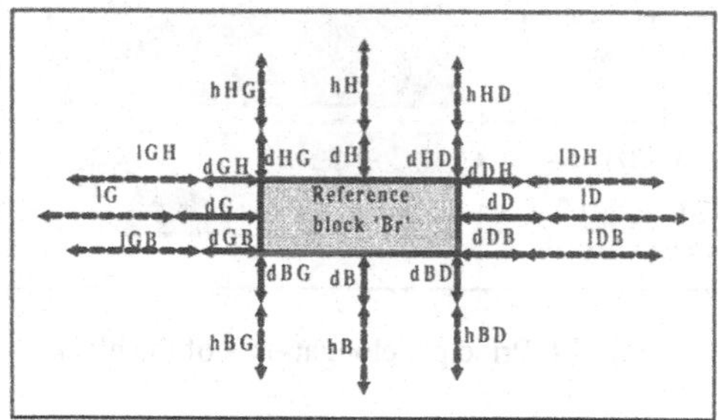

Fig. 11. Vector attributes

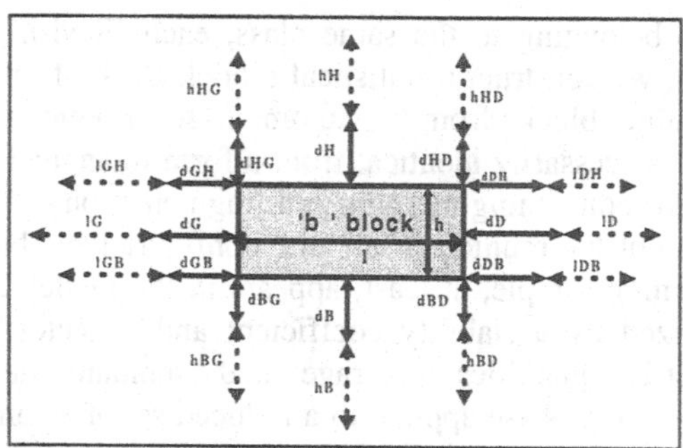

Fig. 12. Block attributes in F_1 Form

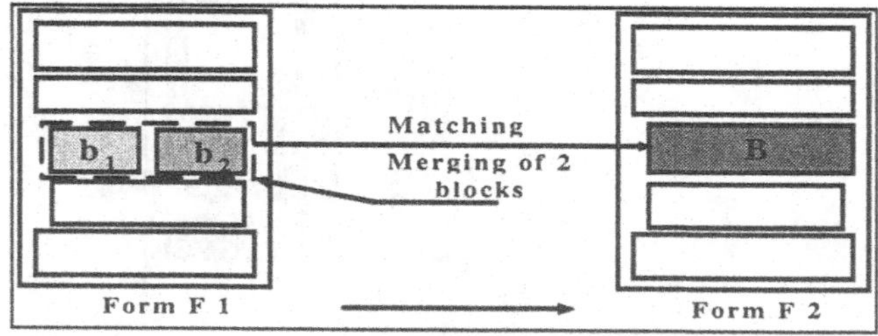

Fig. 13. Merging on the right

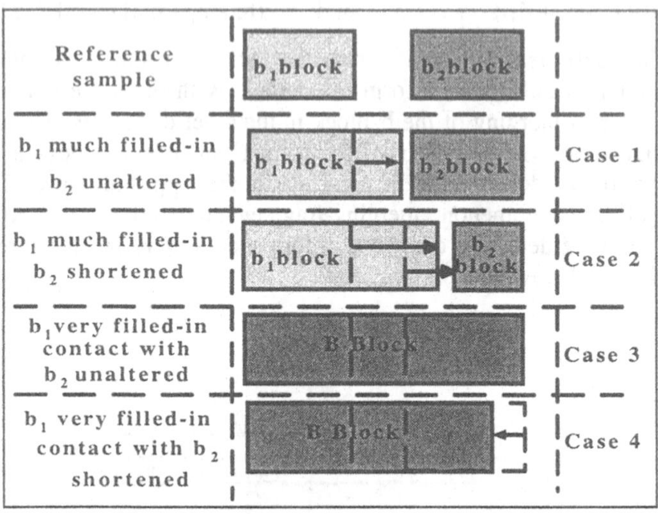

Fig. 14. Principal elongation's of the block

4.2 Form Models Construction

From N forms belonging to the same class, each filled-in by a different writer without constraint, we construct a statistical model. Each of these forms is described by a set of descending blocks from the automatic form segmentation. The number of these blocks is not necessarily identical from a form to another because of the above mentioned problems concerning merging and fragmentation of blocks. One can notice that this model is not the reunion of all the configurations, but every block having appeared in a learning sample, at least, appears in the model. A block of the model will be characterized by a stability coefficient and a vector constructed by using statistical geometric quantities (average and standard deviation). Figure 16, summarizes the learning phase applied to a reduced set of 4 samples in order to form the model of one class.

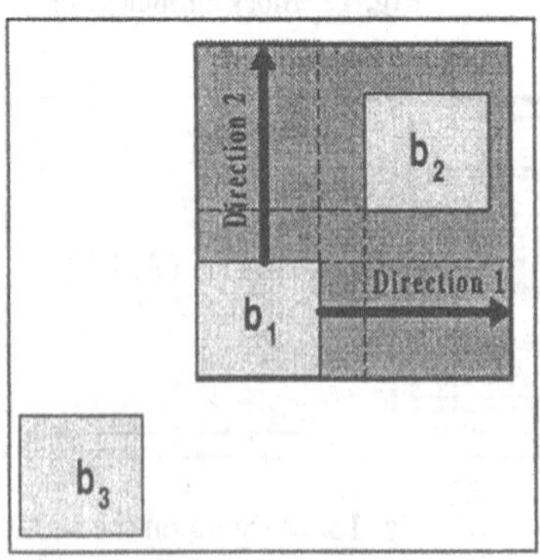

Fig. 15. Merging of the b_1 block with the b_2 to the Northeast

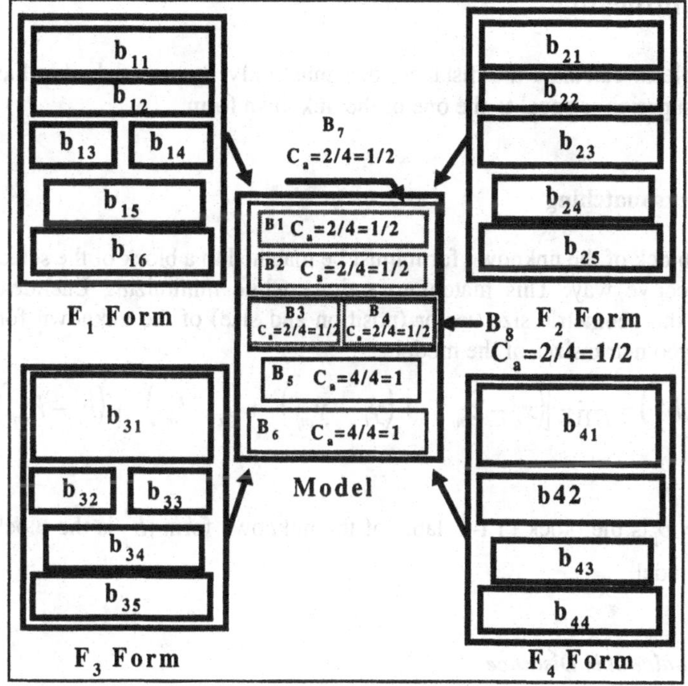

Fig.16. Example of the training done on 4 forms

The correspondence between blocks of different forms of a given class is established according to the following criteria: the Euclidean distance between centers of two matched blocks must be minimal and have the same behavior with its neighbors during merging or fragmentation, if needed. A coefficient of apparition of every block for one same class is calculated:

$$C_a = \frac{N_a}{N_t} \tag{5}$$

where N_a is the number of samples in the class containing the block and N_t is the total number of samples of the class under test. To each block that participates to form the model, we associate a feature vector V_c : $V_c = \{x_m, y_m, l_m, h_m, \sigma_x, \sigma_y, \sigma_l, \sigma_h\}$

where $x_m = \frac{1}{N_a}\sum_{i=1}^{N_a} x_i$, $\sigma_x^2 = \frac{1}{N_a}\sum_{i=1}^{N_a}(x_i - x_m)^2$, the expressions of the other elements can easily deduced, x_m and y_m (resp. l_m and h_m)represent the mean value of the coordinates of the gravity center (resp. the lengths of horizontal and vertical sides) of blocks matched, σ_x and σ_y (resp. σ_l and σ_h) are the standard deviations of the coordinates of the gravity center (resp. the lengths of horizontal and vertical sides) of blocks matched.

5 Identification

To be able to calculate the distance, one must only keep models that have a block number superior or equal to the one of the unknown form.

5.1 Blocks matching

Each block of the unknown form must be matched to a block of the selected model, by a bijective way. This matching is done while minimizing Euclidean distance between the geometric size vector (position and size) of the unknown form and the average geometric sizes of the model.

$$d(b_i, b_j^k) = \min_j \left[(x_i - x_{mj})^2 + (y_i - y_{mj})^2 + (l_i - l_{mj})^2 + (h_i - h_{mj})^2 \right] \tag{6}$$

where b_i is the block of i-th label of the unknown form ; b_j^k is the block of label j of k-th model.

5.2 *Mahalanobis Distance*

When the model presents a single configuration, the description vector always has the same dimension N. The probability to getting jointly the unknown form F and the M_k model is:

$$\Pr ob(F, M_k) = \Pr ob(M_k) \cdot \Pr ob(F / M_k) \tag{7}$$

While supposing that feature follow Gaussian law, the expression of the probability of getting the unknown form F knowing the M_k model is given as:

$$\Pr ob(F / M_k) = \frac{1}{[2\pi]^{N/2} |\Sigma_k|^{1/2}} \exp\left(-\frac{1}{2}\right) \left[(X - X_k)^t \Sigma_k^{-1} (X - X_k) \right] \tag{8}$$

where X is the features vector of the unknown form F ; X_k is average feature vector of the model k and Σ_k is covariance matrices of the k model (N*N dimension). The distance of Mahalanobis only keeps the part of the formula that joins the unknown shape to the model :

$$dist(F, M_k) = \left[(X - X_k)^t \Sigma_k^{-1} (X - X_k) \right]^{1/2} \tag{9}$$

When there is statistical independence of the variables intra-block, the covariance matrix Σ_i becomes diagonal because of the statistical independence of variables and the expression of the distance becomes:

$$d(F,C)=\left[\sum_{i=1}^{N}\left(\frac{(x_i-x_{mi})^2}{\sigma_{xi}^2}+\frac{(y_i-y_{mi})^2}{\sigma_{yi}^2}+\frac{(l_i-l_{mi})^2}{\sigma_{li}^2}+\frac{(h_i-h_{mi})^2}{\sigma_{hi}^2}\right)\right]^{1/2} \quad \textbf{(10)}$$

5.3 Weighted statistical distance

The expression of the Mahalanobis distance contains a sum of the relative terms of each block, due to the inter-block independence. Using the probability to get a configuration C, knowing the model M_k, increases the distance. Since blocks are treated simultaneously on independent way, in the expression of the distance and in the construction of models, it appears more natural to ponder every term of the distance by a coefficient that varies in inverse sense of the stability coefficient (i.e. of the probability of apparition of the block). The expression of the weighted statistical distance becomes:

5.4 *Decision: affectation to a class or rejection*

The decision of affectation to a class is taken according to a double criteria: i) the distance to the model representing the class must be as small as possible. ii) this distance must be small enough to avoid rejection.

6 Experimental Results and Conclusion

The learning basis is made up of 50 classes. Each contains twenty forms which are filled by different writers. The recognition is tested using 4 new elements for each class. In addition, 4 unlearned class samples are used. All the elements of the 4 unlearned classes were rejected. Figure 17 illustrates samples for 4 different classes. A recognition rate of 97% was obtained.

References

1. D. Doermann, A. Rosenfeld, E, Rivlin : The Function of documents, *Proc. of ICDAR'97*, Ulm, Germany (1997) 1077-1081.
2. J. Mao, M. Abayan, K. Mohiuddin: A Model-Based Form Processing Sub-System, *Proc. of ICPR'96*, Vienna, Austria (1996) 691-695.
3. L. Y .Tseng, R.C. Chen: The Recognition of Form Documents Based on Three Types of Line Segments, *Proc. of ICDAR '97*, Ulm, Germany (1997) 71-75.
4. Y. Ishitani, "Model Matching Based on Association Graph for Form Image Understanding, Proc. of *ICDAR'95*, Montreal, Canada (1995) 287-292.
5. C.D. Yan, Y.Y Tang, C.Y. suen: Form Understanding System Based on Form Description Language. *Proc. of ICDAR'91*,Saint Malo, France (1991) 283-293

6. J. Yuan, Y. Y. Tang, C. Y. Suen: Four Directional Adjacency Graphs (FDAG) and Their Application in Locating Field in Forms. *Proc of ICDAR'95*, Montreal, Canada (1995) 752-755
7. F. Cesarini, M. Gori, S. Marinai, G. Soda: A System for Data Extraction from Forms of Known Class. Proc. of ICDAR'95, Montreal, Canada (1995) 1136-1140
8. U. Bohnacker, J. Schacht, T. Yücel: Matching form lines Based on a Heuristic Search ", *Proc. of ICDAR* '97, Ulm, Germany, (1997) 86-90.
9. F. Dubiel, A. Dengel.:FormClass-A System For OCR Free identification Of Forms. DAS'96, USA (1996) 189-208
10. P. Héroux, S. Diana, A. Ribert, E. Trupin:Etude de Méthodes de Classification pour l'Identification Automatique de Classes de Formulaires. *Proc. of CIFED'98*, Quebec, Canada (1998) 463-472
11. S. Kebairi, B. Taconet, A. Zahour, P. Mercy: Détection Automatique du Type de Formulaire Parmi un Ensemble Appris et Extraction des Données Utiles. CIFED'98, Quebec, Canada (1998) 255-264
12. S. Kebairi, B. Taconet: A System of Automatic Reading of Forms: *Int. Conf. of Pattern Recognition and Information Analysis, PRIP'97*, Minsk Belarus , (1997) 264-270.
13. L. Boukined, B. Taconet, A. Zahour: Recherche de la Structure Physique d'un Document Imprimé par Rectangulation., *Proc. RFIA 91*, France (1991) 1027-1031
14. S.Kebairi, A. Zahour, B. Taconet, L. Boukined: Segmentation of Composite Documents Into Homogenous Blocks. *Proc. IGS'98*, Genova Italy (1997) 111-112
15. J.F. Allen: Maintaing Knowledge About Temporel Intervals. Communication of the ACM, 26 (11), (1983) 832-843
16. H. Walischewski: Automatic Knowledge Acquisition for Spatial Document Interpretation. *Proc. of ICDAR'97*, Ulm, Germany (1997) 243-247

DOSSIER de CANDIDATURE à l'I.U.T. du HAVRE

DÉCISION DU JURY : NE RIEN INSCRIRE DANS CE CADRE

☐ LISTE PRINCIPALE ☐ LISTE COMPLÉMENTAIRE
☒ REFUSÉ (E)

COLLER ICI UNE PHOTO D'IDENTITÉ RÉCENTE (avec de la colle)

(remplir impérativement à l'encre noire)

ÉTAT CIVIL N° enregistrement Minitel

1 ☒ Monsieur 2 ☐ Madame 3 ☐ Mademoiselle N° INE

NOM (suivi de épouse pour les femmes mariées)

PRÉNOMS

NÉ (E) LE ... 19 ... à ... Chantilly

NATIONALITÉ : F française

ADRESSE

COMMUNE

CODE POSTAL ... BUREAU DISTRIBUTEUR ou pays Chantilly

TÉL

SITUATION FAMILIALE : ☐ CÉLIBATAIRE ☐ MARIÉ (E) ☐ AUTRE

SITUATION MILITAIRE : ☐ SURSITAIRE ☐ DÉGAGÉ SM ☐ EN COURS

SITUATION DES PARENTS :

NOM

ADRESSE

COMMUNE

CODE POSTAL ... BUREAU DISTRIBUTEUR ou pays Chantilly

TÉL

Profession du père Agriculteur

Profession de la mère pharmacienne

DÉPARTEMENTS D'ENSEIGNEMENT CHOISIS

IMPORTANT

☐ - Génie Civil (Lilas)
☐ - Gestion des Entreprises et des Administrations (Jaune)
☐ - Génie Electrique et Informatique Industrielle (Bulle)
☐ - Génie Mécanique et Productique (Sable)
☐ - Informatique (Bleu Clair)
☐ - Techniques de Commercialisation (Vert Clair)
☐ - Transport Logistique (Rose)

☒ - Carrières Sociales (Mandarine)
☐ Animation Socio-Culturelle
☒ Travail Social

Indiquez votre préférence en numérotant les options ou cochez une des cases si une seule option vous intéresse

☐ - Information - Communication (Orange)
☐ Information et Documentation d'entreprise
☐ Métiers du livre
☐ Publicité - Marketing

a)

DELTASOFT 43, chemin du Vieux Chêne 38240 Meylan Tél. (16) 76 41 85 08 - Fax (16) 76 90 01 69

Nom ... Fonction chercheur Enseignant

Société Université du havre Service Département T.C

Adresse Place Robert Schuman

Code postal 76610 Ville Le Havre Pays France

Téléphone 02.32.99.24.72 Télécopie 02.32.79.71.91

Pour recevoir des informations complémentaires, indiquez le ou les produits qui vous intéressent :

Plate-forme : MacOS Windows

Graphique :
☒ Axum 4.1
☐ Cricket Graph III
☐ DeltaGraph
☐ KaleidaGraph

Statistiques :
☐ BMDP New System
☒ BMDP New System édition professionnelle
☐ EQS
☐ LogXat
☐ NCSS 6.0
☐ nQuarry
☒ PCSM Plus
☐ StatView
☐ StatXact
☐ SuperANOVA
☐ Systat

Enquête, analyse de données :
☒ Atlas Gis
☐ Cartes et Données
☐ Data Muncher
☐ Le Probabiliste
☐ Le Sphinx Plus 2
☐ Perspective 1 2 3
☐ Prevat
☐ Question
☐ StatBox
☐ Turbo Scan

Aide à la décision :
☐ Alice
☒ Amado
☐ BMDP Diamond
☐ Crystal Ball
☐ Extend

Qualité, gestion de documentaire :
☒ BPS Jobs
☐ BPS QUAL
☐ Dox
☐ Endnote 2 Plus
☐ Optimum

Chimie et mathématique :
☐ CS Chem3D
☒ CS ChemDraw
☐ CS ChemFinder
☐ CS ChemOffice
☐ ChemWindow
☐ Chemintosh
☐ Expressionist
☒ Mathcad Plus

Formation :
☐ Scribe
☒ StatView Student
☒ Student Systat

Réseaux :
☐ Formation Internet
☐ NFS/Share-Interprint
☐ Netoctopus
☒ NetWorks
☐ TCP/Connect II

Bureautique et dessin :
☐ Cordial III
☐ EcoToner
☐ Filigrane
☐ MacDraft
☒ Trans-Linc
☐ Visio 4.0

Echange et Sécurité :
☒ Conversions Plus
☐ Copstalk Windows
☐ DBMS/Copy
☐ FileGuard
☐ MacLink Plus
☐ MacOpener
☒ Personal Backup

DELTASOFT - 43 chemin du Vieux Chêne 38240 Meylan - Tél (16) 76 41 85 08 - Fax (16) 76 90 01 69

b)

DELTASOFT 43, chemin du Vieux Chêne 38240 Meylan
Tél. (16) 76 41 85 08 - Fax (16) 76 90 01 69

Nom ... Fonction ...
Société ... Service ...
Adresse ...
Code postal ... Ville ... Pays ...
Téléphone ... Télécopie ...

Pour recevoir des informations complémentaires, indiquez le ou les produits qui vous intéressent :
Plate-forme : MacOS Windows

Graphique :
- ☒ Axum 4.1
- ☐ Cricket Graph III
- ☐ DeltaGraph
- ☐ KaleidaGraph

Statistiques :
- ☐ BMDP New System
- ☒ BMDP New System édition professionnelle
- ☐ EQS
- ☐ LogXat
- ☐ NCSS 6.0
- ☐ nQuerry
- ☒ PCSM Plus
- ☐ StatView
- ☐ StatXact
- ☐ SuperANOVA
- ☐ Systat

Enquête, analyse de données :
- ☒ Atlas Gis
- ☐ Cartes et Données
- ☐ Data Muncher
- ☐ Le Probabiliste
- ☐ Le Sphinx Plus 2
- ☐ Perspective 1 2 3
- ☐ Prevat
- ☐ Question
- ☐ StatBox
- ☐ Turbo Scan

Aide à la décision :
- ☐ Alice
- ☒ Amado
- ☐ BMDP Diamond
- ☐ Crystal Ball
- ☐ Extend

Qualité, gestion de documentaire :
- ☒ BPS Jobs
- ☐ BPS QUAL
- ☐ Dox
- ☐ Endnote 2 Plus
- ☐ Optimum

Chimie et mathématique :
- ☐ CS Chem3D
- ☒ CS ChemDraw
- ☐ CS ChemFinder
- ☐ CS ChemOffice
- ☐ ChemWindow
- ☐ Chemintosh
- ☐ Expressionist
- ☒ Mathcad Plus

Formation :
- ☐ Scribe
- ☒ StatView Student
- ☒ Student Systat

Réseaux :
- ☐ Formation Internet
- ☐ NFS/Share-Interprint
- ☐ Netoctopus
- ☒ NetWorks
- ☐ TCP/Connect II

Bureautique et dessin :
- ☐ Cordial III
- ☐ EcoToner
- ☐ Filigrane
- ☐ MacDraft
- ☒ Trans-Linc
- ☐ Visio 4.0

Echange et Sécurité :
- ☒ Conversions Plus
- ☐ Copstalk Windows
- ☐ DBMS/Copy
- ☐ FileGuard
- ☐ MacLink Plus
- ☐ MacOpener
- ☒ Personal Backup

DELTASOFT - 43 chemin du Vieux Chêne 38240 Meylan - Tél (16) 76 41 85 08 - Fax (16) 76 90 01 69

c)

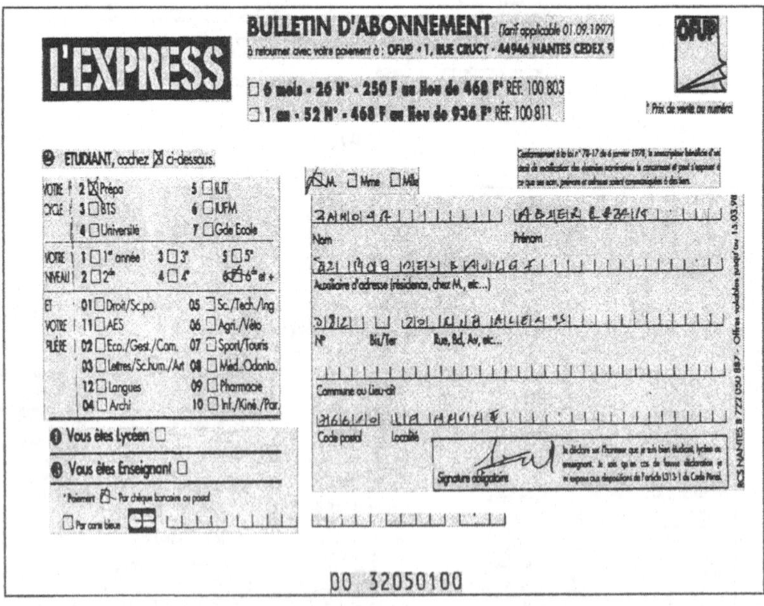

L'EXPRESS

BULLETIN D'ABONNEMENT (Tarif applicable 01.09.1997)
à retourner avec votre paiement à : OFUP - 1, RUE CRUCY - 44946 NANTES CEDEX 9

OFUP

☐ 6 mois - 26 N° - 250 F au lieu de 468 F* RÉF. 100 803
☐ 1 an - 52 N° - 468 F au lieu de 936 F* RÉF. 100 811

*Prix de vente au numéro

ETUDIANT, cochez ☒ ci-dessous.

VOTRE CYCLE: 2 ☒ Prépa, 3 ☐ BTS, 4 ☐ Université, 5 ☐ IUT, 6 ☐ IUFM, 7 ☐ Gde Ecole

VOTRE NIVEAU: 1 ☐ 1ère année, 2 ☐ 2e, 3 ☐ 3e, 4 ☐ 4e, 5 ☐ 5e, 6 ☐ 6e et +

ET VOTRE FILIÈRE: 01 ☐ Droit/Sc.po, 11 ☐ AES, 02 ☐ Eco./Gest./Com., 03 ☐ Lettres/Sc.hum./Art, 12 ☐ Langues, 04 ☐ Archi, 05 ☐ Sc./Tech./Ing, 06 ☐ Agri./Véto, 07 ☐ Sport/Touris, 08 ☐ Méd./Odonto., 09 ☐ Pharmacie, 10 ☐ Inf./Kiné./Par.

Vous êtes Lycéen ☐

Vous êtes Enseignant ☐

*Paiement ☐ Par chèque bancaire ou postal ☐ Par carte bleue

☒ M. ☐ Mme ☐ Mlle

Nom / Prénom

Auxiliaire d'adresse (résidence, chez M., etc...)

N° / Bis/Ter / Rue, Bd, Av, etc...

Commune ou Lieu-dit

Code postal / Localité

Signature obligatoire

00 32050100

d)

Fig. 17. Four segmented samples for 4 different classes. The c) sample is very close to the d) sample

Structure Analysis of Low Resolution Fax Cover Pages

Young-Kyu Lim, Hee-Joong Kang, Chang Ahn and Seong-Whan Lee

Center for Artificial Vision Research, Korea University,
Anam-dong, Seongbuk-ku, Seoul 136-701, Korea
{yklim,hjkang,cahn,swlee}@image.korea.ac.kr

Abstract. The increase in the use of faxed documents calls for the need to handle them automatically and intelligently for efficient storage, retrieval and interpretation. A lot of work has been accomplished for page segmentation in high resolution document images. But conventional methods for page segmentation are not suitable for faxed document processing. The well-known difficulties in faxed document processing are concerned with low resolution images and non-standardized formats. In this paper, we propose an effective structure analysis method for low resolution fax cover pages, based on region segmentation and keyword recognition. The main advantages of the proposed method are its capability of accommodating various types of fax cover pages and its fast processing speed. We divide fax cover pages into three regions – header, sender/recipient information and message – to easily identify the recipient's field. The recipient's name is then extracted through the recognition of keyword. The proposed method was tested on 164 fax cover pages. The experimental results show that the proposed method works well on the various types of fax cover pages.

1 Introduction

The need for automatic faxed document management is rapidly growing as faxed document transmission increase in its volume. It is a matter of course that documents transmitted through fax machines are internally encoded in a standard fax image format. It can be easily transformed into computer readable format. So, a faxed document image can be treated in the same way as many other document images. Many studies on document image processing have been accomplished and reported [1,2]. But the conventional methods for document image processing are not suitable for faxed document processing due to the low resolution and absence of standardized formats within faxed documents images.

A fax cover page is usually accompanies the documents being transmitted. It carries the important information regarding sender, recipient, comments, date, fax and phone numbers, etc. For many fax-related applications such as the intelligent fax server, fax-to-email and fax on demand, the recipient's name needs to be correctly extracted and recognized. Figure 1 shows an application area of this research, called an automatic fax router.

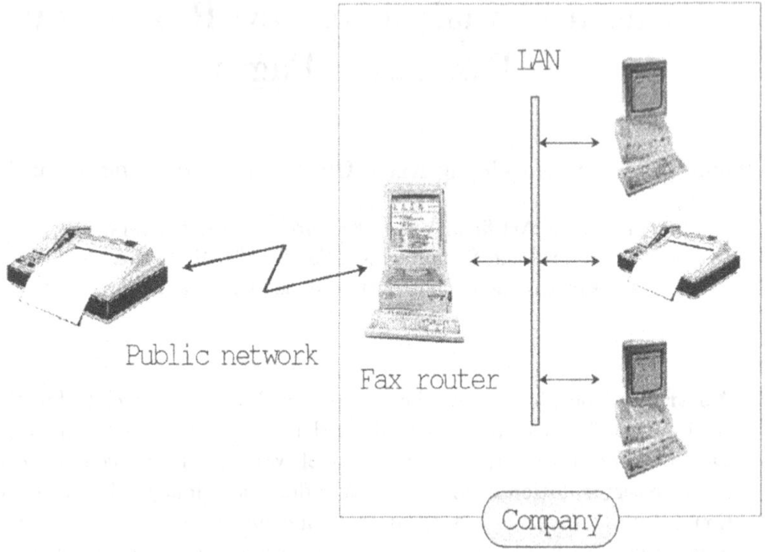

Fig. 1. Automatic fax router

Some related research has been reported in the literature. Li et al. [3] directly recognized names and addresses on fax cover pages using a scheme which strongly couples text recognition and block segmentation. Akiyama [4] performs addressee recognition on documents written in Kanji characters using address indicators like the keyword "TO:" and a double underline. Ricker et al. [5] primarily described order forms in processing faxed documents. The existing methods depend heavily on the performance of the character recognizer and are also restricted by the format characteristic of fax cover sheets such as the existence of field indicators like the double underline. But the difficulty in recognizing low resolution faxed characters demands more robust and efficient techniques.

In this paper, we propose an improved method to extract the recipient's name in low resolution faxed cover pages. The main advantages of the proposed methods are its capability of accommodating various types of fax cover pages and its fast processing speed. At first, the whole image is divided into three regions, which are defined as header, sender/recipient information and message. After the image has been divided, the recipient's field is detected by seeking only through the sender/recipient information region, which contains the target. The keyword is extracted and recognized. Multi-layer backpropagation neural networks are used for character recognition. The recipient's name is identified by comparing the result from character recognition with candidate names in the lexicon.

This paper is organized as follows. Section 2 describes in detail the proposed structure analysis method we adopted for low resolution fax cover pages. Section 3 shows experimental results and analysis for the fax cover pages we collected. Finally, section 4 gives a brief conclusion and directions for future work.

2 Proposed Structure Analysis Method

The images of fax cover pages are inherently of low resolution and the quality is degraded. The approaches that depend heavily on character recognition are not expected to produce good results. In case of Hangul which is Korean, it is necessary to have a more powerful character recognizer. This is not a feasible suggestion in terms of overall system performance. So, we propose an efficient and fast structure analysis method for fax cover pages, based on region segmentation and keyword recognition. This method is able to reduce the dependency on the character recognition result. The whole schematic of the proposed method is shown in Figure 2.

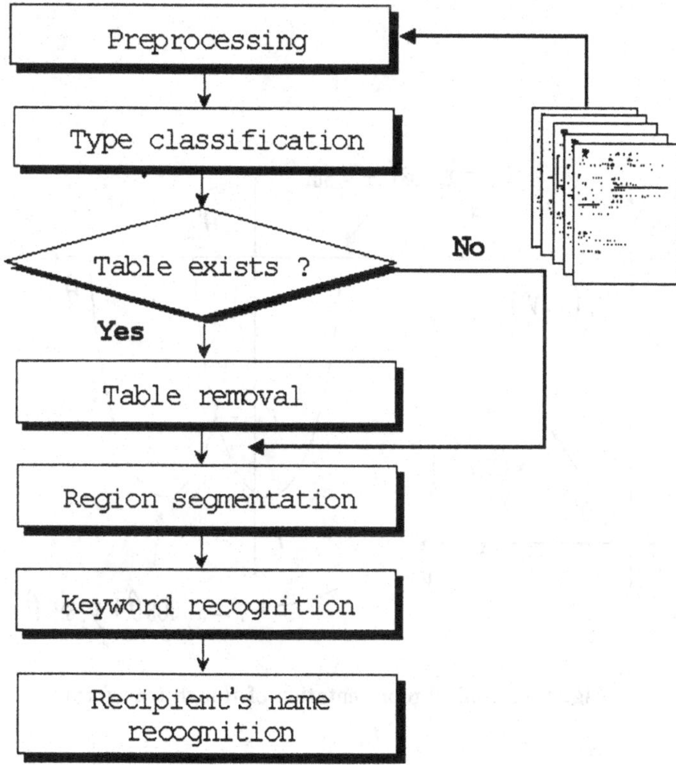

Fig. 2. Schematic of the proposed method

In order to extract information from the fax cover pages, connected components should first be generated. A connected component is a region where black pixels are connected by 8-connectivity [6]. The bounding boxes of connected components are the basic feature used in this system.

2.1 Preprocessing

Preprocessing is done in order to remove noise in images and restore degraded images [7,8,9]. In particular, skew correction is one of the most important tasks in preprocessing. Most existing structure analysis methods do not handle fax cover pages with skew. Applying a Hough transform to one point of the connected components, we designed a computationally efficient skew detection algorithm.

The Hough transform is one of the most popular voting methods for skew detection, line detection, circle fitting problems, etc. [10]. A set of points in x-y axes is mapped into Hough space using the following equation. Figure 3 shows the graphical representation of the Hough transform.

$$\rho = x \sin\theta + y \cos\theta \tag{1}$$

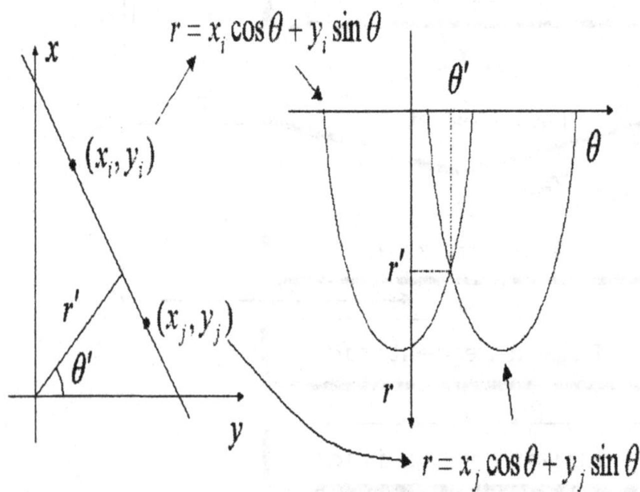

Fig. 3. Graphical representation of Hough transform

We represent the parameter space as an array of accumulators that stand for discrete parameter values. Each of the points in the image votes for several parameters, according to the transform equation. To find the parameters that characterize the line, we should detect peaks in the parameter space.

Since the computation time of Hough transform is proportional to the number of the input pixels, we use only the bottom-right point of the connected components to reduce its cost [11].

2.2 Type classification of fax cover pages

In this section, we describe the method for classifying the fax cover pages. It is important to develop adequate and fast processing methods for the various types. We classify fax cover pages into two types. Type I includes unstructured fax cover pages without tables and type II are structured ones with tables. Figure 4 illustrates the types of fax cover pages discussed in this paper. Figure 4(a) shows examples of type I and (b) shows those of type II. The existence of a table is the key feature for type classification on the given fax cover pages. Existing methods do not handle fax cover pages with tables, but the proposed method overcomes this restriction.

There are many objects in fax cover pages – text, table, isolated lines, images, etc. The bounding box of connected components should be investigated for object classification [12]. Two thresholds, width-threshold (T_w) and height-threshold (T_h), are used for object classification. In the process of object classification, we need to check through the connected components in order to find out if there is any table object among them. When we investigated a large of fax cover pages in practice, there were seldom complex forms of table in them. It enabled us to use a simple algorithm for type classification of fax cover pages.

Figure 5 shows the geometric definition of connected components. This definition will be used in the remainder of this paper. The condition for extracting table candidates is given in Eq. (2). By investigating the connected components to see whether or not they satisfy Eq. (2), images or tables will be extracted as candidates.

$$TableCandidates(CC) = \begin{cases} True, & if \;\; W > T_w \text{ and } H > T_h \\ False, & otherwise. \end{cases} \tag{2}$$

The most identifiable feature of tables in an image is the existence of lines. The ratio of black pixels to a connected component is also used for identification of tables. A table consists of inner and outer lines, as shown in Figure 6. The lines can be detected by histogram value of vertical and horizontal direction[13]. The lines may include noise that distorts their original shape, making it difficult to find them, so run-length smoothing and the number of continuous black pixels with appropriate threshold are used for accurate detection.

The necessary features for the type classification of fax cover pages are as follows.

- Histogram

  The histogram feature of a connected component is defined by projecting the black pixels of the skeleton into x- and y-axes and then accumulating the number of black pixels in each point of the x and y axes. This feature is used for detecting lines with similar length.

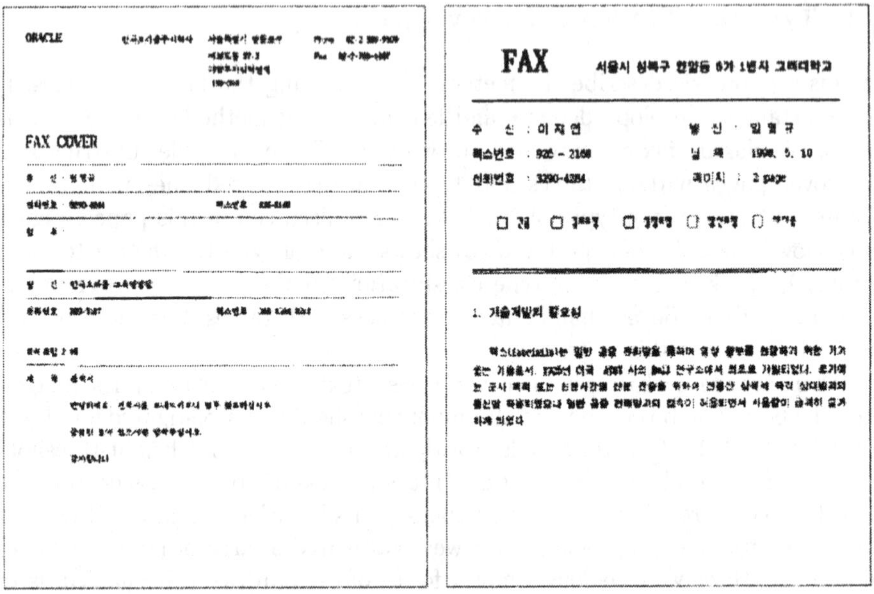

(a)

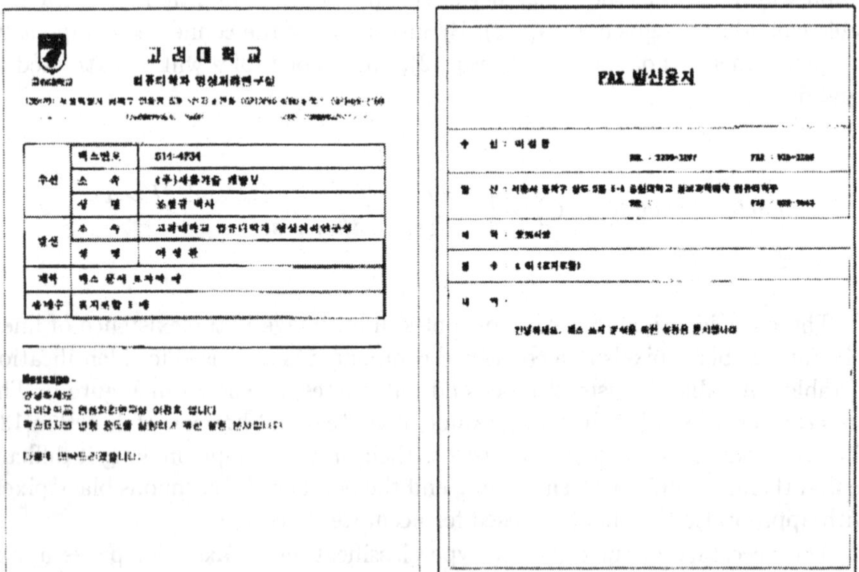

(b)

Fig. 4. Examples of fax cover pages. a) Unstructured fax cover pages. b) Structured fax cover pages.

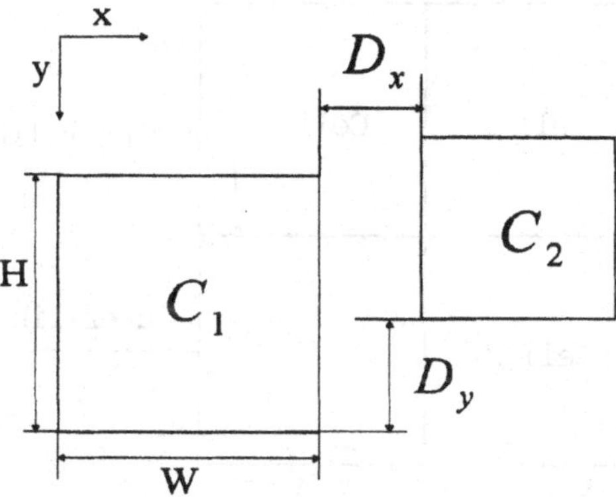

Fig. 5. Geometric definition of the connected components

$$X = \sum_{i=1}^{W} N_i, Y = \sum_{j=1}^{H} N_j \tag{3}$$

where W is the height of a connected component and H is the width of a connected component.

- Density

  The density of a connected component is defined by the summation of all the black pixels within the connected component.

$$D = \sum_{i,j=1}^{M} C_{ij} \tag{4}$$

  where if a pixel point (i, j) is a black pixel, $C_{ij} = 1$; otherwise, $C_{ij} = 0$.

- Ratio

  The ratio of a connected component is the number of black pixels to the area.

$$R = \frac{D}{H * W} \tag{5}$$

  If the ratio of black pixels to a connected component is larger than threshold, this connected component will be classified as an image.

After a table has been extracted, the inner and outer lines of the table are removed.

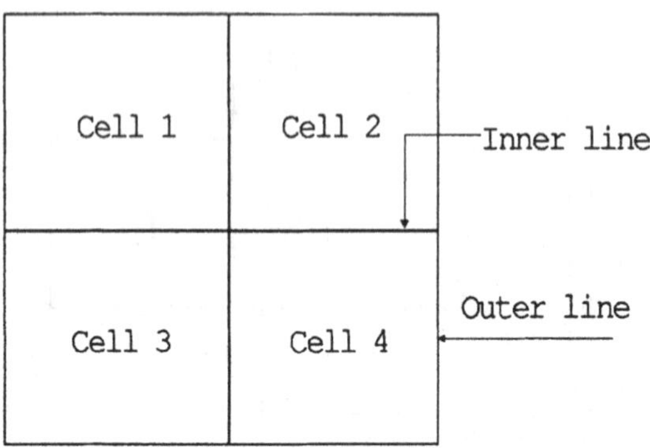

Fig. 6. The basic features of a table

2.3 Region segmentation

After identifying the type of fax cover pages, region segmentation is proceeded as a next step. Most fax cover pages are divided into three regions. We call the separated regions as header, sender/recipient information and message, as shown in Figure 7.

The header usually contains a company logo or graphics. The sender/recipient information contains the information pertinent to fax transmission, and the message contains comments. The primary goal of region segmentation is to isolate the sender/recipient information region. In most document processing systems, the module with the longest time is the character recognition module. In addition, it has an effect on the performance of keyword extraction and recognition in the next stage, in cases of where similar words exist. Therefore, the procedure of segmentation increases the overall system performance and helps to reduce the amount of data to be processed. Until the end of this paper, the sender/recipient information region will be referred to the SRI region.

In most fax cover pages, a region separator takes the form of a long box or single bold line. Finding the region separator is not an easy task due to noise or distortion during fax transmission. First, run length smoothing is applied for restoration. The connected component(CC) is determined to be a region separator if it satisfies Eq. (6).

$$Separator(CC) = \begin{cases} True, & if \;\; H < T_h \text{ and } W > T_w \\ False, & otherwise. \end{cases} \tag{6}$$

If we discern a number of components satisfying the above conditions during analysis, the components will later be discriminated. Usually, the first and the last component will be the candidates for the region separators.

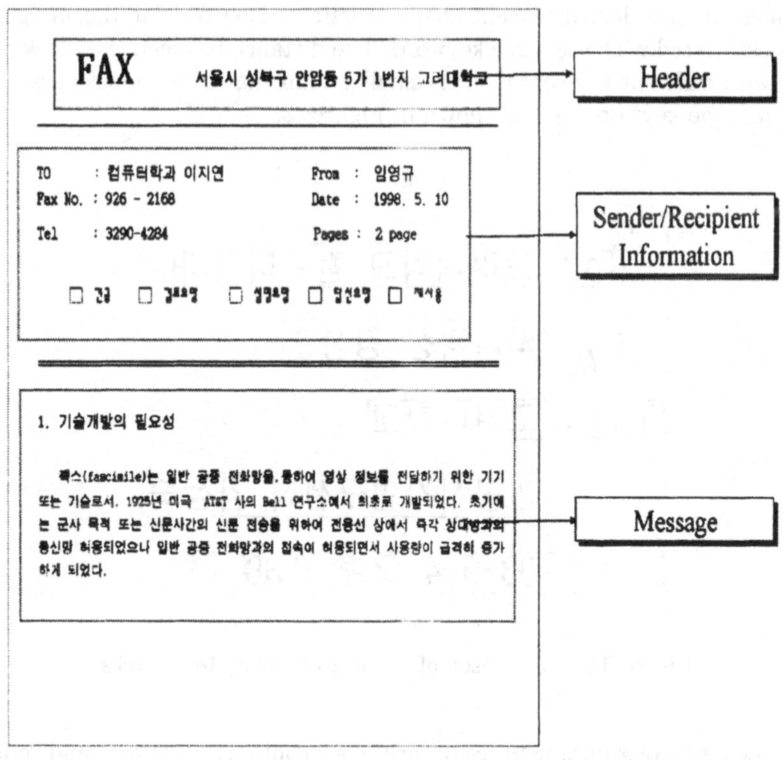

Fig. 7. Region segmentation of a fax cover page

2.4 Keyword extraction and recognition

Most of the useful information appears in the SRI region after region segmentation. The SRI region contains various fields related to fax transmission such as sender's name, recipient's name, fax number, etc. To easily detect the type of fields, the connected components within each field are grouped with a block corresponding to its keyword, using Eq. 7 [13].

$$Merge(C1, C2) = \begin{cases} True, & if \;\; D_x < T_x \text{ and } D_y < T_y \\ False, & otherwise. \end{cases} \tag{7}$$

where D_x is the horizontal distance between two connected components, D_y is the vertical distance between connected components.

There are two formats in unstructured fax cover pages as shown in Fig. 4(a), called one column and semi-two column. The format is determined using the distance between connected components in process of grouping. Where some blocks are located closely together, not only the distance but also the relationship between the blocks has to be investigated. Some blocks may contain two or more text lines. We use left-alignment characteristic of keyword for the merging of blocks associated with the same keyword. The distance between the blocks associated with different keywords(D_d) is smaller than that of the blocks associated with the same keyword(D_s) as shown in Figure 8.

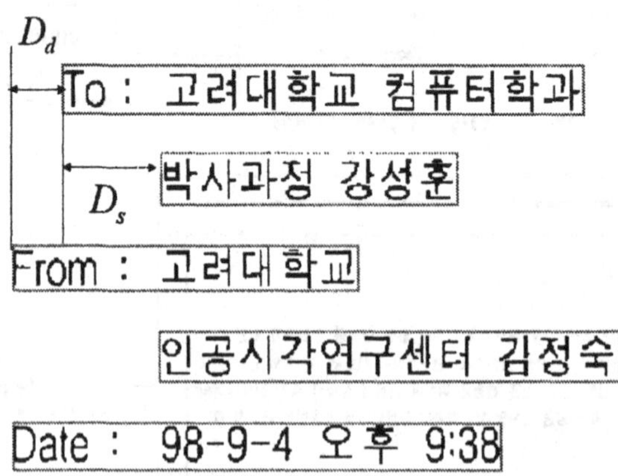

Fig. 8. The comparison of distances between text blocks

As the result of grouping process, each block contains a keyword and contents related to that keyword as shown in Figure 9. A keyword can be easily extracted, provided that the keyword is always located on the left-most side of each block.

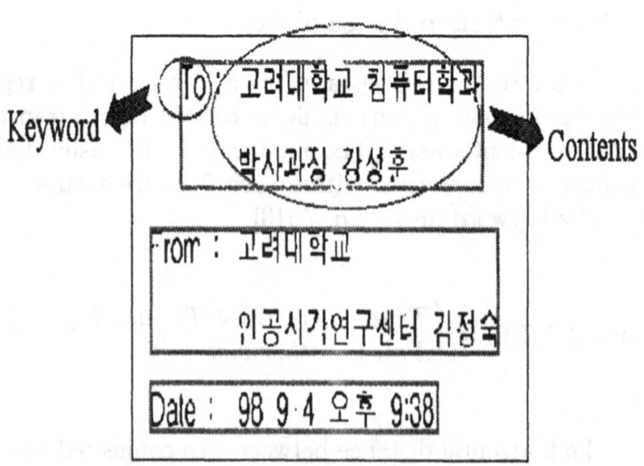

Fig. 9. Example of blocks

Keyword recognition and identification are performed by combination of the small predefined keyword-lexicon with the character recognizer. Korean characters usually consist of three units, called chosung, jungsung and jongsung. Keyword matching entails finding word similarities by comparing the predefined keyword with the recognition results. The similarity is calculated by using the distance between units, which has been defined in advance. The HMM-based approaches have been reported for faxed word recognition [15]. But it does not suitable to korean language. So, the recognition of keywords is done by the Hangul character recognizer, based on multi-layer backpropagation neural network, which shows good performance on low resolution faxed characters [16].

The algorithm of the keyword matching is given below.

```
Let the result of recognition be W and the similarity array be S[i]
For all the predefined keywords in lexicon (W[i]) {
    Segment each keyword into three units
    Calculate euclidean distance(W,W[i]) between three units
    save the distance in S[i]
}
Find minimum in S[i]
```

The characters within each block are connected and form a linked-list. If a keyword can not be recognized on the left-most side in a block, all the remaining characters in the block are skipped without recognition. This enables fast searching and recognition of keywords. Figure 10 shows the whole process of extracting the recipient's field on fax cover page.

2.5 Identification of the recipient's name

The recipient's name on fax cover pages appears in the block including the recipient's keyword. A field indicator like the colon is sometimes followed by the recipient's keyword. Sometimes, a fax cover page without a colon may also exist; therefore it is necessary to check whether a field indicator exists or not. The existence of field indicator is determined using the average size of characters within the block and then the recipient's name is recognized.

There are various pieces of information in the recipient's field like duties, department, etc. This system requires the extraction of only the name in the recipient's field. This is carried out by using word similarity within a small lexicon containing the names of personnel employed by the company or the institution, based on the properties of Korean names. A Korean name usually consists of 2-4 Hangul characters, so the length of a word is first used for comparison to check whether it is a name candidate or not. An extracted word is verified by using a method similar to the keyword matching algorithm.

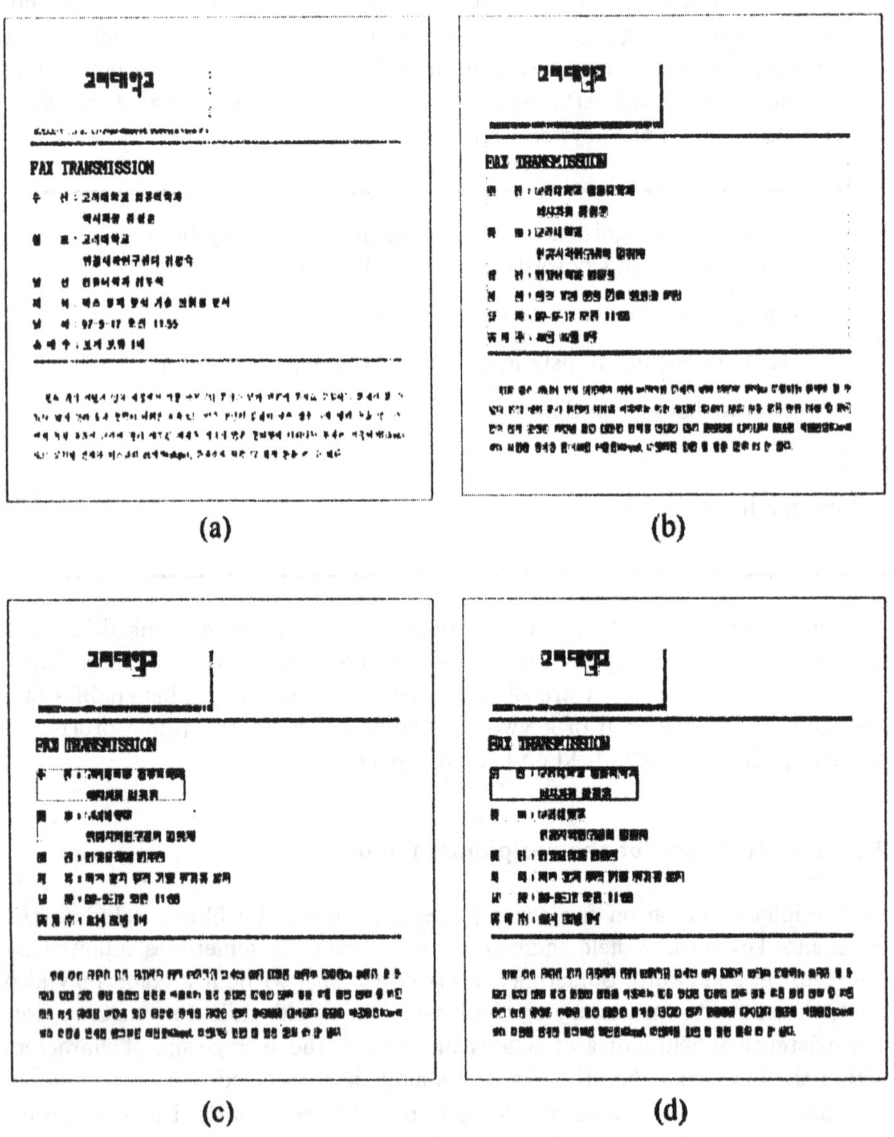

Fig. 10. Process of extracting the recipient's field. a) Input image. b) Region segmentation. c) Grouping. d) Keyword recognition.

As the recipient's name cannot always be recognized correctly by the difficulties of low resolution faxed character recognition, postprocessing is required [17]. It is carried out by confusion matrix.

3 Experimental Results and Analysis

The proposed method was implemented with MS Visual C++ 1.52 on a Pentium 166MHz machine. We collected 164 fax cover sheets which were scanned by facsimile in 2 modes (fine and normal). The test data has resolutions of 200 by 200 dpi in fine mode and 200 by 100 dpi in normal mode, respectively. The examples of test data were shown in Figure 4 in section 2. Table 1 and 2 show the experimental results of the proposed method on two different types of fax cover pages. In Table 2, F_r, F_k and F_n mean the number of failure in region segmentation, failure in keyword recognition and failure in recipient's name recognition respectively.

The experimental results show that the proposed method appeared to work better on fax cover pages scanned in fine mode than on those scanned in normal mode. The result of error analysis allows us to infer that most of errors occurred in the process of keyword recognition or recipient's name recognition. This result is mainly due to the difficulty of low resolution faxed character recognition.

Table 1. Experimental results of the proposed method

Item	Type I		Type II	
(mode)	Fine	Normal	Fine	Normal
# of Total	74	74	8	8
# of Success	69	62	6	5
# of Failure	5	12	2	3

Table 2. Error Analysis

Item	Type I		Type II	
(mode)	Fine	Normal	Fine	Normal
F_r	1	3	0	0
F_k	1	3	1	2
F_n	3	6	1	1

4 Conclusion

In this paper, we proposed an effective structure analysis method for low resolution fax cover pages, based on region segmentation and keyword recognition. The major contribution of the proposed method is the reduction of the dependency on character recognition by using region segmentation and keyword verification based on distance measure. It can enable fast and correct recognition of the recipient's name.

Experimental results confirmed that the proposed method worked well on various types of fax cover pages. We also showed that the fax cover pages were correctly analyzed when the keyword recognition was poor.

In the future, we will extend our research to handwritten fax cover page recognition.

Acknowledgments

This research was supported by Creative Research Initiatives of the Korea Ministry of Science and Technology.

References

1. S.-W. Lee, Character Recognition: Theory and Practice, Hongneung Publisher, Seoul, 1993. (in Korean)
2. J. Li and S. N. Srihari: Location of Name and Address on Fax Cover Pages. Proc. of 3rd Int. Conf. on Document Analysis and Recognition, Montreal, Canada, August 1995, pp. 756-759.
3. Y. Y. Tang, S.-W. Lee and C. Y. Suen: Automatic Document Processing: A Survey. Pattern Recognition, Vol. 29, No. 12, 1996, pp. 1931-1952.
4. T. Akiyama: Addressee Recognition for Automated FAX Mail Distribution. Proc. of SPIE Conference on Document Recognition(III), Vol. 2660, San Jose, California, January 1996, pp. 677-680.
5. G. Ricker and A. Winkler: Recognition of Faxed Documents. Proc. of SPIE Conference on Document Recognition, Vol. 2181, San Jose, California, February 1994, pp. 371-377.
6. J. Ha, R. M. Haralick and I. T. Philips: Document Page Decomposition by the Bounding-Box Projection Technique. Proc. of 3rd Int. Conf. on Document Analysis and Recognition, Montreal, Canada, August 1995, pp. 1119-1122.
7. M. Y. Yoon, S.-W. Lee and J. S. Kim: Faxed Image Restoration Using Kalman Filtering. Proc. 3rd Int. Conf. on Document Analysis and Recognition, Montreal, Canada, August 1995, pp. 677-680.
8. J. C Handley and E. R. Dougherty: Optimal Nonlinear Fax Restoration. Proc. of SPIE Conference on Document Recognition, Vol. 2181, San Jose, California, February 1994, pp. 232-235.
9. J. Liang and R. M. Haralick: Document Image Restoration Using Binary Morphological Filters. Proc. of SPIE Conference on Document Recognition(III), Vol. 2660, San Jose, California, January 1996, pp. 274-285.

10. B. Yu and A. Jain: A Robust and Fast Skew Detection Algorithm for Generic Documents. Pattern Recognition, Vol. 29, 1996, pp. 1599-1629.
11. D. S. Kim and S.-W. Lee: An Efficient Skew Correction and Character Segmentation Method for Constructing Digital Libraries from Mixed Documents. Proc. of The 23rd KISS Fall Conference, Vol. 23, Taegu, Korea, April 1996, pp. 293-206. (in Korean)
12. K. Fan and L. Wang: Classification of Document Block Using Density Features and Connectivity Histogram. Pattern Recognition Letters, Vol. 16, 1995, pp. 955-962.
13. S. W. Lam, L. Javanbakht and S. N. Srihari: Anatomy of a From Reader. Proc. of the 2th Int. Conf. on Document Analysis and Recognition, Tsukuba Science City, Japan, October 1993, pp. 506-509.
14. Y. Katsuyama and S. Naoi: Fast Title Extraction Method for Business Documents. Proc. of SPIE Conference on Document Recognition(IV), Vol 3027, San Jose, California.February 1997, pp. 192-201.
15. A. J. Elms, S. Procter and J. Illingworth: The Advantage of Using HMM-based Approach for Faxed Word Recognition. International Journal on Document Analysis and Recognition, Vol. 1, No.1, 1998, pp. 18-36.
16. D. S. Kim and S.-W. Lee: Performance Comparison of Two Methods for Low Resolution Printed Hangul Recognition. Proc. of The 23rd KISS Fall Conference, Vol. 23, Seoul, Korea, October 1996, pp. 587-590. (in Korean)
17. S.-W. Lee and E. S. Kim: Efficient Postprocessing Algorithms for Error Correction in Handwritten Hangul Address and Human Name Recognition. Pattern Recognition, Vol. 27, No. 12, 1994, pp. 1-10.

Lexical Search Approach for Character-String Recognition

M. Koga[1], R. Mine[1], H. Sako[1], and H. Fujisawa[1]

Central Research Laboratory, Hitachi, Ltd.
1-280 Higashi-Koigakubo, Kokubunji-shi, Tokyo 185, Japan
{koga, mine, sakou, fujisawa}@crl.hitachi.co.jp

Abstract. A novel method for recognizing character strings, based on a lexical search approach, is presented. In this method, a character string is recognized by searching for a sequence of segmented patterns that fits a string in a lexicon. A remarkable characteristic of this method is that character segmentation and character classification work as subfunctions of the search. The lexical search approach enables the parameters of character classifier to adapt to each segmented pattern. As a result, it improves the recognition accuracy by omitting useless candidates of character classification and by changing the criterion of rejection dynamically. Moreover, the processing time is drastically reduced by using minimum sets of categories for each segmented pattern. The validity of the developed method is shown by the experimental results using a lexicon including 44,700 character strings.

1 Introduction

The importance of optical character readers (OCRs), which are used for form processing, mail sorting, etc., is increasing. Especially, the technology to read sets of words such as names and addresses has become more important.

Many methods for recognizing words have been proposed. They are categorized into two groups: segmentation based methods and non-segmentation based methods. Non segmentation based methods such as HMM approaches or holistic approaches are powerful for words of Roman alphabets. However, they are not so successful for Chinese or Japanese characters so far in most cases. On the other hand, segmentation based methods perform rather good results for both.

In general, a process of a conventional segmentation based method consists of three stages: character segmentation, character classification, and linguistic processing as shown in Fig. 1. At each stage *a priori* knowledge, such as arrangement of characters, shape of characters, and sequence of characters, is used. Collaboration of these stages can improve the accuracy of recognition, because different types of *a priori* knowledge are available in the final decision. For example, the method presented in [3] uses character classification to select the best segmentation candidates. An example of collaboration of character classification and linguistic processing is presented in [6]. A method which uses the result of linguistic processing to select a sequence of patterns is presented in [2].

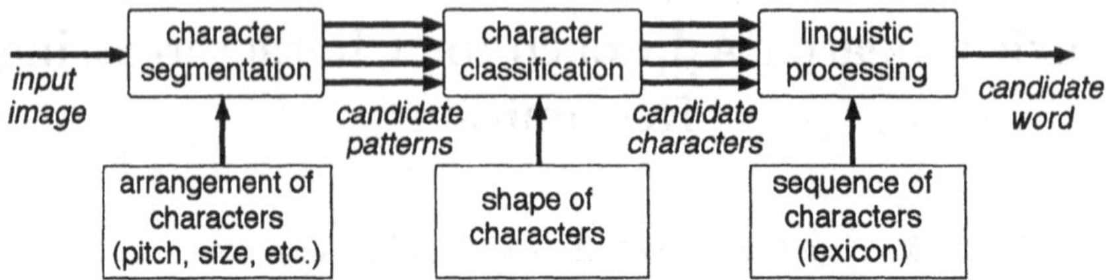

Fig. 1. Data flow model of the conventional word recognition methods.

The common strategy of these methods is the multiple hypothesis generation and testing. A stage sends multiple candidates to the following stages. The candidates are tested and the best one is selected in the following stages. Therefore, a lexicon is available only at the end of the whole process in this kind of methods.

In this paper, a new approach named "lexical search approach" is presented. It is such a top-down approach that the linguistic processing gives hypotheses of character categories to segmentation and classification. This approach has the potential to reduce the processing time and to improve recognition accuracy drastically. The approach is expected to be effective both for handwritten and machine printed strings. Similar ideas have been proposed [4][7] for word recognition of Roman alphabets. We applied the method to the recognition of names of places in Japan. We think this paper describes the first attempt to apply such an idea to a language in which a large number of characters are used. An improved technique to cope with the enormousness of characters is presented in the following sections. In addition, experimental results that show advantages of the method are presented.

2 Concept of lexical search approach

We call such an approach "lexical search approach" that linguistic processing referring to lexicon controls character segmentation and character classification. As shown in Fig. 2, the data flow of the approach is completely different from that of the conventional approach. Linguistic processing gives the character segmentation information about the position where the next pattern may appear. Character segmentation extracts candidate patterns according to the information. Then character classification tests each segmented pattern immediately and decide whether it is acceptable contextually. Here the parameters of the character classifier is adapted dynamically to each pattern referring to the lexicon.

Accuracy and processing time of recognition can be improved by using the lexicon in the early stage of recognition. For example, suppose a lexicon includes the names of the counties in the world. In a conventional method, all candidate patterns should be classified into 26 categories (A to Z). However, if the first characters of a word is recognized as "J", then the following patterns should be classified only as "A" or "O", because "JAPAN", "JAMAICA", and "JORDAN" are the only words whose first characters are "J". The number of categories can

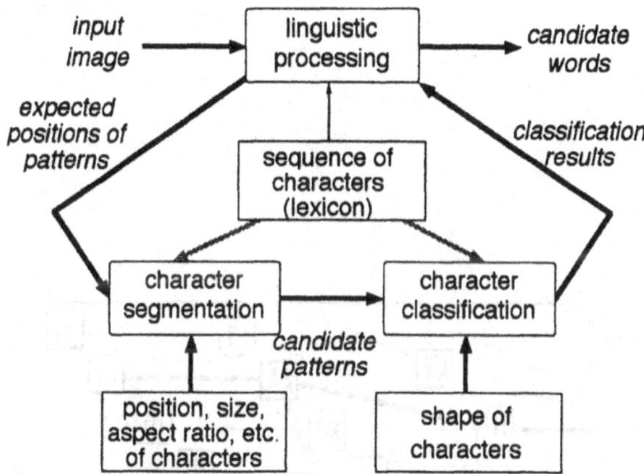

Fig. 2. Data flow models of the developed method.

be reduced from 26 to 2, and accuracy and speed can be improved. It is also possible to change the classification algorithm and parameters according to the set of possible categories for the following patterns.

Figure 3 illustrates the relationship among an input image, candidate patterns, and a lexicon. A name of a city in Japan, "川越市", is used as an example of an input image. The character-strings recognition is a process finding correspondence of patterns and characters in a word (as shown by gray arrows).

Some features of the proposed method are shown here. The candidate patterns are represented in terms of a graph named "segmentation hypothesis graph". Each arc represents a candidate pattern. Nodes represent boundaries of candidate patterns. As most Japanese characters consist of more than one connected components, many candidate patterns can be generated as shown.

Lexicon is represented as a Trie [1] named "lexicon tree" in our method, as illustrated in the figure. This kind of data structure is necessary to cope with the big lexicon where a large number of character categories are used. A path from the root to one of the leaves represents a word. In this example, "川口市", "川越市", "川崎市", "川西市", "川之江市" etc. are included in the lexicon.

3 Character-string recognition method based on lexical search approach

3.1 Overview

Our goal is recognition of phrases which represent names of places in Japan. Each of the phrases consists of a few words. Each of the words is a sequence of three or four Japanese characters in general. Because Japanese words are short, we devised a method to recognize a phrase as one character string.

The developed character-string recognition method has three sub-functions: pre-segmentation, word matching and selection of candidate words (Fig. 4). Pre-segmentation is a technique commonly used in the conventional segmentation

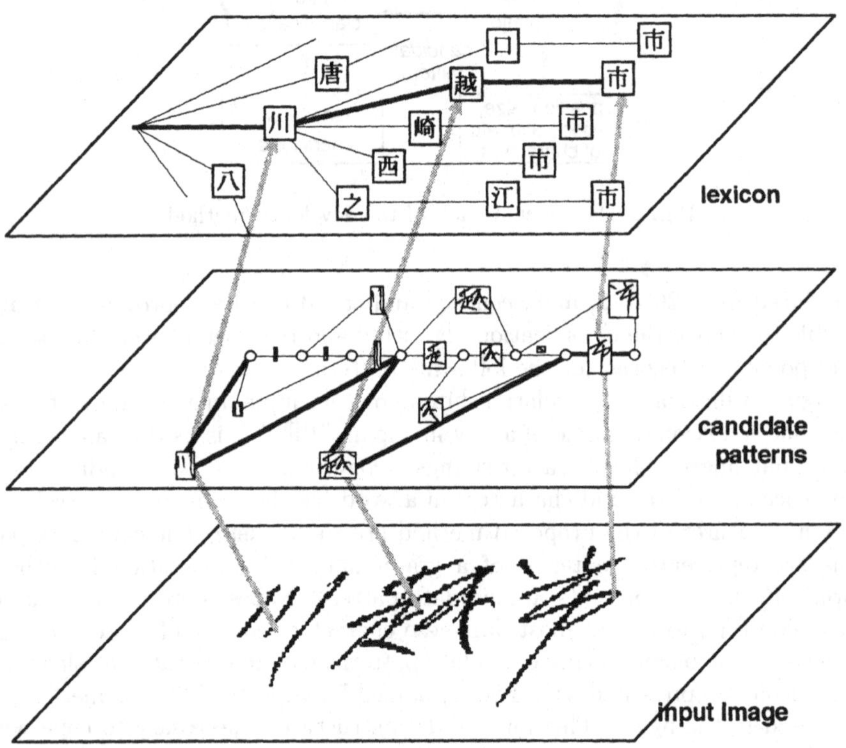

Fig. 3. Relationship among input image, candidate patterns and lexicon.

based methods [2][3]. In the pre-segmentation, a character string is cut into candidate patterns so that correctly segmented patterns are included in the candidates. Word matching is the body of this method. It is a process to search for a sequence of candidate patterns that fits a word in the lexicon. The selection of a candidate pattern is a sub-function of word matching. It selects candidate pattern(s) that can follow the previous one in the sequence. The character classification is also a sub-function of the word matching. It evaluates how candidate patterns fit characters in words. The word matching process outputs the result in terms of a search tree. Then the best candidate word is selected from the search tree.

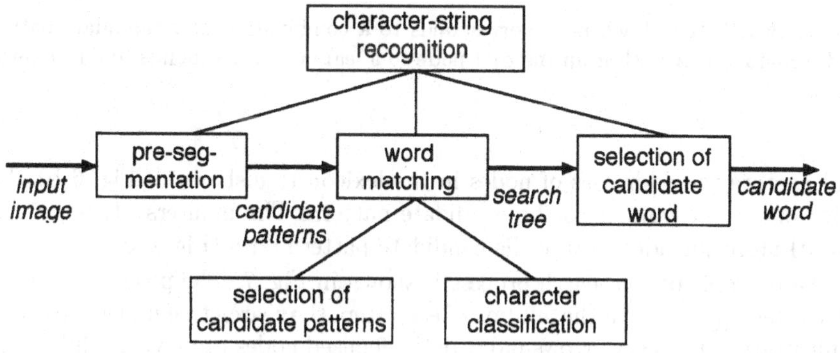

Fig. 4. Function tree of the developed method.

Note that the segmentation process is divided into the pre-segmentation and the selection of the candidate pattern. In the explanation of concept of the lexical search approach, the whole segmentation is done under the control of linguistic processing. However, to reduce processing time, we adopted the pre-segmentation method in this implementation.

3.2 Word Matching

There are many combinations of candidate patterns and characters in the lexicon. In the word matching, a simple breadth-first search algorithm is applied to search for a sequence of patterns that fits a word. A search tree generated from the example shown in Fig. 3 is illustrated in Fig. 5. Each node except the root node corresponds to a combination of a candidate pattern and a character in the lexicon. A recognized word is represented as a path from the root to one of the leaves. In this example, the word "川越市" is recognized.

A more detailed data structure of the tree equivalent to Fig. 5 is shown in Fig. 6(a). Each data record of the nodes has three pointers. The first one is the pointer to the upper node. If the upper node is the root, it points to NULL. The second one is the pointer to the node in the lexicon tree. The pointers A, B, C,

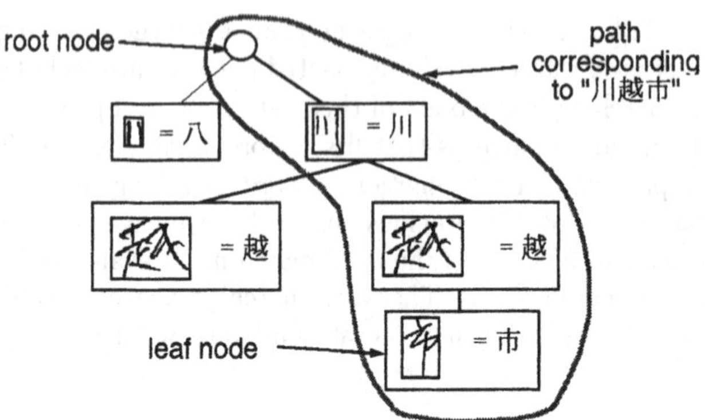

Fig. 5. Search tree. Each node corresponds to a combination of a candidate pattern and a character. A path from the root node to a leaf node corresponds to a recognized word.

and D store the addresses of nodes in the lexicon tree shown in Fig. 6(b). The third one is the pointer to the candidate pattern. The pointers a1, b1, c1, c2, and d1 store the addresses of the candidate pattern data (Fig. 6(c)).

An example of the search process is shown in Fig. 7. The process is divided into 5 steps ((a)-(e)). In the left box of each step, the search tree under processing is illustrated. The gray arrows indicate the focused nodes from which child nodes are being generated. In the middle box, the lexicon tree is illustrated. The gray arrows indicate the characters corresponding to the focused nodes. In the right box, the segmentation hypothesis graph is illustrated. The thick arcs indicate the candidate patterns that can follow the patterns corresponding to the focused nodes.

At the beginning, as shown in Fig. 7(a), the combinations of the first characters of each word and the candidate patterns are tested by character classification. If acceptable combinations are found, nodes for the combinations are generated. In this example, patterns that look like "八" and " 川" respectively are found in the candidate patterns.

Next, the nodes generated in step (a) are focused on in (b) and (c). Combinations of following candidate patterns and following characters in the lexicon are tested. If acceptable combinations are found, child nodes for them are generated (c).

The descendant nodes are generated recursively in the same way as (d) and (e). If a node being focused on corresponds to a leaf in the lexicon tree, then the node is regarded as a leaf and no more child nodes are generated under it (e).

Note that it is not necessary to focus on only the leftmost patterns in the input image at the beginning of the search as shown in (a). If the search starts only from the leftmost patterns, the processing time can be reduced. However, OCR sometimes should find where the target word starts in the text line. In real applications, noise may be included in the text line by error of line segmentation. Unexpected words may exist besides words in the lexicon. The developed method

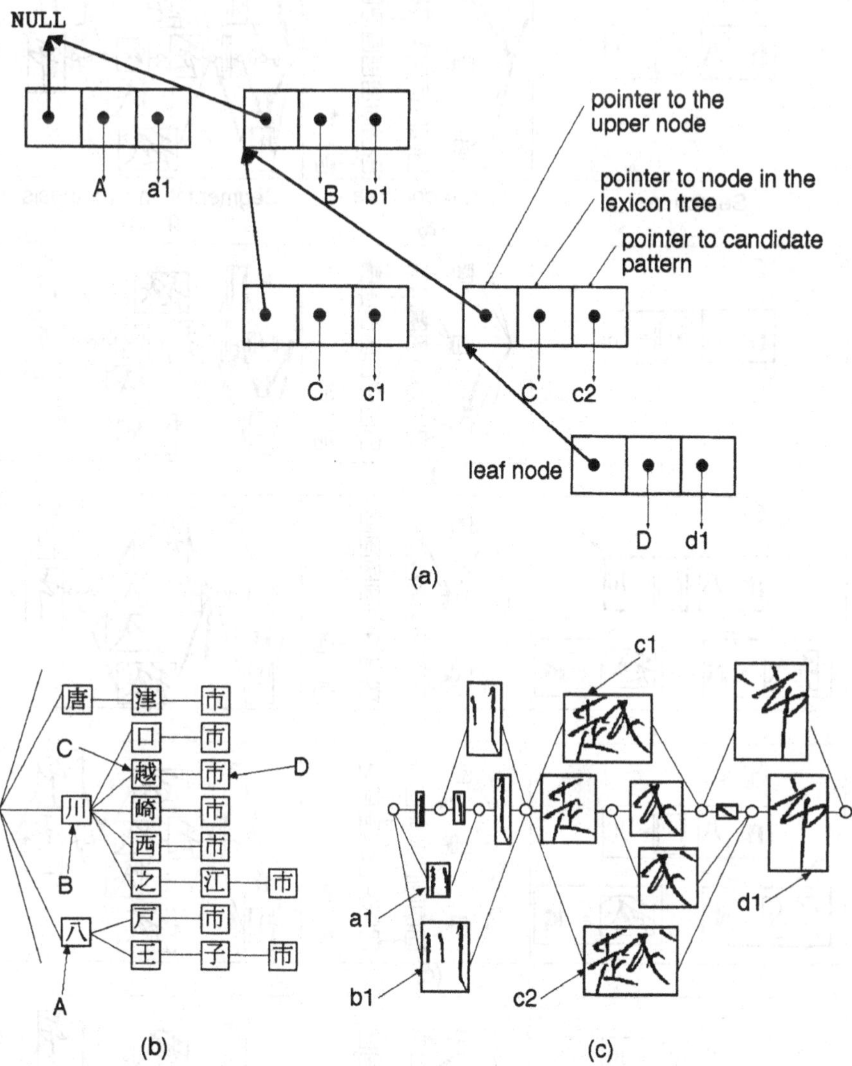

Fig. 6. Data structure of search tree. (a) Search tree. (b) Lexicon tree. (c) Segmentation hypothesis graph.

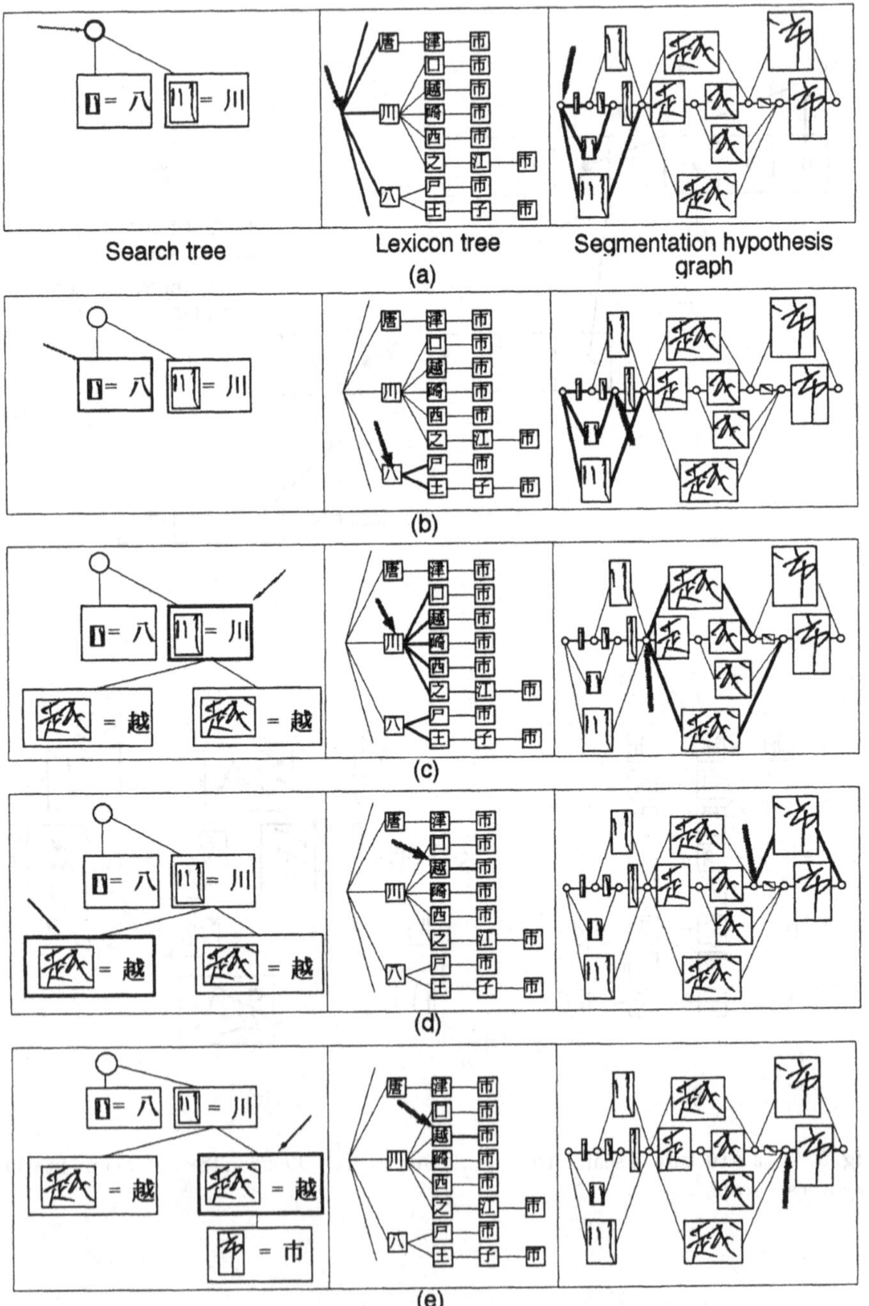

Fig. 7. Example of a search process.

can handle such cases only by checking all candidate patterns at the beginning of the search. Once the first characters of the words are found, the child nodes can be generated in the same way as explained above and the target words can be recognized.

3.3 Lexicon tree

The data structure of the lexicon tree is illustrated in Fig. 8. It is a kind of Trie. A path from the root to a leaf represents a word in the lexicon. Each data record of a node in the lexicon tree consists of a character code, a pointer to the reference patterns and a pointer to the child node pointer table. The child node pointer table is a table of variable size that stores the pointers to the data records of child nodes. If a node is a leaf, the pointer to the child node pointer table points to NULL. The pointer to reference patterns point to the reference patterns used for the character classification. The reference patterns are used when the parent node is focused on in the word matching.

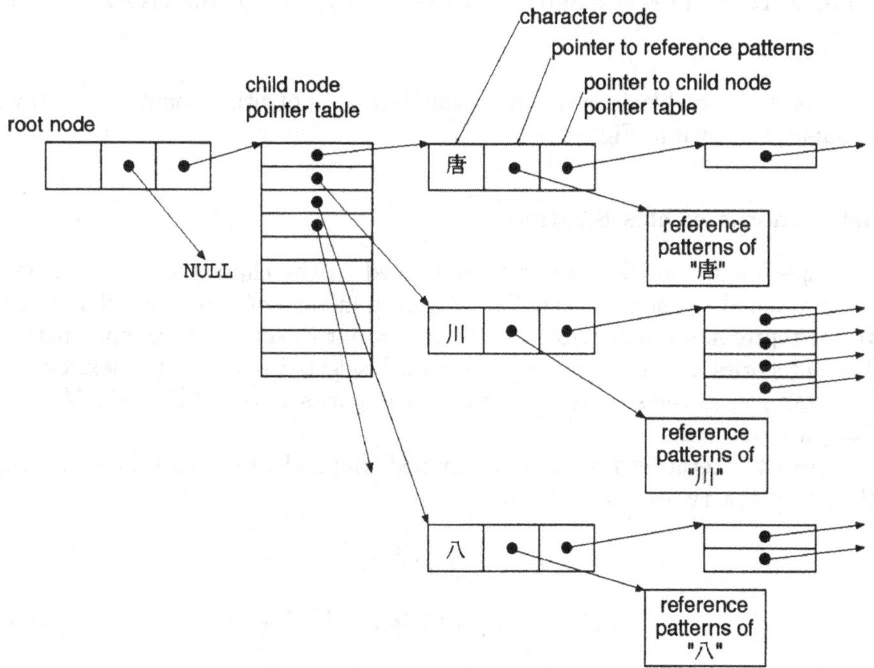

Fig. 8. Data structure of lexicon tree.

The style of the lexicon tree affects the processing time. A plain lexicon tree, which is equivalent to a list of words as in Fig. 9 (a), also can be used for the developed method. However, the nodes of the same characters and the same parent nodes can be merged as in (b) and the tree can be shrunk, and the processing time can be reduced. If the tree is not shrunk, classification of the same pattern into the same set of categories is repeated, while such repetition is avoided with a shrunk lexicon tree. In the case that there are many words in the lexicon, the processing time using plain lexicon tree may be longer even than the conventional method .

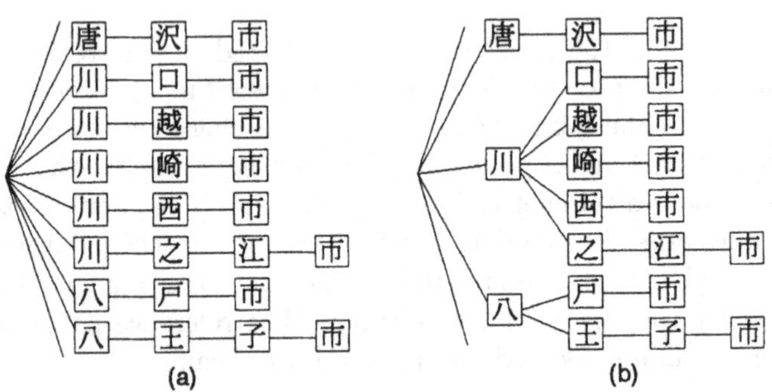

Fig. 9. Types of the lexicon trees. (a) Plain lexicon tree. (b) Shrunk lexicon tree.

A part of a real lexicon tree representing names of cities, counties, and towns in Japan is shown in Fig. 10.

3.4 Character classification

A simple minimum distance method is used in the character classification in the developed method. The similarity is used instead of a distance. The feature vector represents the distribution of the contour direction of an input pattern. The categories of the reference patterns are selected referring the lexicon tree. For example, in the step (c) in Fig. 7, 5 categories ("口", "越", "崎", "西", and "之") are selected.

Special criteria for rejection are applied. Here, the two conditions to accept the i th category are shown below:

$$S_i > \delta \tag{1}$$

$$S_i \geq max\{S_i : 1 \geq j \geq N\} - \varepsilon \tag{2}$$

where
S_i : similarity of i th category
N : number of categories
δ : absolute threshold (constant)
ε : relative threshold (constant)

Condition (1) is used with the intention of selecting the categories whose reference patterns are similar enough to the input patterns. Condition (2) is used with the intention of avoiding the categories that give much smaller similarity

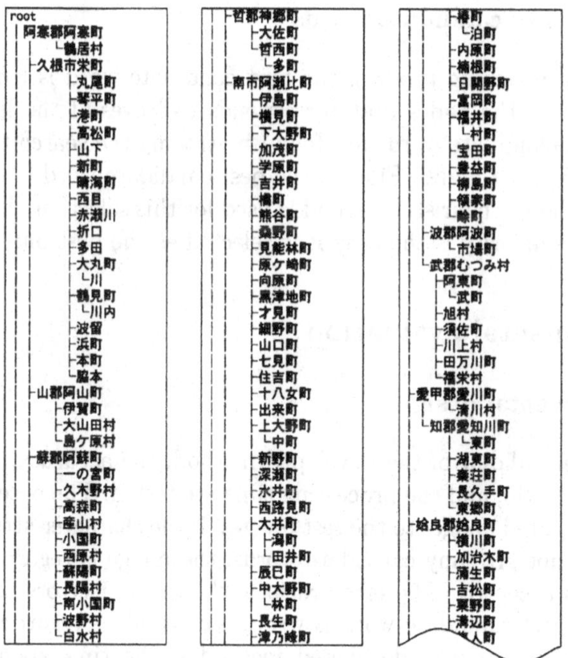

Fig. 10. Example of a lexicon tree that represents names of cities, counties, and towns in Japan. It consists of 44,700 phrases in total.

than others. When more than one categories fulfill the two conditions, all of the categories are accepted. Therefore, if a category gives higher similarity, the condition of rejection becomes severer. This is a good characteristic because a category with lower similarity may cause an error of final recognition result in such a case.

The two parameters, δ and ε , have a significant effect on the processing time and the accuracy of recognition. If δ is larger or ε is smaller, the processing time will become shorter and the error ratio of character string recognition will become lower. If δ is smaller or ε is larger, the acceptance ratio of total recognition will be higher.

The selection of reference patterns by the lexicon can increase the processing speed. More than 4,000 characters are used in the names of the places in Japan. To recognize them by conventional method, all candidate patterns should be classified into the all categories. On the other hand, less categories are needed in the developed method, because the number of characters each of which can appear as the first character of a city name or a county name is only 422. If the category of the first character is fixed, only one or two categories can follow it in most cases. The processing time of the developed method is thus estimated to be 1/100 of that of the conventional method in the best case.

3.5 Selection of candidate words

After the word matching process, the best candidate word is looked for in the search tree. First, the nodes that corresponds to leaves of the lexicon tree are selected. Then candidate words are found by tracing the search tree back using the pointers to upper nodes. Finally, the best candidate word is selected. In the developed method, a heuristic method is used for this selection. The word whose summation of similarity is the largest is selected as the best one.

4 Experimental evaluation

4.1 Experimental design

To evaluate the validity of the developed method, the accuracy, i.e. acceptance ratio and error ratio, and the processing time are tested. The acceptance ratio is the ratio of accepted images to the test images. If the character-string recognition program does not give any candidate words, the image is regarded as rejected; otherwise it is accepted. The error ratio is the ratio of errors to the accepted images. If the first candidate word is wrong, the result is regarded as an error.

The processing time of developed method is the time spent in the word matching including selection of patterns and character classification (see Fig. 4). The processing time of the pre-segmentation and the selection of candidate word is so small, comparing with the character classification, that it is ignored. A workstation with a 160 MHz RISC processor is used for the experiment.

Another character-string recognition program is used to compare the validity of the new method with the conventional method. The program uses the pre-segmentation program same as the new method. The same set of reference patterns is used in the character classification. The processing time of the classification is measured for the comparison to the new method. It classifies all candidate patterns into all categories in the lexicon. The classification is accelerated by a pre-classifier that roughly classify the input patterns before the main classification. Several sequence of candidate patterns are selected by dynamic programing [2] and then interpreted by post-processing [6].

4.2 Lexicon

The lexicon is designed to recognize the names of cities, counties, and towns in Japan. An expression of a Japanese address usually starts with a prefecture name followed by a city name or a county name, and then by the town name. Thus a set of combined words, each of which consists of a city name or a county name, and a town name, are used as the lexicon. If a combined word is longer than five characters, only five characters from the head are used.

The lexicon consists of 44,700 combined words. 1,915 kinds of characters appear in it. There are totally 76,167 nodes in the shrunk lexicon tree (as shown Table. 1).

Table 1. Numbers of nodes in the shrunk lexicon tree used in the experiment

layer Example	1	2	3	4	5
number of nodes	422	1,120	1,806	29,154	43,664

4.3 Test images

As a set of test samples, 1,616 binary images of machine printed character strings (Figs. 11 and 12) are used. A test image consists of several line images. Line segmentation is done previously. A word in the lexicon is included somewhere in the segmented line images of each test image. Note that if the character-string recognition program find a false candidate word at a wrong position, it is regarded as an error.

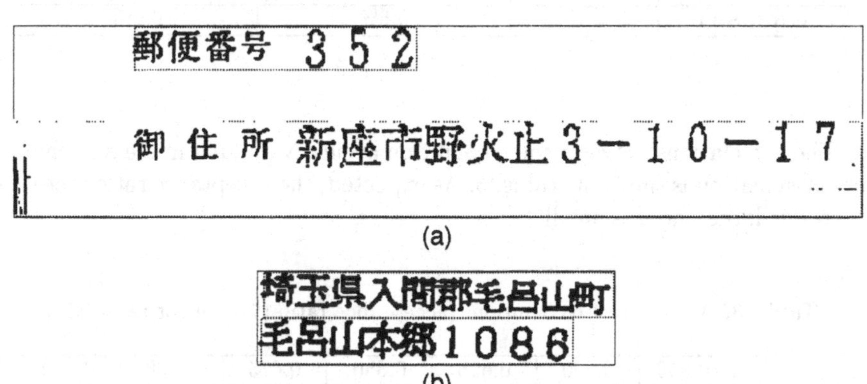

Fig. 11. Accepted test images. (δ = 0.63, ε= 0.05)

Fig. 12. Rejected test images (δ = 0.63, ε= 0.05)

4.4 Experimental results

The processing times and accuracy of recognition of the developed method are listed in Table 2. The processing time of the developed method is much shorter than that of the the conventional method. If the plain lexicon tree is used, the processing time is very long, as expected. If the search starts only at the leftmost patterns of the character strings, the processing time becomes much faster while the acceptance ratio becomes lower. The error ratio of the new method is smaller than the conventional method. Most of the errors of the conventional method come from reading wrong positions.

Table 2. Numbers of nodes in the shrunk lexicon tree used in the experiment

	conventional method	developed method		
		plain lexicon	shrunk lexicon	
	search starting at every position			search starting at the head of the text line
average processing time	0.74 sec	12.3 sec	0.12 sec	0.01 sec
acceptance ratio	72.4%	76.5%		32.6%
error ratio	2.8%	0.6%		0.6%

The correlations between the recognition accuracy and parameters of character classification is shown in Table. 3. As expected, the acceptance ratio increases when ε is large and δ is small.

Table 3. Accuracy of recognition. (acceptance ratio (%) / error ratio (%))

	δ=0.550	0.600	0.625	0.650	0.675	0.700	0.750
ε=0.01	85.7/ 9.7	81.9/1.5	78.1/0.3	73.4/0.2	67.0/0.3	57.7/0.2	32.1/1.2
0.02	87.1/10.9	82.5/1.4	78.9/0.4	74.2/0.3	67.7/0.4	58.2/0.3	32.3/1.2
0.03	88.1/12.0	83.1/1.7	79.6/0.5	74.9/0.3	68.2/0.4	58.7/0.3	32.5/1.2
0.05	87.8/12.9	83.3/2.2	79.9/0.5	75.3/0.3	68.5/0.5	58.9/0.3	32.6/1.1
0.07	86.9/13.9	83.4/2.5	79.8/0.6	75.2/0.4	68.5/0.4	59.1/0.4	32.6/1.1

Examples of test images are shown in Figs. 11 and 12. The results of line segmentation are shown by the doted rectangles. There is no target word in the first line of Fig. 11(a) and there are noises and a pre-print (that means "address") on the left of the target word. The name of prefecture is on the left of the target word in Fig. 11(b). The proposed method could find the target words even in such cases. Figure 12(a) is a rejected example because of failure of pre-segmentation. In this case, characters are touching at so many points that correct boundaries cannot be found. Figure 12(b) is a example of rejected test image because of low similarity. Some strokes are lacking because of the low quality of printing, so the similarity of the pattern is low.

5 Conclusion

The developed method based on the lexical search approach is completely different from conventional methods. In the method, character segmentation and character classification work as sub-functions of word matching. Similar ideas were recently proposed, but we believe this is the first attempt to apply the idea to a language in which a large number of characters are used. This method enables the character classifier to adapt the context, and it has a potential to improve processing speed and accuracy.

Experimental results show the validity of the method. The search using Trie improves the processing time. The mechanism to change the rejection criterion of character classification worked as expected. On the other hand, the method is sometimes not so robust, because the search process can not skip characters that give low similarity or misspelled characters. A simple breadth first search can not handle enormous combinations of patterns and characters if such skip is allowed.

The algorithm is simple and many kinds of extension are possible. Any kinds of character classifier can be adopted to this approach. A sophisticated search algorithm instead of a breadth-first search may improve the performance. Other data structures than the Trie can be used for the approach.

References

1. E. Fredkin, Trie Memory, Commun. ACM, Vol. 3, No. 9, pp. 490 - 500, (1960)
2. H. Murase, Segmentation and Recognition of Hand-Written Character String Using Linguistic Information, Trans. of the Institute of Electronics, Information and Communication Engineers, vol. J69-D No. 9, pp. 1292-1301 (1986 in Japanese)
3. H. Fujisawa et al, Segmentation Methods for Character Recognition: From Segmentation to Document Structure Analysis, Proc. of the IEEE vol. 80, No. 7, (1992)
4. F. Kimura et al, Improvements of a Lexicon Directed Algorithhm for Recognition of Unconstrained Handwritten Words, Proc. of ICDAR '93, pp.18-22(1993)
5. E. Cohen et al, Control Structure for Interpreting Handwritten Addresses, IEEE Trans. PAMI vol. 16. no. 10, pp. 1049-1056 (1994)
6. K. Marukawa et al, A Paper Form Processing System with an Error Correcting Function for Reading Handwritten String, Proc. 3rd Annual Symposium on Document Analysis and Information Retrieval, pp. 469-481 (1994)
7. C. Chen, Lexicon-Driven Word Recognition, proc. of ICDAR '95, pp. 919-922 (1995)
8. J. J. Hull, Incorporating Language Syntax in Visual Text Recognition with a Statistical Model, IEEE Trans. PAMI vol. 18, no. 12, pp. 1251-1256, (1996)
9. R. G. Casey et al, A survey of Methods and Strategies in Character Segmentation, IEEE Trans. PAMI vol. 18, no. 7, pp. 690-706 (1996)
10. P. D. Gader et al, Neural and Fuzzy Methods in Handwriting Recognition, IEEE Computer, Feb. 1997, pp. 79-8 (1997)
11. L. S. Yaeger et al, Combining Neural Networks and Context-Driven Search for Online, Printed Handwriting Recognition in the NEWTON, AI Magazine, Spring 1998, 73-89 (1998)

A Segmentation Method for Touching Handwritten Japanese Characters

Hiromitsu Nishimura[1], Hisashi Ikeda[2] and Yasuaki Nakano[1]

[1] Dept. of Information Engineering, Shinshu University, Nagano, Japan
[2] Central Research Laboratory, Hitachi Ltd., Kokubunji, Japan

Abstract. The purpose of this paper is the segmentation of touching handwritten Japanese characters to enable each segmented character to be recognized. Though segmentation methods cooperating with recognition for the simple characters are known, they are not applicable to complicated characters such as kanji. To estimate the ability of segmentation itself, our method does not use any results of character recognition but segments touching characters using some specific features of character patterns. Linear components in patterns are extracted as features and a segmentation method based on them is proposed. A database, which contains character pattern and ground truth is constructed. In the database the ground truth data describe the correct areas of touching points judged by plural human subjects. As a result of the segmentation experiments, about 64% of touching patterns can be segmented at appropriate points. This correct segmentation rate is automatically calculated consulting the ground truths.

1 Introduction

The demands for the recognition of freely handwritten Japanese characters have become stronger, so as to recognize addresses of letters, manuscripts, memos and so on. In these applications, touching handwritten characters become big problems.

In European languages, words are commonly written in cursive style, so there are character recognition methods (called holistic approach) which identify a pattern as a word without segmenting touching characters.

On the other hand, in Japanese, there is no space between words and the number of combinations of neighboring characters is too big, so that the recognition of touching handwritten characters may be almost impossible if they are not segmented.

For handwritten alphanumeric characters, methods using over-segmentation and multiple hypotheses cooperating with recognition have been reported [1]. For cursive handwritten English word recognition, a method that uses recognition results and lexicon matching has also been reported [3]. For printed word recognition, a segmentation method that uses character sizes has been reported.

In the recognition of handwritten Japanese address characters a method cooperating segmentation, recognition and lexical matching was reported [5]. But the methods coping with touching characters have not been studied deeply.

In this paper, the authors propose a segmentation method that does not use any recognition results, but only uses specific features of patterns. The reason is in that the recognition performance of handwritten kanji characters is not thought high enough to verify the multiple hypotheses.

Using a newly built document database with ground truth data of touching areas, a series of the segmentation experiments was done. The correct segmentation rate was automatically assessed.

1.1 Specific Features of Handwritten Japanese Character Scripts

Handwritten Japanese character scripts have the specific features as shown in Figure 1.

- a: Both vertical (top to bottom) and horizontal (left to right) writing directions exist.
- b: Curved pattern characters (mainly hiragana and Arabic numerals) and linear pattern characters (kanji and katakana) are used.
- c: Character sizes are not uniform.
  - c1: Character sizes of numerals are much smaller than kanji
  - c2: Kanji characters are usually bigger than hiragana characters
- d: Kanji characters are complicated and constituted of many strokes.

In this paper, we deal with not general handwritten Japanese characters but only handwritten Japanese address characters.

The segmentation methods [2] [3] [4] using “Contour following analysis”, “Character size”, “Peripheral distribution”, which are proposed for the recognition of English handwritten address characters, are not appropriate, because of the specific features of Japanese characters stated above.

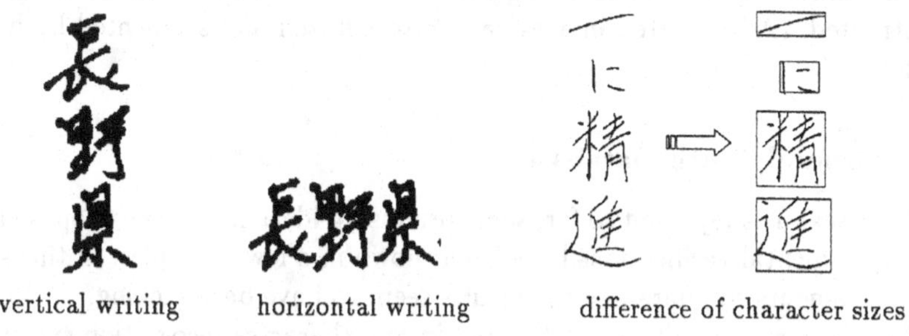

Fig. 1. Examples of handwritten Japanese character script

1.2 Proposed Method

As stated in the condition b in the previous section, there are kanji, hiragana, katakana and alphanumerical characters in handwritten Japanese scripts. If we restrict ourselves on the addresses on the mails, however, most of the characters are kanji. Kanji are mainly constructed with linear components. Thus most of touching characters are found between kanji. In the many touching cases, the last stroke of the preceding character extends too long and touches to the one of strokes of the next character.

In this paper, we assume that a kanji touches with another kanji. Under the assumption, a method to estimate linear components and segment touching patterns is proposed.

2 Database

A Japanese address character database is supplied by Postal Administrator Laboratory for the research encouragement. Since it is not clear how many touching patterns are included in the database, another database fitted to the purpose of the research is needed.

By the reason, the database stated in the section 2.1 is prepared and used in this research.

2.1 The Database for Segmentation Experiments

Data collected for segmentation experiments consist of 8,000 images written by 10 subjects with ball-point pens and fiber-tipped pens in both vertical and horizontal styles. At the collection, the subjects were not instructed to write touching characters intentionally. By forcing the subjects write patterns into rather smaller regions, however, the touching characters were generated in natural manners.

After digitizing the 8,000 images with the resolution of 200 dpi, each of them was examined by human subjects if it includes touching characters. Thus a collection consisting of 2,487 touching patterns selected from the 8,000 images was constructed. (All collected images can be recognized and segmented by human subject.)

2.2 Ground Truth Database

In the researches reported so far, some promising ideas have been proposed, but the experimental verifications have been shown in a few examples. In this sense, the assessments to guarantee the results seem to have been lacking.

In this paper, results are not tested in any character recognition system. So the progresses in character recognition rate can not evaluate the propriety of segmentations.

In this paper, ground truth data judged by human subjects have been made in order to assess the results of the proposed method automatically.

To make the ground truth database, each original scanned pattern was displayed on the computer screens and four subjects were forced to pick the touching areas using the mouses. The point clicked as the touching one was converted to a small square region including the point. The results given by four subjects were merged and an area corresponding to the touching point was generated by a majority logic.

2.3 Possibilities of Recognition by Segmentation

A touching pattern can not be recognized in a usual Japanese character recognition system, because such a usual system is designed only to recognize each segmented character. If a touching pattern is segmented correctly, each segmented pattern may be considered as recognizable.

But not all the segmented patterns can be recognized even if the correct segmentation is done. The reason may be in that touching characters might be deformed heavily so as not to be identified after the segmentations. Besides, the recognition method may not be complete.

As a result, the correct segmentation rate will not completely agree with the recognition rate improvement. It is expected, however, that many correctly segmented patterns have high possibility to be recognized correctly, thus a higher recognition rate may be induced.

3 Segmentation Using Straight Line Components

In the steps explained below, the segmentation lines in the patterns are estimated.

As the precondition, the patterns to be segmented should be extracted from preprocessing stage. By extracting conected regions from an address image, some of them are judged to have too large widths or heights. They can be the touching regions of the two components belonging to the different characters. Each of such conected regions is supplied to the segmentation unit.

3.1 Estimation of the Linewidths and Pattern Normalization

Addresses in mails are written with various character sizes and with various kinds of pens. To make the proposed method robust, it is necessary to normalize the linewidths of patterns.

In the Figure 2, to estimate the linewidth of a pattern, the length in the direction perpendicular to every contour point independently in every small block is estimated. Then the frequency distribution along the stroke is calculated. From the maximum point of the frequency distribution the linewidth of every small block is estimated.

For patterns having too large linewidth, the proposed method may search many surplus linear components from the patterns. To avoid surplus searches, patterns having a large linewidth are preprocessed by thinning.

The thinning method is not the usual "thinning" which converts patterns to those having one pixel linewidth. Our method normalizes the patterns having too large linewidths to those having the standard width. In the following algorithm, two formulae are examined independently in vertical and horizontal directions. In the algorithm

m, n: the estimated and standard linewidths of a character,
X: abscissa, Y: ordinate, O: input image, N: normalized image,
O (x, y), N (x, y): current coordinates in images,
Value of the pixel: 1 for black pixel, 0 for white pixel.

Algorithm

$$\textit{Vertical thinning}\begin{cases} \textit{if } O(x,y+u)=1 \ \textit{for } u=\{-(m-n),\ldots,(m-n)\} \\ \qquad\qquad N(x,y)=1, \\ \textit{else} \qquad N(x,y)=0, \end{cases}$$

$$\textit{Horizontal thinning}\begin{cases} \textit{if } O(x+u,y)=1 \ \textit{for } u=\{-(m-n),\ldots,(m-n)\} \\ \qquad\qquad N(x,y)=1, \\ \textit{else} \qquad N(x,y)=0. \end{cases}$$

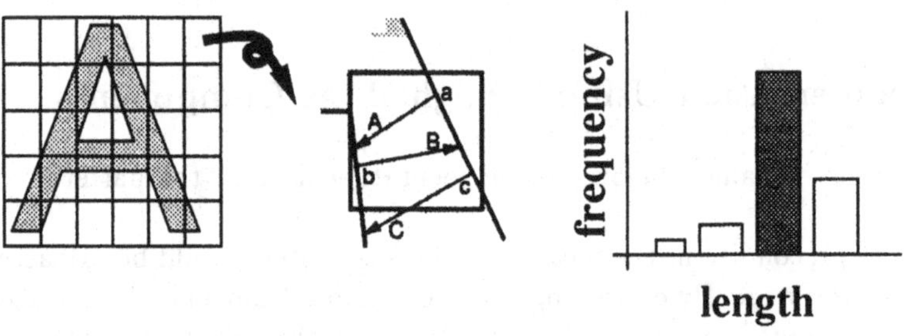

Fig. 2. Estimation of the linewidth of a written character

3.2 Extraction of Linear Components

Since the touching patterns to be segmented are mainly constructed of linear components, extraction of linear components is necessary. In this paper, we estimate linear components from Freeman-code strings extracted from contours of patterns.

As is well known, Freeman-code has only eight values of resolution of the directions that are rather poor. So, we adopt the following condition C to extract linear components in more subtle directions. After extractions of linear components, the extracted linear components are quantized into the eight directions.

If the following five conditions are satisfied for a part of the contour, it is extracted as a candidate of a linear component.
Algorithm

A: If same Freeman-code continues for more than a threshold, the continuation is estimated as a linear component.
B: If some other codes contained in the sequence of the same code and their number is less than a threshold, the continuation including the other codes is estimated as a linear component.
C: When A and B do not produce a string of a linear segment, averaging operation is tested. If the averaged value of some continuous codes is close to the value of the mode of the codes, the continuation is estimated as a linear component.
D: If the length of a linear components estimated by A, B and C is smaller than a threshold, the result is rejected.
E: Linear components are extended along the estimated direction. If the pixels on the extension line have the value "1", they are added to the linear components.

3.3 Generation of Simplified Patterns and Estimation of Potential Segmentation Areas

From a hypothesis that the potential segmentation areas in complicated patterns are to be estimated by a macroscopic viewpoint, simplified patterns are generated.

The simplified pattern is generated by overlapping the extracted linear components, thickening the overlapped area and dilating it. By using simplified patterns, many surplus segmentation lines are suppressed.

The segmentation areas are estimated by extracting crossing points of linear component from the simplified patterns.

If the area around the crossing point has more pixels in the overlapped area than a threshold, the square region around the crossing point with a prescribed edge is estimated as a potential segmentation area.

An example is shown in Figure 3, where the leftmost shows the original image, the center the simplified pattern and the rightmost the potential segmentation areas.

3.4 Estimation of Segmentation Lines

In the step explained below, segmentation lines in potential segmentation area estimated in section 3.3 is extracted.

A potential segmentation area is searched by the scanning line to the direction of character writing. The uppermost (leftmost) point and lowermost (rightmost) point is determined along the every scanning line. Tentative segmentation

Fig. 3. Estimation of potential segmentation areas

lines are estimated by linking the uppermost (leftmost) and lowermost (rightmost) points. So the number of the tentative segmentation is the number of the combination of those two points.

If a tentative segmentation line estimated above does not satisfy the following conditions, it is rejected.

1. The tentative segmentation line segments a conected region.
2. The numbers in pixels of the segmented areas exceed a threshold.

The shortest tentative segmentation line along the all estimated lines is decided as the segmentation line.

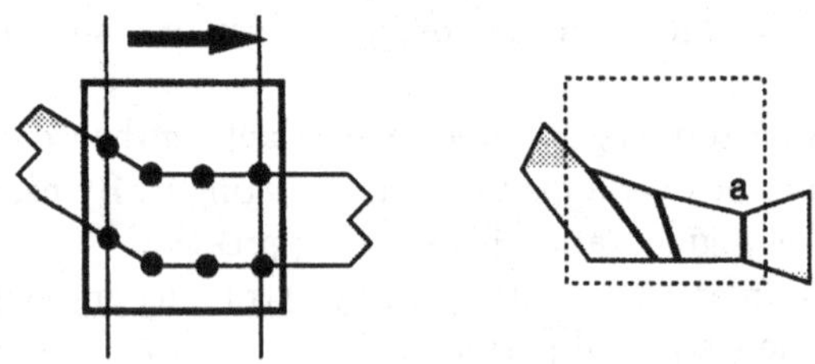

Fig. 4. Example of estimation of segmentation lines

3.5 Reduction of the Surplus Segmentation Lines and Segmentation

By the algorithm explained so far, potential lines for the segmentation are extracted. But many surplus segmentation lines are included in them. Since the combination of the image fragments after the segmentation is fed to the character recognition unit, the number of the combination should be minimum from the viewpoint of the recognition time. Therefore, surplus segmentation lines should be reduced.

The surplus segmentation lines are reduced by scoring. Each estimated segmentation line is scored by the following formula.

$(\Sigma(Pixels\ in\ segmented\ area)) \times (Pixels\ in\ original\ area)$

There are two reasons for adopting the scoring formula.

1. The larger continuous area is, the more probable it is to be segmented.
2. The closer a segmentation line to the center of a continuous area is, the more feasible it is.

Each segmentation result is assessed by the comparison with the ground truth data.

Table 1. The distribution of all estimated correct segmentation lines on score rank

$$P = \frac{number\ of\ reduced\ segmentation\ lines}{number\ of\ all\ segmentation\ lines}$$

score rank	P	correct segmentation rate
3	16.3%	25.1%
5	25.8%	40.9%
7	33.1%	48.0%
9	38.2%	51.9%
∞	100%	64.3%

4 Experimental Results

4.1 Automatic Assessment

Automatic assessing system is constructed using the ground truth database stated in section 2.2. In the system, if a part of estimated segmentation lines is included in a ground truth data, the segmentation line is judged as the appropriate segmentation line. If any part of the line is not included in the ground truth area, the segmentation line is estimated as inappropriate.

4.2 Experiment and Assessment

Table 1 shows the comparison of the elimination rate of candidates and the correct segmentation rate as the function of candidate number. Between the result marked as "∞" and that marked as "9", it can be seen that by using the scoring the number of segmentation lines is reduced by 61.8% at the cost of 12.4% decrease of the detection rate. From the observation, the reduction method is considered to be effective.

It may be doubtful, however, that the automatic assessing system works exactly or not. To evaluate the correctness of the results, all segmentation results are also judged by human subjects. The results are shown in Table 2. In Table 2, each result is judged by the following rules. If it seems correct, label it "correct". If it seems incorrect, but the segmented patterns seem to be recognizable, label it "recognizable". If no segmentation lines are detected, but the original image seems recognizable, label it "failed but recognizable". If no segmentation lines are detected or only surplus segmentation lines are detected (false alarm), label it "failure".

Namely, the former three cases are labeled as the segmentations are proper and the last case is labeled as the segmentations are false. Though there is a little difference in four subject answers, "correct segmentation" is about 60% which is very close to the automatic assessed result.

Table 2. Human assessment for segmentation results

	subject1	subject2	subject3	subject4
correct	66.4%	63.0%	60.3%	53.0%
recognizable	13.3(79.7)%	13.2(76.2)%	19.8(80.1)%	20.6(73.6)%
failed but recognizable	4.1(83.8)%	7.5(83.6)%	4.0(84.1)%	5.1(78.7)%
failure	16.2%	16.4%	15.9%	21.3%

(The percentage in the parentheses denotes the sum.)

5 Concluding Remarks

About a half of the tested data of the database was segmented correctly by the proposed system. The automatic assessing system judges correct answers strictly. Since the assessing is too strict, some segmentation lines close to the ground truth areas are classified as failures even if they may be able to segment the touching patterns so as to enable each segmented character to be recognized. To evaluate the possibility, we made four subjects assess the suitability of the results. From the results about 80% of the touching patterns are segmented properly.

Though the correct segmentation rate does not completely agree with recognition rate improvement as stated in section 2.3, it is highly possible that the recognition system rate will be improved.

61.8% of the surplus estimated segmentation lines are reduced by the proposed scoring method at the cost of 12.4% correct segmentation rate reduction as shown in Table 1.

Using the proposed method, many touching handwritten Japanese characters are segmented, without so many surplus segmentations, so as to enable each segmented character be recognized.

Acknowledgments

The authors appreciate many beneficial advices by Dr. Hiromichi Fujisawa and Dr. Hiroshi Sakou both at Central Research Laboratory, Hitachi Ltd. The authors appreciate the cooperation given by the members of Nakano-Maruyama Laboratory of Shinshu University.

References

1. H.Fujisawa, Y.Nakano and K.Kurino: Segmentation Methods for Character Recognition: From Segmentation to Document Structure Analysis. Proc. of IEEE. **80–7** (1992) 1079–1092
2. Hidefumi Ino, Kazuki Saruta, Nei Kato and Yoshiaki Nemoto: Handwritten Address Segmentation Algorithm Based on Stroke Information. ISSN. **38–2** 1997
3. Hirobumi Yamada and Yasuaki Nakano: Cursive Handwritten Word Recognition Using Multiple Segmentation Determined by Contour Analysis. IEICE. Trans. INF&SYSTE. **E79–D–5** (1996)
4. Masaomi Nakajima and Yuji Yonekura: Handwritten Character Segmentation Using Smoothing Histgram and Discriminant Analysys. IEICE. Trans. INF&SYSTE. **J78–D–2–7** (1995)
5. Yayoi Kobayashi and Jun Tsukumo: Handwritten Characters Recognition Using Contexts. IEICE. Trans. **PRU91–67** (1991) 39–46 (In Japanese)

Cursive Handwritten Word Recognition by Integrating Multiple Classifiers

Kenichi Maruyama[1], Makoto Kobayashi[1], Hirobumi Yamada[2] and Yasuaki Nakano[1]

[1] Dept. of Information Engineering, Shinshu University, Nagano, Japan
[2] Faculty of Engineering, Toyohashi University of Technology, Tenpakuchou, Toyohashi, Aichi, Japan

Abstract. This paper proposes a method for cursive handwritten word recognition. In the traditional research, many cursive handwritten word recognition systems used a single method for character recognition. In this research, we propose a method integrating multiple character classifier to improve word recognition rate combining the results of them. As a result of the experiment using two classifiers, word recognition rate is improved than from those using a single character classifier.

1 Introduction

In a traditional method of word recognition, strings that are combined from the results of character recognition for patterns formed by segmenting a word image are matched to each entry of a lexicon. Thus, to improve a word recognition rate, it is most important to improve character recognition rate because it is most important for correct classes to be at higher rank. But it is difficult to improve the recognition rate of a classifier because usually the performance of the classifier reaches to its highest potential.

To improve word recognition rate fixing a single character classifier, increasing the number of candidates obtained from the classifier may be thought as effective. But if candidates from character recognition increase, wrong candidates will increase as well as the correct ones. There is possibility that the increase of wrong candidates has a bad influence on a word recognition rate.

On the other hand, in recognition of printed English characters and handwritten numerals, it is reported that recognition rate is improved by integrating multiple recognition methods [1] [2]. In this research, we propose a method to integrate multiple classifiers at the character recognition stage in the word recognition system. To evaluate the effectiveness of the proposed method, we test the integration of two character classifiers, i.e., the pattern matching based on directional feature patterns [5] and HMM (Hidden Markov Models) [7].

Recently, a similar approach is proposed by Sinha et al. [3] and discusses the optimal combination by a statistical method. Our paper proposes a more practical combination method.

2 Approach

The system used in this research is based on Yamada's research [4]. As illustrated in Figure 1, this paper proposes a method using multiple classifiers at the character recognition stage and integrating the results. A newly developed character classifier using HMM is used as well as the one used in the previous paper [4].

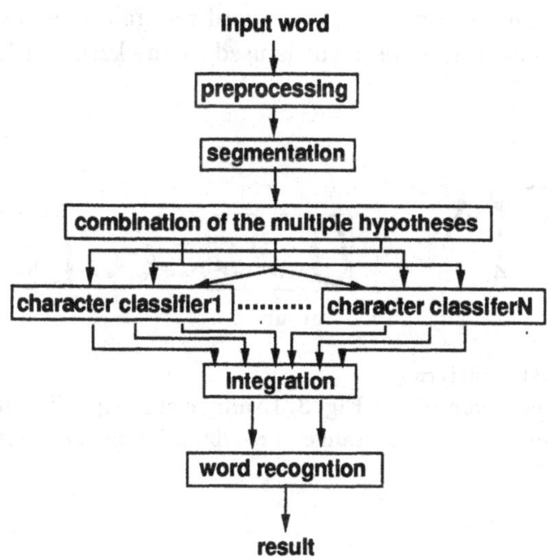

Fig. 1. Flowchart of the proposed system

2.1 Preprocessing

An input word is binarized and normalized in the inclination. Then the contour is extracted for further analysis.

2.2 Segmentation

Candidates of segmentation points are estimated on the left and the right ends of character–like shapes by a contour analysis. Since there is possibility that the simple curve line linking two candidates is a ligature, a middle point of the estimated ligature is added as a candidate of segmentation point.

2.3 Combination and Multiple Hypotheses

Neighboring pattern fragments segmented as candidates are combined to make a hypothesis of a character pattern. Combination of pattern fragments is limited by the number of fragments and the total length of contour. Combined patterns are assembled into a group.

A group is a set of pattern fragments which are combined around a major pattern which is not a ligature. Example of major patterns are painted black in Figure 2. Figure 3 shows an example of groups generated from pattern fragments shown in Figure 2.

Each combined pattern is given a number, which is called a pattern number. The pattern number will be used at the word recognition stage. These numbers basically show which major fragment is used as the kernel of the combination.

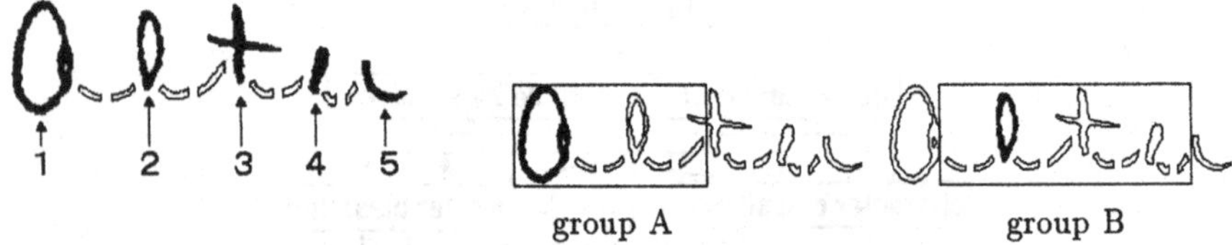

Fig. 2. Segmented pattern fragments (a pattern painted black shows a major)

Fig. 3. Example of groups (The rectangles show the range of combination in each group)

2.4 Character Recognition

Two character classifiers are used in this paper. They are the pattern matching based on directional feature patterns [5] and HMM [7]. The details of two classifiers will be stated in chapters 4 and 5.

Each method outputs three candidates for a combination hypothesis and the results for all hypotheses generated from a same group are merged. If the classes for the different patterns in a group coincide, the result having the largest similarity is adopted.

Word recognition stage uses the result obtained by integrating two methods and does not distinguish uppercase and lowercase characters. So, the outputs from both character classifiers are case insensitive.

2.5 Word Recognition

Word recognition uses the results of character recognition. A set of segmentation points having the smallest penalty is calculated to each word in a lexicon. Figure 4 shows an example but many results are not shown for the simplicity. In Figure 4, each rectangle shows a combination of patterns. For example the string (5, C) in a rectangle shows that "C" is the fifth rank for the combination hypothesis. The combination is given a penalty calculated as the average of the rank of each rectangle.

For the word in the example of Figure 4, the penalty of "ALTA" is $(2+2+1+1)/4 = 1.5$ combining (2, A)(2, L)(1, T)(1, A) and lower than the penalties of all other words in the lexicon. Thus "ALTA" is the first rank in the word recognition. In the same way, ten candidates are outputted and sorted in the ascending order of penalties.

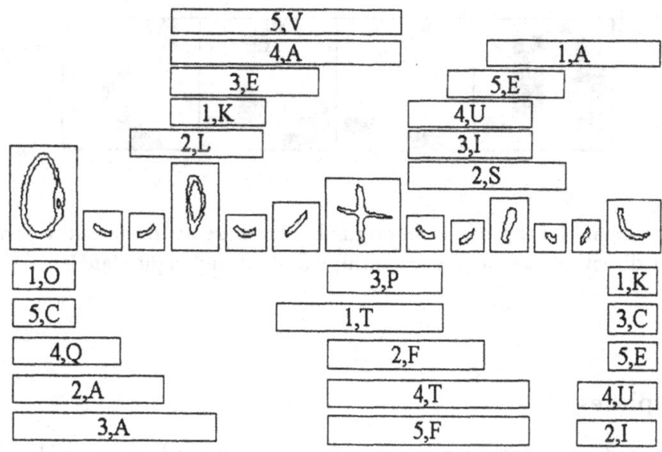

Fig. 4. Example of word recognition

3 Character Classifier Using the Pattern Matching Based on Directional Feature Patterns

The pattern matching based on directional feature patterns (abbreviated as the pattern matching hereafter) is known as an effective method in handwritten kanji recognition [5].

The size of the input pattern sent to the recognition unit is normalized to 64 × 64 pixels. At the same time, the inclination of the input pattern is corrected. The normalized pattern is partitioned into 8 × 8 blocks. Four patterns emphasizing in four directions (vertical, horizontal, left slant, right slant) at every block are formed (Figure 5). Pattern matching using these four patterns is executed. A similarity for a pattern is the average of similarities on four directional patterns. The similarities are calculated with templates of all classes and the several similarities from the top are selected.

Three candidates are outputted in the descending order of similarities for each segmented pattern. Candidates for patterns generated from the same group are merged and sorted in the descending order of similarities.

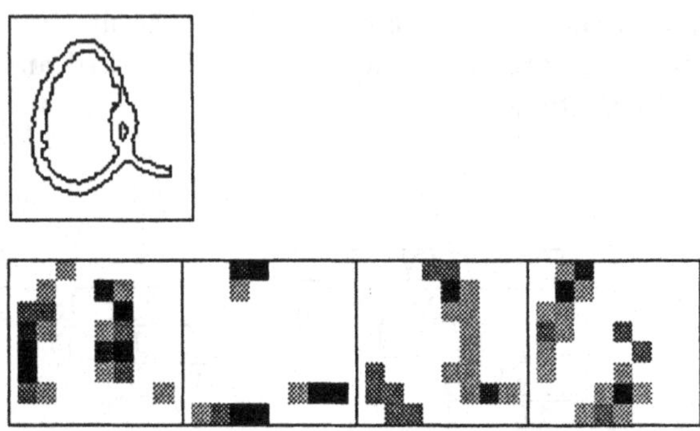

Fig. 5. Patterns at the top row is an original. Those are at the second row are emphasized in four direction (vertical, horizontal, left slant and right slant)

3.1 Templates

Templates used in matching are made from averaging features of learning samples. Some characters have variant shapes, so multiple templates are generated for such a character class by a clustering technique. Total number of templates for 52 alphabets (uppercase and lowercase characters) is 426. In the outputs of recognition uppercase and lowercase are not distinguished in the output, so the number of different classes is 26.

4 Character Recognition Using Hidden Markov Models

In this research, same as the pattern matching method explained in the previous chapter, each input pattern is normalized to 64 × 64 pixels and the inclination is corrected.

4.1 HMM

Though 2–dimensional HMM methods are proposed and tested for character recognition [6] [12], we adopted 1–dimensional HMM, which has become mature in speech recognition [7].

The elements of HMM consist of several states and arcs of state transition shown in Figure 6. Each arc has state transition probability and output probability where $A = \{a_{ij}\}$: set of probabilities of transition from S_i to S_j, $B = \{b_{ij}(k)\}$:

set of probabilities of outputting symbol k when state is transited from S_i to S_j, $\pi = \{\pi_i\}$: set of initial state probability. For convenience, we use the compact notation $\lambda = (A, B, \pi)$ to indicate the complete parameter set of the model.

Given the observation sequence $O = O_1 O_2 \cdots O_T$ and HMM λ, we can compute $P(O \mid \lambda)$, the probability of the observation sequence outputted from the HMM λ.

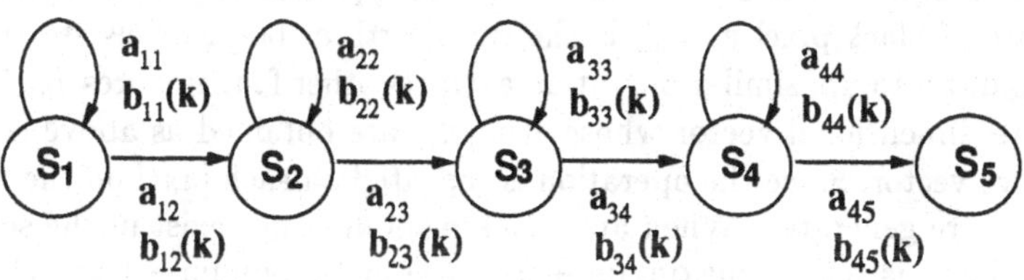

Fig. 6. Hidden Markov Model

4.2 Learning of HMM

Given the parameters of HMM $\lambda = (A, B, \pi)$ and the observation sequences $O = \{O^{(1)}, O^{(2)}, \cdots, O^{(K)}\}$, we can estimate the parameters which maximize

$$P(O \mid \lambda) = \prod_{k=1}^{K} P(O^{(k)} \mid \lambda),$$

where K is the number of different symbols [7].

Using this learning method, we construct an HMM to each character class. Thus, 52 HMMs are constructed corresponding to A–Z and a–z. The sample number used in learning is 12,050.

4.3 Recognition

Using HMMs constructed by the learning, recognition is executed. Given the observation sequence obtained from an unknown character pattern, probability of outputting this sequence at each HMM is calculated. The recognition result is a set the classes corresponding to high probabilities outputted from the HMMs.

When the result of character recognition is outputted, uppercase letters are substituted to the corresponding lowercase letters to make the result case insensitive. Same as the pattern matching, three candidates for a group are outputted by sorting the results in descending order of probabilities.

4.4 Feature Extraction

In this research, we adopt 1–dimensional HMM using a symbol string extracted from thin rectangles obtained by slicing a character pattern. Features used in the research are shown in Figure 7.

By scanning the normalized pattern vertically up to down four features f_1, f_2, f_3, f_4 are extracted. Here f_1 is the first y coordinate of black pixel and f_2 is the run length of black pixels starting from f_1. Similarly f_3 is the second y coordinate of black pixel and f_4 is the run length of black pixels starting from f_3. Next, down to up, similar operation extracts other four features f_5, f_6, f_7, f_8. The eight–dimensional vector whose elements are obtained as above is used as the feature vector. Since the operation is repeated on each pixel on the abscissa, 64 vectors are generated. When any black pixel does not exist in the searching, the coordinate is set to (maximum + 1 = 64) or (minimum − 1 = −1) and the length is set to 0.

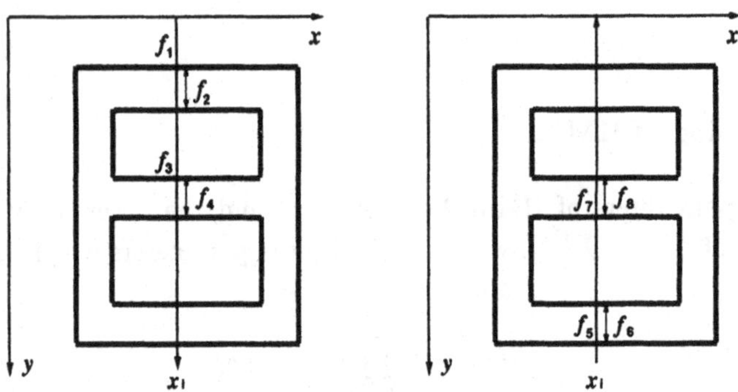

Fig. 7. Feature extraction of HMM

4.5 Vector Quantization

A feature vector is converted into a symbol using vector quantization [7].

We compare a feature vector with the codebook which is the set of vectors generated in advance and represent the vector by the index of the codebook vector whose distance is minimal.

The codebook itself is generated by clustering feature vectors from a learning sample set. Size of codebook is 128. In this manner, a character sample is changed into a symbol sequence.

5 Character Recognition Rate

Table 1 shows character recognition rate using the pattern matching and HMM. The size of the test set is 2,744. These samples are segmented manually from the test set used for word recognition. Uppercase and lowercase letters are not distinguished. The result of the HMM classifier is on the learning pattern set, or, in other words, HMMs are generated from the test set.

Table 1. Character recognition rate using the pattern matching and HMM

	size of test set	recognition rate	cumulative recognition rate	
	2,744		2	3
the pattern matching		56.6%	71.9%	78.1%
HMM		66.0%	83.7%	90.9%

6 Character Recognition Integrating Two Classifiers

Results obtained by the pattern matching classifier and HMM classifier are integrated. In this integration, it must be noted that two classifiers use different measures: the pattern matching uses similarity and HMM uses probability. As the result, the measures cannot be used in the integration, but only the orders in a result of recognition can be used.

The method of integration is as follows. Assume that an array *combi*$[i]$ is the table of results (orders) after integration of two classifiers, *pattern*$[j]$ that of the pattern matching and *hmm*$[k]$ that of HMM. (Here, i, j, k denotes the size of array, $i = j + k$.)

An element of the array *combi* shows the order after integration which represents penalty for each candidate class.

1. Substitute each element of *pattern* into an odd number element of *combi* in turn: $combi[2m - 1] = pattern[m] \quad (m = 1, 2, \cdots, j)$.
2. Substitute each element of *hmm* into an even number element of *combi* in turn: $combi[2n] = hmm[n] \quad (n = 1, 2, \cdots, k)$.
3. If either array ends before the last element comes, the rests of opposite array are added to the bottom.

In the present status, the pattern matching has better performance, so it is given the higher priority.

Next, it is tested whether the same characters are duplicated in *combi*. The candidate having the higher penalty is deleted in the case that candidates have the same character class and the same pattern number. In these cases, it is considered that these candidates have high reliability because both classifiers support them. To reflect this conjecture, the remained candidate (a candidate having low penalty) is promoted. The promotion is done by interchanging the candidate with the one rank higher candidate. But, the interchange is not done in the case that the one rank higher candidate has already been promoted.

7 Result of Word Recognition

To improve word recognition rate fixing a single character classifier, increasing the number of candidates obtained from the classifier may be thought as effective. To test this conjecture, an experiment is executed by changing the number of the candidates at the result of the recognition stage.

Table 2 shows the change of word recognition rate when the number of candidates obtained from the pattern matching classifier is increased. It can be seen from the result that even if candidates from character recognition increase, word recognition rate is not improved but sometimes deteriorated. The reason may be as follows. The increase of the candidates may sometimes increase "imposters" and deteriorate the word recognition.

Table 3 shows word recognition rate using the pattern matching, HMM and integration of two classifiers. For the pattern matching and HMM classifiers, output number of the character recognition stage is set to 3, by the consideration on Table 2.

In Table 2 and 3, the size of the test set is 175 and the lexicon size is 115.

Table 2. A variation of word recognition rate depending on candidates of character recognition using the pattern matching

	test set size	recognition rate	cumulative recognition rate	
	175		5	10
three candidates		62.9%	88.6%	93.7%
five candidates		61.7%	85.7%	92.0%

8 Discussion

From a result mentioned in the previous chapter using the proposed method, it is shown that word recognition rate is improved by integrating two character classifiers in comparison with word recognition rate using a single usage of either classifier.

The recognition time using two classifiers is sum of two classifiers if the recognition is executed successively. Using parallel operation, however, the recognition

Table 3. Word recognition rate of single classifiers and integration

	test set size	recognition rate	cumulative recognition rate	
	175		5	10
the pattern matching		62.9%	88.6%	93.7%
HMM		57.1%	86.3%	90.3%
integrating two classifiers		79.4%	92.6%	95.4%

time does not increase. But the cost of two OCR's in speed or space is the negative aspect of the method.

It must be noted that the recognition rate by HMM is on the learning set. To test the ability of the HMM on the test set, another codebook is learned from the other sample set. Table 4 shows the result using the codebook. The improvement the integration is not so good, but cumulative recognition rate within best ten candidates is improved.

The reason of the poor recognition performance of HMM for the test set may be the lack of learning amount. By enhancing the learning, word recognition rate for the test set is experimentally be improved.

Table 4. Word recognition rate with integrating the pattern matching and HMM using patterns for the test set

recognition rate	cumulative recognition rate	
	5	10
62.9%	87.4%	94.2%

9 Conclusion

This paper proposes a method using multiple classifiers in cursive handwritten word recognition method cooperating with segmentation, character recognition and word recognition. An experimental system is developed using the pattern matching based on directional feature patterns and HMM as character classifiers and a series of experiments is executed on cursive handwritten words included in CEDAR databases. Setting a lexicon size 115, 175 cursive handwritten words are recognized. Though first rank recognition rate using only the pattern matching is 62.9% and that using only HMM is 57.1%, the first rank recognition rate is improved to 79.4% by integrating two classifiers. This result shows that the proposed method is effective. In the future, it is planned to improve character recognition rate using HMM and verify the effect by integrating more than two character recognition classifiers.

Acknowledgement

We use CEDAR database made by and supplied from the Center of Excellence for Document Analysis and Recognition of SUNY at Buffalo.
We appreciate many advices by Prof. Minoru Maruyama and Dr. Hidetoshi Miyao of Information Engineering Department of Shinshu University.

References

1. Rice, S. et al: A Report on the Accuracy of OCR Devices. ISRI Technical Report. Information Science Research Institute. University of Nevada. Las Vegas (1992) 1–6
2. Matsui, T. et al: State of the Art of Handwritten Numeral Recognition in Japan. Proc. 2nd Int. Conference on Document Analysis and Recognition (1993) 391–396
3. P. Sinha and J. Mao: Combining Multiple OCRs for Optimizing Word Recognition. Proc.14th ICPR. Brisbane, Australia (1998) 436–438
4. Hirobumi Yamada and Yasuaki Nakano: Cursive Handwritten Word Recognition Using Multiple Segmentation Determined by Contour Analysis. IEICE Trans.INF&SYSTE. **vol.E79–D–5** (1996)
5. S. Mori, C. Y. Suen and K. Yamamoto: Historical Review of OCR Research and Development. Proc. IEEE. **80(7)** (1992) 1029–1058
6. G. E. Kopec and P. A. Chou: Document Image Decording Using Malkov Source Models. IEEE Trans. on PAMI. **16(6)** (1994) 602–617
7. Lawrence R. Rabiner: A Tutrial on Hidden Markov Models and Selected Applications in Speech Recognition. Proc.IEEE. **77(2)** (1989) 257–286
8. J. C. Simon: Off–line cursive word recognition. Proc. IEEE **80(7)** (1992) 1150–1161
9. R. M. Bozinovic and S. N. Srihari: Off–line cursive footnote word recognition. IEEE Trans. on PAMI. **11(1)** (1989) 68–83
10. A. Kundu and P. Bahl: Recognition of Handwritten Script : A Hidden Markov Model Based Approach. Proc. Int. Conf. on Acoustics. Speech. and Signal Processing. New York City. USA. (1998) 928–931
11. H. –S. Park and S. –W. Lee: Off–line Recognition of Large–set Handwritten Characters with Multiple Hidden Markov Models. Pattern Recognition. **29(2)** (1996) 231–244
12. H. –S. Park and S. –W. Lee:A truly 2–D hidden Markov model for off–line handwritten character recognition. Pattern Recognition. **31(12)** (1998) 1849–1864

Segmentation of Touching Characters in Formulas

Masayuki Okamoto, Syougo Sakaguchi and Tadashi Suzuki

Dept. of Information Engineering, Shinshu University,
500 Wakasato, Nagano, 380-8553, JAPAN

Abstract. Segmentation of touching characters in mathematical formulas needs a different method from the one for text lines, because these characters may occur in horizontal, vertical or diagonal directions.Our segmentation method is based on the projection profiles of a given binary image and minimal points of the blurred image obtained by applying the Gaussian kernel to the original image.

1 Introduction

Formula recognition is of interest in digitization of scientific documents. We have proposed two types of methods for formula recognition [1,2]. This paper describes the extension of our methods for formulas which contain touching characters. A number of segmentation methods of touching characters in text lines have been proposed in the literatures. These methods can be applied for character strings printed in only one direction; horizontal or vertical (e.g., in Japanese documents). In mathematical formulas, characters or symbols are placed in horizontal, vertical or diagonal directions. This fact means we need a new segmentation method for the touching character problem in formulas.

It is common to use features based on a vertical projection in the character segmentation of text lines. The horizontal and vertical projection profiles are also useful to estimate positions for character segmentation in formulas. However most characters or symbols in formulas are printed in slanted form, there are many cases where touching characters can be separated adequately only by a slant line not a horizontal or vertical line. This line can be estimated from minimal points of the blurred image obtained by applying the Gaussian kernel to the binary image. These points are located at the valley between blurred blob components which correspond to each character.

Since the decision whether a given blob is touching characters or not is very difficult, we use a simple criterion that if a classifier rejects the blob, we consider the blob consists of two characters. Then both of horizontal and vertical segmentation are tried, and the classification for each separated component is carried out again. Finally, the average scores for both of the components are compared between two segmentations, and the one which have the higher score is adopted. In this paper, the type of touching characters we examine and the segmentation algorithm are described in next Section 2. Experimental results and performance issues are discussed in Section 3.

2 Segmentation

In our formula recognition system, before structure analysis of a formula, each blob of symbol or character components as a single connected component is classified. At this step, if the score of classifier is less than a priori value, then we assume the blob consists of touching characters. As shown in the Fig.1, typical occurrences of touching characters are grouped into three groups; horizontal, vertical or diagonal adjacency. Although the relative positions of horizontal and diagonal touching characters are different, they can be separated horizontally. Then, from now on, we will examine a segmentation method which separates touching characters in horizontal and vertical directions.

Horizontally adjacent Diagonally adjacent Vertically adjacent

Fig. 1. Typical occurrences of touching characters

Fig.2 shows a binary image of blob with its horizontal and vertical projection HP and VP defined as the functions mapping a vertical or horizontal position to the number of blob pixels in the horizontal or vertical direction correspondingly at that position. In the literature [3], it is reported that the ratio of the second difference, $VP(x-1) - 2 * VP(x) + VP(x+1)$ to the value $VP(x)$ is useful for estimation of breakpoint of touching characters in normal text. We also have found that this criterion is valid for formulas.

Our criteria for the breakpoint are as follows.

(1) Horizontal segmentation

"In the middle part (80%) of the blob, the horizontal breakpoint is the position where the value of VP is lowest and the second difference is positive".

(2)Vertical segmentation

The vertical breakpoint can be estimated similarly. But in our observation of touching characters in formulas, vertical touching characters often occur when a horizontally elongated symbol (e.g., horizontal bar of a fraction or horizontal line segment of symbol $\sum$ etc.) and characters are printed closely. For these cases, it is also suitable to estimate the breakpoint by rapid change of the value HP. The criterion for the vertical breakpoint is the following.

Fig. 2. Horizontal and vertical projection profiles. The gray lines show estimated breakpoints

"In the middle part (80%) of the blob, the vertical breakpoint is the position where the ratio $HP(y)/HP(y+1)$ is less than θ_1 or greater than θ_2. If there is no such point, the breakpoint is estimated in the same way as in the case of the horizontal segmentation".

In the above criteria, the reason we examine only the some extent of middle part of a blob is to exclude the possibility that the blob may be segmented into extremely a large component and a small one.

The blob of touching characters in a text printed with the Roman font can be separated by a vertical line at a breakpoint. However in formulas, most characters are printed with italic font, therefore there are many cases touching characters can not be separated by the vertical line. A proper line which separate a merged blob into two components can be estimated by the valley between them corresponding to each character in the gray-scale image of the given blob. Fig.3 shows the blurred blob of Fig.2 obtained by applying the Gaussian kernel as a point spread function to the original binary image.

$$g(x,y) = \frac{1}{\sqrt{2\pi\sigma^2}} e^{-\frac{x^2+y^2}{2\sigma^2}} \tag{1}$$

Some advantages in character segmentation problem using gray-scale image are stated in the literatures [4,5]. In the literature [4], small value of σ is used to approximate stroke lines of a character, but large one is used to outline its

Fig. 3. Blurred blob of Fig.2. Pixels marked with "x" show horizontal minimal points

shape and position in the literature [5]. We also adopt a large value of σ which corresponds to the number of pixels larger than the width of strokes and smaller than the size of characters. In order to estimate the cutting line, we calculate the minimal points in the gray-scale image horizontally and vertically. In Fig.3, pixels marked with "x" show the horizontal minimal points. This figure shows that minimal points of the blurred blob locate in the valley between two characters and can be used to estimate a cutting line. Fig.4 shows the horizontal cutting line at the breakpoint obtained by using the method of least square from the minimal points near it.

The both of components segmented by the cutting lines are fed to the classifier and their average scores are calculated in horizontal and vertical segmentation. Then the segmentation having the higher average score is adopted.

3 Experiments and Remarks

The method described so far was implemented in the C Language and incorporated into our formula recognition system [2]. Some experiments were carried

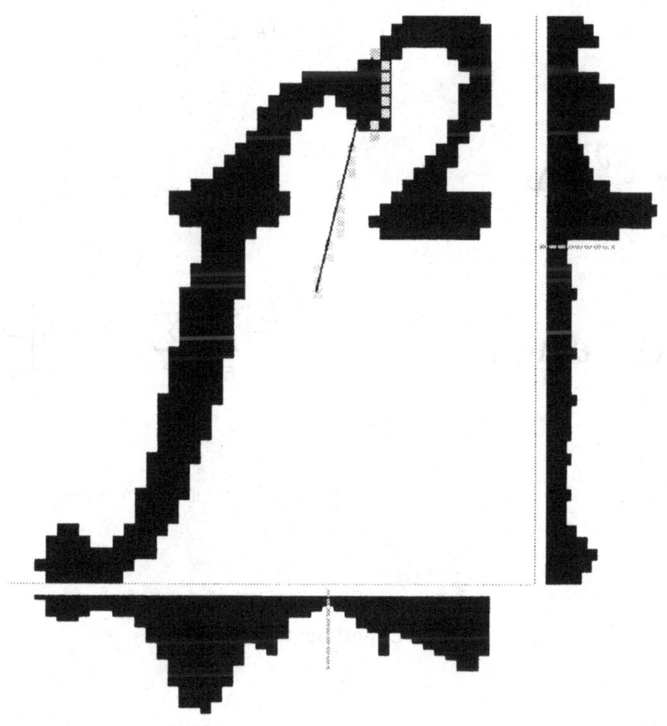

Fig. 4. Estimation of a cutting line in horizontal segmentation

out for formulas scanned from some kinds of printed journals. Fig.5 shows the recognition results for inputed images which contain horizontal, vertical and diagonal touching characters. In our system, the decision whether a given blob should be segmented or not depends on the score of the first stage classifier for every connected components in formulas. In Fig.5, every score for blobs of touching characters is less than a predetermined value and segmentations for them were tried. Finally, each segmented component has higher score than the original blob, and all the formulas in Fig.5 are recognized correctly. Our method of segmentation is very simple and can be executed very fast. We are currently investigating how to segment touching characters where more than three characters are merged.

Scanned images	Recognition results
$-1 \leq \frac{\iint fg}{\sqrt{\iint f^2}\sqrt{\iint g^2}} \leq 1$	$-1 \leq \frac{\int\int fg}{\sqrt{\int\int f^2}\sqrt{\int\int g^2}} \leq 1$
$\theta_i = \frac{2\pi i}{N}$	$\theta_i = \frac{2\pi i}{N}$
$\Delta x_i' = \Delta x_i + \frac{\partial u_i}{\partial x_j} \Delta x_j$	$\Delta x_i' = \Delta x_i + \frac{\partial u_i}{\partial x_j} \Delta x_j$
$-\sum_{i \in I_k} \left[\sum_{j=1}^{n} w_{ij} z_j + \theta_i \right] \Delta x_i(t)$	$-\sum_{i \in I_k} \left[\sum_{j=1}^{n} w_{ij} z_j + \theta_1 \right] \Delta x_i(t)$

Fig. 5. Experimental results

References

1. Okamoto, M., Miao, B.: Recognition of Mathematical Expressions by Using Layout Structure of Symbols. Proc. of ICDAR'91 (1991) 242-250
2. Okamoto, M., Higashi, H.: Structure Analysis and Recognition of Mathematical Expressions. Proc. of ICDAR'95 (1995) 430-437
3. Kahan, S., Pavlidis, T., Baird, H.S.: On the Recognition of Printed Characters of Any Font and Size. IEEE Trans. of PAMI, **9**, 2 (1987)
4. Wang, L., Pavlidis, T.: Direct Gray-Scale Extraction of Feature for Character Recognition. IEEE Trans. of PAMI, **15**, 10 (1993) 1053-1067
5. Nako, K., Takamatsu, R., Sato, M., Kawarada, H.: A New Character Segmentation Method for Handwritten Documents Based on Differential Structure of Blurred Document Image. Technical Report of IEICE, PRU93-131 (1994) 9-16

The *Address*Script™ Recognition System for Handwritten Envelopes

Alexander Filatov, Vadim Nikitin, Alexander Volgunin, and Pavel Zelinsky

ParaScript, LLC, 7105 La Vista Place, Niwot, CO 80503 USA
Tel: (303) 381-3125, Fax: (303) 381-3101,
E-mail: filatov@parascript.com, Web Site: www.parascript.com

Abstract. This paper presents *Address*Script - a system for handwritten postal address recognition for US mail. Key aspects of *Address*Script technology, such as system control flow, cursive handwriting recognition, and postal database are described. Special attention is paid to the powerful character recognizer and the intensive usage of context, which becomes available during the recognition process. The algorithm of confidence level calculation is presented. Laboratory test results on a blind test set of 50,000 images of live hand-written mail pieces demonstrate a 64% finalization rate for error rates below USPS restrictions.

1 Introduction

Mail sorting is one of the most valuable applications of document analysis and handwriting recognition. About 36 million of handwritten envelopes are processed daily by the United States Postal Service (USPS). The USPS uses the Remote Computer Reader (RCR) developed by Lockheed Martin Postal Systems to process handwritten and machine print mail pieces. Current recognition system deployed throughout the United States last year provides about 25% read rate [1]. Lockheed Martin Postal Systems continues to improve the RCR system. Within this work they have successfully integrated the Parascript *Address*Script product into the RCR. Subsequent tests have demonstrated a significant increase in the RCR read rate. USPS has contracted with Lockheed Martin Postal Systems to deploy the new RCR version with the integrated *Address*Script product throughout the United States.

For mail-sorting purposes all information presented in the destination address block of each mail piece is encoded by a string of digits (up to eleven digits) called Delivery Point Sequence Code (DPS). The first five digits are referred to as the ZIP Code. A ZIP Add-On Code is a four-digit number that follows the five-digit ZIP Code. The five-digit ZIP Code divides the U.S. into major geographical areas. The ZIP Add-On Code identifies a small geographical delivery area that is serviceable by a single carrier. The last two digits of the DPS uniquely identify each carrier delivery point. The Five-digit ZIP Code is usually written on an envelope. The ZIP Add-on Code may be extracted from the USPS Delivery Point File for a given ZIP Code, street number and street name. The last two digits of the DPS generally represent the last two digits of a street number.

The interpretation of hand-written addresses is a difficult problem of document analysis and handwriting recognition. Addresses may be written in different styles: city, state, and ZIP Code may occupy one, two, or three lines; the ZIP Code may contain five or nine digits; the last line of an address block may contain other information (e.g. "Attn.", "USA" etc.); street address may occupy one or two lines. There are several different address structures: street, PO Box, rural route addressing, etc. Very often an address is written in cursive so the handprint recognition technology alone can not meet the needs of address interpretation. Figure 1 shows examples of an address block.

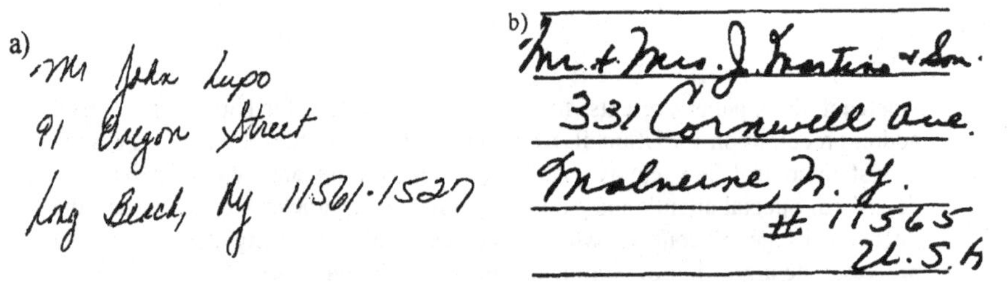

Fig. 1. Examples of address block images.

*Address*Script is a system intended for the recognition of handwritten U.S. postal addresses. Significant increase in the finalization rate compared to the published result [1] is achieved due to the following major factors:

Powerful recognition engine. Our Script Recognizer combines the Holistic Word Recognizer (HWR) intended for cursive recognition and the Analytical Word Recognizer (AWR) intended primarily for recognition of numbers and hand-printed words. AWR was tested on hand-written numerals contained in the CEDAR database [2] and achieved a 99.54% recognition rate, which is the highest rate ever reported on this database.

Extensive use of the context, which becomes available during the recognition. The idea was to adapt the system to an address being recognized. For example, street address block parsing is performed after ZIP Code recognition since the ZIP Code recognition results provide additional information, which can be used for street address parsing. This information includes the percentage of each address type (street, PO Box, rural route), minimum and maximum street number length for ZIP Code, etc.

Reliable determination of the recognition answer correctness. Neural network is used to calculate the confidence level for a particular answer. The neural network takes the information collected at all stages of the previous recognition process as input and outputs the probability of the answer correctness.

2 *Address*Script Recognition Technology

It is necessary to have a powerful recognition engine to deal with real-life handwriting. The core of the *Address*Script technology is a Script Recognizer

(Figure 2). It is a combination of two recognizers: Holistic Word Recognizer [2] and Analytical Word Recognizer [3].

Fig. 2. The structure of the Script Recognizer.

2.1 Holistic Word Recognizer

The strength of the HWR is the ability to recognize cursive handwriting. It can also recognize hand printed information or a combination of handwriting and hand print.

The input to the HWR is an image of a whole word or a phrase written in one string, and a lexicon. The output is a list of probable answers with their respective similarity scores.

The recognition approach can be classified as a holistic one. This means that a word is recognized as a whole without segmentation to the character level. Recognition consists of two stages: a) feature extraction and feature ordering in a linear sequence, b) matching the feature representation of an input phrase to all lexicon entry representations.

The set of features reflects the importance of vertical extremums, which are the most stable elements of writing. It includes eight features to describe maximums (and corresponding eight features for minimums): *arc, arc with a right (left) free end, cusp*, three *long cusps* (upper, upper-right, upper-left), *loop.* Also we use *cross*, *dot*, *dash*, *right (left) arrow*, and several features to describe holes of different shapes (the feature set is described in detail in [2]). Every feature has a height attribute determined by the vertical location of the feature relative to the guidelines (the body of the word). We introduce a measure of similarity between different types (and different heights) of features. This provides a high flexibility in the matching process necessary for the recognition of sloppy handwriting.

Each lexicon entry representation is generated dynamically via concatenation of predefined letter representations. Letters are described by a linear sequence of features. Each letter can have several feature representations (four on the average), so each lexicon entry has a lot of feature representations. The length of the sequence may vary from one feature per letter up to ten features.

Dynamic programming based on a string edit distance is used to match an input word representation with all lexicon entry representations.

2.2 Analytical Word Recognizer

The Analytical Word Recognizer is primarily intended for the recognition of numbers and hand-printed words. AWR has two stages: segmentation and recognition. At the segmentation stage a graph describing the shape of an input word is built. Then the graph is segmented into separate symbols. Obviously, it is not always possible to find the correct segmentation variant without recognition. Therefore, we use a multi-variant segmentation approach. A thorough analysis of the segmentation variants before recognition allows consideration of less than two variants per symbol on the average. After that the recognizer determines the best alternative.

Table 1. Recognition rate on *goodbs* data of the CEDAR database for different error rates.

Error rate	Recognition rate
0.0	93.80
0.05	96.24
0.10	98.14
0.20	99.18
Without Reject	99.54

Table 1 shows AWR test results on handwritten numerals from the CEDAR database. These data were collected from live mail in the U.S. [4]. The directory *goodbs,* containing 2213 samples, is widely used to compare different recognition systems. We did not use these samples for training. AWR obtained 99.54% recognition rate, which is the highest rate ever reported on this database (Table 2).

Table 2. Published systems (recognition rate without reject).

System	Recognition rate
T.M. Ha, H. Bunke [5]	99.09
D.S. Lee, S.N. Srihari [6]	98.87
S. Knerr, S. Sperduti [7]	97.6

Three classifiers inside AWR perform the symbol recognition stage: graph-based character classifier (GRC) [3] and two neural network classifiers based on different features.

2.3 Graph-Based Character Classifier

GRC recognizes input symbols involving an algorithm of matching input symbol graphs with previously defined symbol prototypes. The symbol prototype consists of the symbol graph and the description of its elements (geometrical characteristics of edges, mutual position of edges and nodes, etc.). An obligatory subgraph is defined in each prototype graph. For each element of the obligatory subgraph a match should be found in the input graph.

Each input symbol graph may contain elements that have their analogs in the prototype and the extra elements. The input symbol graph is transformed according to prototype rules to reduce extra elements. The transformations are fulfilled until a one-to-one match is achieved between the input graph and the prototype graph or its obligatory subgraph.

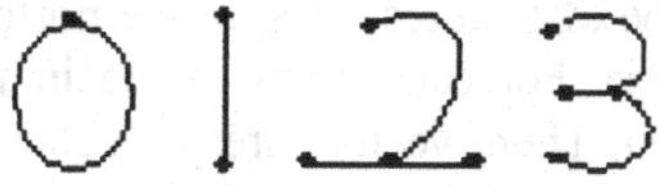

Fig. 3. Examples of symbol prototypes

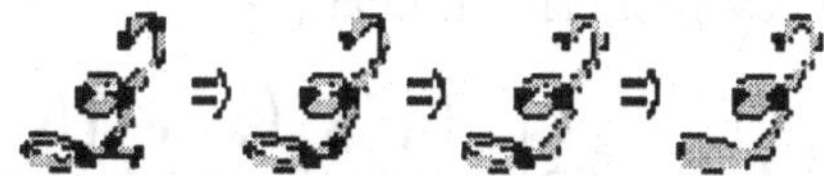

Fig. 4. The sequence of transformations of an input character graph during the matching process.

The estimate of a match between a transformed input graph and the prototype graph is based on the descriptions of the prototype elements and allows certain differences between an original input graph and a prototype.

2.4 Neural Network Classifier

The Neural Network (NN) classifier is intended for recognition of a segment, which is expected to be one character or a few characters written as a whole.

Neural networks are used at the segmentation stage, for character recognition, and for the calculation of the final confidence level for an answer. *Address*Script uses six neural networks: 2 – for digit classification, 2 – for letter classification, 1 – to discriminate between letters and digits, 1 – for confidence level calculation. Here we will discuss the neural network classifiers used for character recognition. To improve the recognition performance *Address*Script uses several NN classifiers to recognize the same character. These NN classifiers use different feature representations of the image as input. Then, the output of the NN classifiers is analyzed, and vector of probability estimations for each class is calculated. The combination of classifiers based on different features reduces the classification error rate because such classifiers rarely produce same errors on the same image.

Our work on NN classifiers has its origin from the NN classifier initially developed by I. Lossev, N. Bagotskaya and coworkers from Paragraph International.

Feature Extraction. We use two main types of features for the character classification.

The first type of features is Fourier descriptors. First, we represent the image as a two dimensional curve. It can be either the contour or the skeleton of an image. Then, the curve is smoothed, and the descriptors are calculated as Fourier coefficients of the x(t) and y(t) – parameterized representation of the curve. We use a different number of coefficients (20-30) depending on the recognition task.

To build the second type of features we split the normalized box of a symbol into 3x3 evenly distributed cells. For each point of the image border within a cell the tangent vector is calculated. Then, vectors are projected on four directions (vertical, horizontal, and two diagonals) and the sums of absolute values of projections over the points of the border form four features corresponding to the cell. So, the total number of features in this case is 36.

Structure of the Neural Network. We use Radial Basis Function (RBF) neural network with one RBF layer for classification:

$$OUT_i = 1 - \prod_{j=1}^{N_i}\left(1 - \exp\left\{-\frac{\left(\mathbf{A}_{ij}^T\mathbf{A}_{ij}\left(\mathbf{x}-\mathbf{c}_{ij}\right),\left(\mathbf{x}-\mathbf{c}_{ij}\right)\right)}{r_{ij}}\right\}\right) \tag{1}$$

where: $\mathbf{x}$ - input vector of features, OUT_i - output weight of class i, N_i - number of RBF neurons for class i, $\mathbf{A}_{ij}$ - weight matrix of j-th neuron of class i, $\mathbf{c}_{ij}$ - center of j-th neuron of class i, and r_{ij} - radius of j-th neuron of class i.

We chose this structure of the neural network based upon the following considerations: The coefficients of this neural network have a clear 'physical' meaning. Vector $\mathbf{c}_{ij}$ corresponding to the neuron can be treated as a vector of features of some 'center' image of the neuron and can be easily visualized. 'Radius' r_{ij} of the neuron shows how 'far' the image can be from the 'center' to still be classified as belonging to the class i. Eigen vectors and corresponding eigen values of the matrix $\mathbf{A}_{ij}^T\mathbf{A}_{ij}$ show the 'directions' and corresponding 'distances' of admissible deviations of the image of the same class from the 'center'. So, this neural network is not a 'black box', and in some cases one can understand how and why one or another result of the classification is produced. We developed special tools for the visualization of the NN.

The proposed structure of the neural network allows us to choose reasonable initial values to the NN coefficients before learning (See more detailed description in the next section). As one can see, the outputs for each class are independent. So, the corresponding parts of the NN can be learned separately. Also, it simplifies the process of tuning of the NN for a new application. Thus, if you need to add one more character class to existing NN it is enough to learn only part of the NN corresponding to the new class. For example, it is necessary to add '#' class to a digit classifier to recognize an apartment number on an envelope successfully.

In some cases, we use modifications of the described structure of NN classifier. For example, matrices $\mathbf{A}_{ij}$ can be unary or diagonal. Such NN classifiers are used when the constraints on the speed of recognition and the memory used by the classifier are more important than the performance of the classification.

Initial Classification. Our experience shows that the choice of initial values of NN coefficients is very important to achieve high performance of the NN classifier. We call this process initial classification. The aim of initial classification is to build neurons ($\mathbf{c}_{ij}, r_{ij}, \mathbf{A}_{ij}$) which produce reasonable output on most of the samples in the learning set. We tried several algorithms of initial classification, but now only two of them are used. Both algorithms consist of two stages.

At the first stage each sample of the class is considered as a candidate to be a neuron 'center' and corresponding neuron coefficients ($\mathbf{c}, r, \mathbf{A}$) are chosen. Let us call samples of the same class native samples of the center candidate and the rest samples the alien ones. The value of $\mathbf{c}$ is always set to the feature vector of the sample. In the first algorithm (isotropic classification), the matrix $\mathbf{A}$ is unary and r is equal to the distance to the nearest alien sample. In the second algorithm (ellipsoidal classification), r is unit but the matrix $\mathbf{A}$ is chosen so that the axes of the ellipsoid $(\mathbf{A}^T\mathbf{A}(\mathbf{x}-\mathbf{c}), \mathbf{x}-\mathbf{c}) = 1$ have maximal length provided that all alien samples were situated outside the ellipsoid.

At the second stage, we choose initial neurons among the built candidates. Each neuron candidate has a set of 'covered' native samples (those being inside the ellipsoid/sphere $(\mathbf{A}^T\mathbf{A}(\mathbf{x}-\mathbf{c}), \mathbf{x}-\mathbf{c}) = r$). The target of the procedure is to choose the candidates which 'cover' the maximal number of native samples. Thus, the problem of the selection of the best center candidates is reduced to the mathematical problem of the selection of the best cover of the set by a predefined number of subsets from a given set of subsets. We use well-known 'greedy' heuristics to find the approximate solution of the problem.

The final performances of NN classifiers built using ellipsoidal classification are close to that of classifiers, based on the isotropic classification. However, ellipsoidal classification is favorable to build neurons corresponding to the rare ways of symbol writing.

Neural Network Learning. We use a gradient relaxation method to learn our NN classifiers. We split the set of samples used for NN learning into a 'train' set, used for gradient relaxation, and 'test' set, used to monitor the performance of the classifier during learning. After each epoch of gradient relaxation, the classifier is tested on the 'test' set. If during some predefined number of epochs, the state of the classifier remains worse than that in the best state, learning is completed. Using the 'test' set eliminates over-learning of the classifier on the 'train' set with the corresponding loss of the generalization ability.

3 System Control Flow

The input of the *Address*Script system is a binary image of an envelope (or an address block). The output is an answer and a confidence level for ZIP5 Code and for the ZIP Add-On Code. Additional output information includes an answer, a confidence level, and field location coordinates for each recognized field: city, state, street number, street name, etc. The overall *Address*Script system control flow is shown in Figure 5.

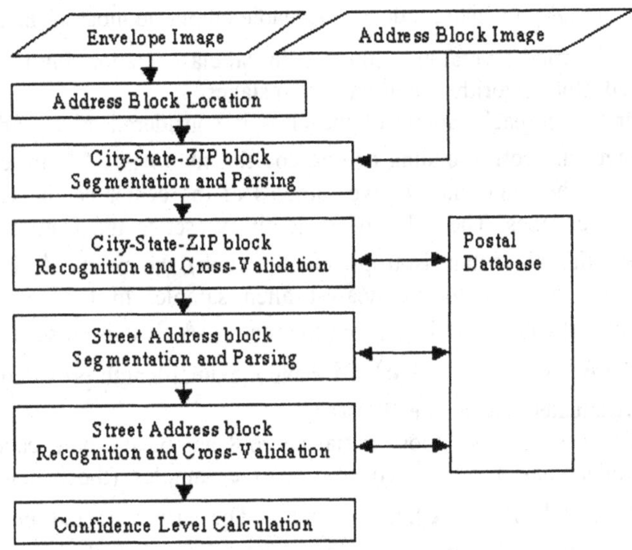

Fig. 5. Overall Control Flow

3.1 Postal Database

Postal database used by *Address*Script system is generated from the USPS City-State and Delivery Point files. Original text files were compacted, and their size was reduced from 15 GB to 670 MB.

The database is queried with a ZIP Code to retrieve all (City, State) pairs; with a ZIP Code and a street number to retrieve all street names and apartment numbers; with a ZIP Code to retrieve all PO Box and rural route numbers.

Aliases of cities (Los Angeles – LA), states (California – CA – Cal), street names, suffixes (Road - Rd), pre- and post-directions (North - N), PO Box and rural route names are stored in the database. The database also contains pre-calculated information about the presence of PO Box, street and high-rise type of addresses in the given ZIP Code, street and PO Box number minimal and maximal values, presence of alphanumeric street numbers and names, etc. This information is used to improve street address block parsing, and to restrict the context for street address recognition.

3.2 City-State-ZIP Block Processing

Our City-State-ZIP block-processing algorithm is described in detail in [8]. Segmentation and parsing module accepts lines of an address block as input. Up to three bottom lines are processed. First, each line is divided into connected components. Next, the algorithm combines all connected components into clusters according to the size, location, and distance between neighbouring components. Clusters are classified as a word, group of characters, separate character (letter or digit), separate letter, separate digit, comma, dash, or noise. We use a neural network, which discriminates between letters and digits at this stage. The parsing algorithm takes a list of clusters as input and provides a list of hypotheses for the city, state, ZIP Code, and 4-digit ZIP Add-On Code. Up to four hypotheses are generated and scored depending on the image complexity. If it is impossible to separate city from state unambiguously, the algorithm composes a long word which includes both city name and state name candidates to reduce the number of segmentation variants. Such a word is recognized with a combined lexicon that consists of city-state pairs.

The correct hypothesis is among the candidates in 91% of the cases. If the correct hypothesis is in the list, it ranks first in 90% of the cases and ranks second in 7% of the cases. Frequently, there is no need to process all segmentation variants. Hypotheses with higher parsing scores are processed first. If the confidence level of a recognized ZIP code is high enough for some hypothesis, the procedure is terminated; otherwise the next segmentation hypothesis is investigated.

The recognition process starts with the ZIP Code. A lexicon of about 42000 ZIP Codes is obtained from the postal database. The algorithm produces a list of ZIP Code candidates (up to 30 answers).

Next, the recognition of city is performed. The postal database is queried by each ZIP Code in the list to obtain a list of city names. Retrieved city names along with their aliases form a lexicon (for example, "MOUNTAIN HEIGHTS", "MTN HEIGHTS", "MOUNTAIN HGTS", and "MT HEIGHTS"). State names and their aliases are also added to the lexicon. After the recognition, the aliases are converted to the standard city name. If the best answer is a state name, the city is considered to be on the previous line. In this case additional parsing hypothesis with city name on the previous line is generated and processed.

After recognition, the city and ZIP Code answer lists are cross-validated using the postal database. A score is calculated as a weighted sum of the city and ZIP Code scores for each valid (city, ZIP Code) pair. The score of the best pair represents the final score of the parsing hypothesis.

The processing of the City-State-ZIP parsing hypotheses is terminated if the score is high enough; otherwise the next hypothesis is processed. The hypothesis with the highest score produces the final result of the City-State-ZIP block recognition.

3.3 Generation of ZIP Code List for Street Address Processing

Street address processing is based on the results of City-State-ZIP block recognition. The algorithm chooses several ZIP Code hypotheses to build a lexicon for street name recognition. The list of ZIP Codes, which is used for further processing includes:

- Several top choices of the ZIP Code obtained after the cross-validation with city recognition results.
- The best ZIP Code hypothesis obtained as a result of the ZIP Code field recognition (before the cross-validation with city recognition results) if its score is significantly higher than the score of the best cross-validated ZIP Code.
- When the ZIP Code has been changed (translated) a writer may still use the old ZIP Code to address a letter. Information concerning ZIP Code translations is stored in the database. There may be several new ZIP Codes instead of the original one. If a ZIP Code in the list is marked as translated, we add a corresponding new ZIP Code to the list.

Up to 5 Zip Codes can be used to build a lexicon for street name recognition.

3.4 Street Address Processing

The street address segmentation and parsing module takes the list of address block lines as input. Up to two lines above the top line of the best City-State-ZIP hypothesis are processed. The street address parsing is based upon the same principles as City-State-ZIP block parsing. The difference is that it uses the postal database information about the presence of PO Boxes, street addresses, and apartments in the list of ZIP Codes, as well as minimal and maximal length of street, apartment and PO Box numbers. The parsing algorithm generates up to four segmentation hypotheses depending on the image complexity. The hypotheses can be one of the following types: PO Box or rural route, Street address, and Street address with apartment.

PO Box or rural route hypotheses consist of name and number components. Street address hypotheses consist of street number and street name components. Hypotheses of a street address with apartment have an additional apartment number component.

The recognition of street numbers, apartment numbers and PO Box / rural route numbers is performed by the Analytical Word Recognizer. Minimal and maximal possible answer values for given ZIP Codes are retrieved from the postal database and used during the recognition. The recognition of street name and PO Box / rural route names is performed by the Script Recognizer and it is lexicon based.

The recognition of PO Box / rural route hypothesis starts with the name component. In this case HWR uses 3 separate lexicons: PO Box names, apartment abbreviations, and rural route names. After the recognition, the best answer is considered. If it came from the lexicon for apartment abbreviations the hypothesis is converted to a street address with an apartment number, otherwise the numeric component is processed.

After the numeric component recognition, the postal database lookup is performed and valid PO Box / rural route answers compose the answer list. The scores of the answers are calculated as a weighted sum of scores of the name and the number.

The processing of street address and street address with apartment number hypotheses starts from the recognition of the street number component. Next, the lexicon of street names is generated. To create the street name lexicon, the postal database is queried with ZIP Code and street number. Depending on the street number confidence level, the postal database is queried either with all street number answers or with the best answer only. The database contains street names in a standard form with abbreviated suffixes, pre- and post-directions (for example, "W OAK DR"). A writer may use non-abbreviated forms, omit or mix up some parts of a street name. Therefore we add to the lexicon:

- Street names with non-abbreviated suffix, pre- and post-directions ("W OAK DRIVE", "WEST OAK DR", "WEST OAK DRIVE")
- Street names without suffix or directions ("W OAK", "WEST OAK", "OAK DR", "OAK DRIVE")
- Street names with substituted suffixes (only frequent replacements such as: Avenue - Street, Drive – Street - "W OAK STREET", "WEST OAK STREET")
- Reversed pre- and post-directions ("OAK DR W", "OAK DRIVE W", "OAK DR WEST", "OAK DRIVE WEST")

Penalties are applied to a score of an answer if the recognition answer is one of the following: street name without suffix, with substituted suffix, with reversed pre- or post-direction. After the recognition, the street aliases are converted to the standard street name.

Next, the apartment number component is processed.

After the recognition of all components, the postal database lookup is performed, and recognition results are cross-validated using the weighted sum of component scores. The hypothesis with the highest score produces the final result of address recognition.

If a writer specifies a 9-digit ZIP Code, 4-digit ZIP Add-On Code is recognized and cross-validated with the ZIP Add-On Code retrieved from the database using the street address recognition results. In real life a writer often applies a wrong ZIP Add-On Code. To handle this situation we perform cross-validation only if a ZIP Add-On Code is found both in the street address answer list and in the digit ZIP Add-On Code answer list. Otherwise, 4-digit ZIP Add-On Code written on the envelope is ignored.

4 The System Adaptability

In this system we tried to use the context, which becomes available during the recognition in the most efficient way. The idea was to adapt the system to the address being recognized. What does this mean? There are two possible sources of information. First, when we generated our Postal Database we accumulated various data available for every ZIP5 Code. This information includes:

- Percentage of each address type: PO Box, street address, street address with secondary information (apartments), rural route, etc. It is used for street address block parsing to generate (or not to generate) some doubtful parsing variants.

- Minimal and maximal street number and PO Box number. They are used for street address block parsing and for street number (PO Box number) recognition (both at segmentation and recognition stages).
- Presence of an alphanumeric street number, street name, or PO Box number. This information should be taken into account to avoid mistakes in street address block parsing. At this stage we use a special neural network, which has been trained to discriminate between letters and digits. In the case of an alphanumeric street number, street name, or PO Box number it is necessary to be careful about interpreting the neural network results.
- This information is also used to apply appropriate neural networks for the recognition.
- Percentage of street names with and without pre-directions, post-directions. It is used for street address block parsing.

Second, we accumulate information concerning peculiarities of a given address at each recognition stage and then we try to use it in subsequent stages. Let us consider two examples:

- Street suffix absence. The analysis is conducted during the street address block parsing and the information is passed to the monitor program. It influences the lexicon for street name recognition. There are three possible solutions depending on this information: to include street names with and without suffix in the lexicon, to include only street names with a suffix, to include only street names without a suffix.
- An apartment number written on a separate line. Sometimes people write a street address in two lines with apartment number written on the second line. It is difficult to parse this street address correctly because it looks like a PO Box address (a name, and after that a number). In this case, recognition can help to detect the parsing mistake. We add apartment names (apartment, apt. suite, #, etc.) into the lexicon for PO Box name and rural route name reading. If after PO Box name recognition the best answer is one of the apartment names, the street address parsing is called again with the corresponding information.

5 Confidence Level Calculation

It is important to get a reliable estimate of answer correctness. Current restrictions of the USPS on error rate are as follows: five-digit ZIP Code error rate should be less than 1%, and ZIP Add-On Code error rate should be less than 2%. The error rate is calculated as a ratio between the number of accepted wrong answers and the total number of accepted answers.

We need a specific reject procedure to achieve the highest possible accept rate provided that the error rate is lower than a priori defined value. It is not convenient to have an output of the reject procedure in the form of 'accepted' or 'rejected' because it demands that the reject procedure be tuned to each specific error rate. To solve this problem, the recognizer outputs a confidence value associated with each recognition answer. If it is necessary to provide a certain error rate, one should choose an appropriate threshold and consider the answers with the confidence levels higher and lower than the threshold as accepted and rejected respectively.

We use the neural network described above to calculate the confidence level of an answer. The neural network takes the information collected at all stages of the previous recognition process as input. It includes:

- The confidence of address block location
- The confidence of city-state-ZIP block and street address block parsing
- The confidence of recognition of each specific field (city, ZIP5, ZIP Add-On Code, street number, street name, etc.)
- The confidence of ZIP5 calculated after cross-validation of city field and ZIP5 field recognition results
- The confidence of the whole street address block calculated after cross-validation between street number and street name recognition results (or PO Box number and PO Box name, etc.)
- The difference in scores between the final answer and the best answer from all the other segmentation variants for the street address block
- Street address type (PO Box, rural route, street address, street address with secondary information)

The length of the input vector is 14. Output is the only value – probability of the answer correctness. Sample set size is 75,000 input vectors (generated in the process of recognition). It is divided in two parts: 65,000 - training samples, 10,000 - verification samples (see neural net learning details above). The confidence level of each specific field is an output from the Script Recognizer. The procedure of its calculation is described in [9].

6 Performance

The *Address*Script software has been implemented in the C programming language and developed under the Microsoft Windows NT environment. The size of the executable code is less than 4 MB. The size of the running code fits 32 MB. The average processing time of one envelope is less than 750 ms on a Pentium II – 300 MHz.

Table 3. Performance of the AddressScript system at various confidence level thresholds.

Finalization rate	Five-digit ZIP error	ZIP Add-On error	DPS error
64.0	0.8	2.0	0.2
61.8	0.7	1.5	0.2
56.5	0.5	0.9	0.1
51.0	0.4	0.5	0.1

The laboratory testing of the system was conducted on a blind test set of 50,000 images of live hand-written mail pieces (Table 3). The system has achieved a 64% finalization rate (finalization rate may be lower under real life operation). This result compares favorably with 25% finalization rate reported in [1]. Finalization rate means the percentage of accepted images (all the other images should be sent to an operator for manual treatment). The error rate is calculated as the number of errors among finalized images divided by the total number of finalized images. It is calculated separately for the five-digit ZIP Code, ZIP Add-On Code, and the last 2 digits of the DPS Code. The reason is that the costs of these errors are different. The most expensive is five-digit ZIP Code error because in this case the letter will be sent far from the correct destination. ZIP Add-On Code error is cheaper than five-digit ZIP Code error and the cheapest is a DPS error. If several errors occur simultaneously, only the most expensive one is taken into account. Current USPS error rate restrictions are: less than 1% for ZIP5 errors, and less than 2% for ZIP Add-On Code errors.

7 Conclusions

We have described *Address*Script - a system for handwritten postal address recognition for US mail. The average processing time of one envelope is less than 750 ms on a Pentium II – 300 MHz. The system has achieved a 64% finalization rate while being tested on a blind test set of 50,000 images of live hand-written mail pieces. The corresponding Five-digit ZIP error rate is 0.8%, ZIP Add-On error is 2.0%, and DPS error is 0.2%. These error rates are below current USPS requirements.

Significant increase in finalization rate compared to the published result [1] is achieved due to the following major factors:

- Powerful recognition engine, based on the combination of the Holistic Word Recognizer intended for cursive recognition and Analytical Word Recognizer intended primarily for number recognition and hand-printed word recognition.
- Extensive use of the context, which becomes available during the recognition.
- Reliable estimation of answer correctness based on the information collected at all stages of the previous recognition process.

New RCR systems with the integrated *Address*Script product were deployed in more than forty USPS sites throughout the United States by the end of August 1998. It is scheduled to deploy more than 160 new RCR systems by the end of 1998.

References

1. Srihari, S.N. and Kuebert, E.J.: Integration of Hand-Written Address Interpretation Technology into the United States Postal Service Remote Computer Reader System. Proc. of the 4th Int. Conf. on Document Analysis and Recognition. Ulm, Germany. (1997) 892-896

2. Dzuba, G., Filatov, A., Gershuny, D., and Kil, I.: Handwritten Word Recognition – The Approach Proved by Practice. Proc. of the 6th Int. Workshop on Frontiers in Handwriting Recognition. Taejon, Korea. (1998) 99-111
3. Filatov, A., Gitis, A., and Kil, I.: Graph-Based Handwritten Digit String Recognition. Proc. of 3rd Int. Conf. on Document Analysis and Recognition. Montreal, Canada. (1995) 845-848
4. Fenrich, R. and Hull, J.J.: Concerns in Creation of Image Database. Proc. of the 3rd Int. Workshop on Frontiers in Handwriting Recognition. Buffalo, New York, USA, May 25-27, (1993) 112-121
5. Ha, T.M. and Bunke, H.: Handwritten Numeral Recognition by Perturbation Method. Proc. of the 4th Int. Workshop on Frontiers in Handwriting Recognition. Taipei, Taiwan, Republic of China. Dec. 7-9 (1994) 97-106
6. Lee, D.S. and Srihari, S.N.: Handprinted Digit Recognition: A Comparison of Algorithms. Proc. of the third Int. Workshop on Frontiers in Handwritting Recognition. Buffalo, New York, USA. May 25-27 (1993) 153-162
7. Knerr, S. and Sperduti, S.: Rejection Driven Hierarchy of Neural Network Classifiers. Proc. of 1993 Int. Symp. on Nonlinear Theory and its Applications. Vol. 3. Hawaii. (1993)
8. Dzuba, G., Filatov, A., and Volgunin, A.: Handwritten ZIP Code Recognition. Proc. of the 4th Int. Conf. on Document Analysis and Recognition. Ulm, Germany (1997) 766-770
9. Dzuba, G., Filatov, A., Gershuny, D., Kil, I., and Nikitin, V.: Check Amount Recognition based on the Cross Validation of Courtesy and Legal Amount Fields. In: Impedovo, S., Wang, P.S.P., Bunke, H. (eds.): Automatic Bankcheck Processing. World Scientific. (1997) 177-193

Sorting and Recognizing Cheques and Financial Documents

Ching Y. Suen, Ke Liu, and Nick W. Strathy *AMDG*

Centre for Pattern Recognition and Machine Intelligence
Concordia University, Suite GM–606
1455 de Maisonneuve Blvd West, Montreal, QC, H3G 1M8, Canada
suen@cenparmi.concordia.ca

Abstract. In collaboration with financial institutions and utility companies, we have carried out substantial research on document analysis and handwriting recognition. This paper describes our prototype which can differentiate between cheques and remittance slips, between English and French cheques, and recognize their contents. A new technique of sorting handwritten cheques and financial documents will be described. It is based on the detection of the structural properties printed on such documents. Handwritten numeric amounts are recognized by a multiple–expert system. These systems have been applied to read handwritten cheques and numerous financial documents with a great variety of backgrounds, colours, and designs in real–life environments. Their performance will be presented and analyzed.

1 Introduction

Document analysis and recognition technologies play a very important role in information processing. Each day, billions of business and financial documents have to be processed by computer, e.g. bank cheques and utility bills, school and property tax forms, driver license renewals, income tax returns, drawings and maps, credit card payment slips, and a great variety of subscription and remittance forms. According to recent surveys and our visits to several data–processing centres of banks and utility companies, over 55 billion cheques (at a cost of 25 billion dollars) are processed annually in North America where the amounts are mostly keyed in manually. Hence economically there is an urge to fully automate the process of entering handwritten data into the computer. However, it is a great challenge due to immense variations of handwriting, colour, and designs [1]–[6].

Current research on amount recognition has been mainly devoted to bank cheque processing [7]–[8]. Our study reveals that in real–life applications, a bank cheque to be processed is usually accompanied with one or more financial documents from the customer that also contain the amount information, either in machine printed or in handwritten format, or in both, which is relevant to the amount information on the cheque. To read the amounts from a bank cheque and its associated financial documents and verify whether they are consistent

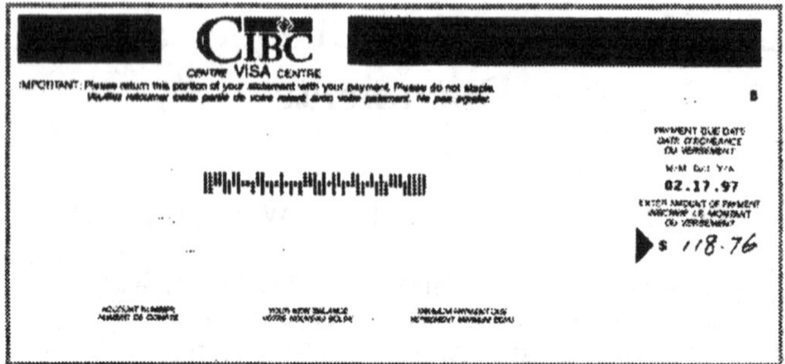

Fig. 1. Sample financial document

or not is an important and necessary process for most banks and utility companies. Therefore, it is very important to have an automatic system which can sort or identify cheques and different documents, and extract and recognize the interested data from them.

In this paper, we first present a novel approach to sort cheques and financial documents and extract data from them. Then, the issues related to amount recognition will be addressed.

2 Sorting Cheques and Financial Documents and Extracting Items

Most existing document processing methods [9]–[10] are based on the analysis of the line features which constitute the layout structures of the documents. Regarding the processing of financial documents, however, some financial documents may be constituted mainly of other kinds of geometrical components such as the regions in different shades, and contain fewer or no lines. Fig. 1 shows a VISA slip used in Canada, in which the rectangle regions and triangle pointer are the geometrical components for the description of the document.

As a result, those methods based only on the analysis of the line features cannot be applied to process financial documents, directly. The financial document processing method should be able to distinguish straight lines and edges of rectangular regions, and to use the geometrical features other than straight lines for the identification of documents. On the other hand, our study indicates that in practice, there are less than one hundred types of financial documents used by a utility company or bank, which means that a *model-driven matching technique* can be employed. Based on the above analysis, a novel approach has been developed for the processing of financial documents, which can be described in four parts, i.e. geometrical feature extraction, model representation, sorting of documents, and item extraction, respectively.

2.1 Extraction of Geometrical Features

The geometrical feature components are extracted from an input document image based on edge analysis since some financial documents such as bank cheques may contain very complicated background pictures. It is reasonable to assume that the skew angle of the scanned input document is within a given range, therefore we can define horizontal lines, vertical lines, and lines in other orientations. Lines other than horizontal or vertical are mainly used for the construction of the triangles and polygons. Hence, the extracted geometrical feature components include horizontal line segments, vertical line segments, triangles, rectangles and polygons.

The extracted geometrical feature components can be represented as set G $= \{C_i\}_0^{N-1}$ where N is the total number of geometrical feature components, C_i indicates the ith geometrical feature component and is described as follows:

$$C_i = \{GT_i, GP_i, GS_i\} \tag{1}$$

where GT_i takes one of values 0, 1, 2, 3, 4 each of which indicates that the type of component is horizontal line segment, vertical line segment, triangle, rectangle and polygon, respectively. GP_i is the representative point of C_i. When the component is a horizontal line or vertical line segment, GP_i is the mid point between the two end points of the segment. Otherwise, the x and y coordinates of GP_i are taken as the average x and y coordinates of the corner points of the triangle, rectangle, or polygon.

GS_i in formula (1) is a set of points, i.e.

$$GS_i = \{P_0, P_1, ..., P_{n_i-1}\}. \tag{2}$$

When the component is a horizontal or vertical line segment, n_i equals 2 and P_0 and P_1 are the two end points of the segments, respectively. In the other cases, n_i equals 3 for a triangle component, 4 for a rectangle component, and the total number of the corner points for a polygonal component. P_k and $P_{(k+1)\%n_i}$, where $0 \leq k < n_i$, are connected to each other through their common edge, and $P_0, P_1, ..., P_{n_i-1}$ are ordered counter-clockwise.

2.2 Model Representation

Model representation is used for training a new type of financial documents. In our approach, the sample document used for training a financial document can be either a blank sample document or a one filled with a customer's handwriting. From our experience, the extra horizontal or vertical lines may be introduced when people write courtesy or legal amounts. Therefore, if a filled document is used for training the system, an inference may be required to discard those horizontal or vertical line segments. The model for the description of a financial document is mainly based on the above set G of geometrical feature components, and will be used for sorting documents and extracting items, respectively.

Model Description for Sorting Documents In order to apply a model–driven technique to find the match between a model and input document, the *dominant geometrical feature component(s)* is defined and determined from the geometrical feature component set G of a training document. In the stage of sorting documents, when a model is compared with the set of geometrical feature components of an input document, the system first tries to find a match between the dominant geometrical feature component(s) of model and a geometrical feature component(s) of the input document. If it is successful, the system will proceed to further match their corresponding geometrical feature components. The model–driven matching method is described in the next subsection.

Several rules have been developed for the determination of dominant geometrical feature component(s) from set G of a training document. If there is a rectangle in G, of which the long edges are long enough(determined based on the width and height of the training document image), the rectangle can be chosen as the dominant geometrical feature component. If there is a line segment either in horizontal or in vertical, whose length is long enough, it can be chosen as the dominant geometrical feature component. If there is a polygon and the length of its longest edge is exceeds a threshold, the polygon can also be chosen as the dominant geometrical feature component.

When a rectangle is determined as the dominant geometrical feature component, the representative point GP of the rectangle is chosen as the original coordinate point of an image plane coordinate system, called *model-image plane coordinate system*. If the long edges are horizontal, the edge direction from left to right of the long edges is defined as the x-axis direction of the model-image plane coordinate system, otherwise, the direction from up to down of the long edges is chosen as the y-axis direction of the coordinate system.

Similarly, a model-image plane coordinate system can be constituted when the dominant geometrical feature component is a horizontal line segment, vertical line segment or polygon.

If the system is unable to determine a dominant geometrical feature component based on the rules described above, an interactive learning process may be required to ask for the labels of two geometrical feature components, which will be used as the dominant geometrical feature components of the model. The representative point of one geometrical feature component will be chosen as the original coordinate point of the model-image plane coordinate system and the direction from this point to the representative point of another geometrical feature component as the x-axis or y-axis direction of the coordinate system, depending on the angle between this direction and that of the x-axis of the document image.

After the dominant geometrical feature components of the model have been determined and the model– image plane coordinate system is built, the coordinates of the representative point GP and the points of set GS of each geometrical feature component are transformed into the coordinates in the model–image plane coordinate system.

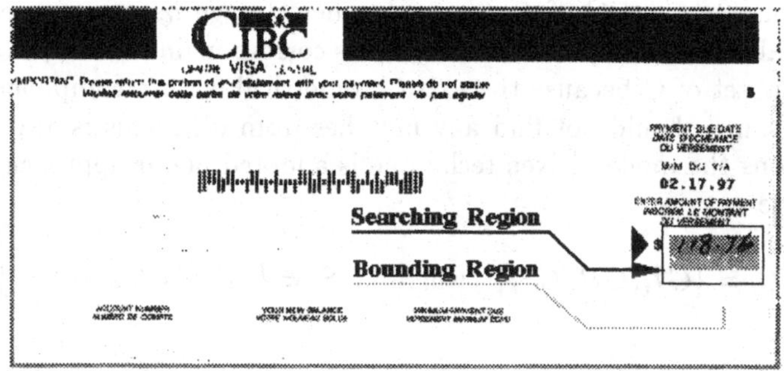

Fig. 2. Searching and bounding regions

Model Description for Item Extraction The second part of model representation is to determine some zones from the training document for the extraction of interested items. As we mentioned before, some financial documents exist neither in table nor in form. Therefore, for these documents, in general, it is impossible to determine the zones for the items automatically, and the knowledge about the positions of interested items is required. Hence, an interactive learning process is needed to incorporate this knowledge.

In our system, after the first part of a model is built, the training system will prompt the original document image, and ask for determining the searching and bounding regions[11], respectively, by selecting four points for each zone using the mouse. The physical meanings of the concepts of searching region and bounding region are: for each item, all its strokes should have their parts inside its corresponding searching region, and the probability of the parts of these strokes going outside of the bounding region of this item should be very low. Fig. 2 shows an example of the determined searching and bounding regions for the numeric amount on the VISA slip.

If more items are to be extracted from the document, their corresponding searching and bounding regions are defined and determined in the same way described above. Besides, the knowledge that whether the handwriting of a item may touch or cross some printed lines or not(for non–table or non-form documents, for example) can also be learned when building model description for the extraction of the item.

The coordinates of the selected points for the searching and bounding regions of each item are also transformed into their corresponding coordinates in the model-image plane coordinate system.

2.3 Sorting Financial Documents

As mentioned before, in practice, extra geometrical feature components such as horizontal or vertical lines may be introduced when people write courtesy or legal amounts on financial documents. Therefore, when the extracted geometrical feature component set G of an input document image I_G is compared with the geometrical feature component set G_m of its corresponding model, G_m may only match a subset of G because the extra geometrical feature components of G, if there are some, should not find any matches from G_m. This is also one of the main reasons the model-driven technique is adopted in our approach.

Suppose

$$C_i = \{GT_i, GP_i, GS_i\} \quad \text{where} \quad GS_i = \{P_0^{(i)}, P_1^{(i)}, ..., P_{n_i-1}^{(i)}\}$$

and

$$C_j = \{GT_j, GP_j, GS_j\} \quad \text{where} \quad GS_j = \{P_0^{(j)}, P_1^{(j)}, ..., P_{n_j-1}^{(j)}\}$$

are two geometrical feature components. Assume that $d(P_1, P_2)$ is the distance between two points on an image plane and, $\alpha(P)$ represents the corner of corner point P of a triangle, rectangle($\alpha(P) = 90^0$ in such case), or polygon. C_i and C_j are said to be *in shape matching* if the followings are true:

1. $GT_i = GT_j$
2. $n_i = n_j$
3. One of the following conditions is true:
   a. $| d(P_0^{(i)}, P_1^{(i)}) - d(P_0^{(j)}, P_1^{(j)}) | < thd$, if $GT_i = GT_j = 0$ or 1;
   b. $(| d(P_{(m+k)\%n_i}^{(i)}, P_{(m+k+1)\%n_i}^{(i)}) - d(P_m^{(j)}, P_{(m+1)\%n_j}^{(j)}) | < thd) \wedge$
   $(| \alpha(P_{(m+k)\%n_i}^{(i)}) - \alpha(P_m^{(j)}) | < th\alpha)$ for $m = 0, 1, ..., n_i - 1$, when $GT_i = GT_j = 2, 3$, or 4, where k is a specific integer such that $0 \le k < n_i$, thd and $th\alpha$ are the given distance and corner thresholds, respectively.

C_i and C_j are said to be *in shape matching under coordinate transformation* T if they are in shape matching and, for the above same integer k, the following two conditions are also true:

4. $d(GP_i, T(GP_j)) < thp$
5. $d(P_{(m+k)\%n_i}^{(i)}, T(P_m^{(j)})) < thp, \quad m = 0, 1, ..., n_i - 1$, where thp is a position distance threshold.

Suppose a model has only one dominant geometrical feature component C^*. A geometrical feature component C is a *candidate geometrical feature component* of C^* if they are in shape matching. When a model has two dominant geometrical feature components C_1^* and C_2^*, geometrical feature components C_1 and C_2 are called the *candidate pair of geometrical feature components* of C_1^* and C_2^*, if C_1^* and C_1 are in shape matching and, C_2^* and C_2 are in shape matching, respectively, and the distance between the representative points of C_1^* and C_2^* is almost the same as the distance between the representative points of C_1 and C_2.

Suppose that $G_m = \{C_{m,i}\}_0^{N_m-1}$ where $C_{m,i} = \{GT_{m,i}, GP_{m,i}, GS_{m,i}\}$ is the set of geometrical feature components associated with the mth model, where $0 \le m < M$ and $G = \{C_i\}_0^{N-1}$ where $C_i = \{GT_i, GP_i, GS_i\}$ is the set of geometrical feature components extracted from the input document. Assume that $N_m^{(j)}, j = 0, \cdots, 4$, indicates the numbers of horizontal line segments, vertical line segments, triangles, rectangles, and polygons contained in G_m, respectively, and $N^{(j)}, j = 0, \cdots, 4$, the numbers of the horizontal line segments, vertical line segments, triangles, rectangles, and polygons contained in G, respectively.

Since the extra geometrical feature components, introduced when people write the courtesy or legal amounts on financial documents, can only be horizontal or vertical line segments, therefore, if G_m is the model of G, the following conditions should be true:

a. $N_m^{(0)} \leq N^{(0)}$, $N_m^{(1)} \leq N^{(1)}$;
b. $N_m^{(2)} = N^{(2)}$, $N_m^{(3)} = N^{(3)}$, $N_m^{(4)} = N^{(4)}$.

The above conditions can greatly reduce the number of models chosen for matching an input document, and can therefore speed up the sorting algorithm.

Based on the above assumptions and descriptions, the algorithm of sorting financial documents can be summarized below.

Sorting Algorithm

Match = -1;
m = 0;
while (m < M) do
if $(N_m^{(0)} \leq N^{(0)}) \wedge (N_m^{(1)} \leq N^{(1)}) \wedge (N_m^{(2)} = N^{(2)}) \wedge (N_m^{(3)} = N^{(3)}) \wedge (N_m^{(4)} = N^{(4)})$
begin
a. *Find a candidate geometrical feature component of the dominant geometrical feature component of G_m, or a candidate pair of geometrical feature components if G_m has two dominant geometrical feature components;*
b. *If no more dominant geometrical feature component exists(or no candidate pair of geometrical feature components), goto f;*
c. *Constitute a coordinate transformation T_m from the model–image plane of G_m to the document image plane based on the correspondence between the dominant geometrical feature component(s) of G_m and the candidate geometrical feature component(pair);*
d. *For each geometrical feature component of G_m, find its corresponding geometrical feature component such that they are in shape matching under T_m. If it is unsuccessful for a geometrical feature component of G_m, goto f;*
e. *Match = m (successful), break;*
f. *m = m + 1;*
end;
else
m = m + 1;

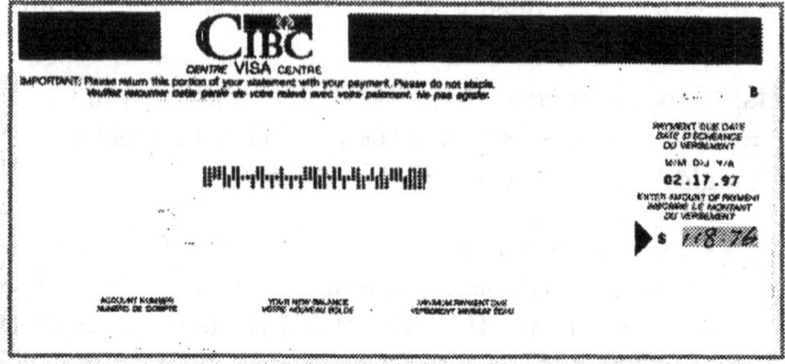

Fig. 3. Extracted digit amount item

If the above algorithm assigns m to $Match$, which is positive, the document image is identified as type m.

2.4 Model–Driven Item Extraction

Once G_m is identified as the model of the input document image I_G, the points selected for the searching and bounding regions of the model document G_m are transformed into, using transformation T_m, the points on document image I_G, which constitute the searching and bounding regions for extracting item(s) from I_G. Then, the item extraction method presented in [11] is applied to extract an item image, which consists of the following steps:

1. Estimate the grey distributions of handwritten strokes by selecting some pixel points on handwritten strokes from the searching region;
2. Trace the connected components of handwritten strokes within the bounding region based on the estimated grey distributions of handwritten strokes, and by selecting initial tracing points from the searching region.
3. Separate strokes from connected table or form lines if necessary.

Fig. 3 shows the extracted item of numeric amount for the VISA slip shown in Fig. 1

2.5 System of Sorting Financial Documents

Based on the proposed approach, techniques and algorithms, an automatic system has been developed for sorting Canadian bank cheques and more than twenty types of financial documents such as phone bills, MasterCard payment remittance forms, VISA payment remittance forms, Cable TV payment remittance forms, and so on, and extracting of the desired handwriting information from them. Fig. 4 illustrates some sample documents that can be processed by our system. Since Canadian bank cheques are printed in a variety of sizes and styles and, we have also developed an effective method [11] of processing Canadian

Fig. 4. Sample financial document images

bank cheques, in which the knowledge about the layout structures of Canadian bank cheques has been incorporated, therefore, in our system, the identification of Canadian bank cheques and the extraction of items from them are still based on the cheque processing method described in [11]. Our system has been used for the sorting of more than ten thousands of Canadian bank cheques and more than eight hundred other financial documents, and reached over 98.5% correct identification rate with 100% reliability.

3 Courtesy Amount Recognition (CAR)

For handwritten U.S. bank cheques the top courtesy amount recognition (CAR) systems typically achieve 60–75 percent raw recognition i.e., with error–detection capability switched off.

What can be done to improve this 25–40 percent recognition failure?

The most significant improvements today are achieved by combining CAR with legal amount recognition (LAR). The top commercial systems claim raw recognition of 80%. The drawback of these systems is that, instead of the 3 or 4 cheques per second processed by a CAR engine, a CAR–LAR engine has difficulty processing more than one cheque per second. In practice, 10 or more high–priced CAR–LAR engines are needed to keep up with a single high–speed scanner (1000 documents per minute).

Although the cost is high, overall recognition performance appears to be improved by combining CAR and LAR, and it is unreasonable to believe that a CAR system alone can be as reliable as a combined system. Nevertheless, CAR performance needs to be maximized, so let us consider some of the factors limiting that performance.

Scan resolution. A significant limiting factor on CAR performance is the scan resolution. Due to the restricted amount of space provided for the amount on North American personal cheques, the characters are often written quite small, especially the cents portion. Since it is difficult for people to write small characters legibly, it is desirable for the scanner to capture as much detail as possible. Commercial systems typically capture images at a maximum resolution of 200 dots per inch (DPI). Historically this has been done to conserve storage space and processing time, however, it is questionable whether this low resolution can any longer be justified given vastly improved storage costs and hardware speeds.

Image binarization. Traditional CAR systems have been developed to operate on binarized cheque images. Often, important information that makes it easier to distinguish the target ink from the cheque background is lost when the image is binarized. However, today's high-speed scanners can provide a grey-level image as well as a binary image. CAR–LAR systems that make use of grey scans are currently pushing recognition percentages into the low eighties.

Segmentation algorithms. Algorithms for grouping together components of broken characters, and for handling characters that touch other characters are problematic. When combined with LAR, a CAR system typically generates multiple segmentation hypotheses for corroboration with legal amount hypotheses. Since current systems cannot always detect spurious segmentations, it is desirable to avoid generating them. The cents portion of the amount on North American cheques is particularly difficult to segment due to the wide range of formats of varying complexity in which it can be written.

Garbage detection. This property of a recognition system is important for ranking segmentation hypotheses. The bulk of garbage detection is performed by the character classifier. Typical classifiers perform very well on the dialect of data they have been trained to recognize, but when required to detect invalid data, for example mis-segmented characters, they become significantly less reliable. This unreliability leads to 'garbage' being accepted as valid data.

3.1 CENPARMI CAR System

A CAR system developed at CENPARMI has been tested on a blind set of 400 real Canadian personal cheques provided by Bell Quebec with results shown in Table 1. Cheques were scanned at 300 DPI, 8-bit grey level. Location, extraction and recognition are fully automatic. The performances from other sources cannot be compared directly since there is no common test set, however the results may be taken as indicative. Talks with Canadian cheque processing companies using top commercial systems indicate that performances at the 1% error level on Canadian cheques are below 50% and sometimes below 40%. To the best of our knowledge, all error rates quoted are for the entire test set, not just the cheques accepted by the particular system.

The CENPARMI performance indicates strong garbage detection capability since a 1% error rate is achieved at a cost of losing just 10% of the raw recognition rate. This capability will be elaborated on in a later section.

Although the CENPARMI system has the advantages of higher resolution and grey–level image capture, the raw recognition rate is only 72%. Raw recognition on training data is currently over 75%, but the types of recognition failures indicate a need to focus more attention on segmentation, target zone extraction, and background removal in that order. One of the more frequently occurring segmentation challenges not yet solved by the system is 'touching fraction lines,' i.e., cents expressed fractionally where the fraction line touches other characters. This occurs in 5–10 percent of personal cheques. Capture of the cents portion from the legal amount is expected to help here also.

Table 1. Courtesy amount recognition.

System	% Correct	% error	Source/Date
CENPARMI	72	raw	1998
	62	1	
	56	0.5	
	51	0.25	
Lucent	44	1	Advertisement, 1998
ParaScript	47	1	Dzuba et al [12], 1997
Mitek	55	1	Houle et al [17], 1996

3.2 Digit Recognition

The results in Tables 2, 3, and 4 indicate that today's CENPARMI digit recognition system, while far from perfect, has surpassed by a significant margin systems from well known sources on three standard test sets. Performance is reported at two error levels, the 'raw' level where no inputs are rejected, and the 0.1% error level where the system is permitted to reject uncertain decisions. Some systems do not report a raw performance, therefore their highest reported recognition rate is quoted here. Quotes for some systems are perhaps out of date, however newer results from these sources have not appeared in the literature.

The CENPARMI digit recognizer consists of multiple neural networks trained by back propagation on about 450,000 digit images. Training takes about 2 to 3 months on a single processor, but is normally shared between processors to reduce the time to a few weeks. For the record, no data from any of the three test sets has been used in any way to train the system. CENPARMI speeds are based on 300 MHz processor speed.

A point of interest is that the CENPARMI system alone appears to perform as well as the combined digit recognition engines of two industry leaders, AEG and Mitek. In a paper by Houle *et al* [17] the recognition rate at 0.1% error rate for the combined engine was 94–95 percent on a large private test set.

Table 2. Digit recognition. Test set = NIST TD1. Size = 58,646 digit images.

System	0% rej	0.10% err	Date	digits/sec
IBM [14]	96.51	< 50	1992	87
AEG [14]	96.57	< 50	1992	34
AT&T [14]	96.84	68	1992	5
Ha et al [16]	97.10	–	1997	6
Mitek [13]	98.6	90	1993	16
Hewlett Packard [18]	98.60	–	1996	–
CENPARMI	99.07	94.45	1998	56

Table 3. Digit recognition. Test set = CEDAR GOODBS. Size = 2213 digit images.

System	0% rej	0.10% err	Date	digits/sec
Kittler et al [19]	98.19	–	1998	–
CEDAR [20]	98.87	–	1993	–
Ha et al [16]	99.09	–	1997	–
CENPARMI	99.77	99.14	1998	54

Table 4. Digit recognition. Test set = Concordia. Size = 2000 digit images.

System	0% rej	0.10% err	Date	digits/sec
Lee [21]	97.10	–	1996	–
Oh et al [22]	97.4	–	1997	–
AEG [15]	98.30	–	1993	–
AEG-CENPARMI 1 [15]	98.50	–	1993	–
AEG-CENPARMI 2 [15]	–	97.55	1993	–
CENPARMI	98.85	97.65	1998	58

3.3 Garbage Detection

Experiments were done at CENPARMI to study and obtain some measure of garbage detection capability of the digit classifier of the CAR system. Although garbage detection is important for evaluating segmentation, it is rarely mentioned in OCR literature except in passing. It has never to our knowledge been quantified.

Motivated by a desire to have a benchmark for garbage detection in order to measure progress, a 'standard garbage test set' for digit recognizers was constructed from materials in the NIST database SD19. All of the isolated letters from the NIST test set were used, but only from classes not often expected to resemble digits.

The resulting test set (dubbed TD1G for Test Data 1 Garbage) contains 13,561 images from classes in the string 'ACEFKLMNPQRVWXacdefhjkmnprtvwx'. Inevitably, some of these images resemble digits quite closely, but the great majority do not. Ideally, a test set for a digit classifier would consist of data from the domain of mis–segmented digits, yet TD1G comes from a domain not radically different from mis–segmented digits. The great advantages of this test set are that it is part of a readily available NIST database and that it is relatively easy to construct.

The performances of two CENPARMI digit classifiers on the NIST digit test set are compared in Table 5. It will be observed that while the raw recognition rate of the 1998 classifier appears to be significantly higher than that of the 1997 classifier, there is not a corresponding improvement at the 0.1% error level. One might be led to conclude that garbage detection capability has not improved significantly. As we will see, this conclusion is not supported by garbage detection benchmarking tests.

The procedure used to benchmark garbage detection capability of a classifier was to measure its error rate on TD1G at a rejection threshold determined from the classifier's performance on the digit test set (TD1). In this case the threshold that gave 0.1% error on TD1 was used for testing the classifier on TD1G. Table 6 gives the performance for each classifier on TD1G. An error occurs whenever a classifier fails to reject a garbage image and instead classifies it as a digit.

Table 6 [1] can be taken as a positive indication of progress in garbage detection since the TD1G error rate of the new classifier is considerably reduced from the old one.

4 Concluding Remarks

This paper presents a new system developed at CENPARMI for sorting and recognizing a great variety of cheques and financial documents. Both the methodologies and the system configuration have been described, and the performances of the major functions on real–life data have been presented.

[1] The performance reported for the same test in two conference proceedings (DAS98, ICMI99 [23]) was incorrect due to a regrettable error in recording experimental results.

Table 5. Digit recognition. Test set = NIST TD1. Size = 58,646 digit images.

System	0% rej	0.10% err
1997	98.90	94.18
1998	99.07	94.45

Table 6. Garbage detection on TD1G (13,561 images) at 0.1% error on TD1.

System	rej	err
1997	86.90	13.10
1998	90.26	9.74

Acknowledgments

This research was supported by the Natural Sciences and Engineering Research Council of Canada, the National Networks of Centres of Excellence program of Canada, and the FCAR program of the Ministry of Education of the province of Quebec.

References

1. G. Lorette. Handwriting Recognition or Reading? Situation at the Dawn of the 3rd Millenium. In *Int. Workshop Frontiers in Handwriting Rec.*, pages 1–13, Taejon, Aug. 1998.
2. J.–H. Chiang and P. D. Gader. Recognition of Handprinted Numerals in VISA Card Application Forms. *Machine Vision and Applications*, 10:144–149, 1997.
3. M. D. Garris, C. L. Wilson, and J. L. Blue. Neural Network-Based Systems for Handprint OCR Applications. *IEEE Trans. Image Processing*, 7:1097–1112, Aug. 1998.
4. I.–S. Oh and C. Y. Suen. Distance Features for Neural Network-Based Recognition of Handwritten Characters. *Int. J. Doc. Analysis and Recognition*, 1:73–88, 1998.
5. S. Bussi and E. Bruzzone. Segmenting Handwritten Character Strings in an ICR System. In*Proc. Int. Workshop on Frontiers in Handwriting Recognition*, pages 189–198, Taejon, Aug. 1998.
6. G. Kaufmann and H. Bunke. Amount Translation and Error Localization in Cheque Processing Using Syntax–Directed Translation. In *Proc. Int. Conf. Pattern Recognition*, pages 1530–1534, Brisbaine, Aug. 1998.
7. L. Lam, C.Y. Suen, et al. Automatic Processing of Information on Cheques. In*Proc. IEEE Int. Conf. on Systems, Man, Cybernetics*, pages 2353–2358, Vancouver, Oct. 1995.
8. S. Impedovo, P.S.P. Wang and H. Bunke (eds). Automatic Bankcheck Processing. World Scientific Publishing Co. Pte. Ltd., Singapore, 1997.

9. L. Y. Tseng and R. C. Chen. recognition and Data Extraction of Form Documents Based on Three Types of Line Segments. *Pattern Recognition*, 31(10):1525–540, 1998.
10. Y.Y. Tang, S. W. Lee, and C. Y. Suen. Automatic Document Processing: A Survey. *Pattern Recognition*, 29(12):1931–952, 1996.
11. K. Liu, C.Y. Suen, M. Cheriet, J. N. Said, C. Nadal and Y.Y Tang. Automatic Extraction of Baselines and Data from Check Images. In Automatic Bankcheck Processing, S. Impedovo, P.S.P. Wang and H. Bunke (eds), World Scientific Publishing Co. Pte. Ltd., Singapore, pp.213–235, 1997.
12. G. Dzuba, A. Filatov, D. Gershuny, I. Kil, and V. Nikitin. Check Amount Recognition Based on the Cross Validation of Courtesy and Legal Amount Fields. *Int. Jour. Patt. Rec. and Art. Intell.*, 11(4):639–655, 1997.
13. J. Geist et al. *The Second Census Optical Character Recognition Systems Conference.* U.S. Department of Commerce, National Institute of Standards and Technology, 1993.
14. R. Allen Wilkinson et al. *The First Census Optical Character Recognition Systems Conference.* U.S. Department of Commerce, National Institute of Standards and Technology, 1992.
15. J. Franke. Experiments with the CENPARMI Data Base Combining Different Approaches. In *Int. Workshop Frontiers in Handwriting Rec.*, pages 305–311, 1993.
16. Thien M. Ha and Horst Bunke. Off-line Handwritten Numeral Recognition by Perturbation Method. *IEEE Trans. Patt. Anal. and Mach. Intell.*, 19(5):535–539, May 1997.
17. G.F. Houle, D. Bradburn Aragon, and R.W. Smith. A Multi–Layered Corroboration–Based Check Reader. In *IAPR Workshop on Document Analysis Systems*, pages 495–543, 1996.
18. Takahiko Kawatani, Hiroyuki Shimizu, and Marc McEachern. Handwriten Numeral Recognition with the Improved LDA Method. In *Int. Conf. on Pattern Recognition*, pages 441–446, 1996.
19. J. Kittler, M. Hatef, R.P.W. Duin, and J. Matas. On Combining Classifiers. *IEEE Trans. Patt. Anal. and Mach. Intell.*, 20(3):226-239, May 1998.
20. D-S. Lee and S.N. Srihari. Handprinted Digit Recognition: A Comparison of Algorithms. In *Proceedings of the 3rd Int. Workshop on Frontiers in Handwriting Rec.*, pages 153–162, Buffalo, N.Y., U.S.A., May 1993.
21. S-W. Lee. Off-line Recognition of Totally Unconstrained Handwritten Numerals Using Multilayer Cluster Neural Network. *IEEE Trans. Patt. Anal. Mach. Intel.*, 18(6):648–652, 1996.
22. I-S. Oh, J-S. Lee, K-C. Hong, and S-M. Choi. Class–Expert Approach to Unconstrained Handwritten Numeral Recognition. In *Int. Workshop Frontiers in Handwriting Rec.*, pages 35–40, 1997.
23. N. W. Strathy. Handwriting Recognition for Cheque Processing. In *Proc. Int. Conf. Multimodal Interface*, pages 47–50, Hong Kong, Jan 1999.

A System for the Automated Reading of Check Amounts - Some Key Ideas

Guido Kaufmann and Horst Bunke

University of Bern, Institut für Informatik und angewandte Mathematik, Neubrückstrasse 10, CH-3012 Bern, Switzerland
{kaufmann, bunke}@iam.unibe.ch

Abstract. In this paper we present a reading system for amounts extracted from bank and postal checks. We focus our description on the legal amount recognition and the combination of the recognition results for the legal and the courtesy amounts. For these tasks we developed and applied several new techniques. In our work we deal with German check amounts. The automated reading of German legal amounts is a great challenge since the literal words the legal amount is constructed of are completely connected. Our system was tested on a database with real checks from the Swiss postal services.

1 Introduction

Automated reading of amounts extracted from postal or bank checks can be divided into three tasks: courtesy amount recognition, legal amount recognition, and subsequent combination of the results of the two recognizers. The combination results in either the recognized amount or a rejection of the check. Since digit and digit string recognition can be performed faster and with higher recognition rates than the reading of handwritten words, the courtesy amount recognizer has become dominant in check reading. The first check reading systems even rely on the recognized courtesy amount only, and ignore the legal amount. In later systems, some of which are still under development, legal amounts are also recognized. Their recognition results are used to verify the hypotheses generated by the courtesy amount recognizer, which helps improving the system's reliability and performance significantly. The recognition of the legal amount is either driven by the results of the courtesy amount recognizer [1], or performed independently [2]. For a good overview of the state-of-the-art in automatic bankcheck processing see the two special issues of the Int. Journal of Pattern Recognition and Artificial Intelligence [3] published on this subject.

This paper presents a system for reading handwritten bankcheck amounts. In the description of the main components we focus on some key ideas and new approaches that have been explored. In our work we are dealing with German amounts. Here recognition is very challenging due to the nature of writing German numbers by words. In contrast to many other languages, such as English and French, the literal words in German that form the legal amount are separated by very small gaps only, or they are completely connected by ligatures.

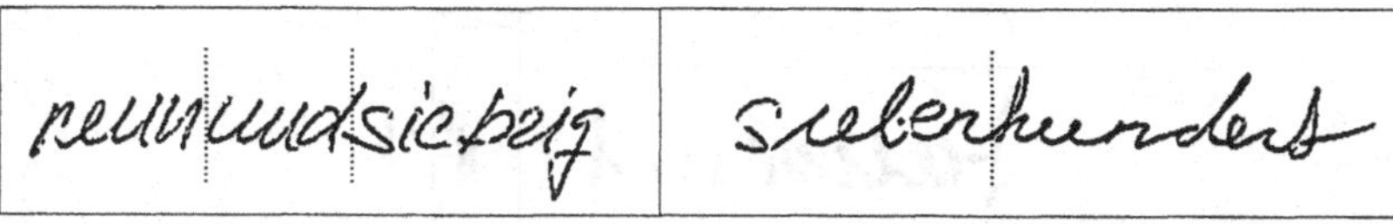

Fig. 1. Two samples of typical German numbers represented by words where the literal words are separated by very small gaps only (left: *neunundsiebzig* (seventy nine)), or completely connected by ligatures (right: *siebenhundert* (seven hundred)). With the dotted lines the hypothetical segmentation positions are marked.

These ligatures and the gaps are not different from those between the characters in a word (Fig. 1). Therefore a recognition approach for the legal amount based on its segmentation into literal words and their subsequent independent recognition is not possible. The legal amount has to be recognized as a whole which leads to a very large vocabulary.

The paper is structured as follows: Section 2 describes the recognition module for the legal amount. We applied a Hidden Markov Model (HMM) based recognition approach, since HMMs are well suited for reading a word without segmenting it into smaller components. For our work this approach was adapted for a segmentation-free recognition of the whole worded amount (consisting of several literal words) by hierarchically building models from simpler literal words. Our HMM-based word recognizer differs from other HMM-based word classifiers described in literature mainly in the type of features extracted from the input pattern. We propose to use the pure bitmap instead of a description of structural or topological elements [1, 4, 5]. In Section 3 the courtesy amount recognizer is presented, where a combined segmentation-based and segmentation-free recognition approach has been implemented. The combination of the recognition results for the courtesy amount and the legal amount is the topic of Section 4. We first describe a method for a systematic translation of recognized legal amounts into digit strings. The strategy of the subsequent combination is based on comparing the ranked lists of the single recognizers and searching for an agreement within the two lists. For checks where no agreement can be found, we propose a new approach to detecting, analyzing and correcting the potential errors of our legal- or courtesy amount recognizer. This means the mismatching subwords and digits are first localized and extracted from the input image. Then a second classifier is applied to those subwords that have been identified as potential errors. Experimental results are described in Section 5. Our system was tested on a database with 1500 real check amounts from Swiss postal services. As the focus of our work is on recognition rather than preprocessing and segmentation, these amounts were manually extracted from checks. Conclusions are presented in Section 6.

Fig. 2. In the feature extraction step a sliding window is further devided into squares (4×4 pixels) whose number of black pixels are counted.

2 Legal Amount Recognition

The process of legal amount recognition is generally divided into segmentation and recognition [2, 7]: In the *segmentation* step the legal amount is split into its literal words; in most languages (English, French, Italian, German, for example) there are 20 to 30 such different literal words[1] the legal amounts are constructed of by concatenation [1, 6, 2]. In the *recognition* step the extracted words are classified. In earlier works in cursive script recognition the techniques applied for the recognition of handwritten words were based on further segmenting the words into individual characters and classifying them. Alternatively, in the last few years Hidden Markov Models (HMMs), widely used in the field of continuous speech recognition for a long time, have been qualifying as an excellent tool also for cursive script recognition. The words are recognized as a whole without any explicit segmentation into characters. Segmentation and recognition are performed jointly and therefore the extremely difficult and error prone segmentation task can be avoided [8]. Sequences of features are implicitly associated with the characters of a word by the HMM.

In the HMM-based legal amount recognizer presented in this section, four different tasks need to be solved, namely, preprocessing, feature extraction, training, and recognition. They will be described in the following subsections.

2.1 Preprocessing and Feature Extraction

In an HMM framework each pattern to be recognized has to be described by a sequence of feature vectors. A common approach to this kind of representation is to scan the image from left to right and to compute at regular positions a feature vector from a vertical strip, called *sliding window* [4] or *frame* [8]. In most recognition systems for cursive handwriting, high-level features, i.e. character fragments, such as lines, curves, or dots are used [1, 4]. In contrast, we explore in our work the use of bitmap-based features, similar to an approach presented in [8]. I.e. the positions of the pixels set within a sliding window are the only information we extract. For that purpose the sliding window (in our work 216×8 pixels) is further split into small subwindows (4×4 pixels). For each subwindow the number of black pixels are counted (Fig. 2). This results in vectors with 108

[1] Analyzing the grammar of German numerals we found 26 different literal words.

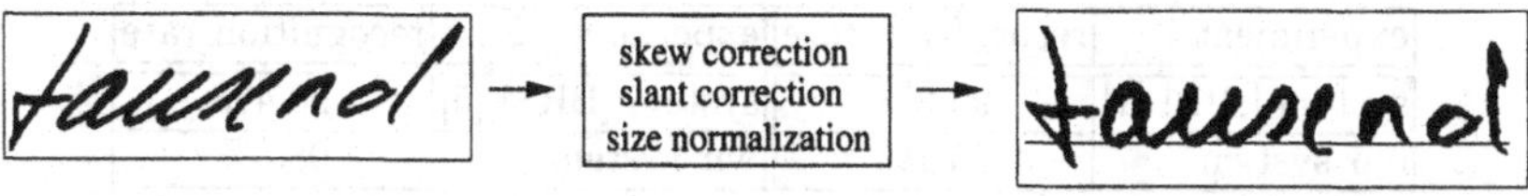

Fig. 3. The normalization steps in the preprocessing step of the legal amount

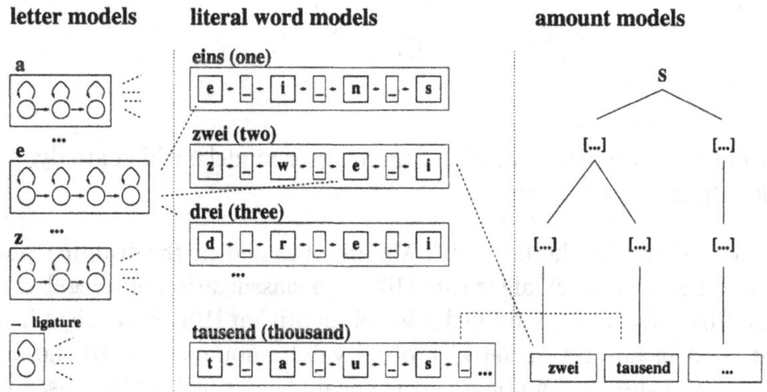

Fig. 4. Graphical illustration of the model building process. The dotted lines are references from the literal word HMMs to the letter HMMs, and from the (amount) word HMMs to the literal word HMMs, respectively.

feature values each. In our work these feature vectors are subsequently reduced by a principal axis transformation to dimension 18.

Working with this simple kind of features no sophisticated structural and topological analysis of the pattern has to be implemented. However, these features require a good normalization in the preprocessing step to eliminate writing variability as much as possible.

In the preprocessing step we apply several algorithms to reduce the effects of typical variations in handwriting, namely, the correction of skewness, slant and size differences (Fig. 3). The corrections are done by estimating the difference of the input word to a standard form and performing the inverse geometric transformation. For further details see [9].

2.2 HMM Model Structure, Training and Recognition

In order to model a legal amount by an HMM, we first define a (linear) HMM for each letter appearing in our words. Then a HMM for each of the literal words is built by concatenating the appropriate letter models. These HMMs are further combined in a hierarchical network, based on the grammar that describes the set of syntactically correct words. Each path in this network represents a valid legal amount. A graphical illustration of this model building process for the legal amounts is shown in Fig. 4. Notice that the letter HMMs are the smallest components and there exists only one HMM per letter regardless of the number of occurrences of the letter in a literal word. The literal word models and the

experiment 1	recognition rate	experiment 2	recognition rate
system [BIP] [1]	90.2%	system [BRS] [5]	98.4%
our system	96.1%	our system	98.8%

Table 1. Comparison of our system with two others HMM-based recognition systems based on structural features.

amount models are concatenations of these letter models, which are dynamically expanded during recognition.

The parameters of the letter HMMs are obtained in the training phase via the standard Baum-Welch algorithm [10]. The classification of a legal amount is performed by means of a modified Viterbi algorithm [10]. It consists in finding the best path in our HMM-network of all valid amounts. Due to the large vocabulary of all valid legal amounts – the vocabulary is further increased because there are very often more than one valid verbal representation for a numeral – an exhaustive search would be too slow. So we use a beam search strategy where paths are dynamically pruned during recognition. This classification algorithm will not necessarily deliver the best path, but only a suboptimal one. However, the search space can be kept reasonably small, allowing a fast search. Both training and recognition of our legal amount recognizer are based on the ISADORA system [5]. The ISADORA system provides flexible HMM-based pattern analysis tools and the possibility to build hierarchically structured models from simpler constituents, as described in the previous paragraph. Besides cursive script recognition, ISADORA has been applied in many other fields, for example, automatic speech recognition and the diagnosis of sensor data from moving vehicles.

In some preliminary tests we examined the quality of the features used in our system, comparing our recognizer with two different systems based on structural features [1, 5]. In the first experiment (see Table 1) a database of 13'000 German literal words collected from 500 different writers was used. This database was divided into five disjoint sets, each consisting of 2'600 words. Each of these sets was once used as a test set, while with the others the HMMs were trained. On this database we compared our system with the one presented in [1].

In the second experiment we worked with a smaller database containing 3000 English words from 5 different writers. This database was collected by the authors of [5] from so-called "cooperative writers". Each person wrote the 150 words of the vocabulary four times. The four data sets of this database were also cyclically used as test and training sets, similarly to the previous experiment.

In both experiments under exactely the same conditions (training/test sets) our system achieved similar or better results (see Table 1).

3 Courtesy Amount Recognition

For courtesy amount reading we adapted a system that was developed (in another project) for the recognition of digit strings. For a detailed description of this system see [11]. In our check reading system the digit recognition subsystem was trained with 50'000 digits collected from Swiss postal data. (These digits are not part of the database used in the experiments described in Section 5.) Working with this recognizer our courtesy amounts had to be restricted to amounts without cent portions. For the reading of Swiss postal checks this was a minor restriction since a cent part does not very often appear on Swiss postal checks.

4 Combination of Legal and Courtesy Amounts

In our system the courtesy and the legal amounts are recognized separately, without using any knowledge of each other. In the combination module the ranked lists of the recognized legal amount and courtesy amount are compared, considering the top L and C ranks of each recognizer, respectively, where L and C are system parameters. If the top ranks match, i.e., if there is an amount common to the top L ranks of the legal amount and the top C ranks of the courtesy amount recognizer, the check is accepted, with this common amount as its result, otherwise it is rejected. Due to the fact that typical confusions of digits generally do not correspond with typical confusions of words, this seems to be a quite promising approach. Since recognition rates for handwritten words are still rather low, though, this yields quite high rejection rates. In the following we describe an approach to lowering the rejection rate without increasing the error rate.

4.1 Amount Translation

Before we can compare the recognized legal and courtesy amounts in the combination step, the legal amounts have to be translated into digit strings. A problem that occurs in the processing of German amounts at this step is that the order of the numeral words does not need to correspond to the digit order. Therefore the translation cannot be done by simply replacing words from left to right by digits or blanks, as in English (for example *seventy nine*: seventy → 7, nine → 9). In German, in the legal amount *neunundsiebzig* (seventy nine, 79) the order of the numeral words that correspond to the digits 7 and 9 (i.e. *siebzig* and *neun*) is reversed. For this translation step we proposed in [12] a systematic and flexible approach, using the technique of syntax-directed translation (SDT). It can easily be adapted to other languages and is especially useful for languages where the ordering problem described above occurs, and many different word representations correspond to the same digit amount.

Our implementation of SDT delivers not only a translation of each recognized legal amount into its corresponding digit string, but also the information for each digit to which word of the legal amount it corresponds. For the example given

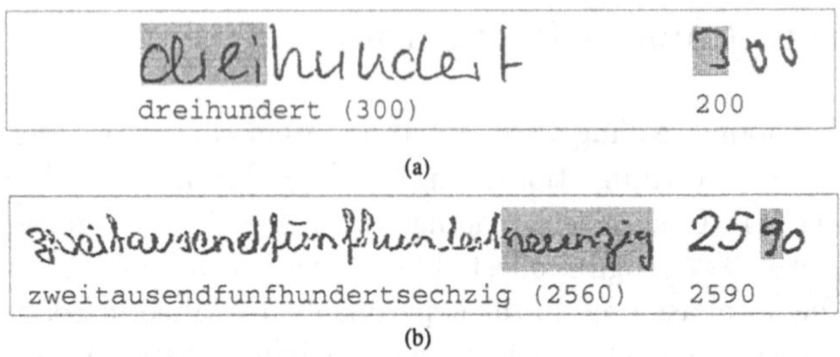

Fig. 5. Two examples of localized mismatching parts.

above, we not only get the digit string *79* as translation of the legal amount *neunundsiebzig* (seventy nine), but also the information that the first word *neun* (nine) corresponds to the second digit of the translated legal amount, i.e. *9*, and the second word *siebzig* (seventy) to the first digit *7*, respectively.

4.2 Localization of Mismatching Parts

In case of a disagreement between the courtesy amount and the translated legal amount this additional translation information is used to detect the cause of the missing correspondence. First, the two digit strings of the courtesy amount and translated legal amount are compared digit by digit. For each mismatching digit in the translated legal amount, the corresponding word in the legal amount is determined. The information needed for this step is provided by the SDT in the translation step. The start and end position of the corresponding word in the image are obtained from the HMM as a byproduct of the recognition process (for further details see [13]).

Two examples of located mismatching parts are shown in Fig 5. In example (a), the correct recognition result for the legal and courtesy amount recognizer is *dreihundert* and *300*, respectively. However, the first digit in the courtesy amount was misrecognized as *2*. As indicated in example (a), the system has correctly located the mismatching subunits. In example (b), the correct legal amount of *zweitausendfünfhundertneunzig* (*2590*) was misrecognized as *zweitausendfünf-hundertsechzig* (*2560*).The mismatching subword *neunzig* (ninety) and the digit *9* are correctly detected and marked.

4.3 Correction of Recognition Errors

The marked words represent potential recognition errors. We call them *potential* errors because we are not completely sure that the disagreement was produced by a recognition error in the legal amount. Actually, there are three different causes that could have led to the disagreement. Either the subword was misclassified, or the corresponding digit, or both of them. Instead of rejecting a check when the legal and courtesy amount do not completely match, we use the images of mismatching subunits for a further post-processing where we try to correct the

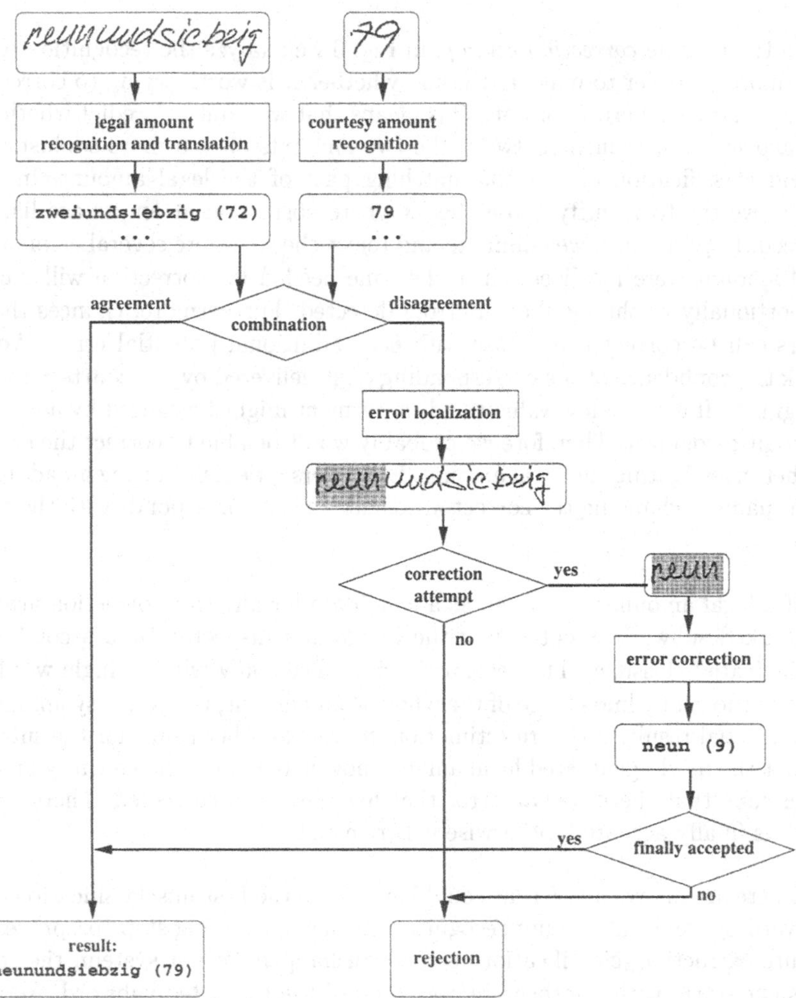

Fig. 6. The general system architecture enhanced by modules for error localization and correction. In the example the legal amount was recognized as *zwei*undsiebzig (seventy two) instead of *neun*undsiebzig (seventy nine). The courtesy amount was correctly recognized as 79. Therefore the first word *neun* (nine) recognized as *zwei* (two) is a potential error and analyzed by the error correction module.

potential errors. Since digit recognition is performed with higher reliability, we focus in our work primarily on the correction of mismatching subwords. In Fig. 6 our enhanced system architecture shown.

In the module *correction attempt* in Fig. 6 we analyze the recognition results once more, in order to make a decision whether it is worth trying to correct the detected potential errors or not. This means that we want to predict whether we can expect an agreement between the two amounts after a more sophisticated, second classification of the non-matching part of the legal amount. In other words, we try to identify those checks where correction attempts are likely to succeed. In particular, we eliminate and reject checks where several errors in the legal amount were localized, since the time needed for correction will increase proportionally to the number of errors detected. Furthermore, chances that all errors can be corrected decrease with each additional potential error. We also check the confidence of the corresponding digit delivered by the courtesy amount recognizer. If it has a low value the disagreement might be caused by an error of the digit recognizer. Therefore we probably won't be able to correct the error by further investigating the legal amount. Even worse, we risk causing an additional error, namely, changing the correct word such that it corresponds with the wrong digit.

If a legal amount is declared as a candidate for an error correction attempt, its marked subword is cut out of the image and inspected by a second, more sophisticated classifier. The second classifier deals only with a single word at a time, without any knowledge of the whole legal amount, the courtesy amount, or the expected result. If this re-estimation delivers another result for the subword, so that the newly generated legal amount now agrees with the courtesy amount, we assume that there was an error that has now been corrected. Therefore the check is finally accepted; otherwise it is rejected.

There are many causes that could have led to the first misclassification of the subword by the legal amount recognizer. In each processing step (preprocessing, feature extraction, classification) errors can happen. In our system, the second classifier starts with another preprocessing of the extracted subword. Actually, the considered subword has already been completely preprocessed in the context of the whole legal amount. However in a second round of preprocessing we might get some better results, for example, for the detection of the reference lines or the correction of skew and slant, since we do it on a local level. In Fig. 7 an example is given. For the legal amount *achtundvierzig* (forty eight) the lower baseline could not be placed properly, since the first subword *acht* (eight) was written skewed relative to the other two subwords *und* (and) and *vierzig* (forty). This problem might have caused the wrong classification of this subword as *zwei* (two). In the error localization step the word was declared as a potential error and the system decided to perform an error correction attempt. After another (local) preprocessing step with skewness correction the baseline was placed in a better position and the word was finally correctly recognized as *acht* (eight).

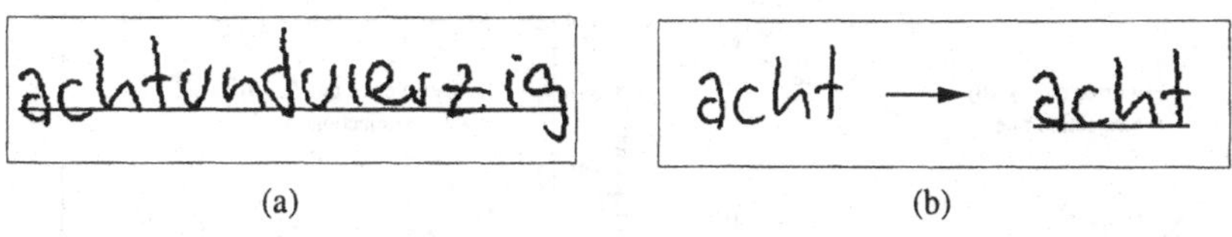

(a) (b)

Fig. 7. The lower baseline for the legal amount was not correctly detected for all subwords (a) which might have led to the recognition error for the first subword *acht* (eight) that was recognized as *zwei* (two). After a local preprocessing (b) with another correction of skewness the baseline was detected properly and the subword was correctly recognized as *acht*.

rank	1	2	3	4	5	10
courtesy amount	79.3%	83.9%	85.7%	86.7%	87.1%	87.7%
legal amount	71.9%	81.3%	84.4%	86.5%	87.5%	88.8%

Table 2. Recognition rates (with zero rejection) of the legal and courtesy amount recognizers on the database used in this work.

5 Experimental Results

For our experiments a test database containing 1500 manually extracted legal and courtesy amounts from real Swiss postal checks was built. In the manual segmentation also the currency characters (for example, *Franken*, *Fr.* or *SFr.*), the cents portion (which is quite rare on Swiss Postal checks), and additional symbols, such as horizontal lines that delimit the amount, were removed.

On this database the individual recognizers for the legal and the courtesy amount achieved the recognition rates presented in Table 2.

We first tested our system with the simple combination strategy described at the beginning of Section 4, where the first L and C ranks are considered. In Fig. 8 (a) the rejection and the error rate for a system with $L = C$ is presented. For $L = C = 1$ (i.e. only the first ranks are considered), our system accepts 58.1% of all checks with an error rate of 0.2%. With more risk, expressed by higher values for L and C, the rejection rate drops while the error rate increases significantly.

If the values for L and C are different, the case where only the first rank of the courtesy amount ($C = 1$) and the best n ranks of the legal amount ($L = n$) are considered is of special interest (Fig. 8 (b)). Here the rejection rate decreases with a higher value for L similar to the previous case, but the error rate does not increase so quickly.

In the two experiments described in the following, we tested the influence of the correction method described in Sections 4.2 and 4.3 on the acceptance and error rates of our system. The difference between the two experiments is the number of ranks of the recognized legal amount (L) that were considered in the combination module. From the results of the courtesy amount recognizer we considered in both experiments only the top rank ($C = 1$).

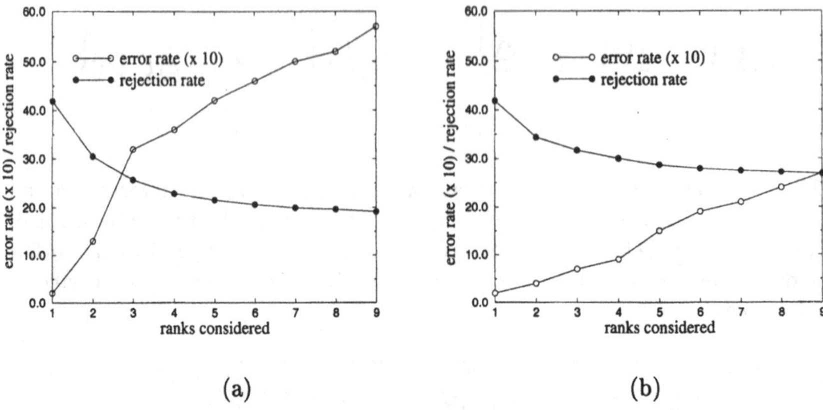

Fig. 8. Recognition rate with different system parameters for the number of ranks considered; (a) $L = C = x$, (b) $C = 1$, $L = x$.

In the first experiment, only the results on the top rank ($L = C = 1$) of each classifier were considered when combining the results (Table 3 (a)). Compared to the system without error correction the acceptance was improved by 7.3% without adding any additional error. In this experiment 251 out of 628 checks underwent correction; 108 of them (43 %) were accepted after reclassification of the localized potential error.

In the second experiment, the top 2 ranks of the legal amount recognizer and the top rank of the courtesy amount recognizer were considered in the combination (Table 3 (b)). With this combination strategy the error rate of the original system was 0.4%. With error correction the improvement in the acceptance rate was 3.2%. Also in this experiment no additional errors were produced, but the improvement was not as high as in the previous experiment.

6 Conclusions

In this paper we presented some key ideas of a check reading system that is currently under development. We focused on the reading of legal amounts and post-processing of the recognition results. For the legal amount recognition we proposed an approach based on Hidden Markov Models. In our system HMMs turned out as an excellent tool, since for German check amounts a segmentation of the legal amount into basic words and their subsequent recognition is very difficult, if not impossible. But also for other languages, where the gaps between subwords are also hard to detect, HMMs' holistic recognition approach is very suitable. In contrast to many other works in this field we didn't use structural features for the description of our words, but the pure bitmap. The bitmap features can be extracted very easily. However, a good normalization by means of preprocessing is required.

Experiment 1: L = C = 1					
	accepted	rejected	error rate	potential errors	
original system	58.1%	41.9%	0.2%	examined	corrected
with error corr.	65.4%	34.6%	0.2%	251	108

(a)

Experiment 2: L = 2 / C = 1					
	accepted	rejected	error rate	potential errors	
original system	65.6%	34.4%	0.4%	examined	corrected
with error corr.	68.8%	31.2%	0.4%	162	47

(b)

Table 3. Rejection and error rate of the system with the new error detection and correction module

For the subtask of translating the legal amount into a digit string, which is needed for the combination of the recognition results, we presented a new, systematic technique based on syntax-directed translation. This method is very flexible and can easily be changed and extended. In our system the translation provides not only the digit string as the translation of the legal amount, but also the corresponding subwords within the legal amount for each digit. This information can be used to localize potential recognition errors in the post-processing of mismatching recognition results.

We finally proposed a new approach for the analysis and correction of detected potential errors. Depending on the combination strategy the rejection rate of the system could be decreased by 17.4%, from 41.9% to 34.6%, or by 9.3%, from 34.4% to 31.2%, respectively, without increasing the error rate. To achieve these improvements only 251 and 162 subwords out of 1500 legal amounts with approximately three subwords each had to be re-estimated in the first and second experiment, respectively. Therefore the overall system throughput doesn't decrease significantly, although the second classifier has a more complex design, and works slower. The proposed architecture for error localization and correction is very general, and can be easily adapted to other check reading systems.

References

1. R. Bippus: 1-Dimensional and Pseudo 2-Dimensional HMMs for the Recognition of German Literal Amounts, *Proc. of the 4th Int. Conference on Document Analysis and Recognition*, Ulm, Germany (1997) 487–490
2. C.Y. Suen, L. Lam, D. Guillevic, N.W. Strathy, M. Cheriet, J.N. Said and R. Fan: Bank Check Processing, *Int. Journal of Imaging Systems and Technology*, Vol. 7 (1996) 392–403
3. S. Impedovo, P.S.P. Wang, H. Bunke (Eds.): Automatic Bankcheck Processing, Special Issue of *Int. Journal of Pattern Recognition and Artificial Intelligence*, Vol. 11, No. 4 and 5 (1997)

4. T. Caesar, J.M. Gloger, E. Mandler: Preprocessing and Feature Extraction for a Handwriting Recognition System, *Proc. of the 2nd Int. Conf. on Document Analysis and Recognition*, Tsukuba, Japan (1993) 408–411
5. H. Bunke, M. Roth, E.G. Schukat-Talamazzini: Off-line Cursive Handwriting Recognition Using Hidden Markov Models, *Pattern Recognition*, Vol. 28, No. 9 (1995) 1399–1413
6. G. Dimauro, S. Impedovo, G. Pirlo and A. Salzo: Automatic Bankcheck Processing: A New Engineered System, in Reference 4, 465–504
7. S. Knerr, V. Anisimov, O. Baret, N. Gorski, D. Price and J.C. Simon: The A2iA Recognition System for Handwritten Checks, *Proc. of Int. Workshop on Document Analysis Systems*, Malvern, Pennsylvania (1996) 431–494
8. J. Makhoul and R. Schwartz and C. LaPre and C. Raphael and I. Bazzi, "Language-Independent and Segmentation-Free Techniques for Optical Character Recognition, *Proc. of Int. Workshop on Document Analysis Systems*, Malvern, Pennsylvania USA (1996) 99–114
9. G. Kaufmann, H. Bunke, T.M. Ha: Recognition of Cursively Handwritten Words Using a Combined Normalization / Perturbation Approach, *Proc. of the 5th Int. Workshop On Frontiers in Handwriting*, University of Essex, England (1996) 17–22
10. L.R. Rabiner, B.H. Juang: An Introduction to Hidden Markov Models, *IEEE ASSP Magazine* (1986) 4–16
11. Thien M. Ha, M. Zimmermann, H. Bunke: Off-line Handwritten Numeral String Recognition by Combining Segmentation-based and Segmentation-free Methods, *Pattern Recognition*, Vol. 31, No. 3 (1997) 257–272
12. G. Kaufmann, H. Bunke: Amount Translation and Error Localization in Check Processing Using Syntax-Directed Translation, *Proc. of Int. Conf. on Pattern Recognition*, Brisbane, Australia (1998) 1530–1534
13. G. Kaufmann, H. Bunke: Error Localization and Correction in Check Processing, *Proc. of Int. Conf. on Frontiers in Handwriting Recognition VI*, Taeduck, Korea (1998) 77–87

A Fast Japanese Word Extraction with Classification to Similarly-Shaped Character Categories and Morphological Analysis

Masaharu Ozaki[1] and Katsuhiko Itonori[2]

[1] Development Center for IT Business
[2] Office Document Products Group
Fuji Xerox Co., Ltd
430 Sakai, Nakai-machi
Ashigara-kami-gun, Kanagawa
259-0157 JAPAN
ozaki@rsl.crl.fujixerox.co.jp[1]
itonori@netg.ksp.fujixerox.co.jp[2]

Abstract. A fast word extraction technique from Japanese document images is described. It classifies each character image not into characters but into categories consisting of similarly shaped characters. Morphological analysis is performed on the sequence of the categories to obtain word candidates. Detailed classification is performed on character images that cannot be identified as single characters. Multi-template methodology and hierarchical classification is combined to make the classifier accurate and fast with low dimensional vectors. As a result of the experiments for the learning samples, the accuracy of classification was 99.3% and the speed was eight times faster than traditional Japanese OCRs. As experimental results for the test samples made from forty newspaper articles, the classification speed is still eight times faster. The morphological analysis greatly decreased character candidates with the fact that 85% of characters were identified as single characters on the newspaper article images.

1 Introduction

Information retrieval from large document image collections is becoming realistic. Fast and accurate word extraction, not character extraction, is required to construct retrieval index. This requirement has led people to develop word recognition techniques. Chen et al. showed a word spotting technique that utilizes upper and lower contour shape of word images [1]. Reiner et al. showed that if characters are classified into a small number of categories based on the characters' geometric size and position, the category sequence can be identified as a single word or a few word candidates [2]. However, these word extraction techniques cannot be directly applied to Japanese text because there is no word separation. Speed and accuracy of Japanese OCRs are not sufficient to be practically used because Japanese has more than 3,000 characters, in common use, including similarly shaped ones. In many studies, such as [3], a word dictionary and morphological analysis are used in post-processing of Japanese OCRs. They improve the accuracy but increase the computational cost. A few studies suggest that linguistic information can be used not only for improvement of accuracy but also for reduction of computational cost. Umeda showed that, for 91% of Japanese words, a character in a word can be chosen correctly from eight candidates if the other characters of the word are known [4]. Kigo showed that anticipation of possible characters from previously recognized ones reduces the computational cost of OCR [5]. These studies suggest that each character image is to be matched not against all of the Japanese characters but smaller number of characters hypothesized from linguistic information.

Being inspired by the techniques shown above, we propose a fast Japanese word extraction technique that is suitable for constructing a word index in document image retrieval systems which handle a large number of document images. The processing model is briefly illustrated in fig.1, being compared with the traditional word extraction process model using an OCR.

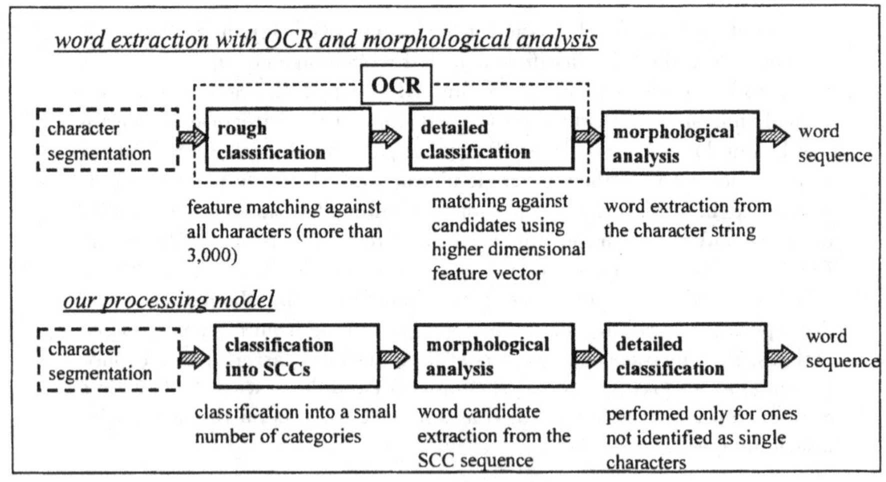

Fig. 1. processing model

Japanese OCRs usually adopt multi-stage classification in order to reduce computational cost. In this classification model, first, each character image is segmented and is sent to the first stage classifier. The first stage classifier picks up candidate characters which are similar to the target character image by feature matching with low dimensional feature vectors. This first stage classification is denoted as rough classification. The consecutive stage classifiers reduce the number of the candidates by feature matching against the candidates with higher dimensional vectors or by applying classification techniques whose computational cost is very high. The last stage classifier picks up the best one from the candidates. In this model, even though it uses low-dimensional feature vectors, the rough classification has to perform the feature matching against all characters in the character set. This process requires much computational cost because the character set usually consists of more than 3,000 characters. Word extraction is done by applying morphological analysis to the recognized characters.

Our model consists of three steps: classification of character images into similarly shaped character categories (denoted as *SCC*s), morphological analysis (denoted as *MA*) of the SCC sequence, and the detailed classification of the images that cannot be identified as single characters. On the first step, each segmented character image is classified into SCCs. On the second step, the MA is performed on the sequence of SCCs. Entries in the word dictionary of the MA are replaced by corresponding SCC representative characters beforehand. Since the MA finds sequences of words that are linguistically correct, the number of the character candidates for SCCs should be reduced. On the third step, character images that cannot be identified as single characters through the first two steps are classified into one of its candidate characters with higher dimensional feature vectors. The feature vector is matched against the candidates' representative vectors and the best-matched character is chosen. Word candidates which do not correspond to the identified characters are eliminated. Finally, the process outputs word sequence extracted from the text image.

This model has some clear advantages from the viewpoint of computational cost. First, classification into SCCs does not require high dimensional feature vectors because similarly shaped characters are merged into SCCs already. Second, the number of character candidates for each of the obtained SCCs can be reduced by the MA. Since computational cost of the MA is much lower than image processing, this also contributes to reduce the computational cost. Third, for characters which are identified as single characters, not only distance calculation but also calculation of the feature vectors can be skipped in the detailed classification, both of which are mandatory for every character image in the traditional OCR processing model.

In the following sections, we describe this technique in more detail. In section 2, construction of the classifier is described. In section 3, the MA and the detailed classification are described. Experimental results are shown in section 4 and we discuss to make this technique more robust in section 5.

2 Construction of Classifier

2.1 Construction of Similarly-Shaped Character Categories

SCCs are constructed by clustering of the character representative vectors. Each character representative vector is calculated as an average vector of its learning samples. We performed an agglomerative hierarchical clustering first on the representative vectors and then performed an iterative optimization of the clusters based on the criteria of minimum sum-of-squared-error [6].

The agglomerative hierarchical clustering is a popular clustering technique. Initially, the process starts with clusters, each of which includes one sample to be clustered. The cluster center is identical to the sample. In our case, the samples to be clustered are representative vectors of characters. Then, among all possible pairs of the clusters, one which has the smallest distance is merged. The center of the merged cluster is calculated as an average vector of the merged samples. This process repeats until the number of clusters becomes the desired one. There are several calculation methods for distance between clusters. We used Euclidean distance between cluster centers.

The iterative optimization is performed by moving samples so that the sum of squared distances between each sample and its cluster center is reduced. In each iteration, the process picks up an arbitrary sample and calculates the variance of the sum of squared distances when it is moved to another cluster. If the process finds some moves can reduce the sum of squared distances, it moves the sample picked up to a cluster that gives the smallest sum. This process repeats until no move can reduce the sum of squared distances.

Fig.2 shows a part of the constructed SCCs used in our experiments. For each constructed SCC, its representative vector is set with an average vector of all learning samples of the characters merged into the SCC.

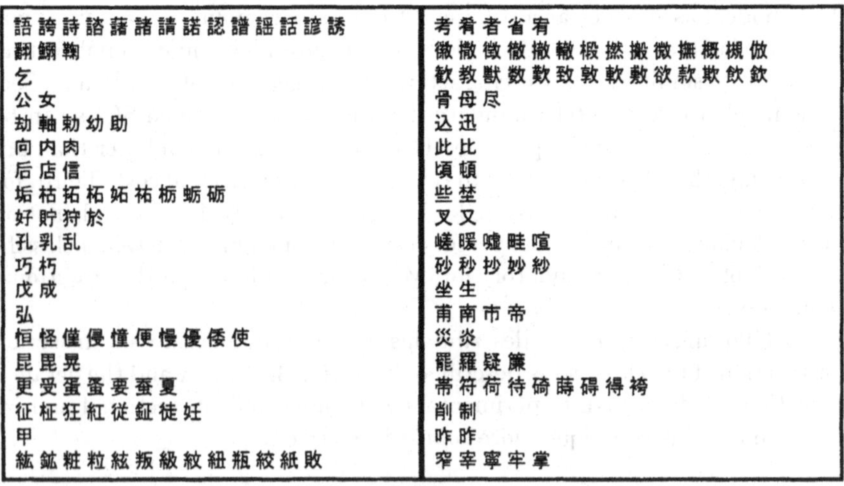

Fig. 2. a part of SCCs. Each horizontal character sequence forms an SCC.

In our experiments, we used peripheral feature vector [7] in the construction of the SCCs and the classification. The feature vector has 64 dimensions. Since similarly shaped characters are merged into the SCCs, we assume that this low dimensional feature vector sufficiently works for the classification into SCCs.

2.2 Dividing Categories

Since SCCs form wider sample distribution area in the feature space than the characters do, misclassification is more likely to occur in feature vectors locating closely to the boundary of the distribution area. To avoid this type of misclassification, we introduced a "multi-template method". The objective of the method is to improve the accuracy of the minimum distance classifier by providing multiple representative vectors for a category having a wide sample distribution. Fig.3 shows effect of the method in the two-dimensional feature space. You can see that misclassification caused by wide sample distributions can be improved by providing multiple representative vectors.

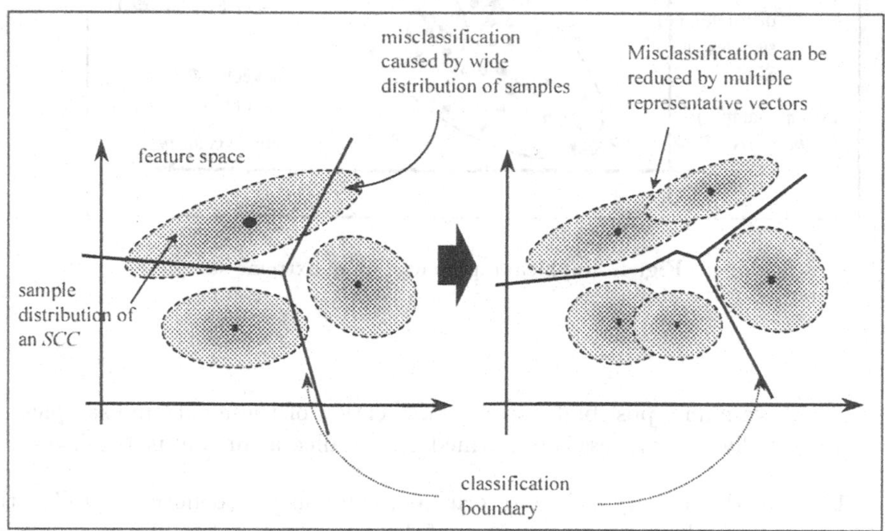

Fig. 3. effect of the multi-template method

In order to obtain multiple representative vectors, we adopt a technique proposed by Omachi et al. [8]. It divides categories having a high possibility of misclassification using principal component analysis (denoted as *PCA*). It approximates the boundary of the distribution area with a multi-dimensional ellipse whose axis directions are principal component vectors and axis lengths are proportional to the principal component eigen values. First, extreme samples are calculated, which are hypothesized samples located on the cross points of the ellipse and their axes. They are calculated with Eq. 1, where $\mathbf{m}$ is the representative vector of the category, $\mathbf{\Phi}_i$ and λ_i are the $i-th$ unit principal component vector and principal component eigen value respectively, and a is a constant value that represents how large we assume the distribution area. Since it is guaranteed from the definition of PCA that there is no covariance among the axes, if we assume the normal distribution of the samples projected on an axis, $a = 3.5$ means more than 99.99% of the samples must exist between the extreme samples. In Fig.4, the meaning of the equation is illustrated.

$$\mathbf{p}_i = \mathbf{m} \pm a\sqrt{\lambda_i}\mathbf{\Phi}_i \tag{1}$$

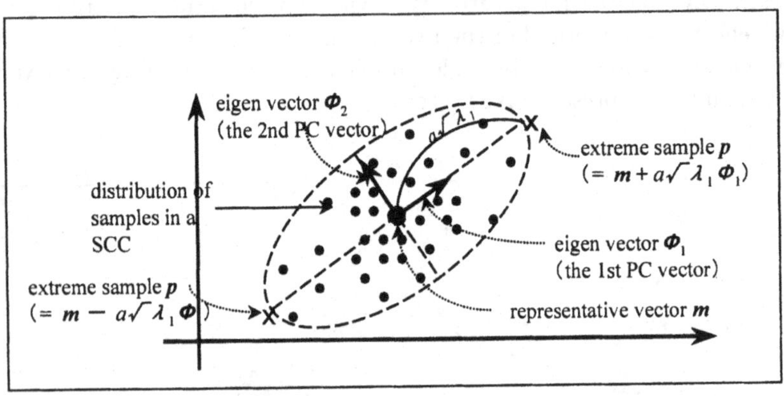

Fig. 4. graphical representation of extreme samples

By examining possibility of misclassification of these extreme samples, the category division process is performed. Its detailed algorithm is as follows:

1. For each category, calculate principal components (denoted as PCs), that is, eigen value and eigen vectors of the covariance matrix obtained from the samples in the category. Keep upper k PCs.
2. Calculate extreme samples for each of the PCs with the Eq. 1.
3. Perform minimum distance classification on all the extreme samples.
4. If an extreme sample is misclassified, keep its corresponding PC as misclassified PC. If no sample is misclassified, end the process.
5. Select a PC that has the largest eigen value from the misclassified ones.
6. Divide the category using k-mean clustering algorithm. Choose samples that are the nearest to the two extreme samples as initial cluster centers for the clustering. Perform PCA on each divided category (denoted as $DSCC$) and calculate its extreme samples. Go back to step 3.

The reason upper k PCs are kept at the step 1 is that the misclassification is more likely to occur for their extreme samples because upper PCs are located further from the center of ellipse than the others. The reason the k-mean clustering algorithm is used is that it tends to gather samples into groups, each of which includes samples near the initial cluster centers. This tendency is useful because the category to be divided should separate along the direction of the PC vector. In the case where the category to be divided has been already divided, all samples of the corresponding SCC are gathered and are clustered again. In this case, in addition to initial cluster centers picked up at the step 6 in the algorithm, the representative vectors of the already divided DSCCs are used as initial cluster centers for k-mean clustering algorithm.

2.3 Reclustering the Divided Categories

The category division process gives good accuracy but the computational cost increases because some SCCs have multiple representative vectors. In order to reduce the number of the distance calculations, we introduced a hierarchical classification technique called "ε-component method" proposed by Ito et al. [9]. Its basic idea is as follows. Clustering is performed on the DSCCs again and their representative vectors are calculated as an average vector of all samples in the reclustered DSCCs (denoted as $RSCC$s). After the reclustering, minimum distance classification into the RSCCs is performed on all learning samples. If misclassification occurs for a sample, the DSCC to which the sample belongs is added to the RSCC to which the sample is misclassified. In this way, we have a hierarchical classification dictionary consisting of the RSCCs and the DSCCs.

Fig.5 illustrates the dictionary construction process and the classification process. In the figure, a SCC consisting of "口" and "四" is divided into three DSCCs and another SCC consisting of "開", "閉" and "聞" is divided into two. These DSCCs are reclustered into two RSCCs. The solid lines between the DSCCs and the RSCCs mean that the DSCCs are merged into the RSCCs through the clustering, and the dashed lines mean that the DSCCs are added to the RSCCs since some samples are misclassified.

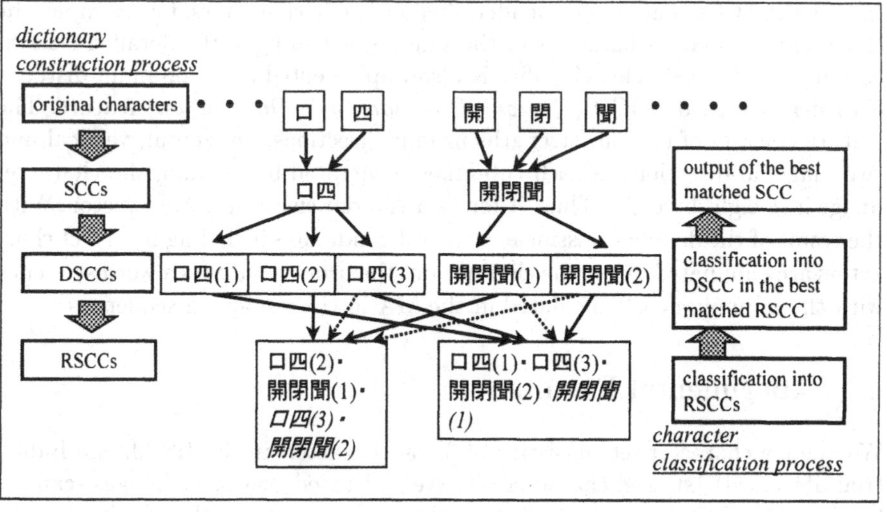

Fig. 5. dictionary construction process and classification process

The classification is performed as follows. First, minimum distance classification of the target character image into the RSCCs is performed and then minimum distance classification into one of the DSCCs in the best-matched RSCC is performed again. Finally, the classifier outputs the SCC correspondent to the best-matched DSCC.

3 Morphological Analysis and Detailed Classification

JUMAN [10], Japanese morphological analysis software, is used in our experimental system. It is based on the minimum cost algorithm. The algorithm examines possible word sequences within allowed cost and outputs all the obtained sequences. The cost is defined for each part of speech (denoted as *POS*) and every possible connection between the POSs. In order to use JUMAN in our experimental system, we replaced all word entries in the MA dictionary with their correspondent SCC representative characters. An arbitrary character in each SCC is chosen for its representative character. A new field is added to the entry to preserve the correspondent actual words. The text unit to be processed by the MA is a part of text separated by the beginning and the end of the text, and punctuation marks. These punctuation marks are obviously word separation marks and they are easily extracted from images with their size and position. After the analysis of the text unit, we get multiple word paths for the SCC sequence. Then, the system collects character candidates for each SCC representative character from the word candidates. Fig.6 shows an example of the MA result. A sequence of the SCC representative characters is obtained in the classification. The morphological analysis is performed on the SCC sequence. In the result of the MA, the first column shows word positions in the text, the second column shows segmented SCC sequences as words, the third column shows actual words, and the fourth and fifth column show their POSs.

For the SCCs that cannot be identified as single characters, for example, the third and the fourth characters of the sample text in fig.6, the detailed classification is performed. This classifier is also implemented as a minimum distance classifier. We used CDCD (*Contour Direction Code Distribution*) feature. The feature consists of contour strengths in four directions, horizontal, vertical and two diagonal directions in each sub-image generated by dividing the character image into eight by eight. Thus, it forms a 256-dimensional feature vector. With the result of the detailed classification, word candidates including incorrect characters are eliminated. After the elimination, the process outputs a word sequence with the minimum cost calculated in the MA in the remaining sequences.

4 Experimental Results

We made a character set consisting of 3,454 characters in the JIS (Japan Industrial Standard) 1st level character set. We generated gray scale images scanned from paper printed in eight fonts to make the learning samples. Each gray image and its blurred one are binarized with different thresholding values. Total

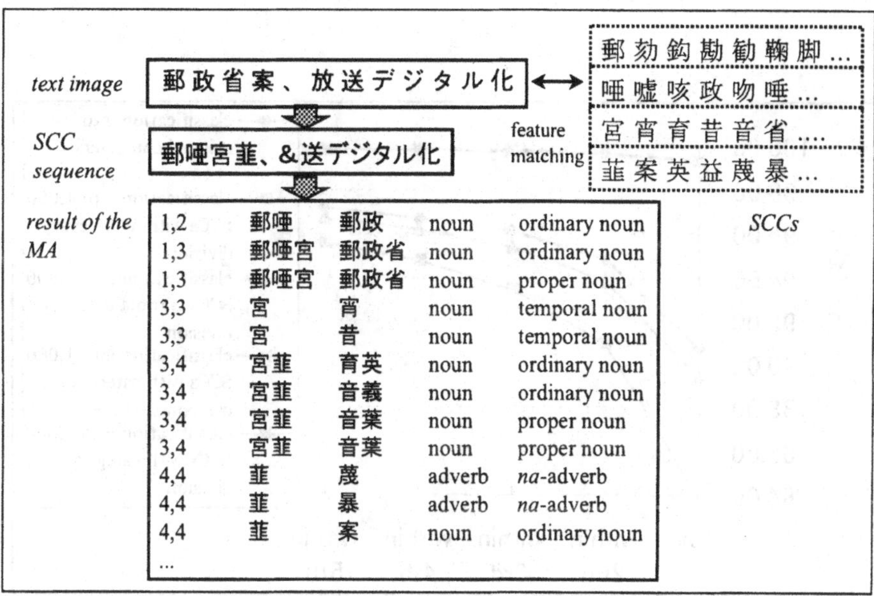

Fig. 6. an example of the word extraction

number of the learning samples is 924,077, and each character has 268 samples on average. We constructed 1,000 and 2,000 SCCs to see their difference. For each of them, we performed the category division process with setting 3.5 for the constant a in the Eq.1 and 3 for k, the number of PCs to be kept. The reclustering process was performed with different numbers of RSCCs. Sample images of actual text were printed with fonts different from ones used for the learning samples. Forty *Nikkei* newspaper articles published in 1994 were used to make the images. The images were printed in a fixed pitch so that no character segmentation error occurred.

First, we examined effect of the category division for accuracy improvement. Fig.7 shows cumulative classification accuracy. It shows the classification accuracy into original character set, and the classification accuracy into SCCs with and without the category division. Table 1 shows the comparison of their top choice accuracy. As you can see, the classification accuracy into SCCs without the category division was not so good as one into the original character set. However, the accuracy of the classification into SCCs with the category division were more than 99% in both of 1,000 and 2,000 SCCs. Note that the both results are overlapped in the graph.

To examine the computational cost, we measured two numbers of the distance calculations while the learning samples are classified: K_m and K_r, the maximum number and the average number of distance calculations respectively. Fig.8 shows the relations of the two numbers with different number of the RSCCs (denoted

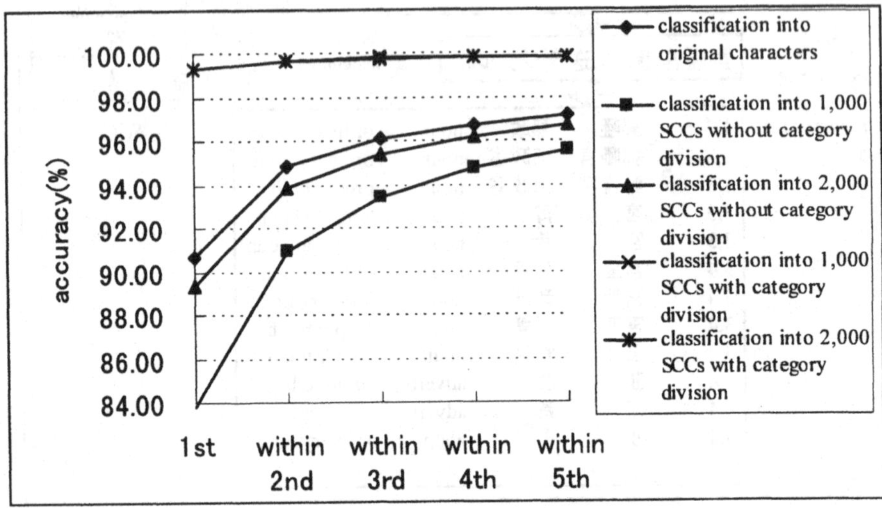

Fig. 7. cumulative accuracy of the classification

Table 1. accuracy of classification for the learning samples

classification target	*category division*	*accuracy(%)*
original characters (3,454)	-	90.7
1,000 SCCs	No	83.8
	Yes	99.3
2,000 SCCs	No	89.4
	Yes	99.3

as N). Focusing on K_r, only 427 distance calculations were required at $N = 200$ for the 1,000 SCCs. This means that the classification was 8 times faster than the rough classification in the OCRs that needs to perform distance calculation 3,454 times. In the 2,000 SCC case, it is performed 7.7 times faster. K_m for the 1,000 SCC was 918 and K_m for the 2,000 SCCs was 1,061 at $N = 200$. They show that the classification was 3 times faster even in the worst case.

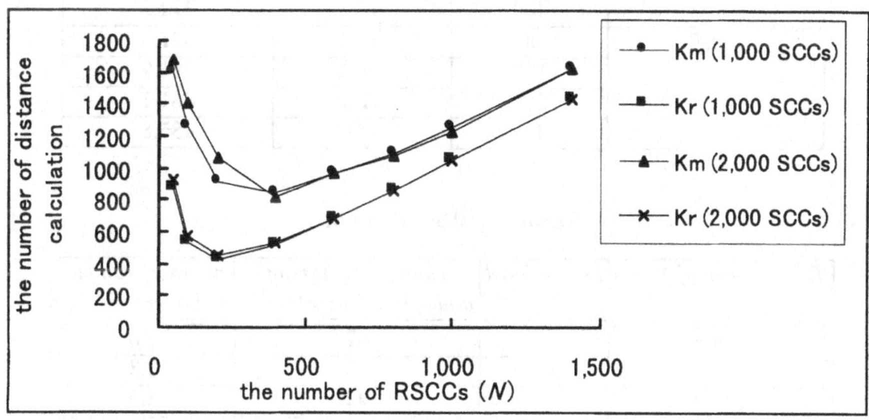

Fig. 8. the number of distance calculations with different numbers of RSCCs

Table 2 shows the result of the accuracy of classification into SCCs for characters on sample text images. The difference between the results obtained with 1,000 and 2,000 SCCs was quite small. The best accuracy 97.6% is obtained at $N = 100$ for 2,000 SCCs. If $N = 100$ is chosen for the best accuracy, the number of distance calculations was 399.3 for 1,000 SCCs and 396.9 for 2,000 SCCs. They show that the classification was performed 8 times faster than the rough classification in the OCRs.

Table 3 shows percentage of character images on the sample text images that have multiple candidates and their average number of the candidates at $N = 100$. If the MA is not applied, 44% of the characters have to be classified into one out of 3.2 character in the 2,000 SCC case. Applying the MA, only 15% of the characters have to be classified into one out of 2.8 character in the 2,000 SCC case. The similar result was seen in the 1,000 SCC case. These results show that the MA greatly decreased character candidates.

The best accuracy of word extraction was 93.3% for the 1,000 SCC case and 93.8% for 2,000 SCC case at $N = 100$. These results were obtained by comparing the extracted words with the ones extracted with the MA from the original text. Thus, this ground truth data may include incorrect words from the human interpretation standpoint. The major reason of the errors was misclassification into SCCs. However, even if the correct SCC sequence is obtained, words that

Table 2. accuracy of classification and average number of distance calculations for sample text images

the number of SCCs	*the number of RSCCs (N)*	*accuracy of classification(%)*	*average number of distance calculation*
1,000	50	97.3	634.1
	100	97.4	399.3
	200	96.7	356.0
	400	97.2	474.3
2,000	50	97.5	621.3
	100	97.6	396.9
	200	97.4	361.1
	400	97.6	485.8

Table 3. effect of the MA

The number of SCCs	*MA applied*	*characters having multiple candidates(%)*	*average number of the candidates*
1,000	No	67	5.0
	Yes	35	3.8
2,000	No	44	3.2
	Yes	15	2.8

are not stored in the MA dictionary cannot be extracted. We did not exclude such errors in the evaluation. Most of the undefined words were ones consisting of *Katakana* characters. Katakana characters are mainly used to represent foreign words phonetically in Japanese. Handling those words is crucial because they are often used as keywords in document retrieval. In addition, even for defined Katakana words, we observed one misinterpretation in the test images. The word "コンパック", which means "Compaq" that is not in the dictionary, was matched with two words in the dictionary, "コンパ" (a drinking party) and "ツタ" (ivy).

5 Discussion

The difference between 1,000 and 2,000 SCCs was very small in both the accuracy of classification and the computational cost. Generally, either overlaps among the sample distribution areas or crossing classification boundary of sample distributions causes misclassification in a minimum distance classifier. The category division process reduces the misclassification caused by the latter reason. For the former reason, we suppose that characters whose sample distributions are overlapped are merged sufficiently into 2,000 SCCs and it would not be necessary to make the number of SCCs smaller. The larger number of SCCs gives us greater advantages in the consecutive morphological analysis and the detailed classification because the possibility of multiple words or character candidates is reduced.

We have some ideas to improve classification accuracy. One of the reasons of the misclassification is that SCCs are not sufficiently divided. In the category division process, DSCCs with a small number of samples are not further divided because PCA cannot be applied to the categories that have the small number of samples. If we have more samples, such categories will be divided into more and the accuracy will become higher. Another reason is that, during the classification, the nearest RSCC to the target character's feature vector does not include its nearest DSCC. In the classification dictionary construction process, DSCCs are included in more than one RSCCs if their samples are misclassified. This guarantees that only the learning samples are correctly classified into RSCCs. In order to improve the classification accuracy, DSCCs should be added to more RSCCs. Therefore, during the dictionary construction process, the DSCC should be added not only to the RSCC to which the sample is misclassified but also to RSCCs whose representative vectors are located close to the misclassified RSCC.

Handling Katakana words is one of the remaining issues. To extract Katakana words accurately, the system should identify a subsequence of the SCC that possibly forms a Katakana word without consulting the dictionary and produce a consistent interpretation of the text.

6 Conclusion

A fast word extraction technique from Japanese document images is proposed. Experimental results show that the classification into SCCs is performed 8 times faster than the rough classification in traditional OCRs with 99.3% accuracy for the learning samples and 97.6% for the actual text images. The morphological analysis greatly decreased character candidates with the fact that 85% of characters on the sample text images were identified as single characters on the newspaper article images. Future works include improvement of the accuracy of classification, and handling of undefined words, in particular, Katakana words.

References

1. Chen, F., et al.: Detecting and Locating Partially Specified Keywords in Scanned Images using Hidden Markov Models, in Proc. of ICDAR93, Tsukuba, Japan, 1993
2. Reiner, J. C., et al.: Document Reconstruction: A Thousand Words from One Picture, in Proc. of SDAIR'95, 1995
3. Kise, K., et al.: A Method of Post-Processing for Character Recognition Based on Syntactic and Semantic Analysis of Sentences, in Trans, of IEICE, Vol. J77-D-II No.11, pp. 2199-2209, 1994 (in Japanese)
4. Umeda, M.: Character Determination Abilities in a Character Recognition System Using Word Dictionary, in Trans. of IEICE, Vol. J72-D-II No. 1, pp. 22-31, 1989 (in Japanese)
5. Kigo, K.: Improving Speed of Japanese OCR through Linguistic Preprocessing, in Proc. of ICDAR93, Tsukuba, Japan, 1993

6. Duda, R. O., and Hart, P. E.: Pattern Classification and Scene Analysis, Wiley-Interscience, 1973
7. Umeda et al.: Classification of Printed Text in Multiple Fonts with Peripheral Feature, in Technical Report of IEICE, PRL78-4, 1978 (in Japanese)
8. Omachi, S., et al.: An Algorithm for Construction of Multi-Template Dictionary for Character Recognition Considering Between-Class Variation, in Trans. of IEICE, Vol.J79-D-II, No. 9, pp. 1525-1533, 1996 (in Japanese)
9. Ito, A., et al.: A Method for Composing the Extended Dictionary in which the Same Character is Involved in the Different Clusters for a Hierarchical Chinese Characters Recognition System, in Trans. of IEICE, Vol. J78-D-II, No. 6, pp. 896-905, 1995 (in Japanese)
10. JUMAN (a User-Extensible Morphological Analyzer for Japanese), `http://www-lab25.kuee.kyoto-u.ac.jp/nl-resource/juman.html`

A Layout-Free Method for Extracting Elements from Document Images

Tsukasa Kochi, Takashi Saitoh

Information and Communication Research and Development Center
32 Research Group, RICOH COMPANY,LTD.
3-2-3 Shinyokohama, Kouhoku-ku, Yokohama-shi, Kanagawa 222-8530, Japan
{kochi, saitoh}@ic.rdc.ricoh.co.jp

Abstract. SGML is a language for defining the layout structure of a document. Various attempts at generating SGML from a document image have not been successful. We focus on extracting some of the important layout elements by using flexible matching strategy and easy model generation. Our proposed approach treats each extracted element as it were independent. Some segmented areas like "title" or "author" are defined locally making the system robust, able to withstand shifting and noise. The system is also easy to operate. Since the system is not full automatic, we need to supply typical models of each component. Our GUI presents the attributes of each segmented area as well as the original bit map images. The color-coded attributes help us to easily edit the extracted component. In experiments with 288 pages of test images, the proposed method is shown to be 95.6% correct for a wide range of documents. By using 145 pages of documents as a learning set, the system recognized 99.2% of feature sets from 148 various types of unknown documents.

1 Introduction

1.1 Background

The increasing use of the Internet and the Intranet has created the need to convert paper documents into digital data so that they can easily be accessed with computer networks. Recently many commercial document management systems have been implemented in offices and libraries. The effective use of systems in office workflow has become very important. When we input documents from a scanner in digital form into such document management systems, we usually give them a file name like `file00xx` and store them in folders. Although it is usual to store original images with OCR text, documents from OCR consist of simple strings of characters and therefore it is difficult to automatically extract important elements from the document, such as title, author, or date of the document.

The most successful system in this field is the business form processing system. Standard business form processing systems first identify the type of input forms and then extract elements from them based on simple comparison of location of their frame lines and elements with a registered model [1] [2]. Although Aoki and Okada [3] presented a form processing system that does not require line properties, it assumes that the extracted elements are positioned in frames. The limitations of business form processing systems are as follows.

1. They can only be used for business forms with distinct frame lines,
2. A limited amount of variation is allowed for the locations of elements.

There have been various attempts to change document images into SGML documents. For example [4] [5] [6] the contents of a document are recognized by referring to models that are usually described by a script language that includes a rule for the relative element arrangement and knowledge of its layout features. Using this knowledge and the OCR results, they tried to structure the whole document, for example Lin [8] presented the logical structure analysis of book document images that generates an SGML document using contents information. The present systems for document image analysis also have some fundamental problems that cannot be avoided.

3. The task of creating models from sample documents requires users to take a lot of time. Walischewski [7] provided an automatic method for creating models but it requires a large number of learning images to improve the model accuracy.
4. One error causes other errors in understanding the document structure because models have been defined by complex structures of document elements depending on each other. Walischewski [7] and Tang [9] had developed a model with attributed directed graph of the document layout.

These problems have made it difficult to use document structure analysis systems for a wide range of documents.

1.2 Summary of the work

This paper addresses automatic element extraction for scanned documents by using layout feature matching. The design goals of this work are to solve the problems of the present systems for document image analysis:

1. The proposed method is robust against shifting or noise.
2. The proposed system can be easily used for various types of document.

To realize our design goals, this work provides a user-friendly interface and a simple method for creating models for flexible matching to extract documentary elements. Since the proposed method can extract important elements, from a practical point of view, our results can directly support the functions of document maintenance system such as keyword retrieval and title registration. As a result, the proposed method can be used for any type of document by changing the models for every type of document but the basic algorithm for extracting elements does not have to be changed.

Figure 1 shows an overview of the system operation. The system consists of three modules, the details of which are described in the following and in Figure 1.

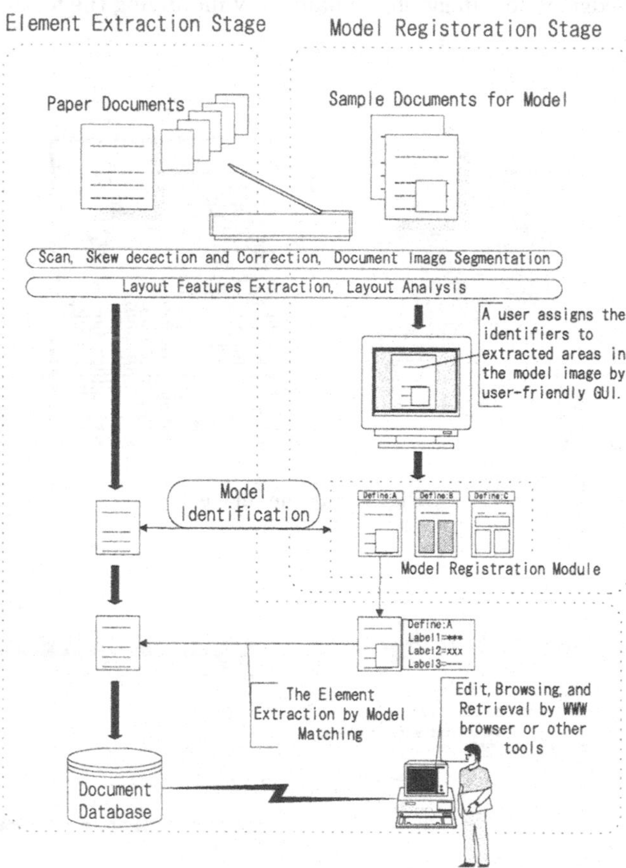

Fig. 1. Overview of system operation

1. **Feature Extraction** The system segments the digitized image of the document before model construction and the element extraction stages.
2. **Model Construction and Registration** A user must assign identifiers to the extracted areas with a GUI and then store the model registration module with them. The model construction procedure concludes with these steps.
3. **Element Extraction** The input data for this module are the segmented images and models. If the model registration has more than one model, the system identifies the input image with the most suitable model in the

model registration module. Then, the system tries to extract elements from the image of the document referring to the model defined by the layout features of each element. Finally, the system outputs the candidate lines of character strings, resulting from the element extraction from the image to the document filing system database. If necessary, the system can improve its knowledge of documents by dynamically modifying the features and their relations.

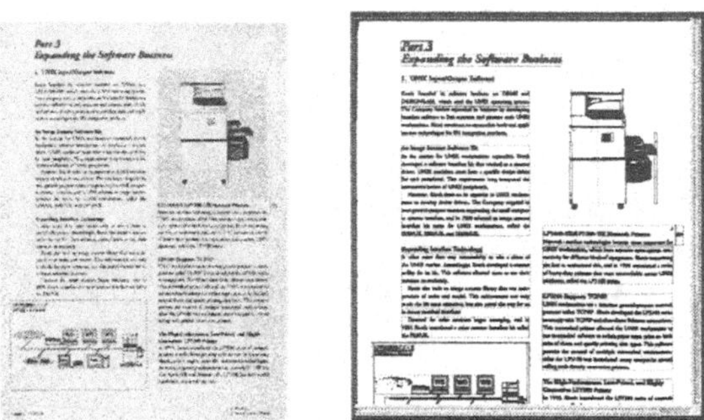

Fig. 2. Sample image

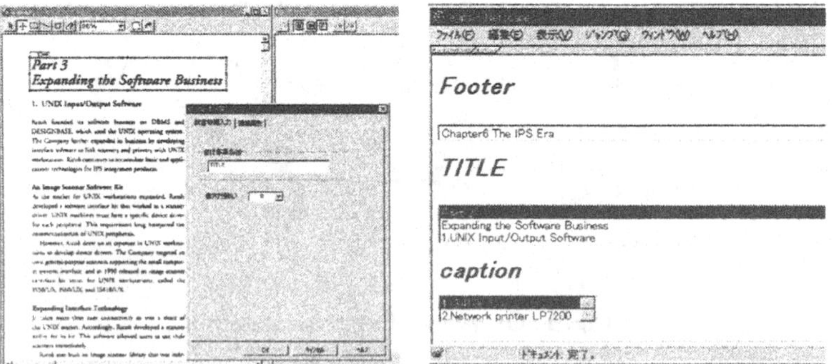

Figure 3: GUI for creating a model Figure 4: Result of extracting

Since the system has too many components to be shown in detail in this paper, we focus on feature extraction, model construction, and element extraction. This paper is organized as follows. Section 2 presents the layout features of document images. Section 3 defines the schema for constructing models and their specifications. Section 4 gives the strategies used in element extraction. Section

5 describes the outline of the learning system. Section 6 shows the experimental results. Section 7 concludes the paper.

2 Feature Extraction

The feature extraction module follows the document segmentation process. The document image is segmented into area blocks containing lines and character blocks. Saitoh's procedure [10] is used for this purpose. After segmentation, the font type is determined for each line of characters. Hull's procedure [11] is used for the font recognition.

The layout features of the images are obtained by using these procedures. The features have three components, (i) page feature, (ii) area feature, and (iii) line feature. Examples of page features are printed page size, number of areas, and line direction. We use well-known layout features as area and line features such as coordinates, character size, font, and indent. The details of the method for extracting these layout features are skipped because these features are extracted easily by any other well known page segmentation method.

3 Model Construction

In order to provide a user-friendly method for creating models for extracting elements, the models should be structured to be as simple as possible. Our model mainly consists of two parts: the first part is the page data for the whole page image, and the second is the list structure of the segmented area of the document. Each area includes lines, and also each line includes characters.

If we make a model for extracting the title of the page shown in Figure 2, we need only assign title area to the identifier `'TITLE'` by using the GUI shown in Figure 3. Table 1 presents the elements definitions in this case.

Table 1. Elements definition

Name	coordinates	Size	Font	Max	···
`'TITLE'`	(415, 303, 1896, 416)	112	1	-1	···
`'Footer'`	(135, 4103, 484, 4114)	40	0	1	···
`'caption'`	(2491, 4059, 2904, 4148)	40	0	1	···

3.1 Example of a Model

Figure 5 shows an example of a model whose element definition is shown in Table 1. The two lines from the top of Figure 5 define the page data on the model document. The list structure for the areas begins at the third line. The third line gives the area data that define the extracted element named `'Footer'`.

The next line gives data of the element. The other extracted elements, '`caption`' and '`TITLE`' are given in a similar way.


```
<!DOCTYPE page SAMPLE >
<page number=1 image=IMAGE width=3296 height=4677 num_area=36 line_dir=0>
<area id=0 kd=4 label="Footer" max=1 nline=1 xs=135 ys=4103 xe=484 ye=4144 sz=40 ls=0 font=0 column=0 cp=9>
<line num=0 len=13 cp=6 lp=-1 sz=27 xs=139 ys=4106 xe=482 ye=4143>Chapter6 The IPS Era</line>
</area>
<area id=1 kd=16 label="caption" max=1 nline=2 xs=2491 ys=4059 xe=2904 ye=4148 sz=40 ls=0 font=0 column=0 cp=4>
<line num=1 len=7 cp=7 lp=-1 sz=27 xs=2497 ys=4063 xe=2687 ye=4090>1. IS4100/UX</line>
<line num=2 len=19 cp=3 lp=57 sz=28 xs=2492 ys=4109 xe=2900 ye=4147>2. Network printer LP7200</line>
</area>
<area id=2 kd=16 label="" max=-1 nline=1 xs=415 ys=191 xe=700 ye=276 sz=80 ls=0 font=0 column=0 cp=9>
<line num=3 len=5 cp=7 lp=-1 sz=76 xs=419 ys=195 xe=697 ye=273>Part3</line>
</area>
<area id=3 kd=16 label="TITLE" max=-1 nline=1 xs=415 ys=303 xe=1896 ye=416 sz=112 ls=0 font=1 column=22 cp=10>
<line num=4 len=16 cp=7 lp=-1 sz=108 xs=418 ys=305 xe=1894 ye=413>Expanding the software Business</line>
</area>
```


Figure 5: Elements definition

3.2 Simple Model

Our models have only the descriptions of the layout features. They do not contain neither rules nor relations among elements. Other known methods can recognize the logical document structure by using a rule-base. However rule construction requires users to follow a very complex set of procedures to apply the rule to a wide range of documents.

In Figure 5, the extracted elements are defined in the 3rd, 6th, and 13th line. It is clear that our model has a simple structure for expressing document layout information because each definition line has simple options for the layout features of the area, such as `id=N`, `kd=N`, `label='name'`, `max=N` , etc. The simple structure of a model would cause no side effects among the nearby elements. Furthermore, by using computer learning methods and testing a couple numbers of sample images, the system can dynamically improve its performance. This learning system is described in Section 5.

4 Element Extraction

In this section, the main algorithm for extracting elements will be described. The input data for this module are the results from document segmentation module and a suitable model for the input document. The output data of this module are candidates of extracted element par lines. How to use the extracted candidates basically depends on the end-users, so the output candidates are simply stored in HTML form in this module.

4.1 Steps of Extracting Elements

As shown in Figure 6, as mentioned before, a plurality of the models is generated for various types of documents. In step 1, a new document is input, and the input document image is divided into areas, then predetermined layout features are extracted. In step 3, the type of input document is detected and the suitable model for the input document is selected. In step 4 through step 8, candidates sentences corresponding to each element are extracted according to the model. Figure 7 shows the idea for model matching based on layout features. An extraction error occurring in an element would not influence other element extractions. These steps show that elements are extracted gradually from areas to lines. This strategy has two advantages. One is that it enables effective thresholds, and the other advantage is that the system is robust against fatal errors in the document segmentation module. For example, illegal composition or division of segmented lines. If the system requires higher accuracy, the candidates for lines are sorted again according to the regularity of an element arrangement in a document.

Finally the output are stored in HTML form. Figure 4 shows the extracting results.

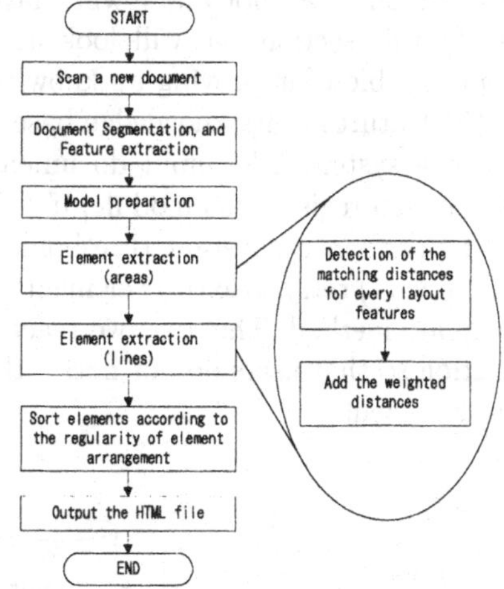

Figure 6: Flow of element extraction

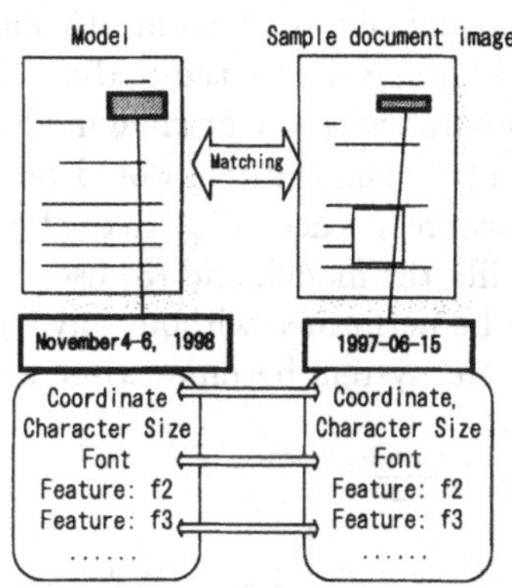

Figure 7: Idea of the model matching

4.2 Concrete Matching Strategy

Here the concrete strategy on the element matching is presented referring to Figure 7. This figure illustrates the retrieval of a segmented area from the input document image, corresponding to the DATE field, "November 4-6, 1998", in the model. The layout features in this figure: location, character size, and font type are automatically extracted with general segmentation methods. The DATE field in the left hand is matched with every segmented sentence in the right hand document in order to determine the distance. The distance s_{e_i} for an element e_i is brought through Mahalanobis distance of the features:

$$d_{e_i}^2 = \sum \frac{|f_i|^2}{v_i}$$

where $|f_i|$ denotes the matching distance for each layout feature and v_i denotes the variance to denote a proper weight for each layout feature.

Although this method can recognize logical elements in a document accurately, the system does not use linguistic information from OCR. Thus extraction costs are low, and moreover we can achieve a high accuracy even if we do not know the character direction or what language are using, because there is no need to recognize errors in the OCR. We expect that the system will be improved by using linguistic processing but we do not wish to pursue this issue in this paper.

5 Learning System

In our basic approach to extract elements from document images, a model is made from only a single document. However this model may prevent improving the performance of the system, because the model can not know what layout features the next document might have. In this section, we will look at the learning methods used to make the system capable of improving its knowledge of documents, by dynamically modifying the features in its knowledge base.

Figure 8 shows the outline of the learning system. The input document is compared with the original model stored in model registration module. If a shift in the layout features would be detected more than a constant threshold, the system reacts according to the following choices; (1) retry to extract elements, (2) modify the model, and (3) use a multi-template method. The first two reactions can be performed without any hand-operation so that users do not notice them but the system becomes wiser with every document.

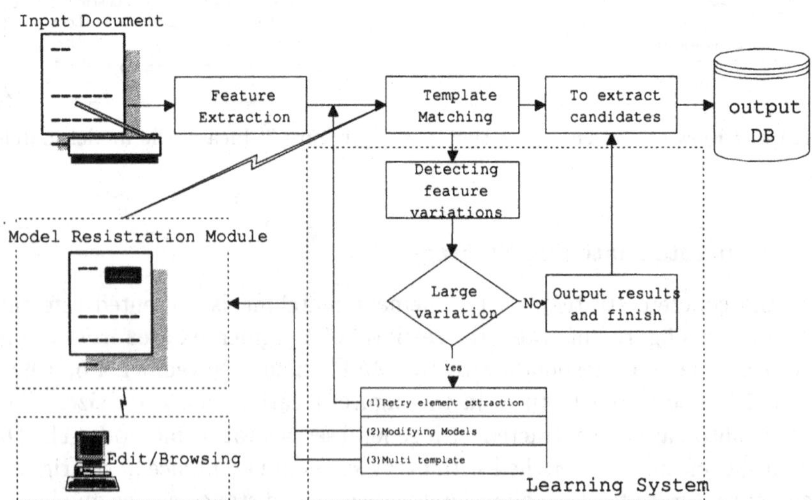

Figure 8: Outline of learning system

6 Experiments

In this section, we present some experiments for extracting elements from the binary images of general documents. We have also compare the performance of the proposed basic algorithm with the performance of the proposed learning method, in terms of the improvement of extraction accuracy for images whose layout features are variable.

6.1 Data Set

In the experiments described in this section, we used an image set containing 288 pages of business letters, reports, technical papers, magazines, and Japanese articles with character strings aligned vertically. In order to estimate the proposed methods for the various kinds of document sets, we classified the sample images into three sets based on their layout features. Table 2 shows the classification of the image set. Sample images for the learning experiments were divided into two sets, for learning and testing, to compare the performance before and the after learning.

6.2 Basic Engine

The first experiment estimates the basic algorithm for the element extraction. The results are tabulated in Table 3. Table3 shows the correct rate for the element extraction and the effectiveness rate, that means the ratio of the number of correct lines found in the extracted candidates over the number of the whole selected candidate lines. The system solved the task of extracting elements from 145 different registered pages of 17 page types. The correct rate for the element extraction from document images was estimated to be 95.6%, and the effectiveness rate for the element extraction was estimated to be 55.5%.

Table 2: Test images

	pages	elements
Small	100	320–331
Normal	83	425
Large	68	287–304
Vertical	37	64–74
Total	288	1096–2232

Table 3: Result of experiment

	Basic		Leaning	
	correct	effect	correct	effect
Small	98.2	67.1	98.2	72.9
Normal	99.2	51.0	99.2	56.0
Large	85.3	43.6	100	44.8
Vertical	100	47.7	100	65.0
Total	95.6	55.5	99.2	61.4

6.3 Learning System

The second experiment was performed to evaluate the improvement of the basic algorithm. New information is automatically added to our knowledge base. Experimental results for the learning method are shown in the right of Table 3. Compared with the results of the basic algorithm shown in the left of Table 3, the correct rate and effectiveness are both improved, especially the correct rate for the images with a large variation in the layout features. This improvement is mainly due to the use of the multi-template method for the documents with discrete variation in the layout features, such as indent and appearance.

7 Conclusion

A system for extracting elements from document images by feature matching has been described. It has the following features;

1. The proposed method is robust against the feature's variations.
2. Creating models is easy because of the user-friendly interface.
3. The system can be used for many types of documents.

We also described the learning method including model modifying and the multi-template for improving the performance of the basic algorithm. Thus the error rate for element extraction has been reduced by 81.1%. The algorithm is effective for images with large shifts in their layout features. Our result shows that out system can directly support the functions of document maintenance system such as keyword retrieval and title registration.

Acknowledgments

The authors thank Dr. Koichi Ejiri and Dr.Hirobumi Nishida for their valuable comments on earlier drafts of this paper.

References

1. T.Watanabe, et al, "Extraction of data from preprinted forms", IEEE Trans. Pattern Analysis and Machine Intelligence, Vol.17, No.4, 1995, pp.432-445.
2. J.Yuan, et al, "Form items extraction by model matching", ICPR'96,1996, pp.691-695.
3. H.Arai, K.Odaka, "Information Acquisition and Storage of Forms in Document Processing", ICDAR,1997, pp.164-169.
4. C.Wenzel, "Supporting Information Extraction from Printed Documents by Lexico-Semantic Pattern Matching", ICDAR, 1997.
5. M.Sharpe, et al, "An Intelligent Document Understanding & Reproduction System", MVA'94,1994, pp.267-271.
6. T.Watanabe, X.Huang, "Automatic Acquisition of Layout Knowledge for Understanding Business Cards", ICDAR, 1997, pp.216-220
7. H.Walischewski, "Automatic Acquisition of Spatial Document Interpretation", ICDAR, 1997, pp.243-247
8. C.Lin, et al, "Logical Structure Analysis of Book Document Images Using Contents Information", ICDAR, 1997, pp.1048-1054.
9. Y.Tang, et al, "Document Processing for Automatic Knowledge Acquisition", IEEE, Transaction on Knowledge and Data Engineering, Vol. 6, No.1, 1994, pp.3-31.
10. T.Saitoh, et al, "Document Image Segmentation and Text Area Ordering" Proceedings of ICDAR, 1993, pp.323-329.
11. S.Khoubyari and J.Hull, "Font Function Word Identification in Document Recognition", CVIU,1996, pp.66-74.

Text-Line Extraction as Selection of Paths in the Neighbor Graph

Koichi Kise[1], Motoi Iwata[1], Andreas Dengel[2], and Keinosuke Matsumoto[1]

[1] Department of Computer and Systems Sciences,
College of Engineering, Osaka Prefecture University,
1-1 Gakuencho, Sakai, Osaka 599-8531, Japan
{kise, iwata, matsu}@ss.cs.osakafu-u.ac.jp

[2] German Research Center for Artificial Intelligence (DFKI, GmbH)
P.O. Box 2080, 67608 Kaiserslautern, Germany
Andreas.Dengel@dfki.de

Abstract. This paper presents a new method of text-line extraction which can be applied to tilted non-rectangular pages. The method is characterized as follows. As the representation of physical structure of a page, we propose the neighbor graph which represents neighbors of connected components. The use of the area Voronoi diagram enables us to extract neighbors without predetermined parameters. Based on the neighbor graph, the task of text-line extraction is considered to be the selection of its paths appropriate as text-lines. We apply simple iterative selection of edges with local examination so as to reduce the computational cost. From experimental results for 50 pages with rectangular and non-rectangular layout, we discuss advantages and limitations of our method.

1 Introduction

Layout analysis is the process of extracting document components such as text-blocks, text-lines, figures and tables as well as identifying layout structure among them. Since the layout analysis is a complex task, it is often decomposed into several sub-tasks. Text-line extraction is an important sub-task, since a large number of documents mainly consist of text-lines.

Existing methods of text-line extraction can be classified from the viewpoint of a class of layout to be processed. An important and the most investigated class would be *rectangular* layout. The layout is rectangular if all document components can be circumscribed by non-overlapping upright rectangles. For this class of layout, various methods such as smearing and projection have been proposed. Some of the methods attain higher accuracy as well as efficiency by fitting algorithms to this class.

In recent years, however, the number of pages beyond this class has been growing as publishing techniques progress. Pages in recent magazines and journals, etc. sometimes include tilted text-lines so as to make them stand out from horizontal ones. In order to extract text-lines from such pages, it is necessary to utilize methods independent of layout as well as skew of text-lines.

Attempts have therefore been made to reduce the assumptions on layout of pages. For black-on-white pages, connected component analysis is often applied to obtain primitives (connected components), and they are merged to form text-lines. Existing methods with connected component analysis are characterized by (1) a representation of physical structure among connected components, and (2) a strategy for merging connected components based on the representation. Some representative methods are as follows: Hough transform with the ρ–θ space[1], distance/angle filtering with k-NN (nearest neighbors)[2], relaxation with low resolution images[3], simulated annealing with pairs of adjacent connected components [4].

In this paper, we propose a new approach for text-line extraction with the help of the *area Voronoi diagram*[5] developed in the field of computational geometry. The area Voronoi diagram enables us to obtain neighbor relations between connected components efficiently. In our method, the neighbor relations are represented by a graph called the *neighbor graph* whose vertices and edges correspond to connected components and neighbor relations, respectively. Based on the neighbor graph, the task of text-line extraction is considered to be the selection of its *paths* appropriate as text-lines. In order to keep the computational cost low, the method selects paths by iterative extension of edges based only on local examination. From experimental results for 50 images with rectangular and non-rectangular layout, we discuss advantages and limitations of the method.

2 Representation of Physical Structure

2.1 Area Voronoi Diagram

The physical structure of a binary document image can be represented by *neighbor* relations among connected components. In this paper, we employ the neighbors of connected components defined by the *area Voronoi diagram.*

The area Voronoi diagram is a generalization of the ordinary (point) Voronoi diagram[5]. While the point Voronoi diagram is generated from a set of *points*, the area Voronoi diagram is generated from a set of *non-overlapping figures.*

The definition of the area Voronoi Diagram is as follows. Let $G = \{g_1, ..., g_n\}$ be a set of non-overlapping figures in the 2-dimensional plane, and $d(p, g_i)$ be the Euclidean distance between a point p and a figure g_i defined by

$$d(p, g_i) = \min_{q \in g_i} d(p, q) \ , \tag{1}$$

where q is a point on the contour of g_i and $d(p, q)$ is the Euclidean distance between p and q. Then a Voronoi region $V(g_i)$ and the area Voronoi diagram $V(G)$ are defined by

$$V(g_i) = \{p | d(p, g_i) \le d(p, g_j), \forall j \ne i\} \ , \tag{2}$$

$$V(G) = \{V(g_1), ..., V(g_n)\} \ . \tag{3}$$

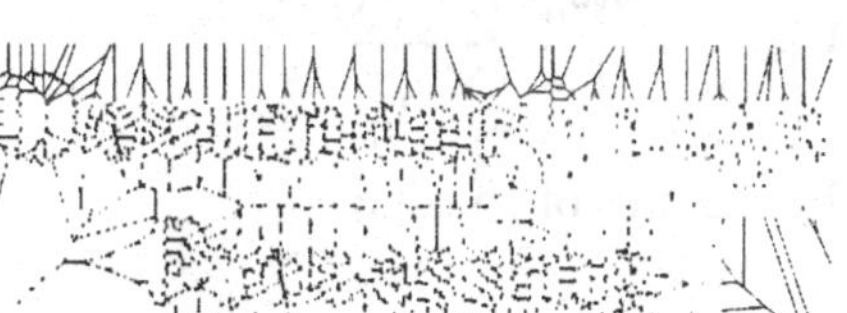

(a) original image

(b) sample points

(c) point Voronoi diagram

(d) area Voronoi diagram

(e) neighbor graph

(f) text-lines

Fig. 1. The Area Voronoi diagram and the neighbor graph.

The boundaries of Voronoi regions are called *Voronoi edges*.

It is known that the area Voronoi diagram can be approximately constructed from the point Voronoi diagram in the following manner[5]:

step 1 Generate the point Voronoi diagram from the points $P = P_1 \cup ... \cup P_n$ where P_i be a set of points lying on the contour of g_i.
step 2 Delete Voronoi edges generated from points on the same figure.

Although a Voronoi edge in the area Voronoi diagram may be a complex curve, that of the approximated version consists of line segments, which are the approximation of the curve. In this paper, the approximated version is referred to as the area Voronoi diagram for simplicity.

The above algorithm enables us to construct the area Voronoi diagram directly from a binary image[6]. By applying labeling, contour following and sampling procedures to a binary image, points on contours of connected components are obtained as shown in Fig. 1(b). The point and area Voronoi diagrams are constructed using these points as shown in Fig. 1(c) and (d), respectively.

2.2 Neighbor Graph

The area Voronoi diagram can be interpreted as the representation of neighbor relations among connected components based on the Euclidean distance: a pair

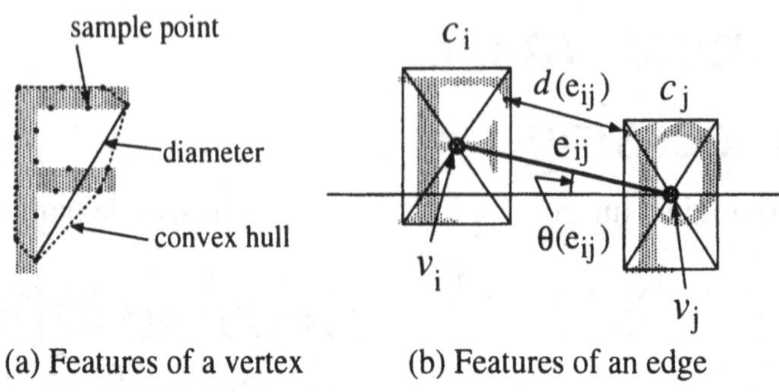

Fig. 2. Features.

of connected components which share a Voronoi edge on their Voronoi regions are neighbors with each other.

In our method, the neighbor relations are explicitly represented by a graph called the neighbor graph. The neighbor graph $\langle V, E \rangle$ is a graph in which a vertex $v_i \in V$ corresponds to a connected component c_i, and an edge $e_{ij} \in E$ between vertices v_i and v_j corresponds to a Voronoi edge shared by connected components c_i and c_j. In other words, an edge e_{ij} represents the neighbor relation between connected components c_i and c_j. The neighbor graph for the area Voronoi diagram in Fig. 1(d) is shown in Fig. 1(e).

It is worth noting that, in ordinary cases, a text-line can be represented by a *path* of a neighbor graph as shown in Fig. 1(f). In such cases, therefore, all we have to do to extract text-lines is to select the appropriate paths from the neighbor graph.

2.3 Features

In order to select the appropriate paths, we utilize the features shown in Fig. 2.

Let $P = \{p_1, ..., p_n\}$ be sample points on the contour of a connected component c. The features of a vertex v (a connected component c) are defined using these points as follows:

area $a(v)$ **:** The area $a(v)$ is the area of the convex hull of P.

diameter $D(v)$ **:** The diameter $D(v)$ is the distance between the farthest pair of points in P:

$$D(v) = \max_{p_i, p_j \in P} d(p_i, p_j) \ . \tag{4}$$

The area is utilized, for example, to distinguish characters from larger connected components in figures. The diameter is useful to distinguish characters from thin ruled lines whose areas are close to those of characters.

Features of an edge e_{ij} are illustrated in Fig. 2(b).

distance $d(e_{ij})$ **:** The distance $d(e_{ij})$ is defined by

$$d(e_{ij}) = \min_{p_1 \in P_1, p_2 \in P_2} d(p_1, p_2) \ . \tag{5}$$

where P_1 and P_2 are the sets of sample points on contours of connected components c_1 and c_2, respectively.

angle $\theta(e_{ij})$: Let v_i and v_j be the centroids of the minimum upright bounding boxes of connected components c_i and c_j, respectively. The angle $\theta(e_{ij})$ [degree] is the angle of the line segment $\overline{v_i v_j}$ to the horizontal line.

3 Text-Line Extraction

3.1 Overview

The method of text-line extraction consists of three steps: (1) generation of the neighbor graph, (2) extraction of seeds and (3) extension of seeds. Figure 3 shows results of these steps.

The first step is to generate the neighbor graph from an input binary image. All the features described in Sect. 2.3 are also calculated in this step.

Text-lines are extracted at the succeeding steps based on the assumptions that:

(A1) Every text-line is represented by a path in the neighbor graph, [1] i.e., $(v_1, e_{12}, v_2, ..., e_{m-1,m}, v_m)$ where $v_i \in V$, $e_{ij} \in E$, and $v_i \neq v_j$ if $i \neq j$,

(A2) Every text-line consists of connected components of approximately equal size and shape,

(A3) Every text-line is linear.

In order to get a clue to extract text-lines, we extract *seeds* from the neighbor graph at the second step. A seed is a path of the neighbor graph which seems a part of a text-line with confidence. Since a seed contains no loops and branches, we can estimate the orientation of a text-line.

At the last step, seeds are extended to obtain complete text-lines based on the estimated orientation. To extend seeds reliably without the help of time-consuming process such as relaxation, we apply simple iterative extension with a varying criterion. Since seeds are short and thus unreliable at early stages of the iteration, we apply a strict criterion. At later stages, on the other hand, a criterion is relaxed to obtain complete text-lines. An edge to be merged with a seed is selected based on local examination of edges which connect with a seed at its end. Details of each step are described below.

3.2 Generation of the Neighbor Graph

Pixels on contours of connected components are selected with a sampling rate R. These pixels are utilized as sample points for the construction of the area Voronoi diagram. In this process, a connected component is eliminated as noise if its area is less than or equal to T_n. Next, the area Voronoi diagram is transformed into the neighbor graph. Figure 3(b) illustrates an example of the neighbor graph.

[1] To be precise, a text-line is represented not by a path, but by a connected subgraph of the neighbor graph, since a path excludes small dots of characters (e.g., i, j). In most cases, however, such dots can be easily included in a text-line by, for example, constructing a convex hull of connected components in a path.

(a) original image (b) neighbor graph

(c) seeds (d) extracted text-lines

Fig. 3. Results of each step. The image (a), which is artificially tilted by 10°, contains 5433 connected components. The number of edges in (b), (c) and (d) is 8343 (100%), 1231 (15%) and 2575 (31%), respectively. The total computation time was 6.36 sec. with a Pentium II 300MHz PC.

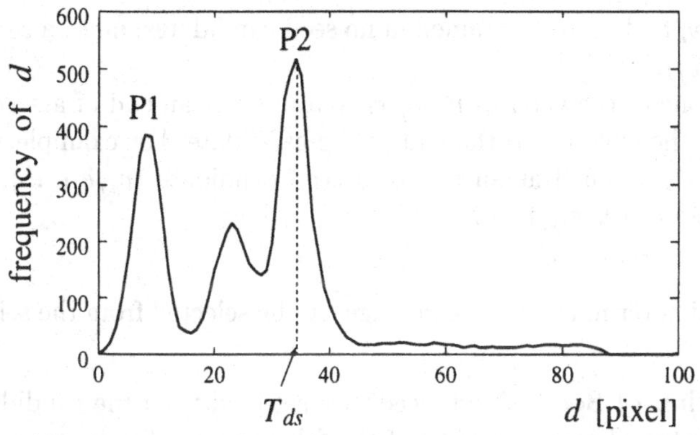

Fig. 4. Frequency distribution of the distance d.

3.3 Extraction of Seeds

This step consists of the following three sub-steps: initial filtering of edges, extraction of seed candidates and identification of seeds.

Initial Filtering of Edges The neighbor graph generally includes superfluous edges which violate the assumption (A2). In this sub-step, such edges are deleted. An edge e_{ij} between vertices v_i and v_j is deleted from the neighbor graph if it satisfies one of the following equations:

$$\frac{\min(a(v_i), a(v_j))}{\max(a(v_i), a(v_j))} \leq T_a \ , \tag{6}$$

$$\frac{\min(D(v_i), D(v_j))}{\max(D(v_i), D(v_j))} \leq T_D \ , \tag{7}$$

where T_a and T_D are thresholds. After the deletion of superfluous edges, isolated vertices are also deleted.

Extraction of Seed Candidates In general, a connected component is closest to that in the same text-line. Thus a group of connected components close with one another can be a candidate of a seed.

Since seeds should be a part or a whole of a text-line, we first select edges whose distances are less than or equal to the estimated inter-line gap T_{ds} of body text regions. Figure 4 illustrates the frequency distribution for the edges in Fig. 3(b). There exist two apparent peaks P_1 and P_2 near the origin: P_1 and P_2 correspond to inter-character and inter-line gaps, respectively. Thus the value of T_{ds} is set to the distance for the peak P_2.

Then the selected edges are connected to form seed candidates. An edge e_{ij} between vertices v_i and v_j is tested in the ascending order of the distance $d(e_{ij})$ as follows:

1. If both v_i and v_j are contained in no seed candidates, make a seed candidate (v_i, e_{ij}, v_j).
2. If only one of the vertices v_i, v_j is contained at an end of a seed candidate, connect the edge e_{ij} to the end of the candidate. For example, when a vertex v_j is contained at an end of a seed candidate $(v_j, e_{jk}, ...)$, update the candidate to $(v_i, e_{ij}, v_j, e_{jk}, ...)$.
3. Otherwise, skip e_{ij}.

The extraction terminates when no edge can be selected from the selected edges.

Identification of Seeds Next, seeds are selected from the candidates. A candidate r is selected as a seed if all of the following conditions are satisfied:

1. It consists of more than one edge.
2. $\text{Var}_\theta(r) \leq T_{v\theta}$ and $\text{Var}_d(r) \leq T_{vd}$, where $\text{Var}_\theta(r)$ and $\text{Var}_d(r)$ are the variance of distances and that of angles of edges in r, respectively, and $T_{v\theta}$, T_{vd} are thresholds.

The first condition indicates that a seed candidate consisting of a single edge is less reliable. The second condition represents that connected components in a seed should be arranged approximately linear as well as at approximately even intervals.

After the selection, the following features of a seed s are calculated:

distance $d(s)$ **:** $d(s) = \sum_{e \in E_s} d(e)/|E_s|$, where E_s is a set of edges in a seed.
angle $\theta(s)$ **:** Consider a line segment which connects both ends of a seed s. $\theta(s)$ [degree] is the angle of the line segment to the horizontal line.

3.4 Extension of Seeds

Finally, seeds are extended iteratively using a criterion varying with the current number of times of iteration n. Figure 5 shows the algorithm of this step: at each time of iteration, each seed s is extended as much as possible by selecting an edge connecting at each end of s, and merging the selected edge with s. The function "Select_Edge(s,v_i,n)" selects an edge e_{ij} to be merged with s at a vertex v_i depending on the current number of times of iteration n. This function returns ϕ (no edge) if there exists no appropriate edge. The function "Merge_Edge(s,v_i,e_{ij})" merges the selected edge e_{ij} with the seed s at its end v_i if $e_{ij} \neq \phi$; otherwise, it returns s.

The point of the algorithm is how to select the appropriate edge to be merged with a seed s in the function "Select_Edge". In order to keep the computational cost low, it is desirable to select the edge only by local examination of edges.

Figure 6 illustrates a seed to be extended. The method selects the first "acceptable" edge from the sorted list of K-best edges $(e_1, ..., e_K)$ as follows.

First, we obtain E_v, i.e., a set of all edges which are contained in no seeds and connect with a seed s only at its end v. If an edge $e \in E_v$ is between the seed s and a different seed s', e must also be at an end of s'. In the case of Fig. 6,

```
for n = 1 to N do
  for all seed s ∈ S(the set of seeds) do
    if the seed s exists in S then
      repeat
        v1 ← a vertex at an end of s
        v2 ← a vertex at the other end of s
        s_old ← s
        e_1x ← Select_Edge(s,v1,n)
        e_2y ← Select_Edge(s,v2,n)
        s ← Merge_Edge(s,v1,e_1x)
        s ← Merge_Edge(s,v2,e_2y)
        if s_old ≠ s then
          Delete from S all seeds which share edges of s
          Add s in S
          Recalculate features of s
        end if
      until s_old = s
    end if
  end for
end for
```

Fig. 5. Extension of seeds.

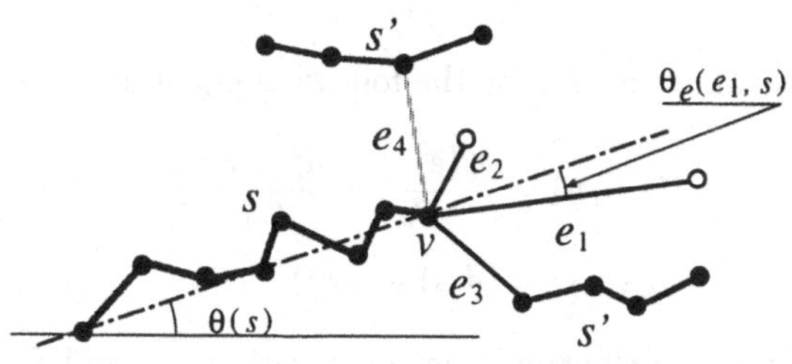

Fig. 6. Selection of K-best edges.

$E_v = \{e_1, e_2, e_3\}$. Then, the list $(e_1, ..., e_K)$ is generated from the elements of E_v by sorting them in the ascending order of the difference of angles

$$\theta_e(e_i, s) = |\theta(e_i) - \theta(s)| \ . \tag{8}$$

The number of elements K is less than or equal to $K_{\max}$. In Fig. 6, the list (e_1, e_2) is obtained with $K_{\max} = 2$.

Next, we select the acceptable edge from the list. If an edge is between connected components in a word, the distance of the edge is generally small but its angle may not close to that of the seed due to the presence of ascenders and descenders. On the other hand, if an edge is between words, the distance is larger but the angle is more closer to that of the seed. The criterion for the acceptable

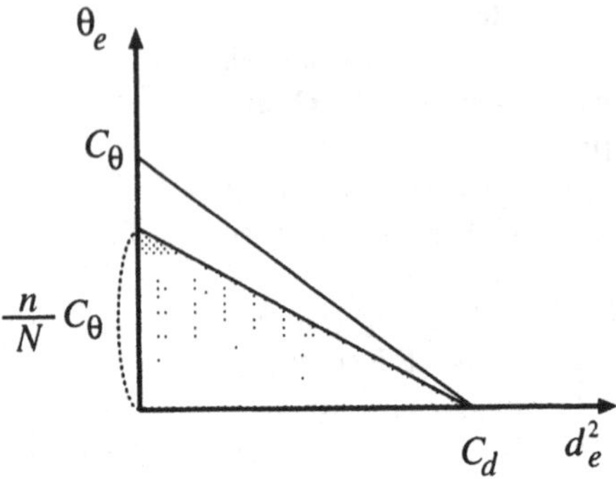

Fig. 7. d_e^2-θ_e plane.

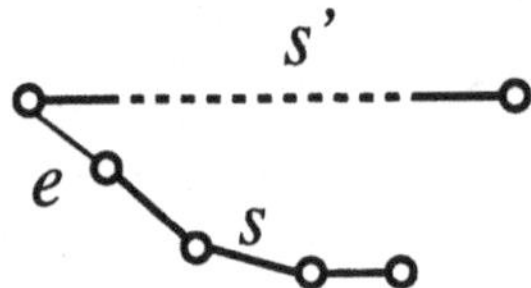

Fig. 8. Necessity of a test with a different seed s'. The edge e is acceptable from s but not from s'.

edges encodes the above nature by the following equations:

$$J(e,s,n) = \frac{\theta_e(e,s)}{\frac{n}{N}C_\theta} + \frac{d_e^2(e,s)}{C_d} \leq 1 \ , \tag{9}$$

$$d_e^2(e,s) = (d(s) - d(e))^2 \ , \tag{10}$$

where N is the total number of times of iteration, C_θ and C_d are thresholds. Figure 7 illustrates the d_e^2–θ_e plane in which an edge corresponds to a point; an edge e satisfies (9) if it is in the shaded area. An edge e for a seed s is tested whether (9) is satisfied if e connects only with the seed s. In the case that an edge e is between s and s', $J(e,s',n) \leq 1$ should also be true in order to keep the extended seed linear. Figure 8 shows the situation in which this additional test is required.

After the iteration, the method outputs as text-lines the seeds whose numbers of edges are more than or equal to M.

4 Experimental Results

4.1 Conditions

Experiments were made using a PC with Pentium II 300 MHz CPU and 256 MB real memory. The method was applied to two data sets of 300 dpi images: UW1 and Nonrect. UW1 consists of 25 page images with rectangular layout obtained

Table 1. Values of parameters.

step	neighbor graph		extraction of seeds				extension of seeds				
parameter	R	T_n	T_a	T_D	$T_{v\theta}$	T_{vd}	N	$K_{\max}$	M	C_d	C_θ
value	1/7	64	1/40	1/10	400	50	10	2	3	1600	50

Table 2. Experimental results.

data set	no. of text-lines	correct	error		
			frag.	over-merg.	omission
UW1	1111	89.1%	7.84%	0.63%	2.43%
Nonrect	2975	89.9%	4.00%	4.73%	1.37%
Total	4086	89.7%	5.03%	3.61%	1.66%

from the University of Washington database 1. UW1 includes one-column (22 pages), two-column (2 pages), and three-column (1 page) pages whose layout is rectangular. We applied no skew correction to these images. Nonrect also consists of 25 images obtained by scanning various English magazines, but their layout is non-rectangular: they include document components of arbitrary shape. Nonrect includes one-column (3 pages), two-column (5 pages), three-column (13 pages), and four-column (4 pages) pages. In order to test the robustness against a severe skew, the images in Nonrect were artificially rotated counterclockwise by 10°.

The values of parameters used in the experiments are listed in Table 1. These values were determined using 50 different images: 25 images from the University of Washington database 1 and 25 images from magazines with non-rectangular layout.

4.2 Results and Discussion

Table 2 shows the results of the experiments. In this table, "no. of text-lines" and "correct" indicate the sum of the number of text-lines in each data set and the rate of correctly extracted text-lines, respectively. In the experiments, an extracted text-line is regarded as correct if it is neither fragmented nor merged with different document components, except for omission of small connected components such as hyphens, dots, commas and periods.

For both of the data sets, about 90% of text-lines were correctly extracted. This indicates that the method is capable of extracting text-lines independently of layout and skew.

Figure 9 illustrates examples of the processing results. Figure 9(a) belongs to UW1, and the rest are in Nonrect. Text-lines extracted from these images are shown in Figs. 9(d)–(f). Although a copy noise in Fig. 9(a), parts of figures in Fig. 9(b) and (c) were erroneously extracted, most of the extracted text-lines were correct ones. It is noteworthy that the text-lines with large characters in Fig. 9(a), the tilted text-line on the top right corner of Fig. 9(b) and those on the left edge of Fig. 9(c) were correctly extracted.

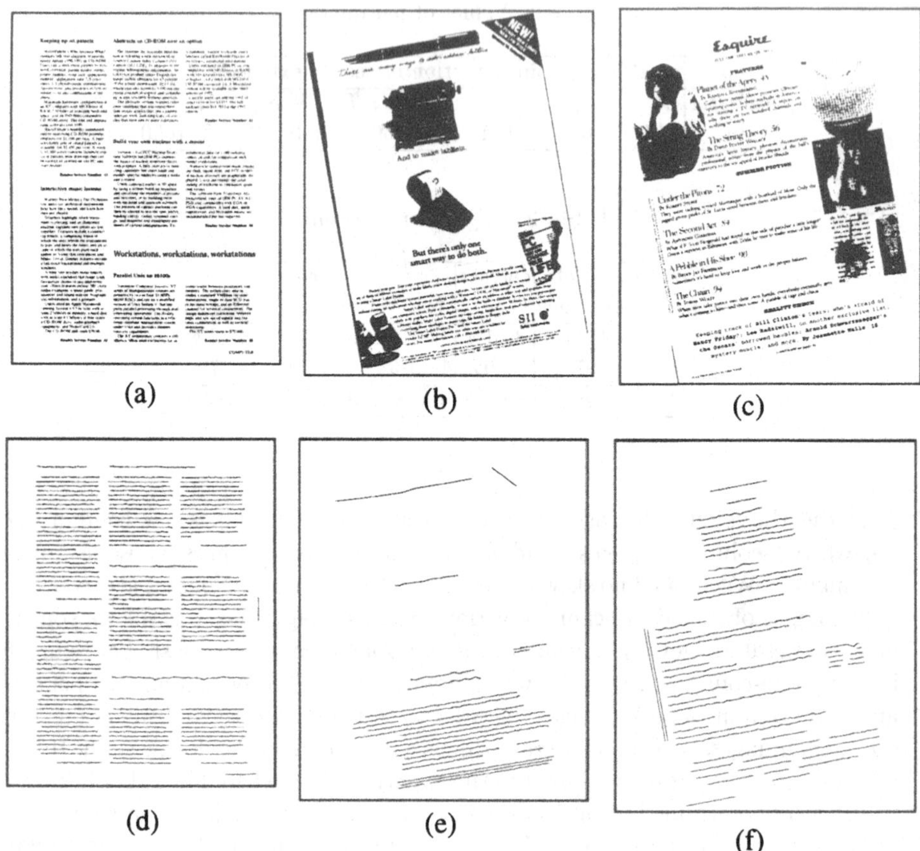

Fig. 9. Examples of processing results.

Errors can be classified into three types: fragmentation, over-merging, and omission of a whole text-line. Rates of the number of errors to the total number of text-lines are shown in Table 2, and examples of these errors are shown in Fig. 10.

Most of the fragmentation errors were due to wide inter-word gaps. A different type of fragmentation was found in text-lines which included equations and chemical symbols: long subscripts, superscripts and consecutive dots (...) severely disturbed the orientation of text-lines, so that edges to be merged could not be found. The fragmentation in UW1 occurred more frequently than that in Nonrect, since images in UW1 contained a larger number of symbols and equations.

Over-merging errors occurred more frequently for Nonrect. This was mainly because inter-column gaps were close to inter-word gaps in two images in Nonrect, one of which is shown in Fig. 10(b). It was also observed that some dotted ruled lines and parts of figures were merged with text-lines.

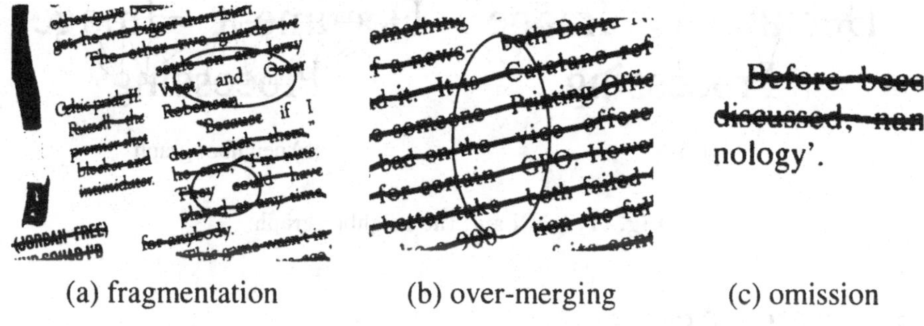

(a) fragmentation (b) over-merging (c) omission

Fig. 10. Examples of errors.

Table 3. Computation time.

labeling, contour following and sampling	3.39 sec. (49.7%)
feature extraction	1.40 sec. (20.5%)
construction of the area Voronoi diagram and the neighbor graph	1.74 sec. (25.5%)
seed extraction and extension	0.28 sec. (4.1%)
others (file I/O etc.)	0.01 sec. (0.2%)
total	6.82 sec.

Note. The ratio of time to the total is shown in parentheses.

Omission occurred in short text-lines located on ends of paragraphs as well as headers and footers. It is difficult for the method to extract short text-lines because the chance of presence of seeds in short text-lines is less than that in long text-lines. Another reason is that the method deletes short text-lines consisting of less than or equal to M edges so as to eliminate noises.

We consider that these errors indicate the limitation of the method which extracts text-lines individually. In order to correct these errors, it is necessary to take account of text-blocks. The parallelness and the alignment of text-lines in a text-block could be fruitful features for correcting these errors.

Let us turn to the discussion about the efficiency of the method. On average, 60,000 sample points were extracted from 8,500 connected components to construct the neighbor graph consisting of 7,000 edges. 2,400 edges were selected as parts of text-lines for an image. The computation time required at each step is listed in Table 3. The process of labeling, contour following and sampling dominated the overall computation time. Although the construction of the area Voronoi diagram and the neighbor graph, and the feature extraction took the second and third longest time, respectively, each of them is about half of the time required by labeling. Thus, we consider that the method is applicable to images that can be labeled in reasonable time. Another important point is that the time consumed by the steps of extraction and extension of seeds was quite small as compared with other steps. This is because the method selects edges based only on the local examination.

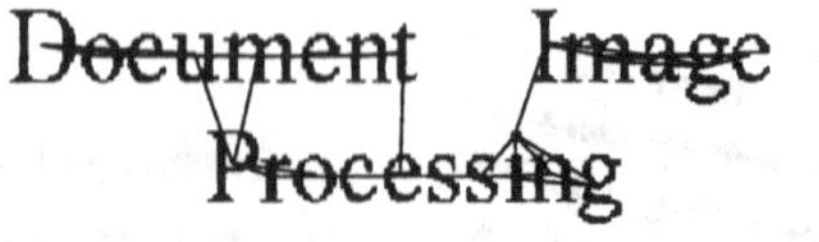

(a) 3-NN

(b) neighbor graph

Fig. 11. k-NN and the neighbor graph.

5 Related Work

In this section, we compare our method with some representative methods [1–4] which are also capable of extracting text-lines independently of layout and skew. We divide the discussion into the comparison of representations of physical structure, and that of strategies of extraction.

5.1 Representations

A representation of physical structure depends on the definition of neighbors of a connected component. A simple definition is that connected components are neighbors with each other if the distance between them is less than a threshold. Some of the methods [3, 4] utilize this definition with modification for efficiency and effectiveness. However, it is necessary for such methods to determine the threshold.

As a representation without the threshold of distance, O'Gorman has utilized k-NN of connected components. Although this representation bears resemblance to the neighbor graph, an important difference is that k-NN requires a predetermined value of k. Figure 11 illustrates 3-NN and the neighbor graph for the same image, which looks like the image in Fig. 1 but the word gap between "Document" and "Image" is wider. As shown in Fig. 11(a), 3-NN does not cover the neighbor relation between "Document" and "Image". In order to obtain the neighbor relation between these two words, it is required to use k-NN with $k \geq 7$; the appropriate value of k varies depending on an image. On the other hand, the neighbor graph in Fig. 11(b) contains all neighbor relations required to extract text-lines without the use of such a parameter.

5.2 Strategies

As a strategy of extraction, a variety of methods have been proposed. These include Hough transform [1], the angle/distance filtering of k-NN [2], relaxation [3], and simulated annealing [4]. In particular, relaxation and simulated annealing are effective for various text-lines, since they pursue globally optimized interpretations. In compensation for the effectiveness, however, they require a large amount of computation time. As compared with these methods, our method is fast but less accurate, since it extracts text-lines only by the local test. In order to improve the accuracy with a little loss of efficiency, it is required to expand the scope of test appropriately. A possible way would be the use of text-blocks — cooperative extraction of text-blocks [6] and text-lines.

6 Conclusion

We have presented the method of representing physical structure of pages by the neighbor graph as well as the method of extracting text-lines based on the representation. The use of the area Voronoi diagram enables us to extract the neighbor relations among connected components without the help of domain-specific parameters. The iterative extension of seeds based only on local selection of edges enables us to keep the method efficient.

From the experimental results for 50 images with a wide variety of layout and severe skew, we have confirmed that the method is capable of extracting text-lines independently of layout and skew. From the analysis of accuracy, however, it has been shown that there exist some limitations of the method which extracts text-lines with only a local evidence.

Future work is to overcome the limitations by developing a method of layout analysis which can cooperatively extract text-blocks and text-lines.

Acknowledgments

This research was supported in part by the Grant-in-Aid for Scientific Research from the Ministry of Education, Science, Sports and Culture, Japan, and The Telecommunication Advancement Foundation.

References

1. L. A. Fletcher and R. Kasturi, A robust algorithm for text string separation from mixed text/graphics images, *IEEE Trans. PAMI*, Vol. 10, No. 6, pp.910–918, 1988.
2. L. O'Gorman, The document spectrum for page layout analysis, *IEEE Trans. Pattern Anal. & Machine Intell.*, Vol. 15, No. 11, pp.1162–1173, 1993.
3. F. Hönes and J. Lichter, Layout extraction of mixed mode documents, *Machine Vision and Applications*, Vol. 7, pp.237–246, 1994.
4. K. Gyohten, T. Sumiya, N. Babaguchi, K. Kakusho and T. Kitahashi, A multi-agent based method for extracting characters and character strings, *IEICE Trans. Information & Systems, Japan*, Vol. E97-D, No. 5, pp.450–455, 1996.
5. K. Sugihara, Approximation of generalized Voronoi diagrams by ordinary Voronoi diagrams, *CVGIP: Graphical Models and Image Processing*, Vol. 55, No.6, pp.522–531, 1993.
6. K. Kise, A. Sato and M. Iwata, Segmentation of page images using the area Voronoi diagram, *Computer Vision and Image Understanding*, Vol.70, No.3, pp.370–382, 1998.

Table Structure Extraction from Form Documents Based on Gradient-Wavelet Scheme

Dihua Xi and Seong-Whan Lee

Center for Artificial Vision Research, Korea University
Anam-dong, Seongbuk-ku, Seoul 136-701, Korea
{dhxi, swlee}@image.korea.ac.kr

Abstract. Based on gradient and wavelet analyses, a novel scheme has been developed to extract table structures from skewed form document images. In this scheme, first, a skewed form document image is rotated according to the angle obtained from the gradient algorithm. Then the deskewed image is decomposed into four sub-images by divisible Multiresolution Analysis(MRA) wavelets. Afterwards, the table structure image which represents the geometric structure of the form can be obtained from the sub-images by a modified wavelet reconstruction algorithm. Meanwhile, another document image without table lines can be produced by Minkowski operation and is referred to as a table free image. Experimental results indicate that this new scheme can be applied to process the skewed form document images with promising achievements.

1 Introduction

A knowledge acquisition bottleneck has become the major barrier to the development and implementation of effective information systems. To mitigate this bottleneck, document processing techniques should be considered to automatically acquire information from various types of documents.

Form document processing is an essential operation in many business and government organizations. Particularly, in financial organizations, millions of financial transactions take place every day. They are associated with conventional form documents such as bank cheques, payment slips, bills, etc. However, there are a number of limitations with current manual operations of the form documents. These include, for example, the cost of information acquisition from printed forms, delay in accessing the stored forms, vulnerability of the stored forms to loss, damage, etc. The cost of information capture from the printed forms can be very high.

For large corporations and government organizations, the cost can be several orders of magnitude[1]. Thus, any development which can improve the processing of such documents will make a significant contribution. A lot of researchers have paid attention to the development of many methods to solve this problem, and some achievements can be found in [1–3].

The form documents may contain tables, and most of significant information is sited in these tables. Therefore, how to extract geometric structures plays an intrinsic role in document analysis. Particularly, the table structure is the main class of the geometric structures in the form documents. And form document image usually has a little skew and slant. This paper presents a gradient based approach for skew correction and a wavelet based approach for table extraction from the form document images. The basic idea is described as the following steps:

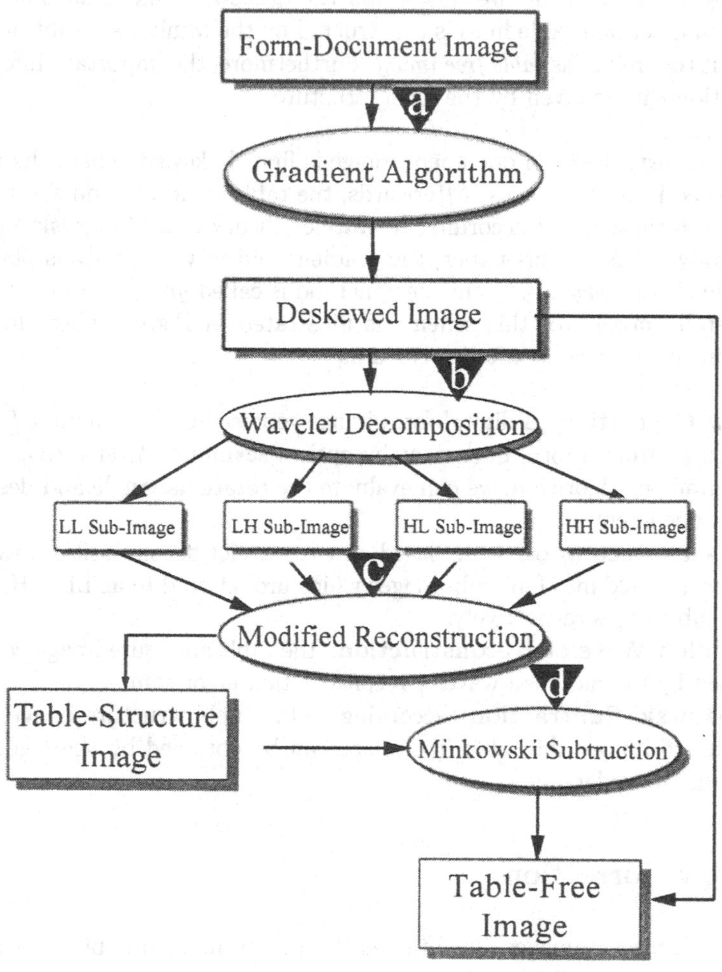

Fig. 1. Diagram of the gradient wavelet scheme for form document analysis.

- Gradient operation is performed on the form document image to evaluate the skew angle. Afterwards, a deskewed image can be obtained by rotating the original form document image.
- The deskewed image is decomposed into four sub-images [4] by the wavelet decomposition algorithm [5].
- According to some of these sub-images, we can reconstruct an image that contains only horizontal and vertical lines from which a particular image can be composed, and is referred to as *table structure image*. Therefore, the table structure of the form document image can be obtained. For this purpose, a modified wavelet reconstruction algorithm will be developed in this paper.
- Using the table structure image and the deskewed image, an image which does not contain table lines is constructed by the Minkowski subtraction [6], and is referred to as *table free image*. Furthermore, the important information position can be given by the form structure.

In summary, the form document image is first deskewed. Then, the image is decomposed into sub-images. Afterwards, the table structure and the table free image are reconstructed according to wavelet theory and Minkowski operation respectively. Thus, in this paper, the gradient and wavelet analysis play major roles. This is the reason why this new method is called *gradient-wavelet scheme*. The overall diagram of this scheme is illustrated in Fig. 1, where four main operations in the scheme are described as

a) **Skew Correction:** a digital form image represented by function $f(m,n)$ is captured from a form document by optical scanning. Afterwards, based on the gradient algorithm, we can evaluate the rotational angle and deskew the form document image.
b) **Wavelet Decomposition:** based on the wavelet decomposition, the image is decomposed into four sub-images which are referred to as LL, LH, HL and HH sub-images respectively.
c) **Modified Wavelet Reconstruction:** the table structure image can be obtained by the modified wavelet reconstruction algorithm.
d) **Minkowski Subtraction:** according to the table structure image and the deskewed image, the table free image can be obtained by the algorithm of the picture difference.

2 Skew Correction

The form document images are obtained through scanning and binarization. The skew correction steps include:

- Noise removal: because scanned images are usually not clean, we used the median filter to remove noise.
- Deskewing: for an image described by f(x,y), the gradient vector $[p,q]^T$ is defined by

$$p = \frac{\partial f(x,y)}{\partial x}, \qquad q = \frac{\partial f(x,y)}{\partial y}.$$

The orientation of this gradient vector is

$$\varphi = \arctan(q/p).$$

For every black point (x, y) in the image, its gradient orientation $\varphi(x, y)$ can be computed or calculated by Eq. (1), Eq. (2), and Eq. (3). Suppose that the region used to computed or calculated $\varphi(x, y)$ is $[x - N, x + N] \times [y - N, y + N]$ and it contains M black points. We have

$$\begin{cases} \overline{x} = \frac{1}{M} \sum_{i=-N}^{N} \sum_{j=-N}^{N} (x+i), & if\ f(x+i,y+j)\ is\ black \\ \overline{y} = \frac{1}{M} \sum_{i=-N}^{N} \sum_{j=-N}^{N} (y+j), & if\ f(x+i,y+j)\ is\ black \end{cases}, \tag{1}$$

$$\mu_{p,q} = \sum_{i=-N}^{N} \sum_{j=-N}^{N} (x+i-\overline{x})^p (y+j-\overline{y})^q, \qquad if\ f(x+i,y+j)\ is\ black, \tag{2}$$

$$\varphi(x,y) = \frac{1}{2} \arctan\left(\frac{2 * \mu_{1,1}}{\mu_{2,0} - \mu_{0,2}}\right). \tag{3}$$

According to above equations, the gradient orientation can be obtained by using $(2N + 1) \times (2N + 1)$ (in our experiment, N=3) filter operation. The range of $\varphi(x,\ y)$ is $[-\frac{\pi}{2}, \frac{\pi}{2})$. Because the orientations of two different points on the table lines are parallel or orthogonal, the range of $\varphi(x,\ y)$ can be transformed into $(-\frac{\pi}{4}, \frac{\pi}{4})$ by

$$\phi(x,y) = \begin{cases} \varphi(x,y), & if\ |\varphi| < \frac{\pi}{4} \\ -sign(\varphi)(\frac{\pi}{2} - |\varphi|), & if\ |\varphi| > \frac{\pi}{4} \end{cases}, \tag{4}$$

where $sign(\varphi)$ is the sign function,

$$sign(x) = \begin{cases} 1, & if\ x > 0 \\ 0, & if\ x = 0 \\ -1, & if\ x < 0 \end{cases}. \tag{5}$$

For detecting the orientation of a skewed form document,a half of the range of φ will be enough. If we have some knowledge about the range of the skew angle, we can reduce the domain of φ even further.

The gradient algorithm is based on the observation of the orientation distribution of all black points in the image. For a skewed form-document image, there will be much more points in the image whose gradient orientations are parallel or perpendicular to the direction of a table line direction. In fact, all points on the table lines have such characteristics. It is obvious to consider that statistical information can be used for skew angle detection. Fig. 2 gives an example shape

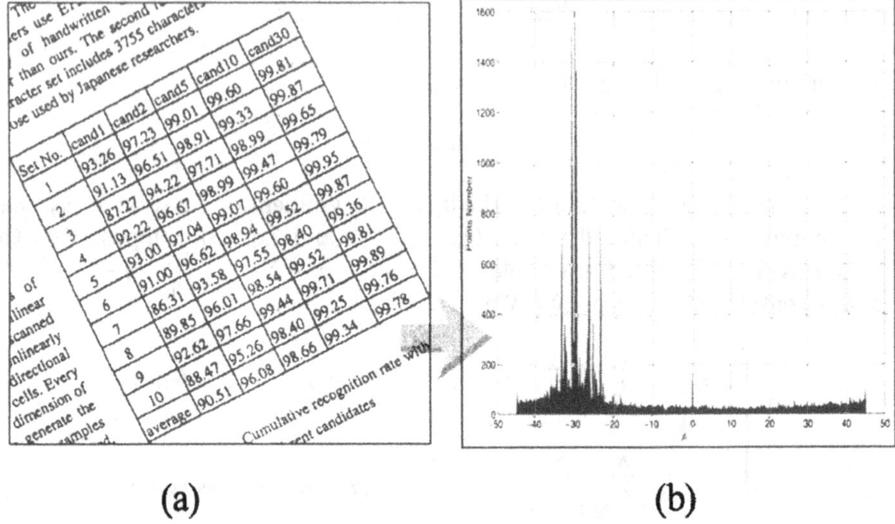

Set No.	cand1	cand2	cand5	cand10	cand30
1	93.26	97.23	99.01	99.60	99.81
2	91.13	96.51	98.91	99.33	99.87
3	87.27	94.22	97.71	98.99	99.65
4	92.22	96.67	98.99	99.47	99.79
5	93.00	97.04	99.07	99.60	99.95
6	91.00	96.62	98.94	99.52	99.87
7	86.31	93.58	97.55	98.40	99.36
8	89.85	96.01	98.54	99.52	99.81
9	92.62	97.66	99.44	99.71	99.89
10	88.47	95.26	98.40	99.25	99.76
average	90.51	96.08	98.66	99.34	99.78

Fig. 2. Example to obtain the skewed angle based on the points distribution histogram on different orientations. (a) Original image of skewed form document. (b) The distribution histogram on different gradient orientations of the original image.

of the gradient orientation histogram of an form-document image. Fig. 2 (a) shows an original image of the skewed document, and (b) gives the histogram of point distribution on different orientations.

Based on the points distribution histogram on different orientations, the gradient algorithm searches for the maximum in the histogram to obtain the skew angle (in Fig. 2, the angle is -29 degrees). By using this skew angle θ, the skewed form document image is aligned by the rotation transformation

$$\begin{cases} x' = & x\cos\theta \; + y\sin\theta \\ y' = & -x\sin\theta + y\cos\theta \end{cases}, \tag{6}$$

where (x, y) is a coordinate before deskewing, and (x', y') is the coordinate after deskewing.

3 Decomposition of Form Document by MRA Wavelet

In this section, the basic concepts of Multiresolution Analysis(MRA) wavelet will be introduced and followed by a description of how the MRA wavelet can be used to decompose the form documents.

3.1 Basic Concepts of MRA Wavelet

Let $\{V_j\}_{j\in Z}$ be a closed subset of $L^2(R)$. It is known that $\{V_j^2\}_{j\in Z}$ is a multiresolution of $L^2(R^2)$ if and only if $\{V_j\}_{j\in Z}$ is a multiresolution of $L^2(R)$, and

$$V_j^2 = V_j \otimes V_j.$$

Let $\varphi(x)$ be a scaling function of $\{V_j\}_{j\in Z}$. Therefore, $\Phi(x,y)=\varphi(x)\varphi(y)$ is a scaling function of $\{V_j^2\}_{j\in Z}$. For every $j\in Z$, the function system

$$\{\Phi_{j,k_1,k_2}=\varphi_{j,k_1}(x)\varphi_{j,k_2}(x)\mid (k_1,k_2)\in Z^2\}$$

becomes an orthonormal basis of V_j^2. Such multiresolution analysis is called divisible MRA.

We can define a wavelet space $W_j^2=(V_j^2)^{\perp}$, namely

$$W_j^2\oplus V_j^2=V_{j-1}^2.$$

From the above analysis, we can easily produce a very significant formula:

$$\begin{aligned}V_{j-1}^2&=V_{j-1}\otimes V_{j-1}\\&=(W_j\oplus V_j)\otimes(W_j\oplus V_j)\\&=(W_j\otimes W_j)\oplus(V_j\otimes W_j)\oplus(W_j\otimes V_j)\oplus(V_j\otimes V_j).\end{aligned}\tag{7}$$

For one-dimensional MRA, because $\varphi(x)$ is the scaling function of $\{V_j\}_{j\in Z}$, we can produce a wavelet function

$$\psi(x)=\sum_{k=-\infty}^{+\infty}g_k\varphi_{-1,k}(x)=2^{-\frac{1}{2}}\sum_{k=-\infty}^{+\infty}g_k\varphi(2x-k)\tag{8}$$

such that for every $j\in Z$, the function system

$$\left\{\psi_{j,k}(x)=2^{-\frac{j}{2}}\psi(2^{-j}x-k)\mid k\in Z\right\}$$

be the orthonormal bases of W_j.

Similar to the one-dimensional MRA, three basic wavelet functions ψ^1,ψ^2,ψ^3 can be produced from the two-dimensional MRA, and described as

$$\begin{cases}\psi^1(x,y)=\psi(x)\varphi(y)\\\psi^2(x,y)=\varphi(x)\psi(y)\\\psi^3(x,y)=\psi(x)\psi(y)\end{cases}.\tag{9}$$

The orthonormal bases of the wavelet space W_j^2 can be obtained from these three single wavelet functions ψ^1,ψ^2,ψ^3 by a dilation (2^j) and a dyadic translation (of $\frac{k}{2^j}$).

3.2 Wavelet Decomposition for Sub-images

The form document image $f(m,n)$ is transformed into four sub-images by the wavelet decomposition. These sub-images are represented by $f_{LL}(m,n)$, $f_{LH}(m,n)$, $f_{HL}(m,n)$, and $f_{HH}(m,n)$ [4]. Mathematically, they are described by

$$\begin{cases} f_{LL}(k_1,k_2) = \sum\limits_{m_1=0}^{2N-1}\sum\limits_{m_2=0}^{2N-1} h_{m_1}h_{m_2}f(m_1+2k_1,\ m_2+2k_2) \\ f_{LH}(k_1,k_2) = \sum\limits_{m_1=0}^{2N-1}\sum\limits_{m_2=0}^{2N-1} h_{m_1}g_{m_2}f(m_1+2k_1,\ m_2+2k_2) \\ f_{HL}(k_1,k_2) = \sum\limits_{m_1=0}^{2N-1}\sum\limits_{m_2=0}^{2N-1} g_{m_1}h_{m_2}f(m_1+2k_1,\ m_2+2k_2) \\ f_{HH}(k_1,k_2) = \sum\limits_{m_1=0}^{2N-1}\sum\limits_{m_2=0}^{2N-1} g_{m_1}g_{m_2}f(m_1+2k_1,\ m_2+2k_2) \end{cases} \tag{10}$$

where $\{h_k\}$ denotes a frequency response which depends on the used wavelet function, and,

$$g_k = (-1)^{2N-k+1}h_{2N-k-1}.$$

In Eq. (10), for a given integer N and a function $f(m,n)$, four functions of the sub-images can be derived. Clearly, the computational complexity of the algorithm increases as N increases. If N is too small, the filtering effect will be dropped. Therefore, we should choose a suitable value for N in our study. Experiments have shown that the results are acceptable when $N=3$ or $N=4$. In this paper, $N=3$ has been chosen for all experiments.

The document image can be regarded as V_{j-1}^2. According to Eq. (7), V_{j-1}^2 can be represented by

$$V_{j-1}^2 = (W_j \otimes W_j) \oplus (V_j \otimes W_j) \oplus (W_j \otimes V_j) \oplus (V_j \otimes V_j).$$

Therefore, the form document image $f(m,n)$ can be divided into four sub-images, namely,

$$f(m,n) = f_{LL} \oplus f_{LH} \oplus f_{HL} \oplus f_{HH}$$

where f_{LL}, f_{LH}, f_{HL} and f_{HH} denote LL sub-image, LH sub-image, HL sub-image and HH sub-image respectively, and can be computed by Eq. (10). The characteristics of these sub-images are described as follows:

- **LL sub-image:** both horizontal and vertical directions are low-frequency. It corresponds to $V_j \otimes V_j$.
- **LH sub-image:** the horizontal direction is low-frequency and the vertical direction is high-frequency. It corresponds to $V_j \otimes W_j$
- **HL sub-image:** the horizontal direction is high-frequency and the vertical direction is low-frequency. It corresponds to $W_j \otimes V_j$.
- **HH sub-image:** both horizontal and vertical directions are high-frequency. It corresponds to $W_j \otimes W_j$.

It is obvious that the LL sub-image has a "smoothing" effect in both directions. The LH sub-image is the result from a filter in which the image has been smoothed in horizontal direction and enhanced in vertical direction. The HL sub-image is the result from a filter in which the image has been enhanced in horizontal direction and smoothed in vertical direction. The HH sub-image has an "enhancing" effect in both directions. Fig. 3 shows the above characteristics of these four sub-images. The original gray level image is shown in Fig. 3(a). Figs. 3(b)-(e) are its sub-images decomposed by Daubechies wavelet. It can be shown that the LH sub-image contains only the lines in horizontal direction, while the HL sub-image contains only the lines in vertical direction. From this example, it can be observed that the horizontal and vertical lines of the image can be extracted from the LH and HL sub-images. Afterwards, the tables which are composed of the horizontal and vertical lines in the form documents can be obtained. Another example is depicted in Fig. 4.

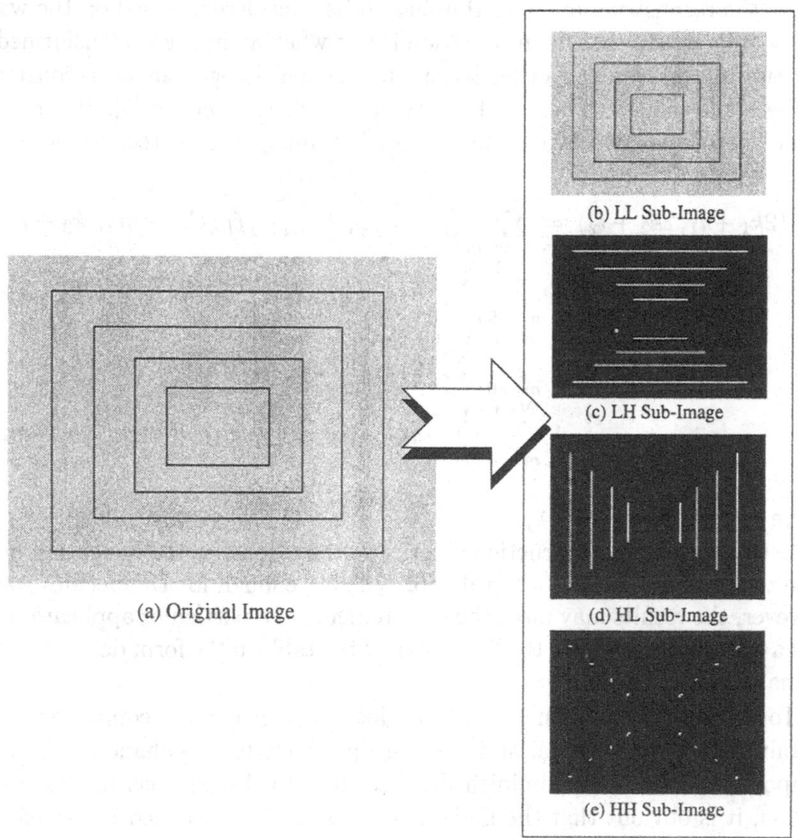

Fig. 3. Example of the decomposition of an image. (a) The original image with several nested squares. (b)-(e) The sub-images which are obtained from the original image by the wavelet decomposition algorithm.

4 Reconstruction of Table Structure Image and Table Free Image

This section is broken into two sub-sections. The first sub-section presents the table extraction processing in accordance with a modified reconstruction algorithm, while the second sub-section describes how to obtain a table free image based on Minkowski operation.

4.1 Composing Table Structure Image by Modified Reconstruction Algorithm

In order to extract the table structure and further to produce the table free image, the reconstruction algorithm has to be considered. Based on the wavelet theory, it is proved that no information is lost when an image is transformed into four sub-images. On the other hand, the original image can be reconstructed by these sub-images. The wavelet reconstruction is given by [5]. Based on the wavelet reconstruction algorithm, the original image can be reconstructed by

$$\begin{aligned} f(2k_1+i_1, 2k_2+i_2) = & \sum_{m_1=0}^{N-1}\sum_{m_2=0}^{N-1} h_{2m_1+i_1} h_{2m_2+i_2} f_{LL}(k_1-m_1,\ k_2-m_2) \\ & + \sum_{m_1=0}^{N-1}\sum_{m_2=0}^{N-1} h_{2m_1+i_1} g_{2m_2+i_2} f_{LH}(k_1-m_1,\ k_2-m_2) \\ & + \sum_{m_1=0}^{N-1}\sum_{m_2=0}^{N-1} g_{2m_1+i_1} h_{2m_2+i_2} f_{HL}(k_1-m_1,\ k_2-m_2) \\ & + \sum_{m_1=0}^{N-1}\sum_{m_2=0}^{N-1} g_{2m_1+i_1} g_{2m_2+i_2} f_{HH}(k_1-m_1,\ k_2-m_2) \end{aligned} \tag{11}$$

where $i_1 \in \{0,1\}, i_2 \in \{0,1\}$.

In this wavelet reconstruction algorithm, the reconstructed image will be very close to the original one if the value of N is big enough for Daubechies wavelet. However, the results may meet the requirements of a particular application when N is a small value because the line width of the table in the form document image is small.

To extract the table lines in a form document image, the components which contain only the horizontal and vertical lines have to be enhanced while other components have to be diminished. According to the analysis in the previous section, it is obvious that the horizontal lines can be enhanced by proliferating the LH sub-image component, while the vertical lines can be enhanced by proliferating the HL sub-image component. Therefore, it seems that the LH and HL sub-images can be used to reconstruct a table structure image which contains mainly table lines of the original image. However, such a table structure image may contain text-noise which has to be removed. Fortunately, the HH sub-image can be severed as a constraint condition to solve this problem, since it contains the main components of the text image. Based on this idea, the wavelet reconstruction algorithm has been modified to achieve the goal. The modified reconstruction algorithm is described as

$$f_{table}(m,n) = \begin{cases} 0 & \text{if } f'_{table}(m,n) < 0 \\ f'_{table}(m,n) & \text{if } f'_{table}(m,n) \geq 0 \end{cases}, \tag{12}$$

where

$$\begin{aligned} & f'(2k_1+i_1, 2k_2+i_2) \\ & = C_1 \sum_{m_1=0}^{N-1} \sum_{m_2=0}^{N-1} h_{2m_1+i_1}\, g_{2m_2+i_2}\, f_{LH}(k_1-m_1,\ k_2-m_2) \\ & + C_2 \sum_{m_1=0}^{N-1} \sum_{m_2=0}^{N-1} g_{2m_1+i_1}\, h_{2m_2+i_2}\, f_{HL}(k_1-m_1,\ k_2-m_2) \\ & - C_3 \sum_{m_1=0}^{N-1} \left| \sum_{m_2=0}^{N-1} g_{2m_1+i_1} g_{2m_2+i_2}\, f_{HH}(k_1-m_1,\ k_2-m_2) \right| \end{aligned} \tag{13}$$

such that C_1, C_2 and C_3 are coefficients, and they should satisfy the condition of $0 < C_1 < C_3$, $0 < C_2 < C_3$.

The modified wavelet reconstruction algorithm is used to extract the lines from the form document image in our research. We have known that the LH and HL sub-images contain the horizontal and the vertical components respectively, while the HH sub-image contains other information which can be used to restrain the "noise" from the image when reconstructing the table structure image. Considering the fact that the magnitude in the HH sub-image is much more smaller than in the HL and LH sub-images, the parameters C_1 and C_2 should be much more smaller than C_3, and absolute is used in the third item in Eq. (13). On the other hand, the table line would be removed if C_3 is too big. Based on our experiments, C_3 can be chosen as 5 to 10 times as C_1 and C_2.

An example of the reconstruction of the table structure image using this modified reconstruction algorithm is illustrated in Fig. 4. The original image which contains texts and lines is shown in Fig. 4(a), the sub-images which were obtained from the original image by the wavelet decomposition are given in Fig. 4(b)-(e), and the table structure image generated by the modified wavelet reconstruction algorithm is given in Fig. 4(f).

4.2 Constituting Table Free Image by Minkowski Subtraction

To produce the table free image, the operation of Minkowski subtraction [6] is applied.

Let A be the set denoting the square object with all its elements denoted by a two-dimensional variable α. Next, let B be the set containing one point and a two-dimensional variable β used to describe this point. The Minkowski addition of two sets A and B, given by the symbol $\oplus$, is

$$A \oplus B = \{\mu \in R^2 : \mu = \alpha + \beta,\ \alpha \in A,\ \beta \in B\}. \tag{14}$$

The dual of the Minkowski addition is the Minkowski subtraction which is defined as

$$A \ominus B = (A^c \oplus B^c)^c. \tag{15}$$

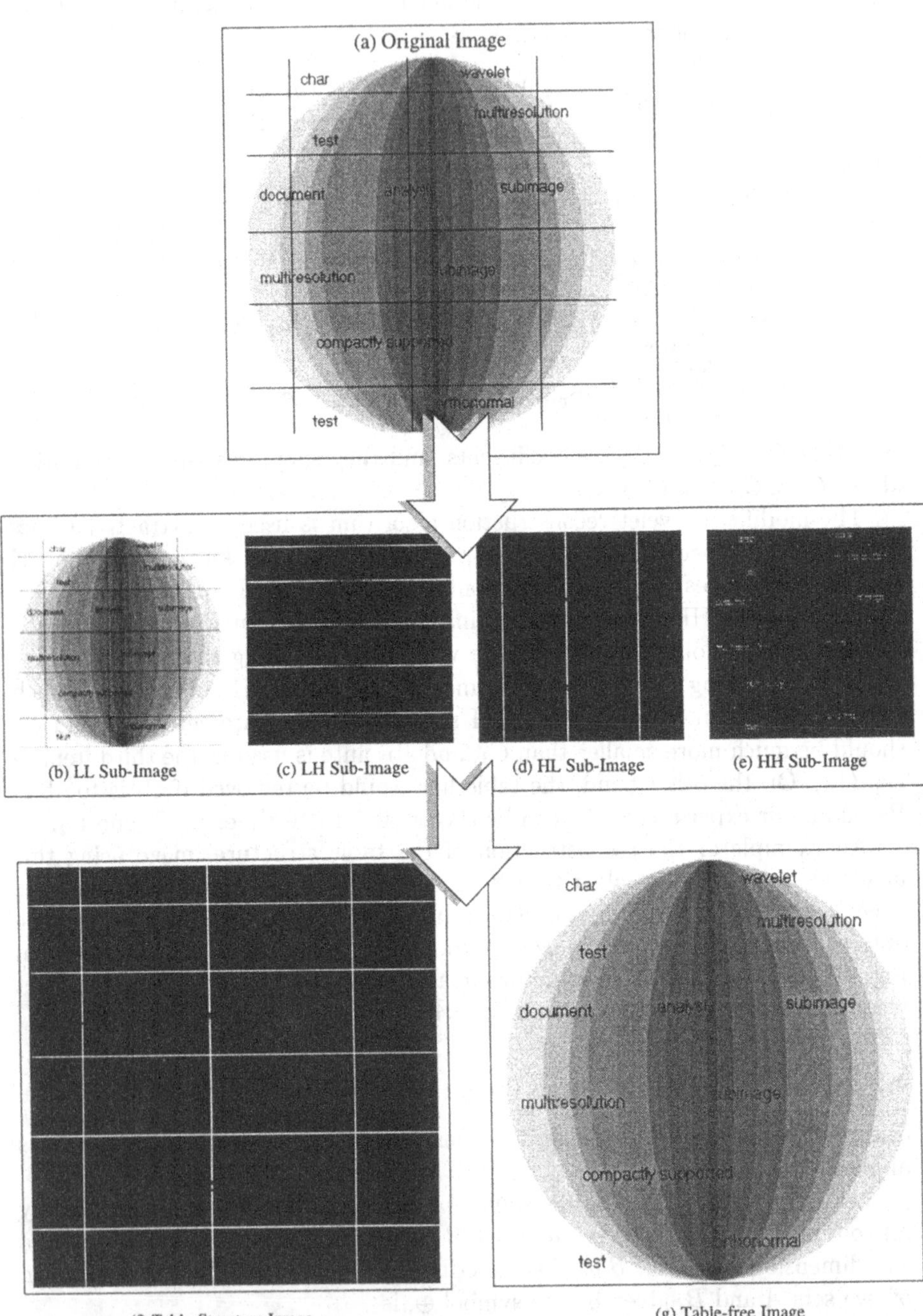

Fig. 4. Example of the wavelet decomposition and reconstruction. (a) The original image. (b)-(e) The sub-images obtained from the original image by the wavelet decomposition. (f) The table structure image generated by modified wavelet reconstruction algorithm. (g) The table free image produced by the original image and the table structure image.

Based on the Minkowski subtraction, the table free image can be generated from the original image and the table structure image. Let $D_{original}$, D_{table}, and D_{text} be a original form document image, a table structure image and a table free image respectively. The table free image can be produced by

$$D_{text} = D_{original} \ominus D_{table}. \tag{16}$$

In accordance with the Eq. (16), we can remove all table lines from the original image. Considering gray-levels of the image, we should replace the certain gray values with the points where the lines have been removed. In this paper, the average gray value of the neighboring points of the replaced pixel has been used.

For a point, $f(i,j)$, on the horizontal lines, the neighborhoods $f(i, j+\alpha)$, where $\alpha = \pm1, \pm2, \pm3$ have been chosen, while, on the vertical lines, the neighborhoods $f(i+\beta, j)$, where $\beta = \pm1, \pm2, \pm3$, have been used. Therefore, the replaced point should be

$$f(i,j) = \begin{cases} \frac{1}{6} \sum\limits_{\alpha=\pm1,2,3} f(i, j+\alpha), & \text{if the point is on the horizontal line} \\ \frac{1}{6} \sum\limits_{\alpha=\pm1,2,3} f(i+\alpha, j), & \text{if the point is on the vertical line.} \end{cases}$$

Fig. 4(g) shows an example of the table free image that was produced by the original image and the table structure image using the Minkowski subtraction.

5 Experiments and Discussion

Experiments have been conducted using a personal computer PC/Pentium II (333MHZ), and the programs have been written in Visual C^{++} 5.0. The form documents were entered into the system by an optical scanner and converted to a monochrome gray scale images(8 bits per pixel). The resolution of digitization in our experiments was 300 DPI.

In our experiments, the gradient algorithm has been used to deskew the form document image, and the value of N in Eq. (1) and Eq. (2) is 3. The Daubechies wavelet has been applied to decompose the form document images. The value of N used in Eq. (10) is 3, i.e., the values of $\{h_k\}$ are listed below:

$$\{h_k\} = \{0.332670 \;\; 0.714816 \;\; 0.630880 \;\; -0.027983 \\ -0.187034 \;\; 0.030841 \;\; 0.032883 \;\; -0.010597\}.$$

Chinese bank form documents has been utilized in our experiments. Fig. 5 and Fig. 6 show the two main process steps in the gradient-wavelet scheme.

The gradient algorithm has been used to deskew the original image, Fig. 5(a). According to the Eq. (1), Eq. (2), and Eq. (3), the distribution histogram of the original image on different orientation is shown in Fig. 5(b). The skew angle is the maximum point in the histogram, which was 12.5 in our example. The deskewed image obtained by Eq. (6) is shown in Fig. 6(a).

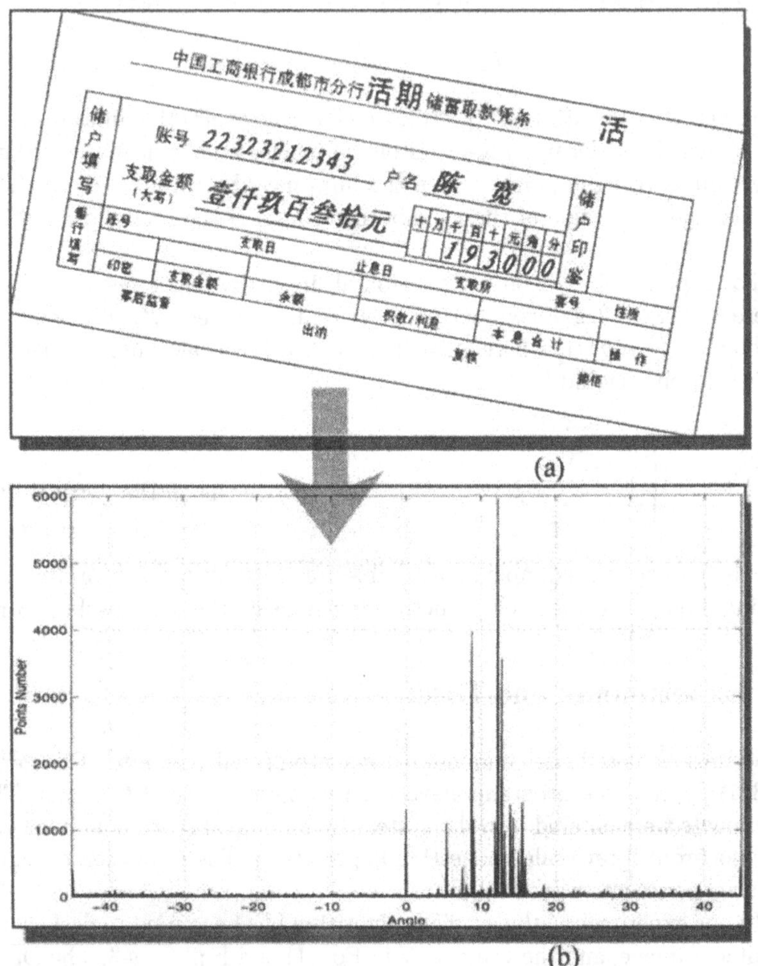

Fig. 5. The points distribution histogram obtained from gradient algorithm on different orientations for the Chinese bank document. (a) Original skewed form document image. (b) The distribution histogram on different gradient orientations of the original image.

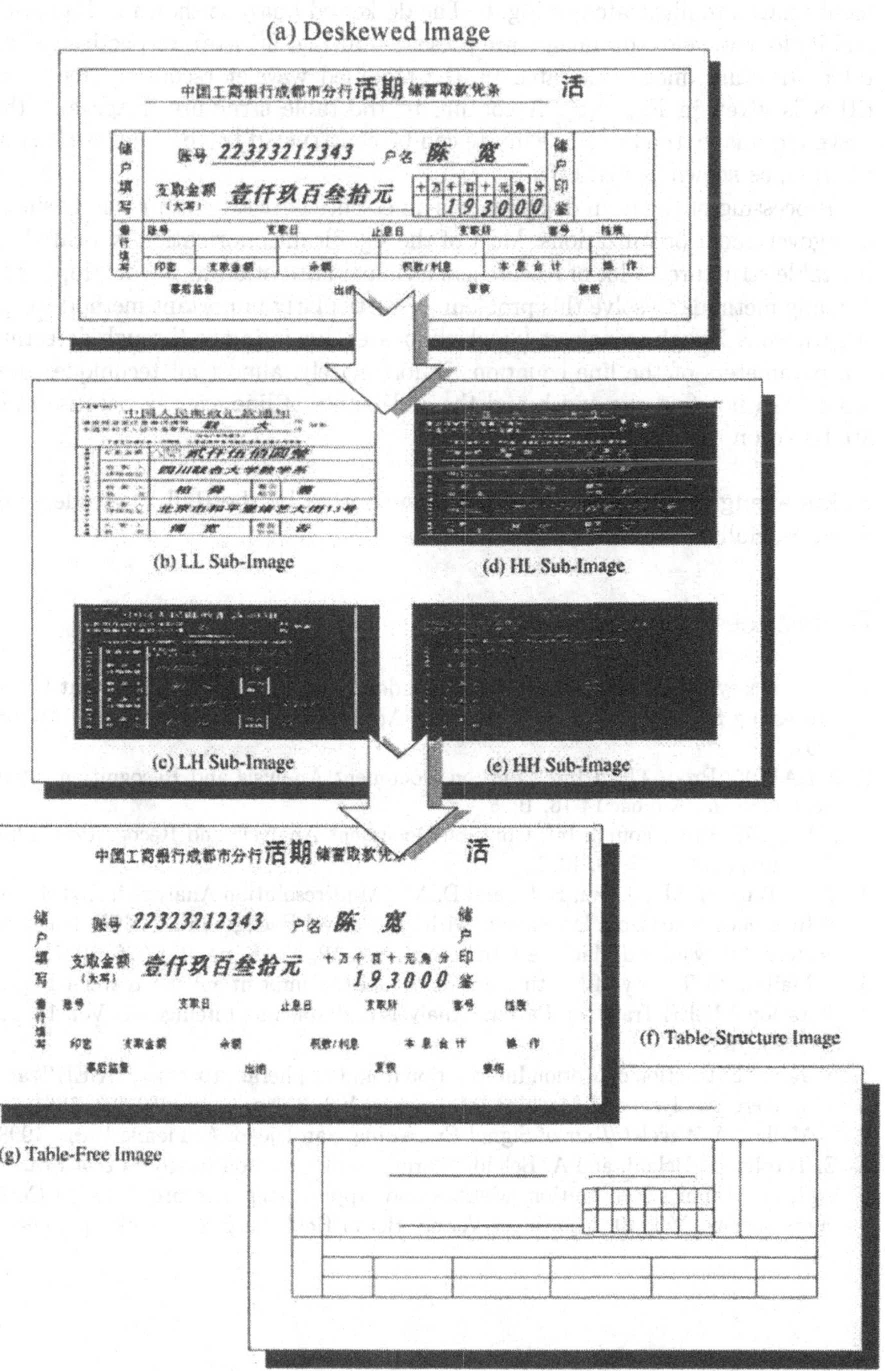

Fig. 6. Wavelet decomposition and reconstruction of Chinese bank document. (a) The deskewed image. (b)-(e) The sub-images obtained from the deskewed image by the wavelet decomposition. (f) The table structure image generated by modified wavelet reconstruction algorithm. (g) The table free image produced by the deskewed image and the table structure image.

Wavelet decomposition and reconstruction of the Chinese bank form document image are illustrated in Fig. 6. The deskewed image is shown in Fig. 6(a), and its four wavelet sub-images are presented in Fig. 6(b)-(e), respectively. The table structure image generated by the modified wavelet reconstruction algorithm is given in Fig. 6(g). According to the table structure image and the deskewed image, the table free image can be constructed by the Minkowski subtraction, as shown in Fig. 6(f).

Processing of the form documents is an essential operation in many business and government organizations. Most of the significant information is located by the table structure. A lot of researchers have paid attention to the developments of many methods to solve this problem. A particularly important method to extract lines is Hough transform [8] which locates line in image through detecting the parameters of the line equation. Unfortunately, almost all techniques presented can not find the width and the end points of line exactly because they are based on the geometry.

Acknowledgement This research was supported by the Hallym Academy of Sciences, Hallym University.

References

1. R. G. Casey, D. R. Ferguson, K. M. Mohiuddin, and E. Walach, "Intelligent Forms Processing System," Machine Vision and Application, Vol. 5, No. 3, pp. 143-155, 1992.
2. ICDAR'95, Proc. Third Int. Conf. on Document Analysis and Recognition, Montreal, Canada, August 14-16, 1995.
3. ICDAR'97. Proc. Fourth Int. Conf. on Document Analysis and Recognition, Ulm-Germany, August 18-20, 1997.
4. Y. Y. Tang, H. Ma, J. Liu, B. Li, and D. Xi, "Multiresolution Analysis in Extraction of Reference Lines from Documents with Gray Level Background," IEEE Trans. on Pattern Analysis and Machine Intelligence, Vol. 19, No. 8, pp. 921-926, 1997.
5. S. Mallat, "A Theory of Multiresolution Signal Decomposition: the Wavelet Representation," IEEE Trans. on Pattern Analysis and Machine Intelligence, Vol. 11, pp. 674-693, 1989.
6. R. Jain, "Extraction of Motion Information from Peripheral Processes," IEEE Trans. on Pattern Analysis and Machine Intelligence, Vol. 3, No. 5, pp. 489-503, 1981.
7. S. Mallat, *A Wavelet Tour of Signal Processing*, San Diego: Academic Press, 1998.
8. E. Turolla, Y. Belaid, and A. Belaid. "Form Item Extraction Based on Line Searching", in Graphics Recognition: Method and Applications, Lecture Notes in Computer Science, Vol. 1072, Springer-Verlag, Berlin Heidelberg New York , pp. 69-79, 1996.

The T-Recs Table Recognition and Analysis System

Thomas Kieninger and Andreas Dengel

DFKI-GmbH, Postfach 2080, 67608 Kaiserslautern, FRG,
Thomas.Kieninger@dfki.de, Andreas.Dengel@dfki.de,
WWW page: http://www.dfki.uni-kl.de/~kieni/t_recs/

Abstract. This paper presents a new approach to table structure recognition as well as to layout analysis. The discussed recognition process differs significantly from existing approaches as it realizes a bottom-up clustering of given word segments, whereas conventional table structure recognizers all rely on the detection of some separators such as delineation or significant white space to analyze a page from the top-down.
The following analysis of the recognized layout elements is based on the construction of a tile structure and detects row- and/or column spanning cells as well as sparse tables with a high degree of confidence.
The overall system is completely domain independent, optionally neglects textual contents and can thus be applied to arbitrary mixed-mode documents (with or without tables) of any language and even operates on low quality OCR documents (e.g. facsimiles).

1 Introduction

Document structure analysis is emerging as a key technology for enabling the intelligent treatment of information and provides the key for an efficient handling of documents. The information inherent to the layout of tables is even more important, since their relational character requires different analysis techniques in the context of document understanding.

This paper presents the approach of *T-Recs*, a system that deals with the identification of tables within arbitrary documents, the isolation of individual table cells and the analysis of the layout to determine a correct row/column mapping.

We start with the initial block clustering – the central idea. Then we point out required postprocessing steps to correct some system inherent errors. While so far we focused on the segmentation, Sect. 4 sketches the analysis of the table cell layout.

1.1 The *T-Recs* Document Model

The *T-Recs* document model has 3 different hierarchically organized structure types and one non-hierarchically embedded auxiliary structure for text lines:

Words are our elementary objects. Their bounding box geometry and optionally their textual contents constitute the input of the system. Formally, a word is described as a triple $W = (T, G, A)$, where T keeps the textual contents, G denotes the bounding box geometry, specified by the quadruple $G = (x_0, y_0, x_1, y_1)$ and A holds the recognized font attributes.

Lines (also referred to as *text lines*) are an initially built aggregation of words that serves as *auxiliary structure* for all following procedures!

They are described as quadruples $L = (W_0, succ, G, A)$, specifying a sorted list of words (with W_0 naming the first word and *succ* the appropriate successor function), the bounding box G and the attributes $A = (linenumber, rownumber, spc\_len)$ that hold the unique *linenumber*, the *logical rownumber* (see Sect. 3.5) and average space width.

Blocks are dynamic aggregations of words. Note that *blocks are not aggregations of lines*! The initial *word-to-block mapping* is made by the central clustering algorithm but is changed by the various postprocessing steps. Blocks thus keep the main segmentation information.

Like lines, blocks are described as quadruple $B = (W_0, succ, G, A)$. The additional block attributes $A = (type, justification, height, nmbwords)$ describe the classification into *type 1* and *2* (see Sect. 3.2), the justification, height (as number of lines) and number of words in the block.

Document The document is defined as quadruple $D = (B_0, succ, G, A)$, where B_0 and *succ* specify a *sorted list of blocks*. The successor function $succ_{doc}(s)$ is defined for *words*, *lines* and *blocks*. The attributes $A = (l\_spc)$ contain the average linespacing.

Significantly large distances between adjacent lines cause the construction of *dummy lines* between them. This prevents the $succ_{doc}(line)$ function from bridging large line spacings as between paragraphs.

In our notation, objects of higher level instances are denoted in a functional way: $block(w_x)$ stands for the associated block of word w_x. The attributes of an object are denoted similarly but with brackets instead of parentheses around the argument. Thus, $fontsize[w_x]$ would describe the *fontsize* attribute of the word w_x. The bounding box geometry $G = (x_0, y_0, x_1, y_1)$ itself is specified by the upper-left and lower-right corner coordinates respectively.

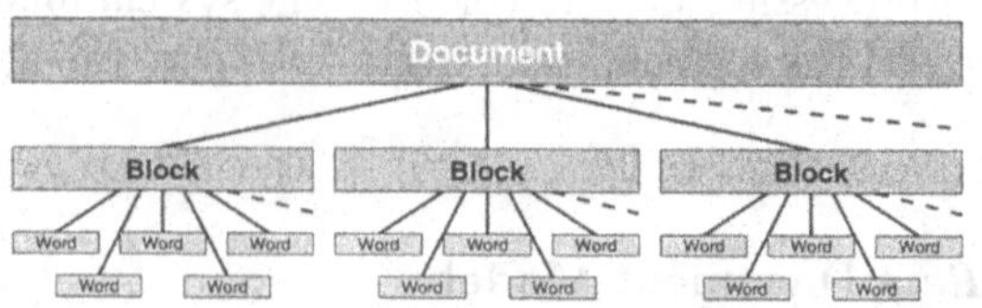

Fig. 1. Document model of the *T-Recs* System (hierarchical part)

Omiting the subordinated textline structure we achieve the hierarchical document model seen in Fig. 1, consisting of *words*, *blocks* and the *document* itself (in bottom-up order). Each object is part of a higher level instance.

2 Segmentation

2.1 Top-Down vs. Bottom-Up

Structure recognition itself is a wide research area and numerous people are addressing this topic. Existing approaches can be divided into systems which are specialized to detect logical objects in a restricted domain such as business letters as described in Dengel [3] or systems which try to identify more general structure elements like paragraphs, headers or lists. Hu [7] and Condit [2] both describe systems of that class. But only a small part of such systems consider the specific problems of tabular structures. They rather focus on objects like *paragraphs*, *headers* and *lists* in the general case or *sender*, *recipient*, *date* and *body* in case of business letters.

The investigation of existing table structure recognition approaches discloses a significant similarity: segmentation can always be characterized as a *top-down* approach that is driven by the detection of separators. Rus and Summers [16] present a system for the segmentation and labeling of general structures, also considering tables where they are able to detect narrow columns, using so-called *White Space Density Graphs* (WDG). Some other approaches relying on sufficiently large white spaces are described by Rahgozar et al. [13] who operates on word segments rather than on the bitmap, Tupaj et al. [18] who takes plain text output of OCR systems as input and Spitz [17] who determines so-called horizontal and vertical *rivers of white space* to define the boundaries of the islands of print material. Others are explicitly looking for ruling lines that determine the table structure. Representatives of this class are Green and Krishnamoorthy [5], who apply a grammar-based analysis on the set of occuring lines to evaluate the table layout, Itonori [8], who only considers the labeling aspects and expects well segmented blocks as input, or Hirayama [6] with his interesting *DP matching method.* Chandran and Kasturi [1] consider both (ruled lines and so-called *white streams*) to determine the layout structure.

T-Recs differs from conventional table segmentation systems as it represents a *bottom-up* approach. The central idea of *T-Recs* is to *not explicitly look for any kind of separators* (lines or spacings) but rather to identify words that belong to the same logical unit. The motivation for this unconventional strategy was twofold:

While typical top-down systems rely on the detection of some evidence to separate layout regions from each other, appropriate table segmentation systems concentrate on either characteristic delineation or conspicuous white spaces. This leads to a somewhat limited applicability of those systems.

The second reason for our design was driven by the insight that a human's way of recognizing a tabular structure within a document is based on the word-segments themselves. When looking at a table, a human never tries to identify textlines which he then divides into fragments of columns nor does he search for a given delineation to decompose layout regions. He rather realizes the blocks and columns directly as aggregations of words.

2.2 The *T-Recs* Bottom-Up Clustering Approach

Elementary to bottom-up approaches is the fact that some ordered elements (words) are aggregated to higher level instances (blocks). Since other bottom-up clustering systems either rely on nearest neighbors [4], run-length smoothing [19] or on the construction of Voronoi diagrams as block separators [12] [10] and thus localize adjacent elements to *all directions*, they will not be able to detect narrow column gaps. In contrast, *T-Recs* limits its search to neighboring words in the previous and next line (relative to the currently inspected item) whose bounding-boxes *horizontally overlap* with the inspected word. This symmetrical, binary relation $ovl(w_1, w_2)$ is given if the projections of the bounding boxes of two words w_1 and w_2 to the x-axis have a common range and if the words are located in subsequent lines:

$$\begin{aligned} ovl(w_1, w_2) \;\Leftrightarrow\; & (x_1[w_1] \geq x_0[w_2]) \wedge (x_0[w_1] \leq x_1[w_2]) \;\wedge \\ & (\, line(w_1) = succ_{doc}(line(w_2)) \;\vee \\ & \;\; line(w_2) = succ_{doc}(line(w_1))\,) \end{aligned}$$

Figure 2 shows a sample block and the area that contains potential overlapping words (gray stripe over the initial word "consists"). The words (or bounding boxes) that are "touched" by this virtual stripe will be clustered to the same block as the initial word.

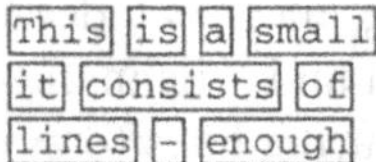

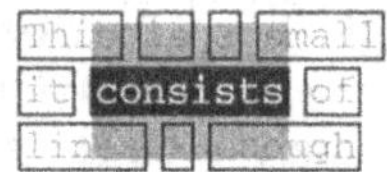

Fig. 2. Vertical neighbors of the word "consists"

Based on this relation, the clustering works as follows:

1. Find an *unexpanded* word $w_x := w_0$ (the *seed*) and create block b_i;
2. Mark *current word* w_x as *expanded* and add it to b_i;
3. Evaluate all *unexpanded* words w_j in $ovl(w_x, w_j)$;
4. For all w_j, make it the *current word* w_x and perform steps 2, 3 and 4;
5. If no more matching words are found, increment i and go to step 1;
6. Stop, if all words are marked as *expanded*.

Blocks are constructed "around" the *block seed* w_0 and can thus be described as transitive hull ovl^* of the overlapping relation. We also write $w_x \sim_{ovl^*} w_y$ if the words belong to the same cluster and define:

$$\begin{aligned} \mathcal{M} &:= \{w_i\} && \text{the set of all words;} \\ [w_0]_{ovl^*} &:= \{w_x | w_x \in \mathcal{M} \wedge w_0 \sim_{ovl^*} w_x\} && \text{the cluster of } w_0; \\ \mathcal{M}|ovl^* &:= \{[w_x]_{ovl^*} | w_x \in \mathcal{M}\} && \text{set of all clusters.} \end{aligned}$$

Since the *ovl* relation is symmetrical, and hence $\sim_{ovl^*}$ is an equivalence relation, it is obvious, that the choice of the block seed has no effect on the clustering result: $w_x \sim_{ovl^*} w_y \rightarrow [w_x]_{ovl^*} = [w_y]_{ovl^*}$

We use the so called *segmentation graph* (Fig. 2, right) to visualize the clustering. The nodes of that graph are the centerpoints of the bounding boxes and an edge between two nodes indicates the overlapping relation between the appropriate words.

Advantages of the *T-Recs* Approach The strengths of *T-Recs* are not directly visible in the context of the above example but at least it is obvious that *T-Recs* is capable of recognizing and clustering regular blocks. It is moreover clear, that isolated blocks will be recognized as isolated elements since their elements do not interleave mutually. An example of a tabular environment with a dense column arrangement is seen in Fig. 3.

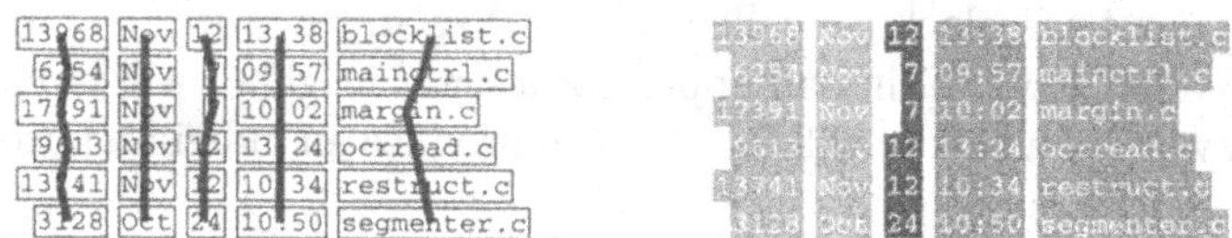

Fig. 3. Segmentation of a tabular environment

A first advantage of this approach compared to top-down systems is the independence of delineations or conspicuous white spaces. We can thus accept any documents regardless of the occurence of the above features.

A second advantage is the independence of accurate vertical or horizontal cuts between block. *T-Recs* is able to segment blocks whose rectangular block bounding boxes intersect. In other words: the block layout is not limited to rectangular shapes. Here we also speak of *Non-Manhattan Layout* [11].

System Inherent Errors Although the results look good on a large collection of documents, we recognize that there are some segmentation errors that are inherent to this approach. Aiming towards the identification of significant features of all mis-segmentations to provide appropriate corrections algorithms, we were able to develop a series of specialized procedures.

Throughout this document we will use Fig. 4 (left) as reference to give examples of the different classes of errors but also for discussing appropriate post-processing procedures. The error classes can be described as follows:

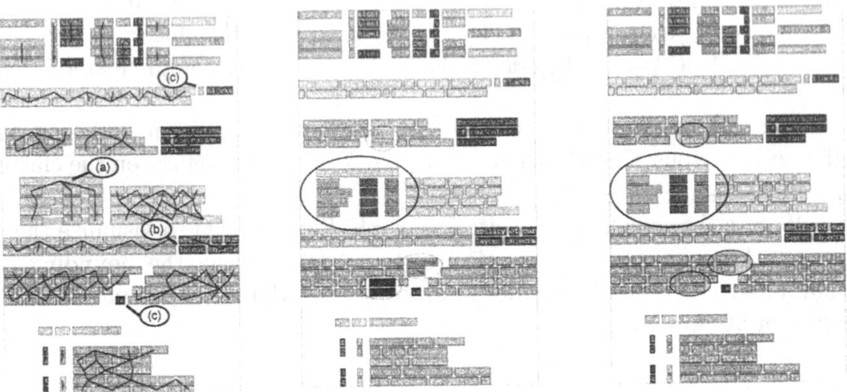

Fig. 4. Initial clustering, intermediate and remaining "split sons"

- Columns that are merged together by a common header which consistently overlaps with the first word of each column (Fig. 4, left: a).
- Blocks that are split into parts by an occasional gap at the same X-position throughout the block (so called *rivers*) (Fig. 4, left: b).
- Words that have neither an upper nor a lower neighbor will remain isolated. Each word of a header will for instance produce an individual, isolated block (Fig. 4, left: c).

The following paragraph discusses ways to escape these inherent errors. Each error-class will have its own postprocessing procedure.

3 Postprocessing Steps

3.1 Isolation of Merged Columns

The first problem that we want to consider are column blocks that are joined together by a common header which spans all the columns. In this case we need to identify the subcolumns. Looking more closely at the segmentation graph, we recognize a significant feature: the words of subcolumns all occur in a *one-to-one* relation. This relation $one_{one}(w_x, w_y)$ is given between two words, if word w_x has exactly one lower overlapping neighbor w_y and w_y has exactly this one upper neighbor w_x. Sequences of such words (as typically found in subcolumns) are especially visually conspicuous. We need to introduce some new functions in order to express this relation formally:

$$w_y = ovl^{first}(w_x) \iff ovl(w_x, w_y) \land \neg\exists w_z : (w_y = succ_{line}(w_z) \land ovl(w_x, w_z))$$

$$w_y = ovl^{first}_{up}(w_x) \iff w_y = ovl^{first}(w_x) \land line(w_x) = succ_{doc}(line(w_y))$$

$$w_y = ovl^{first}_{down}(w_x) \Longleftrightarrow w_y = ovl^{first}(w_x) \wedge line(w_y) = succ_{doc}(line(w_x))$$

Using the above functions, we can define the *one-to-one* relation as follows:

$$\begin{aligned} one_{one}(w_x, w_y) \Longleftrightarrow (\ & w_y = ovl^{first}_{down}(w_x) \wedge \neg ovl(w_x, succ_{line}(w_y)) \wedge \\ & w_x = ovl^{first}_{up}(w_y) \wedge \neg ovl(w_y, succ_{line}(w_x))\ ) \vee \\ & one_{one}(w_y, w_x) \quad \text{(this line ensures symmetry)} \end{aligned}$$

We now separate all *sequences of words* standing in such a one-to-one relation and moreover call them *Split Sons* ($\mathcal{B}^{split}$). No other parametrical limits are applied at that point. The set of words for each of these newly created blocks is characterized as the transitive hull of the one_{one} relation :

$$\mathcal{B}^{split}_{w_x} := [w_x]_{one_{one}^*} := \{w_y | w_y \in \mathcal{M} \wedge w_x \sim_{one_{one}^*} w_y\}$$

The result of this step applied to our reference document is seen in Fig. 4 (center). The interesting regions are marked with ovals.

As expected, this negligent isolation step results in some $\mathcal{B}^{split}$ blocks that are incorrect (small ovals). But the value of each isolated block can best be rated afterwards because the most significant factor for being a proper subcolumn is given by the surrounding columns. As we know, table columns typically occur only in the neighborhood of other columns. The basis for the split sons to remain isolated is calculated on the following features: number of directly adjacent columns; average amount of space to the left and right neighbor; block height; textual or structural similarity of the words (optional).

If the basis of a $\mathcal{B}^{split}$ block does not reach a given threshold, it will be remerged with its father-block. The result of this remerging operation is seen in Fig. 4 (right). The shaded ovals point to the "repaired" blocks.

3.2 Elimination of "Rivers"

In some cases a regular block might show some white space at the same x-position throughout the complete block. These so called *rivers of whitespace* are said to be *bad layout* and are tried to be avoided by modern typesetting programs and wordprocessors. They are more likely to occur in small blocks of only a few lines, using fixed width fonts (e.g. ASCII texts).

Applying the simple heuristics of merging adjacent blocks if the average gap size between the words at the border is not significantly bigger than one space, would end in the loss of isolated table columns with narrow gaps as well. To avoid this error, the merging operation must be applied selectively.

A closer look at the blocks which would be affected points out a very distinctive feature: those table column blocks that we want to prevent from the remerging are all characterized by having at most one word (or token) per line.

We thus classify all blocks into two types: the typical column blocks with one word per line are classified as *type 1*. All others are of *type 2*.

The actual postprocessing step is quite straightforward: we simply merge all (and only!) adjacent type 2 blocks if the white space between the words of the adjacent blocks is not significantly bigger than one space [1]. The intermediate clustering after this merging operation is seen in Fig. 5 (left).

3.3 Clustering of Isolated Words

The third class of errors is caused by words which have neither upper nor lower neighbor and thus would not be clustered to any block. A header would for instance be interpreted as a table of one line height with each word representing one column. In general, words that have neither upper nor lower neighbor might either belong to an isolated line (e.g. a header), stick out of the end of a non-justified block or represent the content of a table cell. For all except the last case the initial clustering algorithm keeps these words isolated by fault.

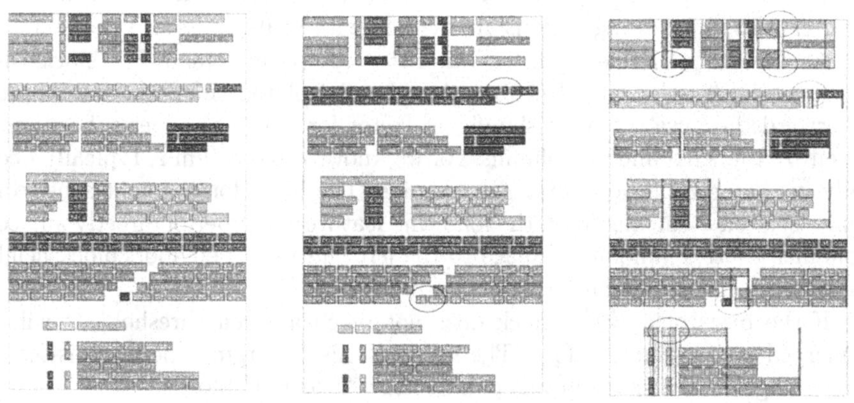

Fig. 5. Closed "Rivers", Reference points and clustered isolated words

We thus have to decide whether an isolated word fits into a table column or not. To gain a global view over all potential columns, we scan through all blocks and wherever a relatively narrow block or at least two blocks in a horizontal neighborhood occur, we assume to be inside a potential table environment and evaluate what we call the corresponding *margin structure* with its *margin points* MP and the *reference points* RP.

Therefore, we visit all blocks sequentially and if a block presumably belongs to a margin structure we evaluate the appropriate block cluster $\mathcal{B}^{b\text{-}clst}$ and the list of *margin points*. These MPs indicate the left and right borders of blocks. An MP can represent more than one block if these blocks are aligned to the

[1] The threshold value used for this comparison is given as an external parameter.

appropriate side. The major attributes of an MP are the accumulated height of its inducing blocks and its type (left or right) which corresponds to the triggering block side and the x-position.

The *reference points* RP are then constructed based on a sorted list (by x position) of margin points. The RPs gather a sequence of MPs with the same type (not interrupted by different type MPs!) and within a threshold x-range. The RPs accumulate the height of the MPs in the *ref_counter* attribute.

The reference points of our sample document are shown in Fig. 5 (center): gray and black bars for the left and right RPs respectively. The dark ovals point towards isolated words that should be bound to their horizontal neighbor. The bright ovals point towards words that should remain isolated.

Thus, every block in a cluster $\mathcal{B}^{b\_clst}$ has one left and one right RP. If any of the appropriate RPs *ref_counter* of a block is smaller than a given limit, it is presumed **not to match** with a surrounding column and will occasionally be merged to surrounding neighbor blocks on the appropriate side.

The effect of this procedure is to select isolated words that do not fit into a surrounding table column for the merging operation. The resulting blocks are seen in Fig. 5 (right). The gray ovals point out the "repaired" parts.

3.4 Delineation Based Block Separation

The intuitive semantics of delineations is an explicit demarcation of the distinct text areas. In the rare case of very dense blocksetting, it might happen, that the initial clustering builds blocks over such delineations. Therefore we apply the following processing steps.

We call a block *strictly cut*, if all endpoints of an intersecting line (or touching lines) are outside of the block bounding box. If one end of a separator is outside and one is inside of the block bounding box (thereby not touching any other separator), we say it is *weakly cut*. In either case the block is subject to further analysis.

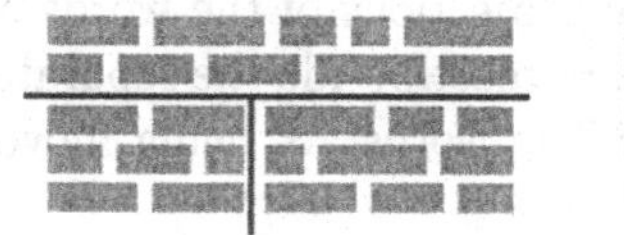
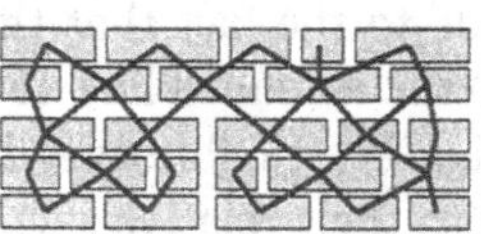

Fig. 6. Separator based splitting of a strictly cut block

Separation of Strictly Cut Blocks In this case, we simply have to decide for each word on which side relative to the separator it is positioned. The words are moved to new blocks accordingly. Figure 6 gives an example of three blocks that are isolated by two separators (left). Due to the dense arrangements of all words of these blocks, the initial clustering of *T-Recs* causes all words to be mapped to one block, as indicated by the segmentation graph (center). The above mentioned operation would achieve the final segmentation (right).

Separation of Weakly Cut Blocks Figures 7 and 8 both show examples of blocks which are weakly cut by a horizontal separator. As the block geometry itself gives no further discriminating information on how to proceed, we need to have a closer look at the words themselves when dealing with *weakly cut* blocks.

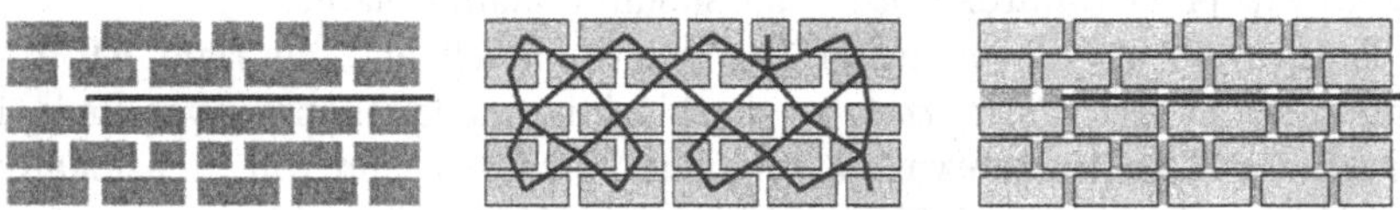

Fig. 7. Example of an unaffected weakly cut block

Even as a human reader we have no intuitive idea how to deal with the situation given in Figure 7. It is not clear, whether to break the block or not and if yes, what to do with the words that are not projected onto the separator. We decided to leave such blocks untouched.

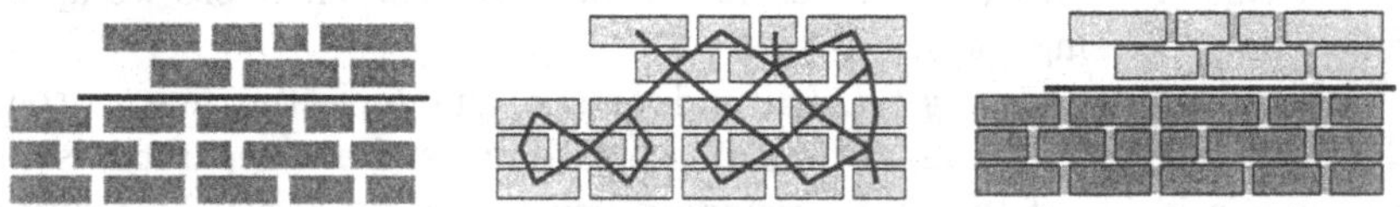

Fig. 8. Example of an affected weakly cut block

The example of Figure 8 is more intuitive: While one endpoint is inside the block bounding box, the decomposition based on the given separator looks nonetheless reasonable. This is due to the fact that the projections of the words on both sides of the separator to the extended line do not meet beside the separator itself. The upcoming operation is straightforward: The words are being moved to separate blocks according to their relative side.

3.5 Unification of Block Abstraction Level

Looking at the type 1 blocks (see Sect. 3.2) we realize that they all represent columns (or parts of a column), whereas type 2 blocks represent atomic textual units. To achieve a homogeneous view, we simply decompose all type 1 blocks into their individual line segments. The resulting structure is seen on the left of Fig. 9.

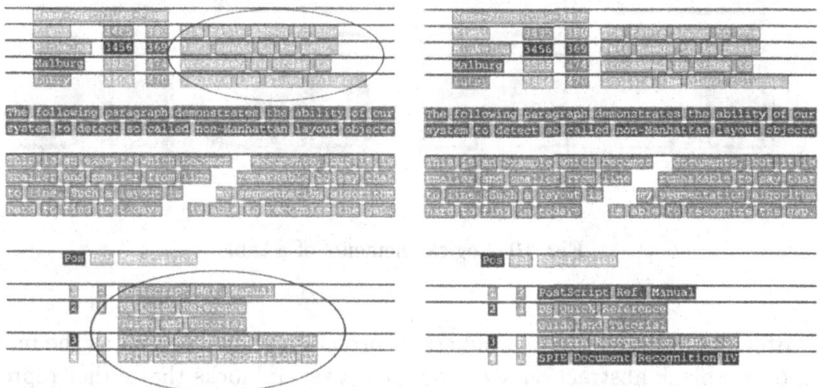

Fig. 9. Decomposed type 1 blocks and type 2 blocks split at row borders

The figure moreover shows some conspicuous black horizontal lines, called (logical) *row borders.* These are triggered by the top edges of those blocks that are standing inside a tabular environment. We might further observe two distinct type 2 blocks (indicated by the gray ovals) which are intersected by some row borders. If such a block is an aggregation of table cells, it will also be decomposed at the edges of the row borders.

To decide whether or not a type 2 block has to be treated like this, we consider that word processors try to fill the existing line space as much as possible. Thus, a word at the beginning of each line would not have fit on the end of the previous line. In this case we say that a block is *properly filled* and conclude that it contains no explicit returns and hence builds a logical entity. The resulting structure which represents the final segmentation result is seen on the right of Fig. 9.

We like to refer to [9] for a detailed description of the postprocessing steps discussed in Sects. 3 and 3.5 and to the online demo of the *T-Recs* system under `http://www.dfki.uni-kl.de/~kieni/t_recs/`

4 Table Layout Analysis

To ensure a common terminology, we need to specify some objects used in the context of tables. To point out the differences between the data *cells* and the table *tiles* we take an example with an empty field as well as a column- and a row spanning data cell as shown in Fig. 10. The block segments are represented by black outlined rectangles. The gray filled rectangles indicate the structures to be explained.

From left to right we see the original *data cells* represented by their bounding boxes. Next we see the *columns* followed by the *rows.* The very right shows the *table tiles*, a regular structure, defined by the combination of rows and columns. The overall structure is called the *table.*

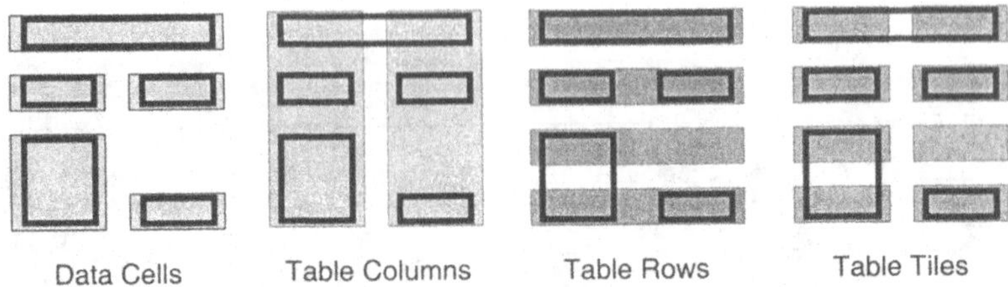

Fig. 10. Logical elements of a table.

After the initial clustering and error correction phases as well as the unification of the block abstraction level, we have a set of blocks that either represent regular paragraphs or table cells. We now need to identify table cell blocks and analyze their structural arrangement.

Wherever two or more blocks occur as horizontal neighbors (indicated by blocks with a dedicated margin structure), we assume a table and construct a structure that we call *table tiles*.

4.1 Construction of Table Tiles

Instead of rule based approaches that perform a bottom-up aggregation of higher level objects, *T-Recs* evaluates a grid of tiles which is fine enough so that each tile covers at most one table cell. Figure 11 (left) shows an example of some blocks (indicated by bright rectangles) and some horizontal and vertical block separators. The horizontal separators are identical to the row borders as described in Sect. 3.5. The vertical separators overlay the areas between right and left margin points as described in Sect. 3.3.

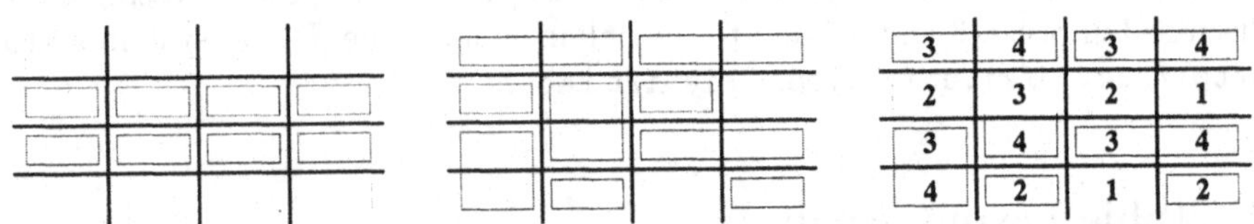

Fig. 11. Tiles of a regular and a degenerated table and appropriate tile classification

The tiles are defined by the grid that is made up of the horizontal and vertical separators and in the case of Fig. 11 (left) they are identical with the blocks of the cells themselves.

It is obvious, that each tile is covered by *at most one table cell* while on the other hand we *do not have any more tiles than needed* to achieve this condition. We can further state, that the tiles are identical to the table cell blocks if the table is dense and none of the cells spans more than one row and column.

In contrast, Fig. 11 (center) shows a degenerate table with various row or column spanning cells and even "missing" cells (i.e. the table is *sparse*). Nonetheless we get the same tile structure as in the example of Fig. 9, indicating 4 rows and 4 columns. Obviously, the tiles are no longer identical to the cells. Again, each tile is covered by at most one cell - but we also realize that some cells touch more than one tile and moreover we see that some tiles remain untouched.

4.2 Internal Structured Representation

The internal representation of the document structure consists of a sequence of regular paragraph blocks and blocks occuring as cells within a table. The latter blocks contain pointers to appropriate tile structures. The presence of tile structures causes the system to handle the appropriate blocks differently than other blocks, i.e. with a function that is designed for that particular purpose. First, we need to identify the different states of a tile:

1. A tile can be left blank (if a table is sparse).
2. A tile can be covered by a block that does not reach to adjacent tiles.
3. A tile can be the first (topmost and leftmost) in a sequence of tiles to be covered by one column and/or row spanning cell.
4. A tile can be the "non-first" in a sequence of tiles to be covered by a column and/or row spanning cell.

Figure 11 (right) shows the center example again, but with numbers in each tile, indicating the appropriate classification according to the numbering of the different states.

4.3 Generating Tagged Output of Tables

Since the current output of *T-Recs* is a HTML document, we briefly summarize the main HTML tags that are used for the definition of tables. All tags specify an environment which ends with the corresponding end-tag. The end-tags are indicated by a slash in front of the actual tag name. An overall table will be nested between a pair of `<TABLE>` and `</TABLE>` tags.

`<TABLE>`	Defines the start of a new table
`<TR>`	Defines begin of a new row of a table
`<TH>`	Defines begin of a header cell
`<TD>`	Defines begin of a data cell
`COLSPAN=`x	Optional Parameter for `<TD...>` and `<TH...>` that defines a cell to span x columns
`ROWSPAN=`y	Optional Parameter for `<TD...>` and `<TH...>` that defines a cell to span y rows

The preparation of the tagged output of tabular environments is done by traversing the tile structure from top to bottom, left to right. The actions performed for each tile are thereby controlled by the discussed state. The following abstract algorithm describes the individual operations:

1. If a new table starts, print "<TABLE>".
2. If current tile is the first one in a new row, print "<TR>".
3. If the status number of the current tile is 1, print "<TD></TD>" to define an empty field.
4. If the status number of the current tile is 2, print "<TD>" .
5. If the status number of the current tile is 3, print "<TD COLSPAN=x ROWSPAN=y>" where x and y denote the number of columns and rows respectively that are covered by the associated block.
6. Skip tiles with a status number of 4.
7. If the status number of the current tile is 2 or 3, print the textual contents of the associated block and the end tag "</TD>".
8. If current tile is the last one the current row (regardless of the state), print "</TR>".
9. If the current table ends, print "</TABLE>"
   else move to next tile and goto step 2.

5 Conclusion and Outlook

While classical character recognition systems do not show recent significant improvements [14] [15], commercial OCR systems focus more and more on the detection of structural information (such as tables) as key technology for their products.

Since benchmarking systems have not yet been developed for tabular structures, we cannot give quantitative statements about *T-Recs* results. But the demonstrated interest of OCR vendors in the *T-Recs* technology might count as proof for being on the right track.

Both of the *T-Recs* subsystems, segmentation and layout analysis, are still subject to further research with the goal of an improved performance. We will for instance implement new heuristics to avoid the misinterpretation of layout objects in business letters as tables.

In order to allow an objective benchmarking of the recognition accuracy we are currently developing a graphical user interface to gather ground truth data. This frontend also allows us to manipulate the layout of given documents while keeping track of the document logic. Thus, it is possible to construct large collections of ground truth data in a ready-to-use format for the actual application (no printing, scanning or OCR process neccessary) which is moreover free of any unwanted noise.

Benchmarking not only allows us to compare different analysis systems but also to document system progress and to optimize predefined system parameters.

References

[1] Surekha Chandran and Rangachar Kasturi: Structural Recognition of Tabulated Data. In *Proc. of International Conference on Document Analysis and Recognition - ICDAR 93*, 1993.

[2] Allen S. Condit: Autotag - A tool for creating Structured Document Collections from Printed Materials. *Master's thesis, Dept. of Computer Science, University of Nevada, Las Vegas*, 1995.

[3] Andreas Dengel: About the Logical Partitioning of Document Images. In *Proceedings SDAIR-94, Int'l Symposium on Document Analysis and Information Retrieval, Las Vegas, NV*, pages 209–218, April 1994.

[4] Lawrence O'Gorman: The Document Spectrum for Bottom-Up Page Layout Analysis. In H. Bunke, editor, *Advances in Structural and Syntactic Pattern Recognition*, pages 270 – 279. World Scientific, 1992.

[5] E. Green and M. Krishnamoorthy: Recognition of Tables using Table Grammars. In *Proc. of the 4-th Symposium on Document Analysis and Information Retrieval - SDAIR95, Las Vegas, Nevada*, 1995.

[6] Yuki Hirayama: A Method for Table Structure Analysis using DP Matching. In *Proc. of International Conference on Document Analysis and Recognition - ICDAR 95, Montreal, Canada*, 1995.

[7] Tao Hu: New Methods for Robust and Efficient Recognition of the Logical Structures in Documents. *PhD thesis, Institute of Informatics of the University of Fribourg, Switzerland*, 1994.

[8] Katsuhiko Itonori: Table Structure Recognition based on Textblock Arrangement and Ruled Line Position. In *Proc. of International Conference on Document Analysis and Recognition - ICDAR 93*, 1993.

[9] Thomas Kieninger: The *T-Recs* Table Converting System. available at http://www.dfki.uni-kl.de/~kieni/doc/trecs3.ps.gz, April 1998.

[10] Koich Kise, Akinori Sato, and Keinosuke Matsumoto: Document Image Segmentation as Selection of Voronoi Edges. In *Proc. of IEEE Computer Society Conference on Computer Vision and Pattern Recognition CVPR 97*, June 1997.

[11] George Nagy and S. Seth: Hierarchical Representation of Optically Scanned Documents. In *Proc. of the 7th Intl. Conference on Pattern Recognition (ICPR)*, 1984.

[12] T. Ohya, M. Iri, and K. Murota: A fast Voronoi Diagram Algorithm with Quaternary Tree Bucketing. In *Information Processing Letters, Vol. 18, No. 4*, 1984.

[13] M. Armon Rahgozar, Zhigang Fan, and Emil V. Rainero: Tabular Document Recognition. In *Proc. of the SPIE Conference on Document Recognition*, 1994.

[14] Stephen Rice, Frank Jenkins, and Thomas Nartker: The Fourth Annual Test of OCR Accuracy. Technical report, Information Science Research Institute (ISRI), Univ. of Nevada, Las Vegas, 1995.

[15] Stephen V. Rice, Frank R. Jenkins, and Thomas A. Nartker: The Fifth Annual Test of OCR Accuracy. Technical report, Information Science Research Institute (ISRI), Univ. of Nevada, Las Vegas, 1996.

[16] Daniela Rus and Kristen Summers: Using White Space for Automated Document Structuring. Technical Report TR 94 - 1452, Department of Computer Science, Cornell University, 1994.

[17] A. Lawrence Spitz: Recognition Processing for Multilingual Documents. In *Proceedings of the International Conference on Electronic Publishing, Document Manipulation & Typography*, Gaithersburg, Maryland, September 1990.

[18] Scott Tupaj, Zhongwen Shi, and Dr. C. Hwa Chang: Extracting Tabular Information from Text Files. Available at http://www.ee.tufts.edu/~hchang/paper1.ps, 1996.

[19] K. Y. Wong, R. G. Casey, and F. M. Wahl: Document Analysis System. *IBM Journal of Research & Developement, 1982*, 26(6):647–656, 1982.

Document Analysis Systems Development and Representation through the Object-Process Methodology

DOV DORI

Information Systems Engineering
Faculty of Industrial Engineering and Management
Technion, Israel Institute of Technology
Haifa 32000, Israel
E-mail: dori@ie.technion.ac.il

Abstract. Object-Process Methodology (OPM) calls for integrated system development, supported by Object-Process CASE Tool – OPCAT – a Computer Aided Software Engineering tool, which supports development and standard representation of industrial systems. OPCAT is designed to provide an Integrated System Engineering Environment (ISEE). Due to their generic nature and comprehensiveness, OPM and OPCAT are suitable for both developing Document Analysis Systems (DAS's) and representing them in a clear and standard way. We present the principles of OPM and show how it can be used as an ISEE for generic DAS development.

1 Introduction

Traditional inputs, such as labor, land and capital, which have played a major role in economics until the last decade, are no longer the major catalysts for economic sustainability and growth. The emerging important resource for the enterprise is an intangible one – the knowledge stored in documents and inside the heads of individuals.

In the last few decades, information has become a prime resource, whose importance is constantly increasing. For lack of a better word, we use the term information to designate a hierarchy of concepts that are built on top of each other. Starting with raw data, stored in ever more powerful and sophisticated machines, from which information is constructed, the hierarchy proceeds to knowledge, which is the result of human and machine information processing, all the way up to expertise. Expertise is the trait of a person who has accumulated and assimilated knowledge to the degree that using natural intelligence, s/he can deduce and generate new knowledge that is useful in the domain. As we climb up this information hierarchy, the emphasis shifts from the power and sophistication of machines to those of human beings.

High technology societies rely heavily on this human resource of natural intelligence and innovativeness. As we proceed toward the 21st century, the quality of this resource depends more and more on information already present in the organization or in its environment. In order to succeed, companies today need to learn how best to find, capture and exploit this precious resource. The ability of an enterprise to develop and make use of Document Management Systems (DMS's) is becoming as crucial s ever. Such systems, of which document analysis systems are but one component, are aimed at that collecting, storing, analyzing and making use of raw data and information through intelligent processing mechanisms. The ultimate goal of such systems from the enterprise viewpoint is to generate useful knowledge that serves its critical success factors. This domain of research and development is emerging as a new area called Knowledge Management (KM), with DMS's providing the infrastructure for KM.

For most enterprises, the knowledge is there, but it is not readily and widely available. In most cases, it does not even have to be created. Rather, it has to be captured. Enterprises have not been capturing "what they know". KM technologies are designed to pave the way to solving this problem. By capturing and finding out what they know, and then disseminating this knowledge to the right people, enterprises will be able to streamline their operations and improve their business processes and customer relationships.

To cope with the challenges and high-level KM requirements, the development of DMS's and general and DAS's in particular, must rely on a sound, integrated systems engineering environment. The Object-Process Methodology (OPM) is proposed here as an ideal infrastructure for this endeavor.

Object-Process Methodology (OPM)

The Object-Process Methodology (OPM) [1], [2], [3], [4] is a system development approach that has been developed to cater to the natural train of thought humans normally apply while trying to understand and build complex systems. In such systems, it is usually the case that structure and behavior are intertwined so tightly, that any separation between them is bound to further complicate the already complex description. Founded on General Systems Theory, OPM is generic and therefore most suitable for specifying systems of virtually any domain. In particular, DAS's are prime candidates for making use of OPM as we show in this work.

OPM incorporates the static-structural and behavioral-procedural aspects of a system into a single unifying model. This approach is counters contemporary object-oriented systems development methods, such as the accepted UML standard [5], which requires no less than eight different models, each with its own . OPM achieves model integration by treating both objects and processes as equally important things (entities) in the system's specification.

In OPM, objects are viewed as persistent, state preserving entities that interact with each other through processes. Processes are transient, transforming entities that affect objects by changing their state, or by generating or consuming objects. This structure-behavior unification into a single model results in synergy of unparalleled expressive power. By incorporating analysis, design, implementation, and deployment within one frame of reference and enabling smooth transitions among theses phases, OPM provides an Integrated Systems Engineering Environment (I SEE).

OPM uses Object Process Diagrams (OPDs) for expressing the objects of a modeled system and the processes that affect them. Figure 1 shows three OPDs, which describe how processes affect objects. This figure, as well as the others in this work, was drawn using OPCAT Version 1.6, which is available from the URL http://iew3.technion.ac.il:8080/~dori/opcathp/index.htm. As Figure 1 shows, objects and processes in an OPD are denoted within rectangles and ellipses, respectively, while object states are marked as round-cornered rectangles

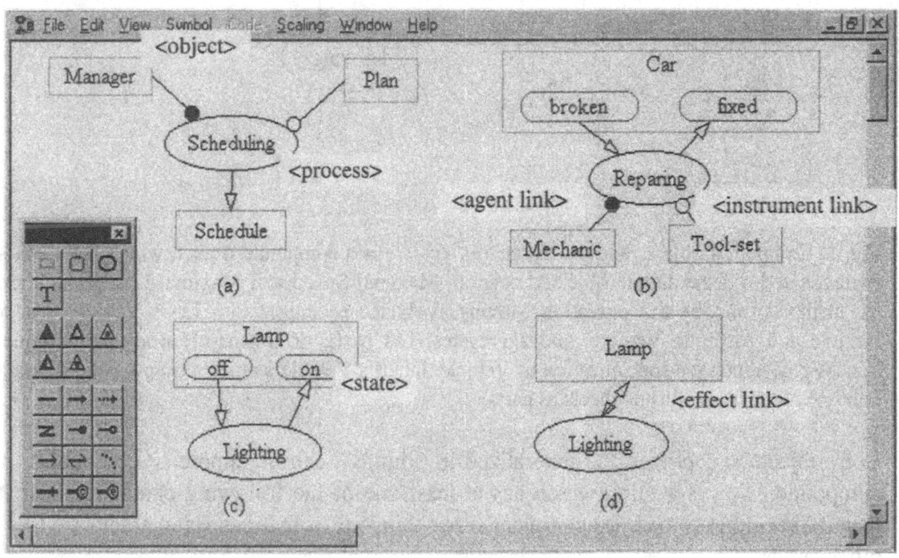

Fig. 1. OPDs showing how processes generate objects and change object states. (a) The object Manager is an agent that generates the object Schedule through the process of Scheduling using Plan as an instrument. (b) The agent Mechanic changes the state of the object Car from "broken" to "fixed" through the process of Repairing using Tool as an instrument. (c) The process Lighting changes the state of the object Lamp from "off" to "on". (d) Suppressing the states of Lamp converts the two effect links yields a single bi-directional effect link.

Two different kinds of links are used in the OPD of Figure 1 to connect objects to processes, depending on the roles that these objects play in the process to which they are linked. Objects may serve as enablers – instruments or intelligent agents, which are involved in the process without changing their state. Objects may also be transformed (change their state, generated, consumed, or affected) as a result of a process acting on them. In this case, the transformation link, denoted by a single- or double-head arrow is used. If a process generates an object, which did not exist prior to the process occurrence, the transformation link is a result link.

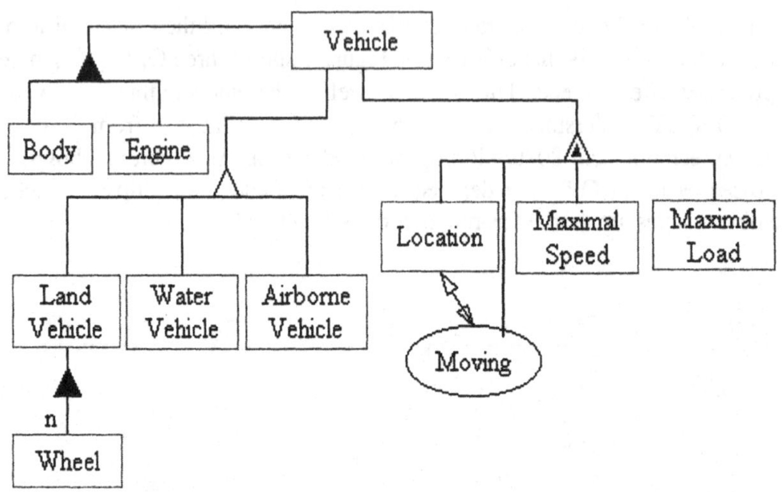

Fig. 2. Compound objects and processes. (a) Vehicle is a compound object, which features (is characterized by) the simple objects Location, Maximal Speed and Maximal Load, which are its attributes, and by the operation Moving. Vehicle specializes into Land Vehicle, Water Vehicle and Airborne Vehicle, and aggregates (has parts, or consist-of) Body and Engine. Land-Vehicle, being a specialization of Vehicle, inherits Vehicle's attributes and parts. Being a Land-Vehicle, it also has n wheels as parts.

Both objects and processes, generalized as "things", can be simple or compound. A compound thing is a thing which has at least one of the following characteristics: It generalizes other things, it aggregates other things pr it features (is characterized by) other things.

Figure 2 shows an example of a compound object. OPM handles the complexity of systems by using recursive seamless scaling. Objects and processes are first presented at a top-level system-environment OPD, which abstracts the key things – objects and processes – that play major roles in the system and its environment. Other, increasingly lower-level OPDs, are zoomed-in views into the details of these compound objects and processes. Selective scaling provides for focusing attention on various system portions at desired detail levels without losing the "big picture".

The time line in an OPD flows from the top of the diagram to its bottom. Hence, the top-to-bottom of process layout in the OPD represents their default execution order. Processes at the same height represent either parallel or mutually exclusive processes, depending on the existence of the logical XOR link between them or lack thereof.

A textual description in a natural-like Object-Process Language (OPL) is automatically extracted from the diagrammatic description. It is used for both customer verification and generation of executable code and database schema. To exemplify this, consider the following example of a generic manufacturing company.

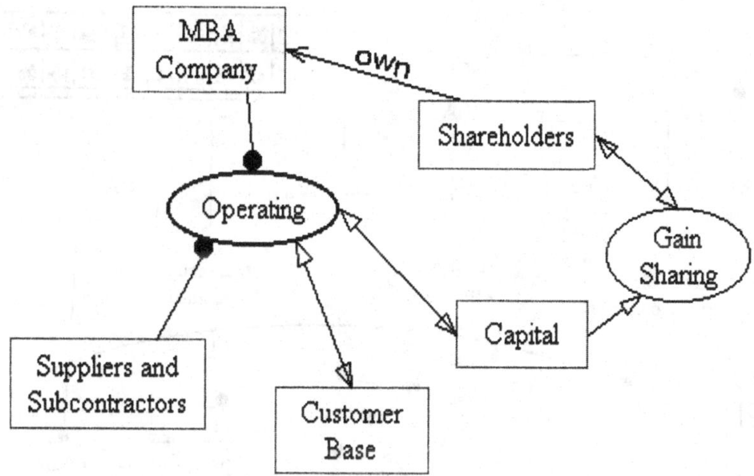

Fig. 3. Top-level Object-Process Diagram of the MBA Company

The Object-Process Language (OPL) set that is equivalent to the OPD of Figure 3 is:

```
  Shareholders own MBA Company.
  Operating is enabled by MBA Company, acting as agent.
  Operating is enabled by Suppliers & Subcontractors,
acting as agent.
  Operating affects Capital and Customer Base.
  Gain Sharing affects Shareholders.
  Gain Sharing consumes Capital.
```

Part of the Object-Process Language (OPL) set that is equivalent to the OPD of Figure 4 is:

```
  Company consists of CEO, CIO, Engineering Department,
Logistics Department, Manufacturing Department, Marketing
Department and Sales Department.
  Managing is enabled by CEO, acting as agent.
  Managing affects MBA Company.
  Operating is enabled by CIO, acting as agent.
  Operating consists of Designing, Manufacturing,
Marketing and Selling.
  Designing is enabled by Engineering Department, acting
as agent.
  Designing is enabled by Marketing Department, acting as
agent.
  Designing consumes capital.
  Designing results in Model.
  Manufacturing is enabled by Model.
  Manufacturing results in Product.
  Manufacturing consumes Capital.
  Marketing is enabled by Product.
  Marketing affects Customer Base.
  Marketing consumes Capital.
  Selling is enabled by Customer Base, acting as agent.
  Selling results Capital.
```

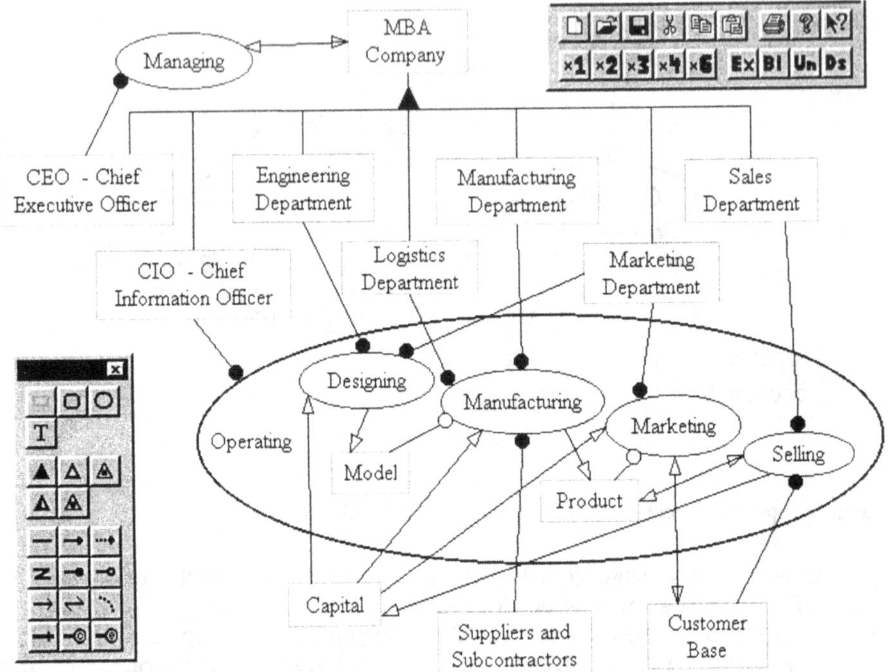

Fig. 4. A zoomed-in Object-Process Diagram, where the object MBA Company is unfolded and the process Operating is inflated.

As the example shows, OPL is designed such that it is very close to English as a natural language, albeit with stringent and limited syntax. The similarity of OPL to the *lingua franca* natural language makes it readable and understandable to humans without the need to learn any programming or pseudo-code-like language. The system's OPL specification resulting from an OPD set is thus amenable to being checked by domain experts, who need not be software experts. Since OPL is close enough to natural English, no prior training is required. This closes the gap between the requirement specification, which the customer usually expresses in prose, and the actual system specification resulting from the OPM analysis and design. On the other hand, the syntax of OPL is well defined and unambiguous. This eliminates the problem of the fuzziness of natural languages and provides a firm basis for executable code generation, database schema definition, control of computer supported collaborative work and other computer based processes. Thus OPL serves two goals. One is to convert the set of Object-Process Diagrams (OPDs) into a natural-language-like text for use as a means for communicating analysis results back to the prospective users and customers, who may be more comfortable with reading text than checking Object-Process Diagrams. The other goal of OPL is to provide the infrastructure needed for code generation, database scheme generation and reverse engineering activities.

OPM is useful for understanding system-related problems, communicating with application experts, preparing documentation, and designing solutions for the modeled system, which, as noted, can be of any domain. OPM has been successfully applied in a variety of areas, including studyware design [6] Computer Integrated Manufacturing [7], R&D Management [8] and real-time systems [9]. In the specific area of DAS, OPM was instrumental in works dealing with the Machine Drawing Understanding System (MDUS) [10, 11], 3-D reconstruction from engineering drawings [12] and content-based image retrieval [13].

2 Document Management System – an OPM Representation

Data, information and knowledge are the three major items in the informatics hierarchy. Knowledge, the highest item, is generated by humans from information, which, in turn, is extracted from data. A document is a human-generated artifact that records a representation of some data, information or knowledge. In the long term, interesting documents from the single enterprise or the entire community viewpoint are those that represent knowledge – a meaningful and useful digest of information and data. A document is the instrument that enables preservation of this knowledge, its transfer to other interested parties and extracting the knowledge through capturing the document and analyzing it.

As the OPD in Figure 5 shows, a Document Management System (DMS) consists of three subsystems: generation, exchange and analysis. The Document Generation Subsystem is the instrument used by the document author to generate the document. The Document Exchange Subsystem is the instrument that enables the communication of the document to its prospective audience, which can be a particular human or organization, or the public at large. Exchanging documents implies a two way subsystem: one that publishes (sends or disseminates) the document, and the other that acquires (receives) it. Once acquired, the document must be analyzed, i.e. properly processed, in order to make the knowledge recorded in it in a representational format that is readily available to humans.

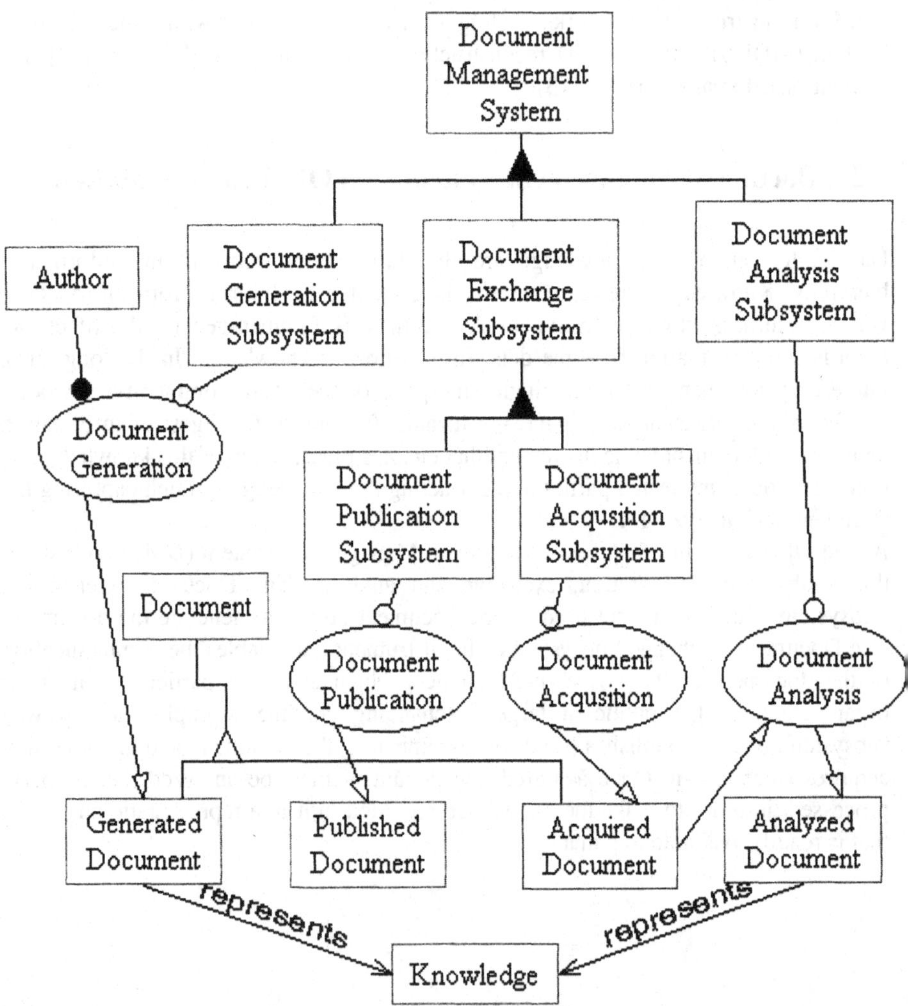

Fig. 5. A top-level OPD of a generic Document Management System showing its three major subsystems and their associated processes.

In the OPD of Figure 5, the two most important Document attributes – Modality and Medium, are specified. Modality has the values analog and digital, while Medium has the values text, image, audio and video. Thus, documents can be recorded in two major different modalities: analog or digital. Documents with analog Modality are paper-based, while those with electronic Modality are electronic-based. As Figure 6 shows, Paper Document can inherit only the text and/or image values of the Medium attribute, while Electronic Document can inherit all the four Medium attribute values.

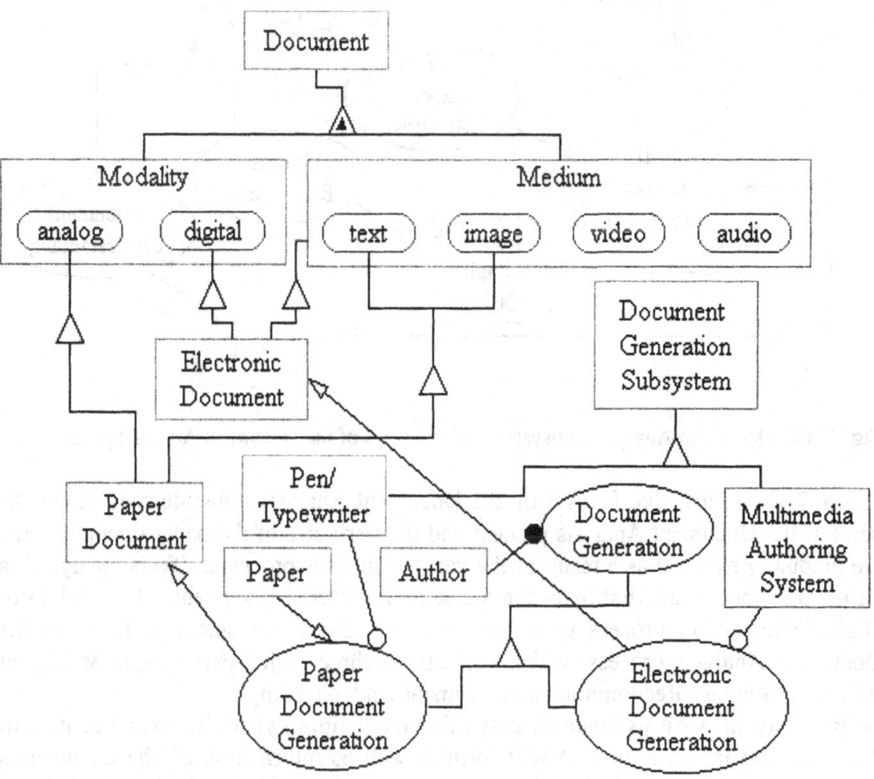

Fig. 6. The attributes of Document and the corresponding specializations of Document Generation and Document Generation Subsystem.

Each modality implies a different implementation of all the three DMS subsystems. Figure 6 shows the attributes of Document and the corresponding specializations of the process Document Generation and the object Document Generation Subsystem. The process Document Generation is enabled by Author, acting as agent. Document Generation Subsystem specializes into Pen/Typewriter, which is the instrument for the Paper Document Generation process, and Multimedia Authoring System, which is the instrument for the Electronic Document Generation process.

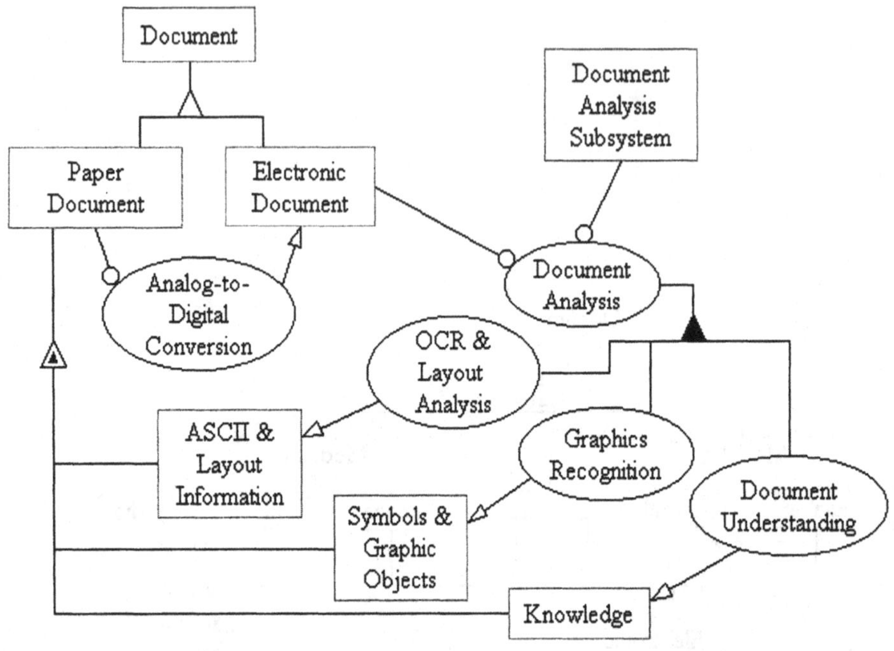

Fig. 7. The Document Analysis Subsystem and the parts of the Document Analysis process.

Figure 7 is an OPD that focuses on the Document Analysis Subsystem. It shows the parts of the Document Analysis process and the attributes of the paper document that are gradually exposed as a result of the various analysis processes. To be analyzed, a Paper Document must first be converted to an Electronic Document. The Analog-to-Digital Conversion process does this. The Electronic Document is input to the Document Analysis process, which consists of three major parts: OCR & Layout Analysis, Graphics Recognition and Document Understanding.

OCR & Layout Analysis (and/or handwriting recognition) yield the textual content of the document information in ASCII form as well as information on the document's layout. Graphics Recognition yields the Document's Symbols & Graphic Objects, while the most sophisticated sub-process – Document Understanding – is aimed at extracting the meaningful knowledge that the original paper document represents in a form that can be best digested by humans. Document Understanding makes use of all the information obtained by the pervious Document Analysis parts and requires a substantial amount of what is known as "artificial intelligence." An example of a high level Document Understanding process is 3-D reconstruction of objects described in engineering drawings. Most contemporary document analysis systems are just beginning to show signs of real document understanding. Indeed, having solved the early analysis tasks, the challenge of current systems is to enhance their high-level understanding capabilities so that they become more intelligent and therefore more useful.

Summary

After introducing Knowledge Management and discussing its emergence as a new engineering discipline, we presented the basic principles of the Object-Process Methodology (OPM), its two major tools – Object-Process Diagrams (OPD) – and its complementary textual equivalent – Object-Process Language (OPL). The OPDs were drawn with OPCAT – Object-Process CASE Tool, which was developed to support OPM-based development.
Having argued that documents of interest represent human knowledge, using OPM we then moved to describing a Document Management System as the tool for handling documents. We distinguished three major components of document management: generation, transmission and analysis, and, using an OPD set, we described the details of each component, its structure and behavior.
The work presented in this paper demonstrates the viability of OPM as a standard vehicle for system specification in general and DAS's in particular. The unification of structure and behavior within a single model is a unique feature of OPM that results in synergy founds in no other systems development method.

Acknowledgement
This work is supported by Technion VPR Fund and the Israeli Ministry of Science.

References

1. D. Dori, Object-Process Analysis: Maintaining the Balance Between System Structure and Behavior. Journal of Logic and Computation. 5(2) 227-249, 1995.
2. D. Dori, Unifying System Structure and Behavior through Object-Process Analysis. Journal of Object-Oriented Analysis, July-August, 66-73, 1996.
3. D. Dori and M. Goodman, On Bridging the Analysis-Design and Structure-Behavior Grand Canyons with Object Paradigms. Report on Object Analysis and Design, 2(5), 25-35, January-February 1996.
4. D. Dori and M. Goodman, From Object-Process Analysis to Object-Process Design, Annals of Software Engineering, 2, 20-25, 1996.
5. Booch, G., Jacobson, I., and Rumbaugh, J., Unified Modeling Language (UML) Notation Guide Version 1.1, Rational Software Corporation, September 1 1997.
6. D. Dori and Y.J. Dori, Object-Process Analysis of a Hypertext Organic Chemistry Studyware, Journal of Computers in Mathematics and Science Teaching, 15, 1/2, (1996),65-84.
7. D. Dori, Object-Process Analysis of Computer Integrated Manufacturing Documentation and Inspection Functions. International Journal of Computer Integrated Manufacturing 9(5), 339-353, 1996.
8. D. Meyersdorf and D. Dori, The R&D Universe and Its Feedback Cycles: an Object-Process Analysis R&D Management, 27 (4), 333-344, 1997.
9. M. Peleg and D. Dori, Extending the Object-Process Methodology to Handle Real-Time Systems. Journal of Object-Oriented Programming (to appear).

10. D. Dori, Representing Pattern Recognition Embedded Systems through Object-Process Diagrams: the Case of the Machine Drawing Understanding System Pattern Recognition Letters 16 (4), 377-384, 1995.

11. D. Dori, Arc Segmentation in the Machine Drawing Understanding Environment IEEE Transactions of Pattern Analysis and Machine Intelligence (T-PAMI) 17 (1), 1057-1068, 1995.

12. D. Dori and M. Weiss, A Scheme for 3D Object Reconstruction from Dimensioned Orthographic Views, Engineering Applications in Artificial Intelligence 9 (1), 53-64, 1996.

13. Dov Dori and Hagit Hel-Or: Semantic Content-Based Image Retrieval Using Object-Process Diagrams. In A. Amin, D. Dori, P. Pudil and H. Freeman (Eds.) Advances in Pattern Recognition, Lecture Notes in Computer Science, Vol. 1451, 230-241, 1998.

Precise Table Recognition by Making Use of Reference Tables

Claudia Wenzel[1] and Wolfgang Tersteegen[2]

[1] German Research Center for Artificial Intelligence (DFKI)
P.O. Box 2080, 67608 Kaiserslautern/Germany
Claudia.Wenzel@dfki.de
[2] University for Applied Sciences of Emden (FHO)
Constantiaplatz 4, 26723 Emden/Germany

Abstract. The ScanTab system represents a knowledge-based approach to table recognition in scanned documents. In contrast to most systems which recognize tables by grouping layout information, our system uses predefined information about which table types may appear in the documents. This enables a very accurate detection able to cope with distorted tables and tables providing little layout information, e.g., no lines, bad alignment, or few rows. Table recognition starts with the detection of the table header. Afterwards, this header is compared with table headers of known reference tables. Having determined the correct reference table, the information kept in the knowledge base is utilized to compute the complete table structure. A graphical user interface allows an easy and fast specification of reference tables.

1 Introduction

Nowadays, document analysis systems cover all kinds of documents, e.g., business letters, books, technical reports, or bank cheques. In all these documents, special treatment is required for recognizing tables and forms because of their specific structure. Meanwhile, form recognition has become tractable and a lot of approaches capture the fix layout conventions of a form sheet automatically. However, table recognition has different characteristics and is harder to solve. The appearance of a table can vary in different ways, e.g., concerning labels above or beneath a table, nested tables, lines, number of entries.

This paper describes an approach dealing with the analysis of German business letters. In this domain, tables appear quite often to structure offers and orders of goods or services. Some examples can be seen in Figure1.

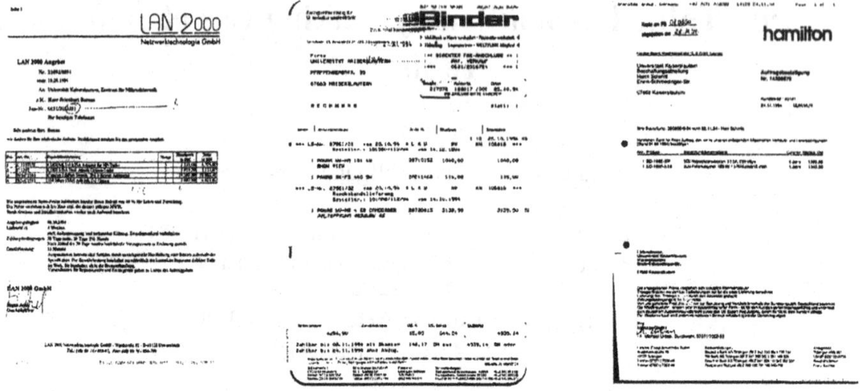

Fig 1. Some exemplary documents containing tables

Our tables are characterized by the following features (revealed by a statistic carried out on 61 documents):

- Most tables have column descriptors (91%).
- Lines are not mandatory (vertical lines 35%, horizontal lines for each row 18%, horizontal lines to separate table header and table entries 56%).
- Most tables contain up to six columns (68%) and are small (37% with one table entry, only 17% more than six entries).
- Cell boundaries are violated (41%) and tables contain text which does not belong to the table (42%).

Because of these bad characteristics, we have chosen a knowledge-based approach to table recognition. That means, we require a certain amount of information about the tables in the domain in advance. By this, we are able to reach high precision and recall values despite the bad table quality.

Our ScanTab system is equipped with a graphical user interface which enables work in two modes: During *reference table specification*, the user specifies table details which are necessary to enter the current table as new table model. During *table recognition*, the current table is recognized based on the knowledge base of reference tables. Both modes start with the same procedure, namely the detection of the table header. This step requires the existence of labels for table columns. The further analysis respectively the specification of a new reference table is guided by the table header.

Table analysis has become a prominent research topic in document analysis since the early 1990's. Most approaches to table recognition described so far utilize purely geometric features (e.g. pixel distribution, line-art) to determine the logical structure of the table. For example, Hori and Dörmann [1] use a method called "box-driven reasoning" to analyze tables with touching characters and broken lines. It is based on the computation of boxes for e.g., cells, characters, bars, and noise. Relations between boxes are extracted to detect missing cell boxes and touching characters. Chandran

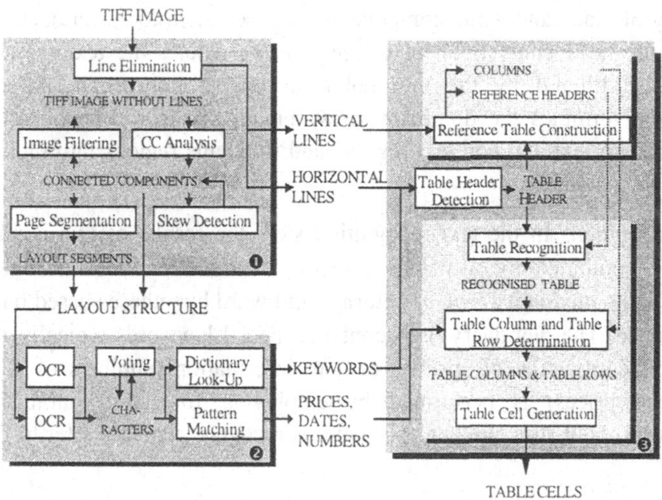

Fig. 2. Processing Model (① Structure analysis, ② Text recognition, ③ Table analysis)

and Kasturi [2] use line information to determine a table's location. Afterwards, horizontal and vertical pixel projection reveals white streams as additional cell boundaries. Then, resulting cells are labeled in a specific format as headings, subheadings, or table entries.

Green and Krishnamoorthy [3] employ visual clues (lines, fonts, textual semantics, data format) to divide a table into cells. Using a table model, the tables logical structure is detected in a subsequent step. Consider Hirayama [4] to read more about bottom-up approaches.

The scenario of the work of Shamilian et al [5] is similar to our system. Their "retargetable table reader" recognizes known predefined table styles. A graphical user interface supports the definition of table styles. It consists of selecting the region of the table, determining field boundaries, and assigning several information to the fields such as name, and so on. After this, documents containing tables in a known layout are analyzed by several steps, namely background suppression, elimination of line-art, table location, table record identification, field location, OCR, and contextual analysis. The kernel of the table recognition procedure is based on text-line projection.

2 Processing Model

This chapter provides an overview on the table analysis procedure. As shown in Figure 2, all documents (already scanned with 300 dpi) are processed by three steps.

Structure Analysis: First, vertical and horizontal lines are removed to reduce the error rate of the page segmentation. All information about line coordinates and line types is separately stored for further use. Next, a *connected component analyzer* generates a hierarchy of black and white components and uses them to detect background texture or noise in the document. Then, *image filtering* deletes the texture while all noisy regions are filtered by the morphological opening operation. Afterwards, *skew detection* determines the dominant skew. Finally, *page segmentation* classifies the document into text and non text regions and segments regions into block, line, word, and character segments.

Text Recognition: In the text recognition step, the results of two commercial OCR tools are combined by a *voting component* which provides a higher accuracy. Subsequently, *dictionary look-up* returns valid word hypotheses based on the weighted edit distance. The dictionary used contains special keywords typically found in table headers. Identification of specific content information (numbers of a fixed format, dates, and prices) is performed by employing finite-state-automata. For more information about structure analysis and text recognition please refer to Baumann et al [6].

Table Analysis: In the third step, table data is extracted. First, the *table header detection* tries to locate the table header by relating the positions of the keywords to each other. If available, horizontal lines are used to improve the generated result. Secondly, the column information of the table is delivered by comparing the table header of an unknown table with table headers of known tables (so-called *reference tables*). This information is also used to create rows. Together with the column borders, they result in the cells of the table. Finally, the contents of the corresponding cells are assigned to their logical objects.

A necessary precondition for our recognition algorithm is a knowledge base of documents containing the same table structures as the documents which are analyzed later-on. For entering a document in this knowledge base, its table header must be localized and column information (e.g. positions of column borders) must be entered.

3 Detecting Table Headers

The detection of the table header is necessary for table cell generation and reference table construction. It is divided in several steps: After reducing the search area and rotating words, a starting point (called pivot-element) for the table header is determined. This starting point is horizontally expanded to establish table boundaries.

3.1 Pre-processing

After the dictionary look-up in the text recognition step is finished, all words are divided into two groups: keywords and other words. Keywords are words contained in the dictionary of known table headers and located within a certain search area. In fact, one can expect different information in special regions of the document, e.g. sender at the top and banking arrangements at the bottom (this is typical for German business letters). Thus, the number of words investigated can be reduced by applying thresholds. Furthermore, pre-processing corrects inclinations by rotating all words within the search area.

3.2 Detection Algorithm

In our domain, table headers consist of a maximum of three text lines. In fact, they often contain only one line. This observation is crucial for the detection algorithm.

The detection starts with the determination of a so-called *pivot element*. Every keyword is supposed to be the pivot element of a table header, provided it has a minimum number of characters. The pivot element sets the maximum expansion of the table header upwards and downwards (calculated from the left top corner respectively the right bottom corner of the pivot element). All other keywords lying in the area calculated are also members of this potential table header. The table header containing the maximum number of keywords ($\max[\text{header}_1,...,\text{header}_n]$) is the final header. However, only those headers with a certain number of words are taken into consideration.

If at this time the table header is not unique, the algorithm computes *sector counters* of these headers. A sector counter counts every word (not only keywords) lying in the same line as the pivot element. The table header with the highest sector counter wins the comparison. At the end, the final table header is filled with all remaining words (non keywords) lying in the area of the corresponding pivot element. This compensates OCR mistakes.

The next part aims at localizing horizontal lines which are members of the final table header. There are either no lines, one or two lines (one or none above and one or none below the header). Lines are used to verify the final boundaries of the header. Therefore, the search area of the pivot element is enlarged which is done separately for the area above and below the pivot element. The algorithm looks sequentially at all lines of the document. It finishes as soon as a line of a certain minimum length is lying in the enlarged area.

If the algorithm is not able to find an upper or lower line for setting table boundaries, the appropriate area (above and below the pivot element) is treated by a different procedure. Therefore, all keywords of the area are counted. If the number of keywords is less then a certain threshold value, all words in this area are removed. So the final size of a table header is between one and three lines. The threshold value guarantees that the words in the area analyzed really belong to the table header. The more keywords exist, the more likely this will be.

3.3 Final Processing

In case the detection algorithm has been successfully completed, word positions are used by a transformation step to generate rows and columns. The final size of the table header is calculated with help of word boundaries and then adjusted by the upper and lower lines. If the table header's width is too small (related to the width of the

Positions-nummer	Menge	Modell-nummer	Beschreibung	Einzelpreis DM	voraussichtl. Lieferdatum
0100	1	A4052A	Upgrades HP9000 Mdl 720 to Mdl 735/125	37.877,00	Ende Nov4
	1	008	Install LAN AUI Interface	0,00	
			Nachlass(41.0%)	-15.529,57	
			Postensumme :	22.347,43	
0200	1	A1986A	720 Aufrüstkit f. einen EISA-Steckplatz	3.475,00	Ende Nov4
	1	0S4	Inst. und HP LAN-Konfiguration	609,00	
			Nachlass(41.0%)	-1.674,44	
			Postensumme :	2.409,56	

Fig. 3. Screenshot of a detected table header

document), table header detection has failed. Figure 3 shows an example of a successfully detected table header.

4 Reference Table Construction

The construction of a reference table starts with the table header detection as already described. It builds the starting point for the following further table specification:

1. OCR errors in the table header can be corrected manually by clicking the incorrect word and typing in the correct one.
2. Vertical table boundaries are generated automatically by using the left boundary of the leftmost word in the table header and by using the right boundary of the rightmost word.
3. Now the user is able to draw vertical lines to correct the table boundaries or to mark boundaries of table columns. Drawing is accomplished by moving the cursor to the intended line position and clicking the right mouse button. Resulting lines are displayed as shown in Figure 3.
4. For each column, the user can specify the orientation of the column entries (left/ right/ none). Moreover, one can specify entries belonging to a certain word class by using regular expressions. This enables the lexical preprocessing to detect and mark such expressions.
5. The user specifies details for the generation of table cells: Each column can be labeled as top-separator, bottom-separator, or repeater. A top-separator is a column in which each line entry marks the beginning of a new table cell (typically for running numbers). A bottom-separator is a column in which each line entry marks the end of a table cell (prices). A repeater column does not contain an entry in each cell. In this case, the intended meaning of the cell is a repetition of the value of the next cell up (dates).
6. Finally, this specification is saved.

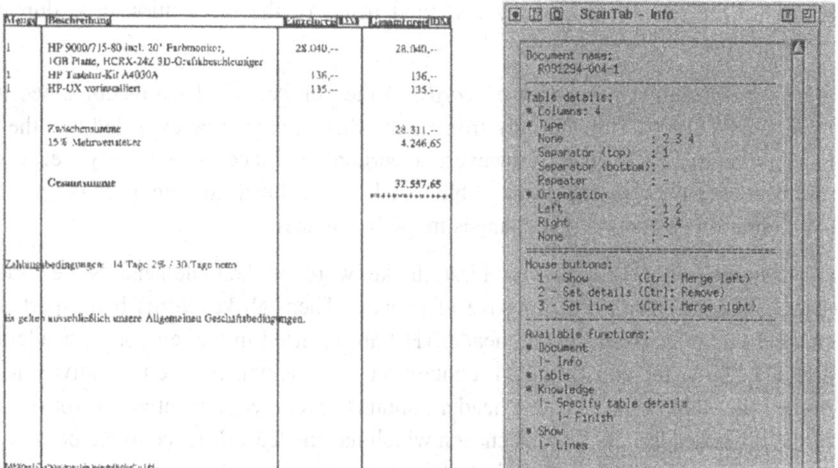

Fig. 4. Final Screenshot for Reference Table Construction

Figure 4 shows a screenshot where all details have been specified. The left window reveals the column boundaries and the right window displays more detailed information. Manual effort for the construction of a reference table takes about 3 minutes.

5 Table Recognition

Table recognition subsumes the assignment of a reference table to an unknown table. It is based on the following observation: It is impossible that two table headers belonging to different table types are identical with regard to keywords and the distances between these keywords. Thus, table recognition is based on a comparison of the table header of the unknown table with table headers of reference tables. In case of successful comparison, information about the table structure can be retrieved from the knowledge base of reference tables and is used for further analysis.

The following subsections describe the corresponding algorithms in more detail.

5.1 Recognition Algorithm

The table header of an unknown table is sequentially compared with all available table headers of the knowledge base. For a final assignment of a reference table, the hereby determined best similarity must be higher than a certain threshold value.

The comparison of two table headers consists of five phases, whereas phase one and phase two only provide yes/no answers which decide on the execution of phase three, four, and five. As a result of that the search area is considerably reduced to speed up the overall procedure. The final result of the recognition procedure is an assignment to a reference table.

(1) Comparison of the number of words: If the number of all words contained in the table headers differs too strongly from each other, it cannot be expected that the table headers match each other. However, a certain tolerance is necessary because the number of words in the same table header is subject to minor changes due to segmentation errors or slight changes in the layout style.

(2) Comparison of the keywords: First, the keywords in the table headers are sorted by the quicksort algorithm to improve efficiency. Then, all keywords being part of the first (H_1) as well as the second header (H_2) are inserted in the temporary headers TH_1 and TH_2. So at the end H_1 and H_2 contain only words which have no equivalent word in the other table header. If one header contains several equivalent words for one word of the other header, the word is chosen which has the least distance to the partner word of the other table header. This phase fails either if the number of the remaining words (that means words without an equivalent) exceeds a certain value or if too few pairs exist.

In order to determine the shift between both headers all word pairs detected are investigated. By calculating an average value out of the distances between the word pairs the influence of some deviating values is decreased. At the end of this phase, TH_1 and TH_2 contain only keywords appearing in both headers.

(3) Distance check: For each word in the headers TH_1 and TH_2 the distance to all other words of the same header is determined. This produces a kind of distance network for the keywords. Next, a counter registers all distances in TH_1 which differ too strongly from the corresponding distances in TH_2. The degree of similarity results from the relation between the final counter value and the overall number of comparisons (used for standardization).

(4) Pattern matching: Goal of this phase is to check the remaining words in H_1 and H_2 (remember phase two) which could not be assigned to a word pair. The following procedure is executed for each word in H_1 with all words in H_2. The check of a pair is done by comparing

1. the similarity of the horizontal and vertical size proportions of the word segments
2. the distances of the word out of H_1 to all keywords in TH_1 with the distances of the word out of H_2 to all other words in TH_2.

The average value of the size and distance correspondence delivers the similarity of both words. If the best similarity exceeds a certain threshold, the comparison was successful and the words are removed from H_1 and H_2.

In case H_1 and H_2 are finally empty, the degree of similarity is set to one. Otherwise, the number of unreferenced words is determined for every table column and weighted according to its share in the total quantity of contained words. The sum of all weights related to the number of words (before execution of phase four) in the bigger one of the two headers H_1 and H_2 supplies the similarity degree.

(5) Calculation of the total similarity: In case all previous phases have been finished, the total similarity of the two headers is calculated on the basis of the similarity values gained in phase three and four. This is done by weighting them differently:

$$\text{similarity}^{\circ}_{\text{total}} = \frac{\left[\sum \text{Words}(TH_1) * \text{similarity}^{\circ}_{\text{phase3}} + \max\left(\sum \text{Words}(H_1), \sum \text{Words}(H_2)\right) * \text{similarity}^{\circ}_{\text{phase4}}\right]}{\left[\sum \text{Words}(TH_1) + \max\left(\sum \text{Words}(H_1), \sum \text{Words}(H_2)\right)\right]} \quad (1)$$

Note that in the formula the number of words of H_1 and H_2 is calculated before execution of phase four.

5.2 Generating Table Cells

Reference table information can be used in the following way for cell generation:

- Shift between both table headers
- Coordinates of column rows (relative to the table header)
- Details about special columns containing *separators* and *repeaters.*

With this information, table cells are generated by using intersections between column lines and row lines caused by the separators. By exclusive treatment of columns with special patterns and by considering the column alignment, influence of text which does not belong to the table can be reduced.

Determination of special columns: In phase one, the special patterns are assigned to those columns with a particular type (separator and repeater*).* All remaining special patterns are treated as normal words. Since it must be expected that some of the coordinates of the column positions are slightly inaccurate, patterns are also accepted if they start or end outside the column borders (only within a certain tolerance).

Filtering of the special columns: Now all special columns are filtered:

1. For each pattern in a column it is counted how many other patterns of this column start (left aligned) respectively end (right aligned) at the same position as the pattern itself (including a certain tolerance once more). The pattern with the highest counter sets the so-called *alignment point.*
2. All pattern of the column with a different alignment point (again in the tolerance range) are removed.
3. Normal words with the same alignment point - lying in the tolerance range - which fit into the column are included in the column.

Creation of row lines: Row line creation is done on the basis of the special columns. In order to determine whether a row line starts or ends a table entry, special columns of the type *separator* are divided in two classes: The first class contains columns where data are at the beginning of an entry while the second class contains data at the end of an entry. A filter unites all lines with a distance less than a certain number of pixels. It is important that both sorts of row lines are filtered separately, because the distance between lines which start an entry and lines which end an entry is normally very small. Of course, if there is only one column with starting lines (resp. ending lines), the filtering is omitted.

Assignment of cell contents: Intersections between column lines and row lines produce the table cells. Afterwards, table data is assigned to them by first processing all cells with data out of special columns. Then all normal words are used to fill the remaining cells.

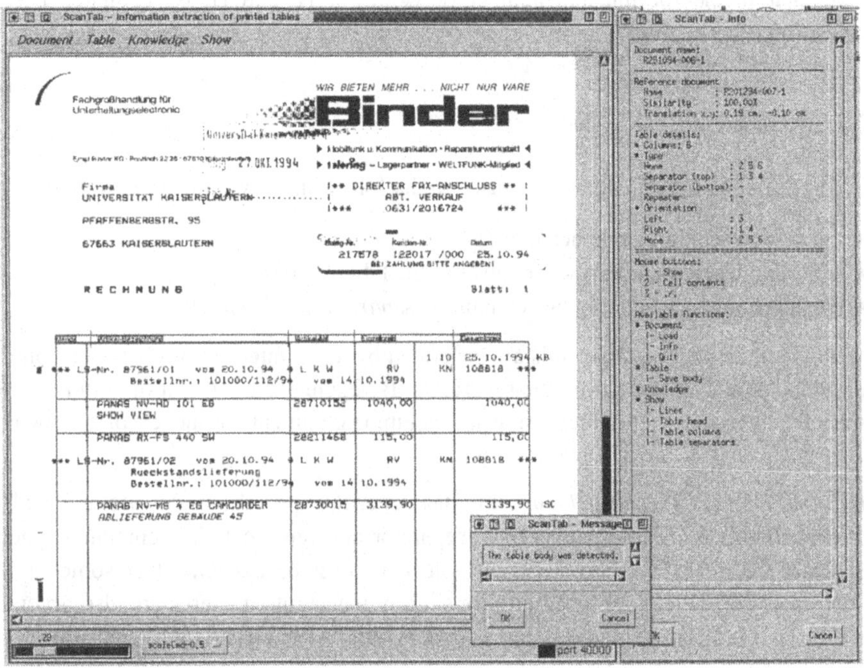

Fig. 5. Screenshot of a table completely analyzed (partial view)

Note that there is also a tolerance range for the dimensions of the table cells. To conclude, Figure 5 shows the result after a complete table analysis.

6 Results

Up to now, our system has been used on a comparatively small set of 99 documents collected at the purchasing department of the University of Kaiserslautern. However, the system's processing steps were determined by testing it on a much larger set but we did not measure the behavior in figures. The set of 99 business letters was divided into three different document clusters:

- 24 documents were used to build up the knowledge base with reference tables (training set)
- 44 documents served as test set for the full analysis process (test set)
- 31 documents were the basis for a special test of the table header detection (without the table recognition) under aggravated circumstances, i.e., we have chosen documents with a high error rate regarding to segmentation and/or character recognition (special set)

Table 1 presents the evaluation results of tests with the test set and the special set in terms of recall and precision.

Table 1. Test results

Document Cluster	Precision	Recall
test set	100%	96%
special set	100%	100%

During the test of the whole analysis procedure for every document out of the training set, two (if available, otherwise one) belonging documents out of the test set with the same table header were processed. Precondition for all documents was that the correctness of the keyword segmentation had to be better than 75%.

The technique for the generation of the table cells delivered good results if no text which does not belong to the table was present. However, if this requirement was not met then the results were often inaccurate. Since due to this distinction the results of cell recognition cannot be classified as correct or incorrect, the precision and recall values are only valid for table header detection and table recognition. So the values for the entire test would be worse if the results for the generation of the table cells would be taken into consideration.

7 Conclusion

We have proposed a system for extracting information of tabular structures. It is especially tailored for tables with little layout conventions and tables containing text not belonging to the table and violating the table layout. To reach a high accuracy, our system is based on the assignment of predefined reference tables to new unknown tables. Moreover, the definition of reference tables allows to integrate information extraction from tabular structures into an extraction procedure for the whole document by assigning semantic labels to columns.

In our opinion, our approach seems very promising. Table header determination and reference table assignment can serve as a very accurate starting point for further analysis. The system tests delivered very good results. However, due to the small basis of documents they cannot be seen as representative. For that purpose it would be necessary to use considerably more documents in another test. The table cell generation needs yet some improvements in order to improve the ability to handle tables with text which does not belong to the table. Furthermore, this procedure can be refined by incorporating ruled line information and a more accurate determination of the table end.

Acknowledgements

This work has been supported by the German federal ministry of education, science, research and technology under contract number 01 IW 807.

References

1. O. Hori, D. S. Dörmann: *Robust Table-form Structure Analysis Based on Box-Driven Reasoning*. Proceedings of the International Conference on Document Analysis and Recognition (ICDAR 95)
2. S. Chandran, R. Kasturi: *Structural Recognition of Tabulated Data*. Proceedings of the International Conference on Document Analysis and Recognition (ICDAR 93)
3. E. Green, M. Krishnamoorthy: *Model-Based Analysis of Printed Tables*. Proceedings of the International Conference on Document Analysis and Recognition (ICDAR 95)
4. Y. Hirayama: *A Method For Table Structure Analysis Using DP Matching*. Proceedings of the International Conference on Document Analysis and Recognition (ICDAR 95)
5. J. Shamilian, H. Baird, T. Wood: *A Retargetable Table Reader*. Proceedings of the International Conference on Document Analysis and Recognition (ICDAR 97)
6. S. Baumann, M. Ben Hadj Ali, A. Dengel, T. Jäger, M. Malburg, A. Weigel, C. Wenzel: *Message Extraction from Printed Documents - A Complete Solution*. Proceedings of the International Conference on Document Analysis and Recognition (ICDAR 97)

Design of an Integrated Environment for the Automated Analysis of Architectural Drawings*

Philippe Dosch[1], Christian Ah-Soon[1], Gérald Masini[1],
Gemma Sánchez[1 2], Karl Tombre[1]

[1] LORIA–CNRS–INPL–INRIA–UHP
B.P. 239, 54506 Vandœuvre-lès-Nancy Cedex, France
{dosch, ahsoon, masini, gsanchez, tombre}@loria.fr
WWW home page: http://www.loria.fr/isa/
[2] Computer Vision Center
Edifici C, Campus Universitat Autònoma de Barcelona
08193 Bellaterra (Barcelona), Catalunya-Spain
gemma@cvc.uab.es
WWW home page: http://www.cvc.uab.es/~gemma/

Abstract. This paper presents the principles which have guided the design of our graphics recognition software environment. A number of applicative modules have been constructed on top of the environment, for the purpose of analyzing architectural drawings. A flexible user interface drives these modules. Our choices are compared with those of similar systems.

1 Introduction

Our research group has been investigating various aspects of graphics recognition techniques for more than ten years: Map analysis [1], symbol recognition [2, 3], dimension analysis [4], conversion of engineering drawings to CAD models [5], and lately interpretation of architectural drawings [6].

During the last two years, we have also conducted a "consolidation" activity, especially for low-level graphics recognition methods [7], in order to build up a set of stable software components, reusable from one application to the other. This work leads to a number of systems engineering issues, that we try to document and comment in this paper. Such design and integration problems are recurrent in the document analysis field, and more generally in the image processing field. Initiatives to solve them gave for instance rise to the *Image Understanding Environment* (IUE) [8, 9].

Figure 1 gives an overview of our three-layered system. The first layer is the ISADORA library (§ 2), which consists of basic graphics recognition methods. They are designed to be as general as possible, *i.e.* to be independent of application fields.

* This work is partially funded by France Telecom / CNET.

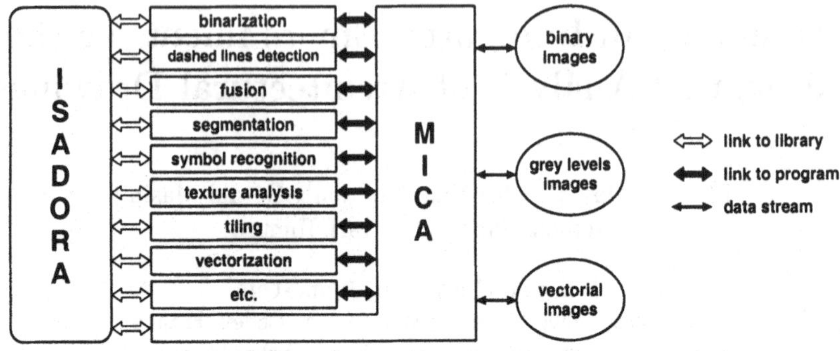

Fig. 1. Overview of our three-layered system.

The second layer includes useful so-called graphics recognition *applications* (§ 3). Low-level applications are more or less sequences of calls to the corresponding modules of the ISADORA library, while higher-level ones are real programs including calls to ISADORA functionalities. All applications are independent programs, which can either be run using a command line or be driven by the user interface.

The third layer is the user interface. In order for a document analysis system to work in practice, the user must be "in the loop": The interface must be tightly connected with the underlying layers, so that the user can easily guide the analysis process, and take quick corrective actions when necessary. The MICA user interface that we propose (§ 4) provides such functionalities. It is also an application, linked with the ISADORA library as the others, but it is able to call applications of the second layer.

Some elements of comparison with other similar environments are given in § 5, before concluding the paper.

2 C++ Classes for Graphics Recognition

Our goal is the construction of a library of stable and reusable data structures, by using an object-oriented language. It rises two main categories of problems. If those related to the design of the components of the library do depend on the specific domain of the library, graphics recognition in our case, we first had to deal with those related to the design of the library itself.

2.1 Prerequisites and Tools

We have been confronted with three typical software engineering requirements. Firstly, the transition from existing code to new code had to be as easy as possible. As we had a lot of old code written in C, C++ appeared to be the ideal choice. It is not necessarily the best object-oriented language, but it is more or less a standard in industry, and it provides to a large extent compatibility with our previous C code.

Secondly, we wanted to use as often as possible available software, preferably public-domain, easy-to-find tools, and *de facto* standards. This explains, for example, why we use Jef Poskanzer's *Portable Bitmap* (PBM) format for image files, DXF for the representation of 2D graphics, and VRML for 3D graphics.

Finally, code reusability and efficiency had to be guaranteed. These two criteria are often antagonistic. Reusability is achieved through C++ thanks to data abstraction and encapsulation, but it sometimes leads to a lot of computation overhead. We therefore allowed ourselves to use well-known "programming tricks", based on low-level C constructions, for efficiency reasons. Since it is based on C, C++ makes it easier to implement such tricks. However, as classes designed in this way are often dependent on the implementation details, tricks have been hidden in so-called *private classes* (with private interfaces), which are not accessible to the common users of the library.

The programming tools had then to be chosen according to the previous criteria. This is out of the scope of this paper, but two points deserve a special attention. We had no intention to code a new set of common data structures like vectors, lists, sets, and so on. The C++ standard library provides most of them in what was previously known as the Standard Template Library (STL), on the notable exception of graphs, for which we decided to use an additional library, LEDA[1], from the *Max-Planck-Institut für Informatik* in Saarbrücken, Germany.

Moreover, a software library is useless without documentation giving detailed information about class interfaces. We chose Malte Zöckler and Roland Wunderling's documentation system, DOC++[2], which is similar to `javadoc` in the JAVA environment. It has low memory requirements and is very easy to use. It automatically generates online browsable HTML and high-quality hardcopy documentation directly from the C++ code by parsing the sources for special comments, that instruct how to create the documentation.

2.2 Class Design

In fact, the principal problem we had to solve is encountered when implementing image processing operations in an object-oriented language. The object-oriented paradigm is based on data encapsulation, *i.e.* describing abstract data types and their interfaces with the clients, whereas image processing generally concerns collections of operators, *i.e.* procedures, to be applied to images.

Let us consider an elementary example. The convolution of an image by a Gaussian yields a new image $J = I \otimes G$. The question is then: Should convolution be defined as a function member of the `Image` class that describes images, or should it be defined as a global operator? Our answer to the question is quite pragmatic, and is close to what is proposed by marketed libraries such as the *Image Vision Library*™ from Silicon Graphics.

The basic idea is very simple. `Image` is the base class of a hierarchy and its derived classes define image types: `BinaryImage`, `GreyLevelImage`, `FloatImage`...

[1] `http://www.mpi-sb.mpg.de/LEDA/`
[2] `http://www.zib.de/Visual/software/doc++/`

Each operation that processes an image of a particular type corresponds to a derived class of the class defining the image type, and is implemented by a constructor of this derived class. Different methods to perform the same conceptual operation can thus be easily implemented through derived classes of an abstract class.

Of course, this paradigm does not only apply to image processing, but also to all analysis and recognition tasks. It has the advantage of meeting understandability requirements [10]: Designers as well as clients of the library write compact and easy-to-read code. The idea may be illustrated with a very common image processing problem, edge detection. A straightforward algorithm can be written using our library in the following way:

```
PgmFile f("image.pgm");      // File containing the original image
GreyLevelImage myImg(f);     // Load it as a grey level image

// Perform Canny operator with sigma == 1.2
CannyGradientImage myDeriv(myImg, 1.2);
// Alternatively, if you choose the Deriche operator,
// comment previous line and uncomment next line
// DericheGradientImage myDeriv(myImg); // with default parameters

LocalGradientMaxima maxG(myDeriv); // Compute maximum of gradient
EdgeMap myEdge(maxG, 0, 5);         // Edge map with double thresholding
LinkedChainsList myChains(myEdge, 1, 0); // Link edges

// And so on... We can perform a polygonal approximation on the chains,
// and then save the segments to a DXF file, etc.
```

This obviously is an idyllic view as, in the general case, additional parameters are needed to accurately perform the different image processings. However, we firmly believe that the general philosophy holds for most low-level and intermediate-level operations in document image processing and graphics recognition applications.

2.3 The Class Hierarchy

ISADORA classes are hierarchically organized as a tree, with a single root named `IsaObject`, which defines information common to all objects, especially error handling facilities. This tree can be viewed as a collection of subtrees grouping together classes according to the different kinds of objects to be handled when designing a document analysis system. Each subtree is itself organized in the same way.

There are three main families of classes. The first one includes classes for image processing (mainly `Mask`, `Histogram` and `Image` subtrees), as graphics processing involves a lot of image processing, at least in the low levels. For instance, see figure 2 for a synthetical view of the `Image` subtree.

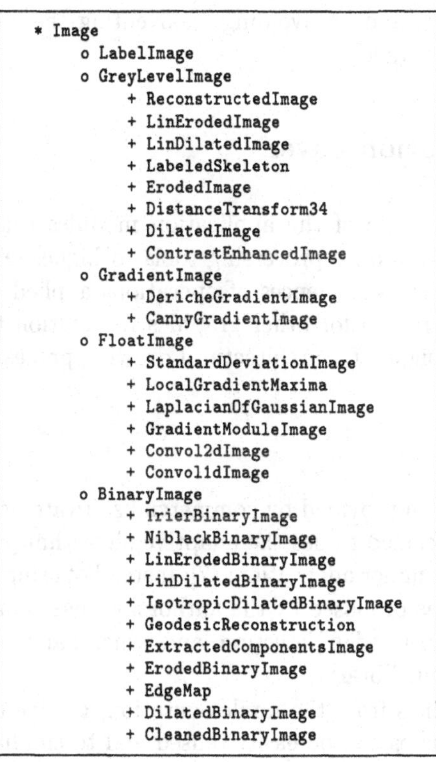

Fig. 2. The subtree of image classes.

All images are represented as arrays of pixels and can be either input data or results of some processing. We intentionally do not use a too general definition, to avoid the complexity found, in particular, in the IUE specifications [8]. Most of the common image processing tools are available: Histogram computing, basic processing using convolutions (Gradient, Laplacian, etc.), mathematical morphology on both binary and grey level images, edge detection (in particular Canny's and Deriche's methods), binary image processing, and so on.

The `Graphics` subtree provides classes for graphics processing, describing all the different kinds of graphical primitives that can be delivered by basic segmentation modules, and also groupings of such primitives, that are delivered by analysis modules: Points, segments, chains of segments, rectangles, arcs of circle, connected components, etc. as well as ordered collections of such objects (cf. § 3.3). They correspond to the semantics level in Koelma and Smeulders' hierarchy (cf. § 5).

Finally, classes for utilities, especially file processing (`IsaFile` subtree), allow graphics or image data to be stored in a selected format (cf. § 2.1).

The interfaces of the usual classes are not especially original, as we describe the fundamental operations in a very classical way. We first of all want to make the programming of complex algorithms easier, by providing a relatively simple design framework and by avoiding "reinventing the wheel" when reusable, efficient tools are available.

3 The Application Layer

Let us now present some of the application modules that we have designed, going from lower-level image processing tools to higher-level ones. The former are basically designed as sequences of operations applied to ISADORA objects. They can be easily reused for other graphics recognition tasks. The latter are more specifically designed for architectural drawing processing.

3.1 Binarization

When the binarization provided by commercial software or hardware is not satisfactory, we have decided to use the adaptive algorithm proposed by Trier and Taxt [11], with some minor adaptations [7]: Instead of using *ad-hoc* filters such as the Sobel gradient, as proposed by the authors, we use Gaussian filtering, which has become standard in edge detection, and which happens to be implemented in a robust way in our library.

Here are some lines from the implementation, to give once again a taste of the way existing classes can be easily reused and to emphasize the processing–through–constructor concept (cf. § 2.2):

```
TrierBinaryImage::TrierBinaryImage(const GreyLevelImage& anImage,
                                   const float postThresh,
                                   const float activityThresh,
                                   const double sigma)
{
  // Compute the Canny gradient of the original image:
  // Convolution by the 1st derivative of a Gaussian
  CannyGradientImage* gradient = new CannyGradientImage(anImage, sigma);
  GradientModuleImage modGrad(*gradient);
  delete gradient;
  // Compute the image activity
  Mask2d aMask2d(3, 1.0);
  double* myMask = aMask2d.mask();
  for (int i = 0; i < aMask2d.width(); i++)
    *myMask++ = (double) 1.0;
  // Compute the Laplacian of the smoothed image
  // by convolving with the Laplacian of a Gaussian
  Convol2dImage* activity = new Convol2dImage(modGrad, aMask2d);
  LaplacianOfGaussianImage* lapImg =
    new LaplacianOfGaussianImage(anImage, sigma);
  ...
}
```

The last steps of the algorithm (not documented here) rely heavily on the LabelImage class, used to label the connected components of a binary image, as explained in next section.

3.2 Text/Graphics Separation

As most text/graphics separation methods are based on analyzing the connected components, we have designed the LabelImage class, whose constructor builds a tree of connected components from a BinaryImage [1]. The tree represents the inclusion relation between components and gives the oriented contours of all the components.

The principle of the algorithm consists in analyzing the input image one row after the other, comparing the current row with the previous one, and storing all necessary information while labeling the black and white runs of the current row. The contours of the connected components are chained "on the fly" and described by Freeman chain codes, instances of the Freeman class.

This class defines just one possible representation of a chain:

```
class Freeman : public GenChain<int> { ... };
```

and the template class GenChain<T> defines a common interface to all kinds of chains (cf. § 3.3). Hence, the Freeman class defines the specific encoding of Freeman chains, and implements the common interface given by GenChain.

Fletcher and Kasturi have proposed one of the most robust text/graphics separation methods of the literature [12]. We therefore suggest that, instead of spending a lot of time on reinventing new methods, which most of the time do not give any real improvements on known methods, research groups do use this method, appropriately changing the parameters, if necessary, to fit the characteristics of the documents to be processed. Then, they will have more time left to concentrate on the really difficult problem of separating touching text and graphics, for which only partial solutions have been presented.

In our implementation, we added an absolute threshold for the size of a text component [7]. We thus end up having three thresholds, but their interpretation is straightforward, and they have proven to be very stable for a family of graphics documents: Once the best values are determined for a certain kind of application, they can be used for all related images.

Figure 3 shows some results obtained on an architectural drawing. As proposed by Fletcher and Kasturi, a string grouping is then performed, using the Hough transform. Further refinement of the graphics part can be obtained by separating thin and thick lines using morphological filtering, which is also available in the image processing part of the ISADORA library.

3.3 Vectorization

Among all the vectorization methods (*i.e.* raster-to-graphics conversion) currently available, our favorite is a skeletonization based on the 3–4 distance trans-

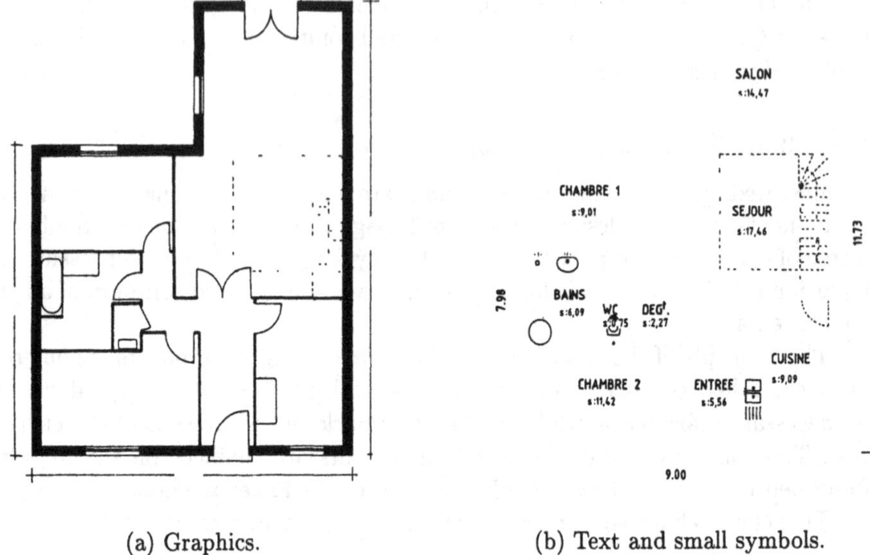

(a) Graphics.

(b) Text and small symbols.

Fig. 3. An example of text/graphics separation using Fletcher and Kasturi's method on the architectural drawing of a simple private house.

form [13], followed by some polygonal approximation [7]. The distance skeleton is implemented by the `LabeledSkeleton` class.

Once a skeleton is computed, the skeleton pixels must be linked into chains. The `LinkedChainsList` class defines a list of linked chains of 2D points. We show here the context of this class, to illustrate how a specific implementation (such as using a list of points to represent a chain) can be encapsulated into a generic, abstract class.

First, the `GenChain` template class provides a generic interface for any chain, independently of the way it is internally represented and coded (note the use of DOC++ special comments).

```
template <class T>
  class GenChain : public Graphics {
public:
  /** Basic constructor. */
  GenChain() {}
  /** Get chain length (number of points). */
  virtual int length() const = 0;
  /** Get first point of chain. */
  virtual GenPoint<T> first() const = 0;
  /** Get last point of chain. */
  virtual GenPoint<T> last() const = 0;
  /** Set iterator to initial position (start of chain). */
```

```
  virtual void setInitialPosition() = 0;
  /** Access next point through iterator.
  The function returns 1 if it is possible to move forward in the chain,
  0 if not. When moving is possible, the new (x,y) translation is stored
  in 'transPoint' and the direction of the new code is stored in 'dir'.
  */
  virtual int next(GenPoint<T>& transPoint, Direction& dir) = 0;
  /** Reverse chain. */
  virtual void reverse() = 0;
  /** Is current chain empty?. */
  virtual int empty() const = 0;
};
```

A possible implementation of such a chain is then obtained by using a list of points provided with an iterator. Of course, the functions of the generic interface must be defined, although these implementations are not given here for the sake of brevity.

```
template <class T>
  class GenLinkedChain : public GenChain<T> {
protected:
  /** The list itself. */
  list< GenPoint<T> > theList;
  /** An iterator on the list. */
  list< GenPoint<T> >::iterator theIter;
public:
  // Implementation of the interface defined by GenChain<T>
  ...
};
```

Finally, the complete result of a chaining can be defined as a list of such chains, with integer coordinates:

```
  class LinkedChainsList : public list< GenLinkedChain<int> >
    { ... };
```

This class is provided with both a general constructor from a `BinaryImage` object, that performs the chaining of any kind of binary image, and a specific constructor from a `LabeledSkeleton` object, that implements a linking algorithm taking the topological properties of the skeleton distance into account.

The skeletonization itself is followed by a polygonal approximation. The way we have designed our library allows us to have several algorithms in store for that. They can be easily tested on any list of objects implementing the generic interface for chains: A contour of a connected component represented by a Freeman code, a contour computed from a grey level image by some edge detector, or a skeleton.

All the polygonal approximation methods use the generic interface provided by class `GenChain<int>`. We have implemented Wall and Danielsson's method

[14], as well as the recursive method proposed by Rosin and West [15], which actually is an evolution of an algorithm first proposed by David Lowe. Both corresponding classes, `WallDanielssonSegList` and `RosinWestSegList`, have a constructor from a `GenChain<int>` object: They can work on any kind of linked chain.

If necessary, vectorization is followed by arc and dashed-line detections, inspired by Dov Dori's ideas [16,17]. The corresponding algorithms are implemented by constructors of classes, in the same way as our other tools.

3.4 Symbols and Textures

A flexible recognition system performs the identification of symbols representing building elements, such as doors or windows [2]. Each symbol is described by a set of constraints on the graphical features of the symbol, using a language we have specifically designed for that purpose.

All the description files are parsed to dynamically create a network representing a compact description of all the symbols. A node of the network represents a constraint. A one-pass symbol detection can subsequently be performed by propagating graphical features (*i.e.* segments and arcs of circle) through the network: When a feature conforms to the constraint of a node, it moves to the adjacent node. The recognized symbols are retrieved from the terminal nodes. They are represented as instances of ISADORA classes and thus can be easily handled by higher-level applications. This method allows the recognition of most of the symbols with a very low computation time (Fig. 4.a).

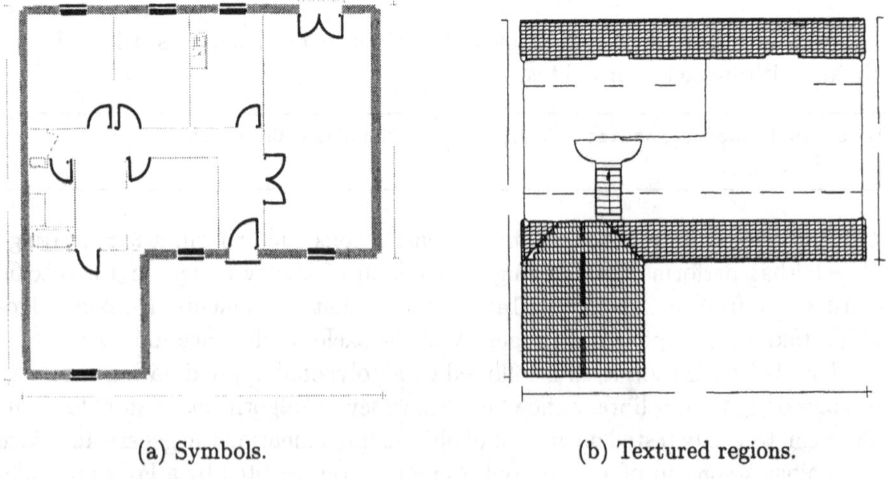

(a) Symbols. (b) Textured regions.

Fig. 4. Symbols and textured regions extracted from the architectural drawings of the first and second levels of the same private house.

Texture detection is also useful, mainly to recognize and locate specific areas representing staircases and pieces of roofs. A texture usually is a structure composed of similar lines presenting a regular repetition. It is made from an element, called a *texel*, placed according to a regular pattern. In our case, texels are straight lines or polygonal shapes.

As textures vary a lot from one drawing to another, we do not use predefined models of regularly structural textures. In fact, we try to find all structures composed as a regular arrangement of a same pattern, whatever this pattern may be.

The method we have integrated in our system results from previous work by one of the authors, at *Universitat Autònoma de Barcelona* [18]. Similar neighboring texels are grouped together using a hierarchical clustering method [19]. The similarity between texels is estimated from their area difference and their shape similarity. The latter is itself computed using the cyclic string edit distance between the boundary strings, proposed by Maes [20], in association with the merge operation of Tsai and Yu [21]. The costs are defined as a weighted sum of an angle cost and a length cost, in a similar way as [22].

The result is a set of regions containing similar neighboring shapes with the same orientation. These regions represent the different textured zones, as illustrated in figure 4.b, where they are displayed as areas surrounded by thick lines.

4 The User Interface

All the processes presented in the previous sections are incorporated into a user-friendly software system, provided with a sophisticated user interface giving a visual feedback about the working of the system.

In fact, it would not be reasonable to run the whole interpretation chain without giving the user any possibility to interact. Indeed, we have to deal with many problems like the noise introduced by artefacts (especially folds) in drawings, by the fact that a same architectural component (door, window, etc.) can be drawn in many different ways, and, of course, by the very limitations of our methods.

A human assistance is anyway required to determine when and how a specific process is to be performed, and to set values to parameters and thresholds of the different applications of the analysis. The user may also want to experiment several applications related to a given problem, in order to be able to select the one giving the best results.

All the applications of the second layer are therefore connected through simple links with what constitutes the third layer of our system, named MICA. In this way, an application can be easily substituted for another or can be upgraded when necessary. Each link is used to transmit the values of the parameters to the corresponding application: Names of images, options, thresholds, etc. Such parameters are set with default values which can be customized by the user.

The interface supplies the following basic functionalities:

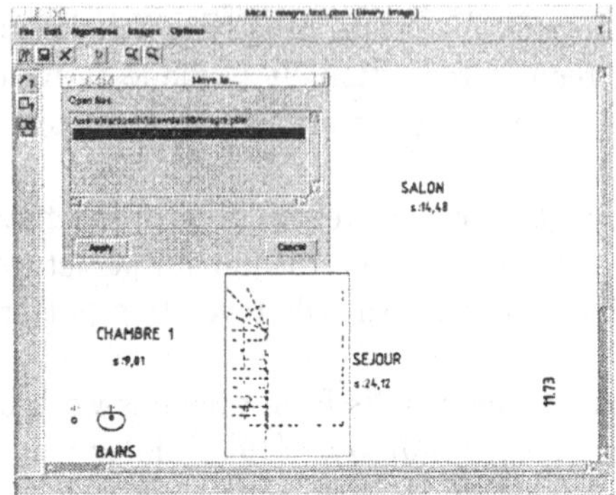

(a) Interactive correction of segmentation results.

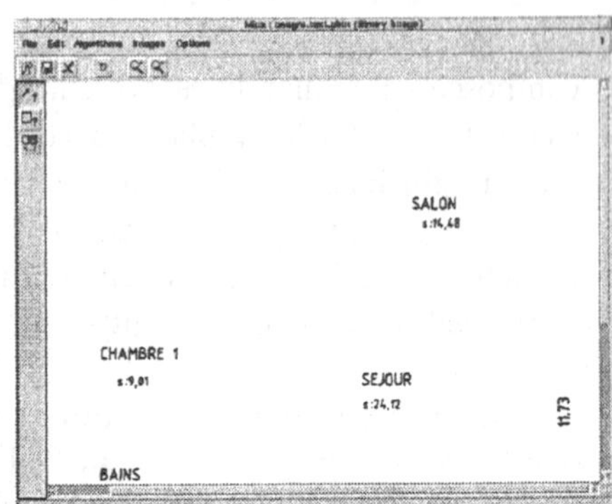

(b) Final text layer.

Fig. 5. Correction of text/graphics segmentation: Some dashes are misinterpreted as hyphens in the text layer (they actually represent stairs) and are moved to the graphics layer by the user.

- Display of the content of all kinds of files, with common editing functionalities like multi-file editing, zooming, and so on.
- Parameter and threshold tuning, after examination of the results of the current application using the display facility.
- Direct manipulation of resulting data, *i.e.* add missing results, delete or alter erroneous results. In particular, special editing operations are supported for both bitmap and vectorial images: Cut and copy of bitmap images, creation and modification of vectorization components. (Fig. 5), etc.

5 Comparison with other Work

We are aware that we are not the only research group working on this topic. For instance, the duality between object-oriented programming and operator-based image processing (cf. § 2.2) has been studied by several teams, most notably in our area. Dov Dori's group, for instance, proposes a similar environment, MDUS, the *Machine Drawing Understanding System* [23], based on the object-process methodology. Our approach is probably more pragmatic than theirs, but the resulting environments are quite comparable.

The TABS system [24] has also been designed according to choices similar to ours, whereas its applications deal with form processing and handwriting recognition. The system is implemented in C++, but the user interface is written in TCL/TK. It also includes a supervision level driven by a blackboard.

A number of people have proposed different solutions, for example Koelma and Smeulders, who designed a library for image processing, with a hierarchy based on the number of dimensions of the image, the form of the pixel representation and the semantics of the image content [25]. Other systems include PhotoPix [26], and Piper and Ritovitz's work on C and C++ classes [27, 28].

In our opinion, a system like Khoros belongs to a different category. Its main strength comes more from the flexibility of its user interface (based on the visual programming paradigm) and from the completeness of its image processing library. Although it seems to be appropriate to teaching or to prototyping, it remains quite slow when used for real applications.

6 Conclusion

We have described a framework for designing reusable graphics recognition software components. It comprises a library of basic image and graphics processing operations, ISADORA, and a set of higher-level graphics recognition applications. A user interface has been added on top of these two layers, to drive the applications.

The design of this software platform first constrained us to deal with software engineering problems: We had to choose tools to be integrated as our programming environment, and to specify detailed programming recommendations to which each member of the research group had to conform. The latter point is particularly important when coding with a programming language like C++, which encourages the use of tricks increasing efficiency.

Some could think that we are not concerned by such problems. On the contrary, it appears that they fully condition the future of a project like ours: Without the long time passed in the careful study of the prerequisites, we could not be able to work together and to achieve a project involving the coding and the integration of a great number of complex methods. This experiment taught us that rigor and simplicity must be privileged, even at the cost of a certain loss of efficiency. The most important fact is that software components are easy to upgrade, to complete and to reuse.

The principles that we have initially chosen to design each separate method and tool allow our group to subsequently develop this environment all together, thus going from single-user programming to group development. Some software engineering problems remain open, but our platform can be considered as operational and we are now experienced enough to progressively solve them. Of course, our research work about graphics recognition is still simultaneously carried on. When methods become mature enough, they are integrated into the common environment, and become thus available to the whole group. We hope this paper has demonstrated the pertinence of our choices.

Ultimately, our work, as well as the others, might end up becoming contributions to the *Image Understanding Environment* (IUE) [8], which aims at providing a sophisticated environment for all kinds of image understanding activities. However, before joining this large effort, we prefer mastering a lower level of complexity by concentrating on our own know-how. We want to prove that we can "serve our own group" before being able to "serve the community".

References

1. D. Antoine, S. Collin, and K. Tombre. Analysis of Technical Documents: The REDRAW System. In H. S. Baird, H. Bunke, and K. Yamamoto, editors, *Structured Document Image Analysis*, pages 385–402. Springer-Verlag, Berlin, 1992.
2. C. Ah-Soon and K. Tombre. Network-Based Recognition of Architectural Symbols. In A. Amin, D. Dori, P. Pudil, and H. Freeman, editors, *Advances in Pattern Recognition (Proceedings of Joint IAPR Workshops SSPR'98 and SPR'98, Sydney, Australia), Lecture Notes in Computer Science 1451*, pages 252–261. Springer-Verlag, Berlin, 1998.
3. A. H. Habacha. Structural Recognition of Disturbed Symbols Using Discrete Relaxation. In *Proceedings of 1st International Conference on Document Analysis, Saint-Malo (France)*, volume 1, pages 170–178, 1991.
4. S. Collin and D. Colnet. Syntactic Analysis of Technical Drawing Dimensions. *International Journal of Pattern Recognition and Artificial Intelligence*, 8(5):1131–1148, 1994.
5. P. Vaxivière and K. Tombre. CELESSTIN: CAD Conversion of Mechanical Drawings. *IEEE COMPUTER Magazine*, 25(7):46–54, July 1992.
6. C. Ah-Soon and K. Tombre. Variations on the Analysis of Architectural Drawings. In *Proceedings of 4th International Conference on Document Analysis and Recognition, Ulm (Germany)*, pages 347–351, 1997.
7. K. Tombre, C. Ah-Soon, Ph. Dosch, A. Habed, and G. Masini. Stable, Robust and Off-the-Shelf Methods for Graphics Recognition. In *Proceedings of the 14th International Conference on Pattern Recognition, Brisbane (Australia)*, pages 406–408, 1998.
8. C. Kohl and J. Mundy. The Development of the Image Understanding Environment. In *Proceedings of IEEE Conference on Computer Vision and Pattern Recognition, Seattle (USA)*, 1994.
9. J. Mundy, T. Binford, T. Boult, A. Hanson, R. Beveridge, R. Haralick, V. Ramesh, C. Kohl, D. Lawton, D. Morgan, K. Price, and T. Strat. The Image Understanding Environment Program. In *Proceedings of IEEE Conference on Computer Vision and Pattern Recognition, Urbana Champaign (USA)*, pages 406–416, 1992.
10. B. Meyer. *Object-Oriented Software Construction, Second Edition*. The Object-Oriented Series. Prentice-Hall, Englewood Cliffs (NJ), USA, 1997.
11. Ø. Due Trier and T. Taxt. Improvement of "Integrated Function Algorithm" for Binarization of Document Images. *Pattern Recognition Letters*, 16(3):277–283, 1995.
12. L. A. Fletcher and R. Kasturi. A Robust Algorithm for Text String Separation from Mixed Text/Graphics Images. *IEEE Transactions on PAMI*, 10(6):910–918, 1988.
13. G. Sanniti di Baja. Well-Shaped, Stable, and Reversible Skeletons from the (3,4)-Distance Transform. *Journal of Visual Communication and Image Representation*, 5(1):107–115, March 1994.
14. K. Wall and P. Danielsson. A Fast Sequential Method for Polygonal Approximation of Digitized Curves. *Computer Vision, Graphics and Image Processing*, 28(2):220–227, 1984.
15. P. L. Rosin and G. A. West. Segmentation of Edges into Lines and Arcs. *Image and Vision Computing*, 7(2):109–114, May 1989.
16. D. Dori. Vector-Based Arc Segmentation in the Machine Drawing Understanding System Environment. In A. L. Spitz and A. Dengel, editors, *Document Analysis Systems*, pages 338–362. World Scientific, 1995.

17. D. Dori, L. Wenyin, and M. Peleg. How to Win a Dashed Line Detection Contest. In R. Kasturi and K. Tombre, editors, *Graphics Recognition—Methods and Applications, Lecture Notes in Computer Science 1072*, pages 286–300. Springer-Verlag, Berlin, 1996.
18. G. Sánchez, J. Lladós, and E. Martí. Segmentation and Analysis of Linial Texture in Planes. In *Proceedings of 7th Spanish National Symposium on Pattern Recognition and Image Analysis, Barcelona, Spain*, volume 1, pages 401–406, 1997.
19. S. W. C. Lam and H. H. S. Ip. Structural Texture Segmentation Using Irregular Pyramid. *Pattern Recognition Letters*, 15(7):691–698, 1994.
20. M. Maes. Polygonal Shape Recognition Using String-Matching Techniques. *Pattern Recognition*, 24(5):433–440, 1991.
21. W. H. Tsai and S. S. Yu. Attributed String Matching with Merging for Shape Recognition. In *Proceedings of 7th International Conference on Pattern Recognition, Montreal (Canada)*, pages 1162–1164, 1984.
22. Y. T. Tsay and W. H. Tsai. Model-Guided Attributed String Matching by Split-and-Merge for Shape Recognition. *International Journal of Pattern Recognition and Artificial Intelligence*, 3(2):159–179, 1989.
23. D. Dori. Representing Pattern Recognition-Embedded Systems Through Object-Process Diagrams—The Case of the Machine Drawing Understanding System. *Pattern Recognition Letters*, 16(4):377–384, 1995.
24. C. Cracknell and A. C. Downton. TABS: Script-Based Software Framework for Research in Image Processing, Analysis and Understanding. *IEE Proceedings - Vision, Image and Signal Processing*, 145(3):194–202, 1998.
25. D. Koelma and A. Smeulders. An Image Processing Library Based on Abstract Image Data-Types in C++. In C. Braccini, L. De Floriani, and G. Vernazza, editors, *Proceedings of 8th International Conference on Image Analysis and Processing, San Remo (Italy), Lecture Notes in Computer Science 974*, pages 97–102. Springer-Verlag, Berlin, 1995.
26. A. A. S. Sol and A. de Albuquerque Araújo. PhotoPix: An Object-Oriented Framework for Digital Image Processing Systems. In C. Braccini, L. De Floriani, and G. Vernazza, editors, *Proceedings of 8th International Conference on Image Analysis and Processing, San Remo (Italy), Lecture Notes in Computer Science 974*, pages 109–114. Springer-Verlag, Berlin, 1995.
27. J. Piper and D. Rutovitz. Data Structures for Image Processing in a C Language and UNIX Environment. *Pattern Recognition Letters*, 3(2):119–130, 1985.
28. J. Piper and D. Rutovitz. An Investigation of Object-Oriented Programming as the Basis for an Image Processing and Analysis System. In *Proceedings of 9th International Conference on Pattern Recognition, Rome (Italy)*, pages 1015–1019, 1988.

An Approach for Processing Mathematical Expressions in Printed Document

B. B. Chaudhuri[1] and U. Garain

Computer Vision & Pattern Recognition Unit
Indian Statistical Institute
203, B. T. Road, Calcutta 700 035, INDIA
e-mail: *bbc@www.isical.ac.in*

Abstract. In this paper, we propose an approach for understanding mathematical expressions in printed document. The system consists of three main components namely (i) detection of mathematical expressions in a document, (ii) recognition of the symbols present in the expression and (iii) meaningful arrangement of the recognized symbols. However, detection of mathematical expressions is done through recognition of symbols. Moreover, some structural features of the expressions are also used for this purpose. For recognition of the symbols a hybrid of feature based and template based recognition techniques is used. The bounding-box coordinates and the size information of the symbols help to determine the spatial relationships among the symbols. A set of predefined grammar rules is used to form the meaningful symbol groups to properly arrange the symbols. Experiments conducted using these approaches on a large number of documents show high accuracy.

1 Introduction

The use of computerized document-handling systems has now become widespread. One of the major applications concerns automatic conversion of text data into a computer readable form. Optical Character Recognition (OCR) systems are used for this purpose. OCR tries to recognize the characters on the document automatically and stores the corresponding ASCII code in a computer-processable file.

In spite of tremendous progress, we have not reached the stage where a printed page can be inserted in a OCR system so that a coded file comparable to the keyed-in version is generated. Many document elements like figures, logos, tables etc may baffle the system. Mathematical formulas and equations also fall into this category. It is a serious lacuna for technical documents since such documents generally contain a large number of such mathematical expressions. One naive approach for handling such documents is to manually key in the mathematical expressions into the computer. This approach is not acceptable when on line document processing is necessary and hence an automatic approach is called for.

---

[1] Author for correspondence.

In this paper, we propose an approach for understanding Mathematical Expressions (MEs) contained in a printed document. Earlier, Blostein and Grbavec [1] presented an interesting, systematic review on mathematical notation recognition. Anderson [2] also discussed the problem of the recognition of 2-D mathematical notations. He manually simulated the symbol recognition step and got an error-free recognition result. For symbol-arrangement Anderson [2] adopted a syntactic method and used coordinate grammars. On the other hand, Grbavec and Blostein [3] used a computational technique called graph rewriting where the information was represented as an attributed graph and the computation proceeded by updating the graph by following the graph-rewriting rules. Regarding the definition of mathematical notations, Martin [4] presented a brief list of notational conventions found in use in technical publications. Later on, Belaid and Haton [5] designed a coordinate grammar that is simpler than that of Anderson. Chang [6] used a structure specification scheme to recognize the structure of MEs. Okamoto et al [7], [8] proposed a recursive projection-profile cutting for arranging the symbols. Larvirotte and Pottier [9] used the graph grammar to recognize the mathematical formulas. H. J. Lee et al [10] proposed a procedure-oriented method for understanding MEs where they utilized thirteen features to represent each symbols. Chou [11] used a stochastic grammar to recognize a large set of mathematical expressions, all of which are drawn from a textbook printed by a known typesetter.

Our proposed approach for processing of MEs is based upon the structural features and the formats of the MEs. Functionally, the system is divided into three parts. The first part deals with the identification of the region containing MEs from the rest of the document. Most of the previous studies in this field do not concentrate on this issue. Our approach increases the speed of the system as once the MEs are identified we can concentrate on them instead of going through the whole document. Identification of ME areas is done through checking the presence of mathematical symbols in the text lines. It also uses some structural features of the expressions found in printed documents. The method for checking the presence of mathematical symbols involves the recognition of such symbols. So, part of the symbol recognition phase is done in this first stage.

In the second step, the system recognizes different symbols of the identified MEs in details. Feature-based approach for recognition of symbols is more flexible for size and style variations of the character font but less reliable for complex-shaped patterns where template matching gives better result. So, we use a hybrid of the two approaches for recognizing the symbols. After character recognition, the recognition engine gives the coded form of the MEs, which is represented by a list of symbols in random order. Apart from recognizing the symbols, the system also stores some format information against each mathematical symbol regarding its size, relative position (bounding box coordinates) in the document image etc.

In the third and final step, the system translates the recognition result into a meaningful character string satisfying the required criteria of a certain publication system, which can be used to recompose the MEs in the system. The method for symbol arrangement employs the format information stored against each symbol in the second step as well as the knowledge of notational conventions of expressing mathematics in a document.

The method for identifying MEs offers the option of storing the ME portion in picture mode for data storage. It also helps to create a database after scanning and interpreting a large collection of technical documents. On the other hand, storing the format information along with the coded form of the MEs also helps in other operations like browsing or automated retrieval where the expressions can be more or less accurately delineated and linked to the text itself. It also helps in structured or hypertext representation of a document.

This paper is organized as follows. In section-2, the results of quantitative survey on the relative abundance of MEs and their structural layout in technical documents are presented. Section-3 describes the procedure for detection of ME areas. Symbol recognition scheme has been described in section-4 while the technique for the re-composition of the MEs are described in section-5. Section-6 presents the test results.

2 MEs in printed document: A quantitative survey

Our approach for processing ME is based on statistical survey and hence it is expected to be robust and efficient. More than 10,000 document pages were manually scanned. The documents are drawn from various engineering and scientific books, journals, proceedings etc. We also studied softwares like LATEX [12] and Microsoft Equation 3.0 [13] that are commonly used for laying out MEs inside a document on Computers.

The study on the relative abundance of the MEs in printed technical documents gives the results summarized as below:

- Total number of pages scanned is 10,400.
- Total number of pages containing at least one ME is 6,700.
- Total number of MEs found is 11,820.
- Average page size is 391.17-sq. cm.
- Average ME size is 17.66-sq. cm.
- The estimated Probability that a page contains at least one ME is 0.64.
- The average number of MEs per page is 1.14.

The last two figures show the high density of MEs in the technical documents. The study also highlights the following facts on the structural features of the MEs:

- Most of the MEs (61%) have ME equation numbers at the right side of the MEs.
- In 47% of the cases the MEs are printed in italic style and in 27% of the cases in boldface.

This study reveals another important fact that the MEs are separated by white spaces which, in general, is wide enough to be distinguished from plain text region. This is supported by the following statistics:

- Average white spacing between two text lines is 0.2 cm and between two text paragraphs, it is 0.27 cm.
- Average white spaces above and below the ME are of height equals to 0.34 cm.

We obtained also the list of different symbols that appear in MEs. We classify these symbols into three groups: i) numerals, ii) English alphabet and words describing mathematical functions, as well as Greek alphabet, iii) mathematical symbols.

During the statistical study we detected 100 mathematical symbols and 40 Greek letters. The most popular mathematical symbols and Greek letters with their % of occurrences are shown in Table-1.

Table 1. Mathematical Symbols and Letters

Sl. No.	Symbol	% of occurrences*	Sl. No.	Symbol	% of occurrences*
1	=	94	21	⊂	4
2	+		22	Π	4
3	- (Minus)	93	23	√	4
4	/		24	θ	4
5	(	60	25	β	4
6	)		26	∈	4
7	Fraction Line	51	27	α	4
8	[	35	28	∇	4
9	]		29	μ	3
10	{	20	30	≠	3
11	}		31	→	3
12	<	18	32	×	3
13	>		33	∀	2
14	*	15	34	∉	2
15	Σ	15	35	%	2
16	∫	12	36	⊕	2
17	~	7	37	⇒	2
18	∪	5	38	δ	2
19	∩	5	39	λ	2
20	⊃	5	40	σ	2

** Out of 11,820 expressions.*

Table 2. Mathematical Keywords

Keywords	% of occurrences*	Keywords	% of occurrences*
Log	5	max	3
Exp	4	min	
Sin		ln	2
Cos	4	prob	2
Tan		avg	2

** Out of 11,820 expressions.*

In the MEs, certain words are found which represent mathematical functions. These are called *mathematical keywords*. The topmost 10 keywords and their percentage of occurrences are given in Table-2.

3 Detection of ME areas

MEs are generally mixed with text in documents. There are two ways in which MEs are found in documents: either as a separate line surrounded by wide white space, or as a part of a normal text line. So, the first step is to detect where the MEs are located in the document. Most of the related works mentioned earlier do not address this problem. Rather, they deal with an isolated ME. Lee and Wang [14] presented a method for extracting MEs in a text document. For this purpose they exploited some basic expression forms but did not provide any detail.

In our approach, we check each text line to decide whether they contain any mathematical symbol listed in Table-1. We adopt some clever approach for such checking to avoid false detection of mathematical symbols due to misrecognition. For example, sometimes letter 'C' may be confused as left parentheses '(', letter 'E' may be confused as square bracket '[', etc. To avoid such confusion for parentheses both the left and right parentheses are searched. For example, to decide that a text line contains square brackets both left '[' and right ']' brackets have to be detected. Presence of curly brackets '{' and '}' is also confirmed in a similar way. Some other similar rules guide this algorithm for searching mathematical symbols in a text line. Whenever a binary operator like '=', '+', '×', or '<' etc. is located in a text line its presence is confirmed by checking left and right side of the operator as binary operator contain two operands one on its left and another on its right side.

Once the presence of some mathematical symbols is confirmed in a text line say, T, it is decided that T contains an ME. At this stage, it is not confirmed whether T contains only ME (i.e. ME is printed as a separate line) or ME along with normal text (i.e. embedded ME). To resolve this confusion, we apply the knowledge extracted from our quantitative survey described in the last section. The survey reveals that the MEs that are not a part of normal text line are separated by white space, which are wide enough to be distinguished from other spacing such as the white spacing between lines or paragraphs etc. So, if T is surrounded by wide white spaces then it is decided that the ME is printed as a separate text line.

We use another important property of MEs to detect them whenever they are in a separate line. Our quantitative survey reveals that in more than 60% cases MEs have equation numbers whenever they are in a separate line. So, if any equation number can be detected in T then immediately it is decided that T contains only ME instead of any normal text. Detection of equation numbers is relatively easy, as these numbers generally have some well defined structured. Normally, they are written at the extreme right side of the line, sometimes succeeded by series of dots or a straight line or blank spaces.

On the other hand, if T is neither surrounded by wide white spaces nor it has any equation number then it is decided that T contains ME along with normal text. In such cases, ME area is detected and then extracted from T. Let W_1 be the first word from the left-hand side that contain one or more mathematical symbols in T. Construction of ME area is started by including W_1. Next the ME area grows towards both left and right side following certain rules. Two such rules are given below:

- If W_1 contains only a binary operator then both the immediate left and right side words are included in the ME area.

- Words adjacent to W_1 (on immediate left and right) are included in the ME area provided they contain:
  - Any mathematical symbol
  - Superscript or subscripts
  - Single or a series of dots
  - Numerals

Applying these rules each word included in an ME area is checked. Fig 1(a) shows a document containing both embedded and separate MEs. Fig. 1(b) shows the extracted ME areas.

4.2. Root-mean-square reconstruction error

Let $P = p_1 p_2 \dots p_K$ be a component segment associated with a static stroke S_i. We define a point sequence $P' = p'_1 p'_2 \dots p'_K$ sampled from S_i that best correspond to P in the following manner:

1. case of straight-line segment
   In this case, we locate $P' \in S_i$ such that $d(p_k, p'_k) = d(p_k, S_i)$, where $d(p_k, S_i)$ denotes Euclidean perpendicular distance between point p_k and line segment S_i.
2. case of arc
   In this case, we locate $P' \in S_i$ such that p'_k is the intersection of arc S_i and the line segment $\overline{p_k o_i}$ where $o_i(x_c, y_c)$ is the center of S_i.

Note that in either case, we always have $p_1 = p'_1$ and $p_K = p'_K$ as a result from our component segmentation.

Based on the above description, we can concatenate point sequences stroke by stroke and component by component. Then we get two point sequences that correspond to each other at script level.

Let $P = p_1 p_2 \dots p_M$ be the point sequence of a script and $P' = p'_1 p'_2 \dots p'_M$ be its correspondent in the reconstructed traces, the root-mean-square reconstruction error at script level is defined as

$$rmse = \frac{1}{H}\sqrt{\frac{1}{M}\sum_{m=1}^{M} d^2(p_m, p'_m)}. \quad (43)$$

where H is the normalized height of the script. Thus, the error can be expressed in percentage compared with H.

(a)

$P = p_1 p_2 \dots p_K$

$P' = p'_1 p'_2 \dots p'_K$

$P' \in S_i$

$d(p_k, p'_k) = d(p_k, S_i)$, $d(p_k, S_i)$

$P' \in S_i$

$o_i(x_c, y_c)$

$p_1 = p'_1$

$p_K = p'_K$

$P = p_1 p_2 \dots p_M$

$P' = p'_1 p'_2 \dots p'_M$

$$rmse = \frac{1}{H}\sqrt{\frac{1}{M}\sum_{m=1}^{M} d^2(p_m, p'_m)}. \quad (43)$$

(b)

Fig. 1. Extraction of Mathematical Expressions

4 Symbol recognition

Design of a recognition engine for mathematical symbols is a difficult task because the engine has to deal with a large character set. The set consists of Roman and Greek letters, operator symbols with a variety of typefaces (normal, bold or italic). Different font sizes are used to designate superscripts, subscripts and limit expressions. To deal with this problem we divide the character set into two groups. The first group, *group-1* includes the following 26 symbols:

"=" "+" "−" "/" "(" ")" "[" "]" "{" "}"
"<" ">" "Σ" "∫" "~" "∪" "∩" "⊂" "⊃" "Π"
"√" "×" "∀" "∈" "Δ" Fraction line

The second group, *group-2* includes the rest of the symbols given in section-2. Earlier we have discussed that ME areas are detected through recognition of mathematical symbols. We observe that the *group-1* symbols have very high rate of occurrence, so error in recognizing the symbols of this group not only affects the overall symbol recognition rate but also the efficiency of the module that detects the ME areas. Hence, we use feature-based approach which is more flexible to size and style variation of the character font than the template based one for recognition of *group-1* symbols. Moreover, these symbols have relatively simple shapes, so recognition through stroke/feature analysis is more efficient.

On the other hand, group-2 mostly includes the Roman and Greek letters which have more complex stroke patterns. For recognition of such symbols we combine the positive aspects of feature based and template based approaches. A run number based normalized template matching technique [15] is used for recognizing the *group-2* symbols.

A word is recognized inside a ME when more than one Roman character is found side by side and the inter-character gap is within a predefined threshold. If the recognition engine finds any word inside the ME it checks the list of *mathematical keywords* (discussed in section-2) for a quicker recognition of the word.

Our run number based template matching technique is more or less invariant to scaling and insensitive to character style variations. But it is found to be sensitive to the italic style of the characters. We find that in 47% of the cases the MEs are printed in italic style. So, we apply an approach for the detection of italic characters [16] and then use our template matching technique on the slant-corrected characters.

During recognition of the symbols the system stores some format information against each mathematical symbol regarding its size, relative position (bounding box coordinates) etc. along with its recognized shape name. These format information are used to categorize a symbol as superscript/subscript, upper or lower limit etc.

5 Arrangement of symbols

After character recognition, a ME is represented by a list of symbols in random order. So, we need to arrange these symbols into a character string satisfying the notational conventions of the 2-D language for mathematical expression. Blostein and Grbavec [1] reviewed four approaches for symbol-arrangement analysis. They are (i) syntactic methods (ii) projection-profile cutting (iii) graph-rewriting and (iv) procedurally coded rules.

In our approach, we first identify the significant spatial relationships among the symbols. For this purpose, we use the bounding-box coordinates, coordinates of the centroids and the size information of the symbols. Grammar rules are used to group the symbols into meaningful units. These grammar rules are made as general as possible. For example, the system covers 20 forms of integrals, including single integrals, line integrals, double (surface) integrals, and triple (volume) integrals, all with various combinations of limits. Similarly, 5 different types of sums with various combinations of limits are covered by the rules.

To identify meaningful symbol groups in a ME we first order the symbols from left to right according to their x and y values of the bounding box coordinates. Superscripts, subscripts, upper or lower limits are identified by their position and size information. Next, grammar rules are applied to form meaningful units. Sometimes, confusion arises regarding the placement of some symbols. For example, in case of a dot "." alternatives like (i) a decimal point (ii) multiplication sign (iii) terminating symbol (i.e. full stop) (iv) sometimes series of dots are placed in between an ME and its number (i.e. equation number) or (v) noise are considered.

Once the meaningful units are identified they are converted into a coded form. Coding of some MEs has been shown in Fig. 2. Fig. 2(a) and Fig. 2(c) show two MEs and their coded forms are shown in Fig. 2(b) and Fig. 2(d), respectively.

$$X = a_0 + a_1 x + a_2 y + a_3 xy + a_4 x^2 + a_5 y^2 + ... + a_{m-1} x^n + a_m y^n \qquad (1)$$

(a)

X = a ₀ + a ₁ x + a ₂ y + a ₃ x y + a ₄ x ² + a ₅ y ² + ... + a _{m-1} x ⁿ + a _m y ⁿ <EQU NO> (1) </EQU NO>

(b)

$$R(C) = \int_0^L \sqrt{(x(s) - P_x)^2 + (y(s) - P_y)^2}\, ds \qquad 2$$

(c)

R(C) = <INTEGRATION> <UPLIM> L </UPLIM> <LOWLIM> 0 </LOWLIM> <SQRT> (x(s) - P _x) ²+ (y(s) - P _y) ² </SQRT> ds </INTEGRATION> <EQU NO> 2 </EQU NO>

(d)

Fig. 2. Coding of Mathematical Expressions

For coding of MEs we follow a coding scheme that has similarity with HTML code. The code uses abbreviated forms to indicate different meaningful groups. For example, the keyword <INTEGRATION> indicates the beginning of a mathematical operation called integration. </INTEGRATION> indicates the end of the operation. Similarly, <SUP>, <SUB>, <UPLIM>, <LOWLIM> indicate the beginning of superscript, subscript, upper limit, lower limit, respectively. <EQU NO> indicates the start of the equation number if it exists for an ME.

6 Test results

Algorithms for detection of ME areas, recognition and arrangement of symbols have been tested on total 80 technical documents containing 82 MEs. Fig. 3 shows some of the test documents. Both clean and degraded versions of the documents are used. The degraded documents are generated by adding synthetic noise. The system performance is evaluated in terms of the performance of each module responsible for various processing.

In 95% cases our algorithm for detecting ME areas properly finds the both the separate and embedded (mixed with text) MEs in a document. Only four MEs (out of 82) have not been properly identified. Two of them are embedded MEs. The rest two MEs have been missed because of the complicated structure of the documents. In these cases, our algorithm fails to analyze the document structure itself.

Earlier it is mentioned that the symbols (*group-1* symbols) with high occurrence rate are recognized through stroke feature analysis. For recognition of other symbols a run-number based normalized template matching technique is used. Both the techniques show high accuracy in recognizing the symbols and the overall correct recognition rate is about 98.3%. Since *group-1* symbols have relatively simple shapes than that of *group-2* symbols, stroke feature analysis shows better result than the template matching technique. The errors in recognition are mainly due to (i) the character font drastically varies from the commonly used fonts (ii) poor quality of the document paper (iii) poor print quality etc.

Rating of symbol arrangement approach is little bit difficult. Sometimes, wrong arrangement of few symbols may drastically change the meaning of the expression even after all other symbols are arranged properly. Hence, to evaluate the approach for symbol arrangement first one has to set a proper evaluation criteria. We emphasis on correct grouping of mathematical symbols. We rate our symbol arrangement approach by examining how many meaningful symbol groups out of all such groups in an ME are properly formed and arranged. We observe that our method for this purpose works well with 92% accuracy. The errors occur mainly due to (i) errors in symbol recognition stage (ii) unavailability of proper grammar rules to represent certain meaningful symbol groups (iii) complication in the structure of some MEs, etc.

It is observed that our system for processing MEs is also efficient in term of execution time. It is implemented on a 166 MHz. Pentium machine with 32 MB Ram using 'C' programming language. Documents are scanned at a resolution of 300 dpi. On an average, the document images are of size 3000X2000 pixels. To process such a document the system on an average takes only 1 min. 6 seconds which also includes the time required for binarizing a gray-level image.

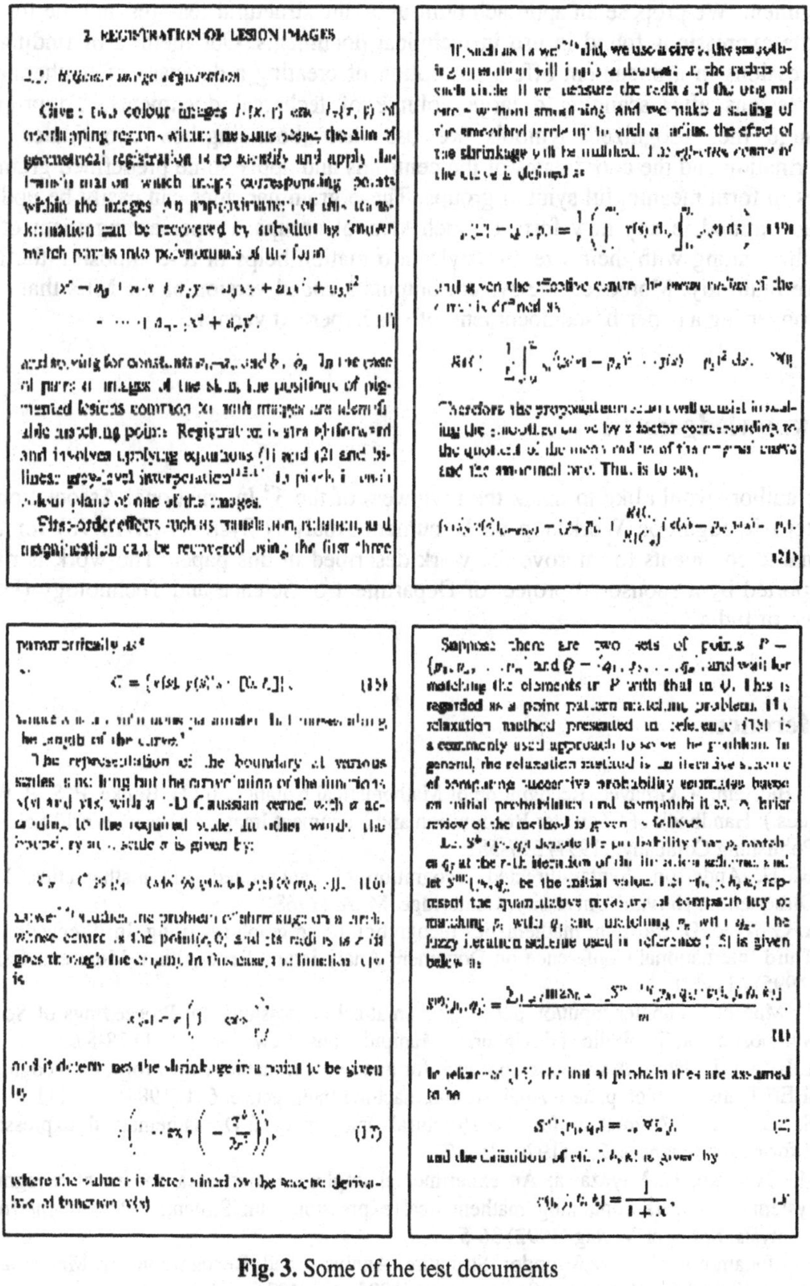

2. REGISTRATION OF LESION IMAGES

[illegible]

Given two colour images $I_1(x, y)$ and $I_2(x, y)$ of overlapping regions within the same scene, the aim of geometrical registration is to identify and apply the transformation which maps corresponding points within the images. An approximation of this transformation can be recovered by substituting known match points into polynomials of the form [illegible]

and solving for constants [illegible]. In the case of pairs of images of the skin, the positions of pigmented lesions common to both images are identifiable matching points. Registration is straightforward and involves applying equations (1) and (2) and bilinear grey-level interpolation [illegible] colour plane of one of the images.

First-order effects such as translation, rotation, and magnification can be recovered using the first three [illegible]

[illegible] we use a circle, the smoothing operation will [illegible] a decrease in the radius of such circle. If we measure the radius of the original curve without smoothing and we make a scaling of the smoothed circle up to such a radius, the effect of the shrinkage will be nullified. The effective centre of the curve is defined as [illegible]

and given the effective centre the mean radius of the curve is defined as [illegible]

Therefore the proposed correction will consist in scaling the smoothed curve by a factor corresponding to the quotient of the mean radius of the original curve and the smoothed one. That is to say, [illegible] (21)

parametrically as [illegible] (15)

[illegible]

The representation of the boundary at various scales is nothing but the convolution of the functions $x(s)$ and $y(s)$ with a 1-D Gaussian kernel with σ according to the required scale. In other words, the boundary at a scale σ is given by: [illegible] (16)

[illegible] goes through the origin. In this case, the function [illegible]

and it determines the shrinkage in a point to be given by [illegible] (17)

where the value [illegible] is determined by the second derivative of function $x(s)$

Suppose there are two sets of points [illegible] and wait for matching the elements in P with that in Q. This is regarded as a point pattern matching problem. The relaxation method presented in reference [illegible] is a commonly used approach to solve the problem. In general, the relaxation method is an iterative scheme of computing successive probability estimates based on initial probabilities and compatibilities. A brief review of the method is given as follows.

[illegible] denote the probability that p_i matches q_j at the r-th iteration of the iteration scheme and let [illegible] be the initial value. Let [illegible] represent the quantitative measure of compatibility of matching p_i with q_j and matching p_h with q_k. The fuzzy iteration scheme used in reference [illegible] is given below as [illegible] (1)

In reference [illegible] the initial probabilities are assumed to be [illegible] (2)

and the definition of [illegible] is given by [illegible]

Fig. 3. Some of the test documents

7 Conclusions

In this paper, we present a system for processing mathematical expressions in printed document. We propose an approach built upon the structural features and the formats of the expressions found in use in technical documents. Our method of finding the expressions in a document offers the option of creating a database of mathematical expressions after scanning a large volume of technical documents. To properly arrange the recognized symbols we use their bounding-box coordinates, size information and the coordinates of the centroids and apply some predefined grammar rules to form meaningful symbol groups. These grammar rules can easily be updated to accommodate any new form of such symbol groups. Proper arrangement of the symbols along with their size and style information helps in re-composing the MEs more faithfully. Moreover, the system outputs a coded version of the MEs that helps in converting a paper-based document into its hypertext version.

Acknowledgement

The authors would like to thank the reviewers of the 3rd International Association for Pattern Recognition Workshop on Document Analysis Systems (DAS'98) for their valuable comments to improve the work described in this paper. The work is partly supported by a sponsored project of Department of Science and Technology (DST), Govt. of India.

References

1. D. Blostein, A. Grbavec: Recognition of Mathematical Notation. In: H. Bunke, P. S. P. Wang (eds.): Handbook of Character Recognition and Document Image Analysis, World Scientific Publishing Company, (1997) 557-582
2. R. H. Anderson: Syntax-directed recognition of handprinted 2-D mathematics. Ph.D. Dissertation. Harvard University, Cambridge, M. A. (1968)
3. A. Grbavec, D. Blostein: mathematics recognition using graph rewriting. In: Proceedings of Third International Conference on Document Analysis and Recognition. Montreal, Canada (1995) 417-421
4. W. Martin: Computer input/output of mathematical expressions. In: Proceedings of Second Symposium on Symbolic and Algebraic Manipulations. New York (1971) 78-87
5. A. Belaid, J. Haton: A syntactic approach for handwritten mathematical formula recognition. IEEE Transaction on pattern Analysis and machine Intelligence. 6, 1 (1984) 105-111
6. S. K. Chang: A method for the structural analysis of 2-D mathematical expressions. Information Sciences. 2, 3 (1970) 253–272
7. M. Okamoto, H. Miyazawa: An experimental implementation of a document recognition system for papers containing mathematical expressions. In: Structured Document Image Analysis. Springer-Verlag (1992) 36-53
8. M. Okamoto, H. Twaakyondo: Structure Analysis and Recognition of Mathematical Expressions. IEEE Computer Society Press (1995) 430-437
9. S. Larvirotte, L. Pottier: Mathematical formula recognition using graph grammar. In: Proceedings of SPIE, Vol. 3305. California, USA (1998)

10. H. Lee, M. Lee: Understanding mathematical expressions using procedure-oriented transformation. Pattern Recognition, 27, 3 (1994) 447–457
11. P. Chou: Recognition of equations using a two-dimensional context-free grammar. In: Proceedings of SPIE Visual Communication and Image Processing IV. Philadelphia PA (1989) 852-863
12. LATEX: A document Presentation System. Addison Wesley Publishing Company, Inc. (1986)
13. Microsoft® Word 97: Copyright © 1983-1996. Microsoft Corporation. USA
14. H. Lee and J. Wang: Design of a mathematical expression recognition system. In: Proceedings of Third International Conference on Document Analysis and Recognition. Montreal, Canada (1995) 1084-1087
15. U. Garain, B. B. Chaudhuri: Compound character recognition by a run number based metric distance. In: Proceedings of SPIE, Vol. 3305. San Jose (1998) 90-97
16. B. B. Chaudhuri, U. Garain: Automatic detection of italic, bold and all-capital words from documents. In: Proceedings of International Conference on Pattern Recognition. Australia (1998) 610-612

A Map Mosaicking Method Using Opportunistic Search Approach with a Blackboard Structure

Jonghyon Yi, Min Suk Lee, and Jaihie Kim

Department of Electrical and Computer Engineering, Yonsei University,
Shinchon-dong, Seodaemoon-gu, Seoul, 120-749, Korea
{johnyi,lms}@seraph.yonsei.ac.kr, jhkim@bubble.yonsei.ac.kr

Abstract. Map mosaicking is to integrate two or more map images having a coincident area by computing the rotational angle, the vertical and horizontal distances a map image has to move to overlap the coincident area. A solution of the problem is represented as a point in the parameter space with three axes: one for the rotational angle and the others for the vertical and horizontal distances. We extract local features from each map image, match them to make feature pairs, and project the feature pairs onto the parameter space. Traditional approaches using parameter spaces have suffered from a huge search space and computing time, for they project all the feature pairs onto the parameter space and search solutions by iterative optimization methods. We propose a new method that can give a solution not projecting all the feature pairs onto the parameter space but search opportunistically in a Blackboard structure.

1 Introduction

When scanning a large map with a flat bed scanner that can scan only documents of restricted size, one should divide the map into several parts, scan them, and then integrate them by adequate methods. Map mosaicking can be considered as finding coincident areas among these partitioned map images and computing the exact transformations among them. To do this manually, one should find some distinguishing marks on one map image, look for the same marks on another, and then overlap these two coincident marks. To mosaic map images automatically, one can follow the same strategy. In order to reduce computation, we used local features[1], rather than the pixels itself. The features should be consistently obtainable from map images regardless of rotation, scaling, and translation of map images. A feature from one map image and another feature from the other map image form a matched feature pair if they are coincident with each other. A matched feature pair implies a possible transformation between two map images.

Finding the optimal transformation is performed on the set of matched feature pairs. The matched feature pairs are positioned in the parameter space, which has axes of two translational parameters, one rotational parameter and one scaling parameter. The optimal transformation is expected to be at the location where feature pairs densely exist. While early studies tried to find optimal transformation by procedural or mathematical methods[1, 2], recent researchers[3, 4] addressed that Hopfield neural networks showed good performances in finding the position representing the optimal transformation. All these approaches try to match all possible feature pairs and suffer from heavy computation. Kim *et al*[4]. used Discrete Hopfield neural network and Continuous Hopfield neural network to solve the search space problem.

We propose a new map mosaicking method that can find the transformation solution with a reduced search space by an opportunistic search approach. We first extract local features from each map images, match them, and calculate the similarity between them. Then we compute transformations of matched feature pairs in order of their similarities, and position them on the parameter space as "points". Two matched feature pairs with high similarities closely located in the parameter space imply high possibility of the transformations of the neighboring positions being a solution transformation. These two matched feature pairs trigger the generation of a "cluster" at the middle of these two pairs in the parameter space. The cluster is defined as a candidate for solution transformation and has a region of predefined size. If a new transformation computed from a matched feature pair is positioned close to the center position of a existing cluster, the transformation is included into the cluster. A cluster which has included sufficient transformations is verified to be the solution transformation. These procedures are executed opportunistically through a blackboard structure[5].

We examine the proposed method by applying it to mosaicking Korean Land Register Map scanned with a resolution of 200 dpi. The result shows that the proposed method can mosaic map images in a opportunistic way, and is applicable to mosaicking map images with small coincident areas. In this paper, we assume that there are only rotational and translational transformations between two map images. However, the proposed method can be extended to scaling transformations without fundamental modifications.

2 Map Mosaicking Method Using Clusters in Parameter Space

2.1 Feature Extraction

Features extracted from map images are roads, crossroads, and districts[6]. Figure 1 shows an example map image and the extracted feature information.

A district feature represented by a polygon has several attributes: the lengths of roadsides, the directions of roadsides, the number of neighboring roads, and the widths of every neighboring roads. A road feature represented by a straight line has following attributes: the width of the road, the length of the road, the number of crossroads connected, and the number of connected roads of each crossroad. A crossroad feature has the number of connected roads, the widths of the each connected road, and the angles between connected roads.

A feature has a vector representation for transformation computation. A road feature itself is a line and has a vector represented by two end points. A crossroad feature has a vector that starts at the crossroad point and ends at the other end

(a) (b)

Fig. 1. An example map image and the extracted feature information.

point of the widest connected road line. A district feature consists of several lines. So, any of these lines is used as a vector representation.

2.2 Matching the Features

Two features selected from each map image are matched and the similarity is computed when they are of same type and satisfy one of the three matching criteria. The *coincident* criterion is satisfied when two features fit exactly each other in all attributes. The *partial* criterion means that one feature is a part of the other. Two features sharing part of attributes satisfy the *sharing* criterion.

Crossroad features can be matched only by coincident matching criterion. District features and road features can have all three matching criteria. Figure 2 shows examples of matching criteria: in (a) two point features coincides in all attributes, in (b) one district feature is totally matched to part of the other district feature, and in (c) and (d) two road features share only half of attributes and satisfy sharing matching criterion.

The similarity between features is computed differently depending on the kind of features and the matching criteria but the idea is that the value is between zero and unity, and a pair of similar features has a value close to unity. The similarity can be calculated easily by Eq. 1. In this equation, A_i means the ith attribute of the feature A of the first map image, and B_j means the jth attribute of the feature B of the second map image. *Val(•)* implies the value of an attribute.

$$Sim(A,B) = \prod_{\text{matched attribute } i,\ j} \frac{\min(Val(A_i), Val(B_j))}{\max(Val(A_i), Val(B_j))} . \qquad (1)$$

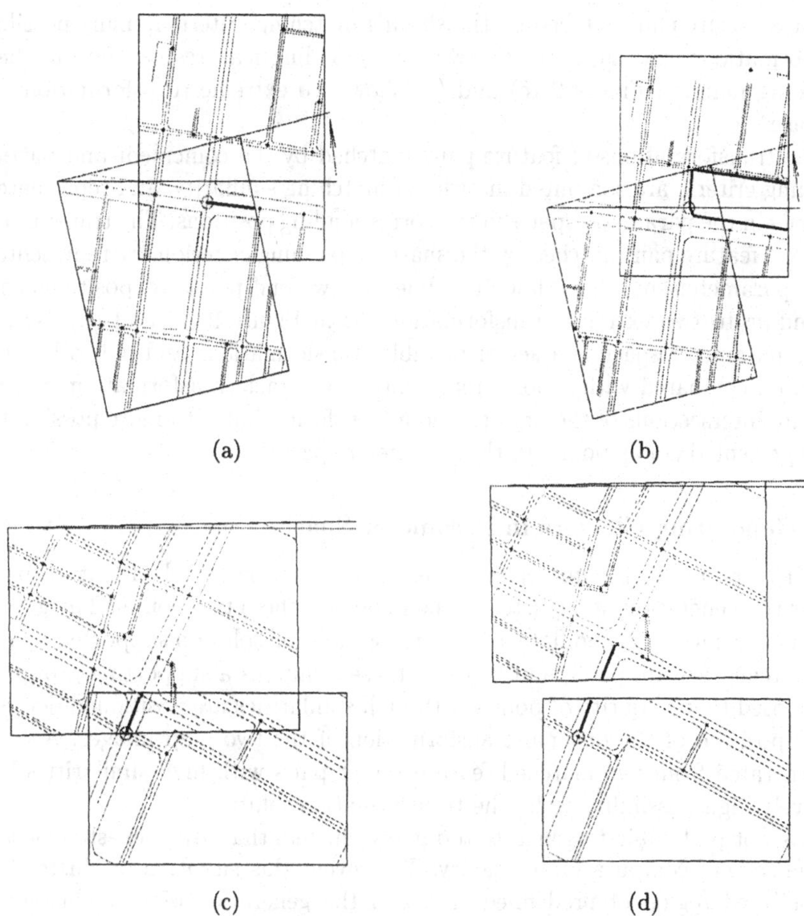

Fig. 2. Examples of matching criteria: (a) coincident criterion of crossroads, (b) partial criterion of districts, and (c) and (d) sharing criterion of roads.

2.3 Computing Transformations from Matched Vector Pairs

Assuming there is only rotational and translational (RT) transformation between two map images, we need a parameter space with three axes: $d\Theta$ axis for rotation angle, dX and dY for horizontal and vertical translation. Then a point ($d\theta$, dx, dy) implies an RT transformation.

For a feature pair, we can compute a transformation between the two features[1]. If two matched features are represented in vector form as $\boldsymbol{v}(x_1, y_1)$, and $\boldsymbol{w}(x_2, y_2)$, the transformation ($d\theta$, dx, dy) is decided as Eq. 2, 3 and 4.

$$d\theta = \angle(\boldsymbol{v}) - \angle(\boldsymbol{w}) \ . \tag{2}$$

$$dx = x_2 - (x_1 \cos d\theta - y_1 \sin d\theta) \ . \tag{3}$$

$$dy = y_2 - (x_1 \sin d\theta + y_1 \cos d\theta) \ . \tag{4}$$

For a feature pair matched by the sharing matching criterion, many possible transformations exist because the two corresponding features can be matched by sliding manner. Figure 2 (c) and (d) show two extreme transformations of this case.

The transformations of feature pairs matched by the coincident and partial matching criteria are computed in order of matching similarity, and represented as points in the parameter space on the corresponding positions. The transformations of a feature pair matched by the sharing matching criterion are represented in the parameter space as a line. The line has two end points at positions corresponding to two extreme transformations as in Figure 2 (c) and (d). A line on the parameter space is a set of possible transformations and it has less information compared with a point representing an exact transformation. So, we compute intersections of the lines to find a transformation with more possibility, and represent them as points in the parameter space.

2.4 Generating Clusters in Parameter Space

Two close points in parameter space, each representing matched feature pair, trigger the generation of a cluster at the middle of these two points. The generated cluster implies a candidate for the transformation solution supported by the two matched feature pairs, and includes these points as a supporting group. It is supposed that majority of points with high similarities are positioned densely at the position of the optimal transformation of the two map images. A cluster generated from two matched feature vector pairs with high similarities has relatively high possibility to be the transformation solution.

It is not preferable to generate too many clusters that are congested closely for the sake of computation efficiency. To prevent this situation, a cluster has a prohibited region of predefined size, and the generation of new clusters is prohibited inside the regions of existing clusters. The size of the prohibited region of clusters determines the precision of the transformation solution search. Figure 3(a) shows an example of generating a cluster from two points in the parameter space. In this figure, the inner circle shaded darkly implies the prohibited region and the outer circle shows the region in which the cluster takes points as its own supporting group.

The cluster c_k to be generated from the two points p_i and p_j has a certainty factor $CF(c_k)$ as Eq. 5. In this equation, $\delta\theta$ and $\delta\tau$ are distances between two points in rotation axis and in translation surface in the parameter space respectively. And $\phi\theta$ and $\phi\tau$ are bias values in rotation axis and in translation surface in the parameter space respectively. The computed certainty factor shows a value closer to unity when two seed points are close to each other and have larger similarities. The certainty factor value determines when the cluster should be generated. The usage of the certainty factor is explained in Chap. 3 in detail.

$$CF(c_k) = \max\left(Sim(p_i), Sim(p_j)\right) \times \left(1 - \frac{\delta\theta(p_i, p_j)}{\phi\theta}\right) \times \left(1 - \frac{\delta\tau(p_i, p_j)}{\phi\tau}\right) . \quad (5)$$

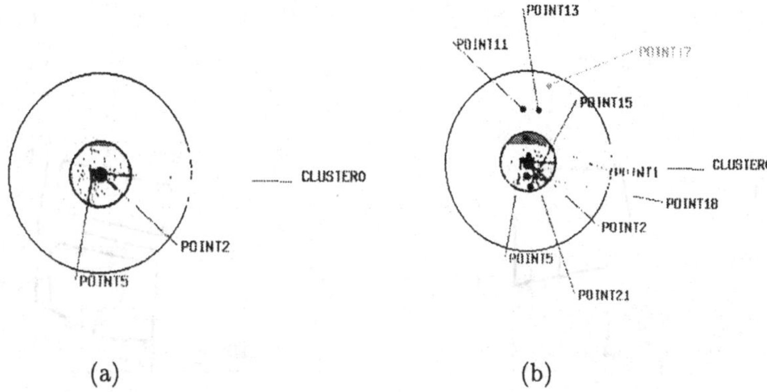

(a) (b)

Fig. 3. Examples of a cluster in the parameter space : (a) the generation of cluster CLUSTER0 from point POINT2 and POINT5, (b) the growth of CLUSTER0

2.5 Growth of Clusters

If a cluster is generated near a existing point or a new point is positioned near the center of a existing cluster, the cluster can include the point into its supporting group. The probability of a cluster being a solution increases by including points into supporting group. The support value defined below determines whether a point in the parameter space should be included into a cluster or not. The support which point p_i has for cluster c_k is given by Eq. 6. It measures how strong a point supports a cluster. It shows a value close to unity when the certainties of p_i and c_k are large and the distance between them is small.

$$Sup_{p_i}(c_k) = Sim(p_i) \times CF(c_k) \times \left(1 - \frac{\delta\theta(p_i, c_k)}{\phi\theta}\right) \times \left(1 - \frac{\delta\tau(p_i, c_k)}{\phi\tau}\right) . \quad (6)$$

Clusters centered at a position where a large amount of points with high similarities are densely located will grow fast, because points with large similarities and close to centers of the clusters have large supporting values for the clusters and will be included early in the computation.

2.6 Cluster Verification

A sufficiently grown cluster is determined to be a solution transformation through the feature comparison. We call this procedure cluster verification. To decide which cluster to verify, we defined the competency. The competency of a cluster c_k is close to unity when the certainty factor of the cluster is close to unity and the supporting group is large as in Eq. 7. Here, $S(c_k)$ is the number of points in the supporting group of c_k and T is the number of matched feature pairs.

$$Comp(c_k) = CF(c_k) \times \frac{S(c_k)}{T} . \quad (7)$$

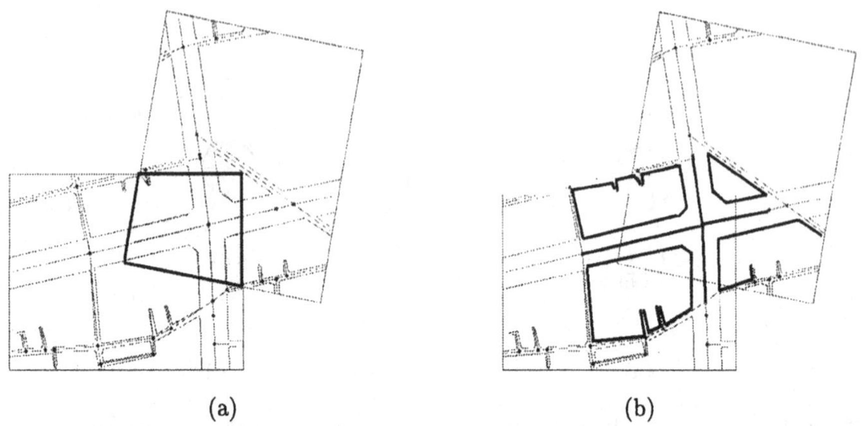

(a) (b)

Fig. 4. (a) Composed feature map image and (b) features engaging into the verification

In the cluster verification procedure, competencies of all clusters are compared and the cluster with the largest competency value is selected. To verify a cluster, the features of one map image as Figure 1(b) is rotated and translated onto the features of the other by the transformation designated by the center of the cluster. Overlapped region exists on the composed feature map image as Figure 4 (a). Then, each feature of one map lying on the overlapped region is matched one to one with the corresponding feature of the other map. Verification result is computed with feature pairs matched for verification. Different from the similarity computation in Section 2.2, verification result is computed by Euclidean distance between matched line segments of each matched feature pair, and given as Eq. 8. In this equation, ϕd is a sufficiently large bias value and $d(f_i, g_j)$ is minimal Euclidean distance between feature f_i of one map and g_j of the other.

$$Verif(c_k) = \prod_{\text{matched feature pair } f_i,\ g_j} \left(1 - \frac{d(f_i, g_j)}{\phi d}\right). \tag{8}$$

The search for transformation solution is finished when the cluster verification result is greater than a predefined threshold. For further reliability, one map image is transformed onto the other and pixel level similarity is computed.

3 Opportunistic Search Using Blackboard Structure

The proposed map mosaicking method is implemented by using blackboard structure to take advantage of the opportunistic reasoning characteristics. The hierarchical data structure in the proposed map mosaicking method is composed of map images, features extracted from the map images, matched feature pairs which is represented as points in the parameter space, clusters in parameter space, and the solution transformation. Figure 5 shows the blackboard structure.

In this figure, a horizontal line designates a layer of hierarchical data structure and the arrows represent knowledge sources. Each knowledge source takes information from the layer where the arrow starts and puts the results on the layer where the arrow ends.

We use following 5 knowledge sources: *Point Generator*, *Cluster Generator*, *Cluster Grower*, *Cluster Verifier*, and *Stopper*. Each knowledge source is composed of a precondition that determines whether the knowledge source is applicable at the situation, and a body that executes appropriate computation. In our implementation, all preconditions of knowledge sources show their priority values on the basis of current blackboard condition, and the controller of the blackboard system chooses a knowledge source that shows largest priority value. The chosen knowledge source does its job and returns the result to the blackboard.

In the blackboard structure, it is very important to define the priorities of knowledge sources. The point generator takes the greatest value among similarity values of matched feature pairs as its priority value, and the cluster generator takes the certainty factor of the cluster to be generated as its priority value. And the cluster grower takes the largest value among support values that points have for clusters. The priority value of cluster verifier takes into account the number of points in the supporting group of the cluster to be verified and is defined as Eq. 9. In this equation, $CF_{best\ cluster}$ and $S_{best\ cluster}$ are the certainty factor and the number of points in supporting group of a cluster with maximal competency value respectively. The precondition value is close to unity when the certainty factor of the cluster is close to unity and the number of points in supporting group is large. The priority value of the stopper has unity when the cluster verification result is greater than a predefined threshold or when there is no solution even after predefined trial of cluster verification and it has zero otherwise.

$$Precondition_{CV} = (CF_{best\ cluster})^{\frac{1}{K}} , \tag{9}$$

$$K = \begin{cases} \frac{S_{best\ cluster}}{4} & \text{when } S_{best\ cluster} \geq 4 \ ; \\ 1 & \text{when } S_{best\ cluster} < 4 \ . \end{cases}$$

When the search for the solution transformation is finished and there is a solution transform, we integrate the two map images by rotating and translating one map image onto the other. The integrated map image may be used for mosaicking with another map image via the same method.

4 Experimental Results

Korean Land Register Maps are used in the experiment. The map image is scanned with the resolution of 200 dpi and in 256 gray levels. The district information, which is represented in light gray color because it is originally in yellow color, is recognized first. Parallel lines between neighboring districts are recognized as roads. And finally the intersection points of elongated road lines are

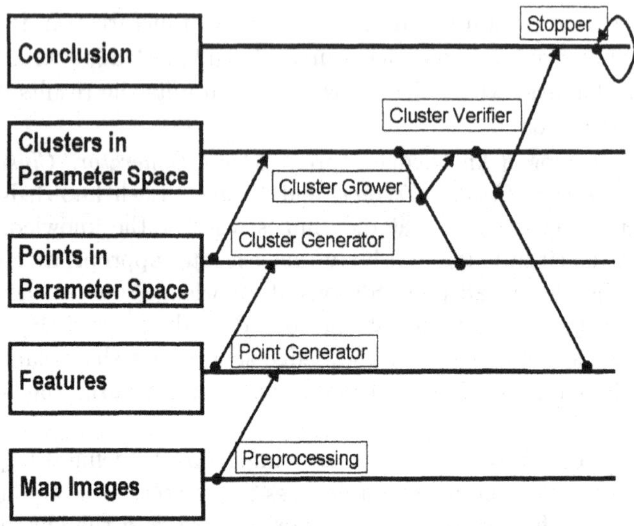

Fig. 5. The blackboard structure for the opportunistic map mosaicking

Table 1. Characteristics of Problem 1, Problem 2 and Problem 3.

Problem1	Image Size	Number of District	Number of Road	Number of Crossroad
Map1	600 x 716	17	26	12
Map2	600 x 716	19	30	13
Problem2				
Map1	808 x 409	9	11	5
Map2	900 x 600	24	35	7
Problem3				
Map1	582 x 732	20	33	18
Map2	782 x 600	23	36	15

recognized as crossroads[6–8]. The experiment was done on Intel Pentium Pro PC of 200 MHz with the operating system Linux 2.0.

Figure 6, 7 and 8 show the examples of the experiment. In each figures, (a), (c) are map images, and (b), (d) are feature images extracted from (a) and (c) respectively. Using the proposed mosaicking method, the integrated feature image (e) is obtained by the solution transformation, and the mosaicked map image is shown in (f). Characteristics of problems are given in Table 1

The summary of the results of Problem 1, 2 and 3 is shown in Table 2. In Problem 1, one can guess the solution easily because of the outstanding local features such as a crossroad. With the proposed method, it takes a lot of computation time in preprocessing and similarity computation because there are many district, road, and crossroad features despite its small image sizes. And it takes relatively small portion of time in the opportunistic search processing because

Table 2. Experimental results of Problem 1, Problem 2 and Problem 3.

	Problem 1	Problem 2	Problem 3
Solution Transformation ($d\theta$: degree, dx and dy : pixel)	$d\theta$: -13.25 dx: -260.45 dy: 485.30	$d\theta$: 2.21 dx: -172.04 dy: -597.73	$d\theta$: 0.17 dx: 143.18 dy: -239.22
# of Points in Parameter Space	22	53	10
# of Clusters in Parameter Space	4	18	7
# of Clusters Verified	1	7	3
Total Time (TA+TB) (second)	42.2	39.0	44.0
Preprocessing Time + Similarity Calculation(TA) (second)	31.0	18.0	37.0
Time Elapsed in Opportunistic Search(TB) (second)	11.2	21.0	7.0
# of Execution of Knowledge Sources	55	178	28

there are large coincident area and maybe because there are many feature pairs matched with high similarities.

In Problem 2, human may feel it hard to find the solution because of little coincident area. Only 18.0 seconds were taken in preprocessing and similarity computation because of small number of features. Large part of processing time was spent in opportunistic search phase trying to verify 7 clusters in parameter space. However, one can expect that it will not be possible to find the solution without the sharing matching criterion defined in this paper.

In Problem 3, because there are very large coincident area and many coincident features, it took less time in opportunistic search compared to other examples. One can see this from the fact that there are 10 points and 7 clusters in parameter space. This means that most of the transformations are congested closely.

5 Conclusion

We proposed a map mosaicking method using clusters in the parameter space and the opportunistic search approach. We showed that the proposed method can find the transformation solution with a reduced search space compared to that of conventional methods using parameter spaces. We adopted a blackboard structure in building the system and realizing the opportunistic search method. By defining "clusters", we were able to manage candidates for transformation solutions, and get a solution transformation with small amount of computation. By using the sharing matching criterion, mosaicking map images that have relatively small coincident area was made possible.

In this paper, we dealt with only two partitioned map images. To integrate more than two images, we can follow the same method discussed previously. First, we select another partitioned map which have coincident area with the previously mosaicked map. Second, we extract features from the selected map.

And we finally apply the same method to the newly generated feature map and the formerly composed feature map as in figure 6(e), 7(e) and 8(e). These steps would be continued until all the partitioned map images are integrated together.

Careful readers may find out that our method is not for searching the "optimal" transformation because we define the prohibited region of a cluster of fixed size. However, we can insist that finding suboptimal transformation solution in short time is more helpful for map mosaicking applications than finding optimal solution with large computation because map images are generally large in size. Furthermore the precision required by an application can be achieved by changing the size of the prohibited region of the cluster.

The opportunistic approach used in this paper is applicable to object recognition, image mosaicking, and also to image registration, in case that robust features are available.

Acknowledgments

This work was supported in part by Korea Science and Engineering Foundation by the Contract 95-0100-11-01-3.

References

1. G. Stockman, S. Kopstein, and S. Benett, "Matching Images to Models for Registration and Object Detection via Clustering," *IEEE Trans. on Pattern Analysis and Machine Intelligence*, Vol. PAMI-4, No. 3, pp. 229-241, May 1982.
2. I. Dowman, V. Vohra, and A. Holmes, "Developments in automated object- image registration," *Integrating photogrammetric techniques with scene analysis and machine vision II*, Orlando, FL, pp. 85-92, Apr. 19-21, 1995.
3. N. M. Nasrabadi, W. Li, "Object Recognition by a Hopfield Neural Network," *IEEE Trans. on Systems, Man, and Cybernetics*, Vol. 21, No. 6, pp. 1523-1535, November/December 1991.
4. J. H. Kim, S. H. Yoon, and K. H. Sohn, "A Robust Boundary-Based Object Recognition In Occlusion Environment By Hybrid Hopfield Neural Networks," *Pattern Recognition* Vol. 29, No. 12, pp. 2047-2060, 1996.
5. Robert Engelmore, Tony Morgan, and H.P. Nii, *Blackboard Systems*, Addison- Wesley Publishing Company, 1988.
6. K. S. Jang, J. Yi, J. Y. Jung, J. Kim, and K. H. Chang, "A Recognition of Map Using the Geometric Relations between Lines and the Structural Information of Objects," *Proc. of IEEE Int'l Conf. on Image Processing*, Santa Barbara, California, pp. 150-153, Oct. 1997.
7. Mark J. Carlotto, "Using maps to automate the classification of remotely- sensed imagery," *Algorithms for multispectral and hyperspectral imagery II*, Orlando, FL, Apr. 9-11, 1996 (A96-42073 11-35), SPIE Proceedings. Vol. 2758, pp. 40-50, 1996.
8. L. Boatto, V. Consorti, M. D. Buono, S. D. Zenzo, V. Eramo, A. Esposito, F. Melcarne, M. Meucci, A. Morelli, M. Mosciatti, S. Scarci, and M. Tucci, "An Interpretation System for Land Register Maps," *IEEE COMPUTER*, pp. 25-32, July 1992.

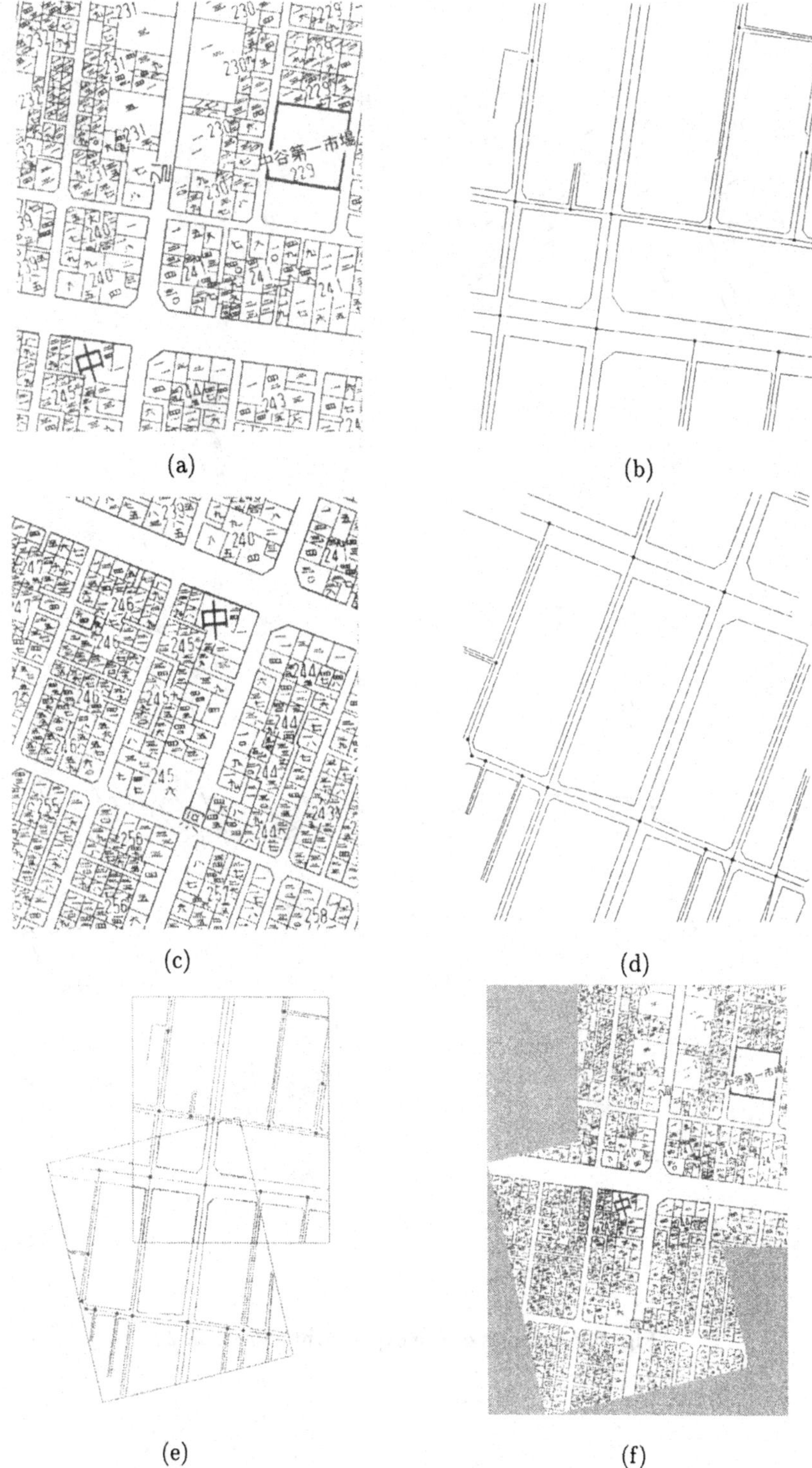

Fig. 6. Examples of the experiment : Problem 1

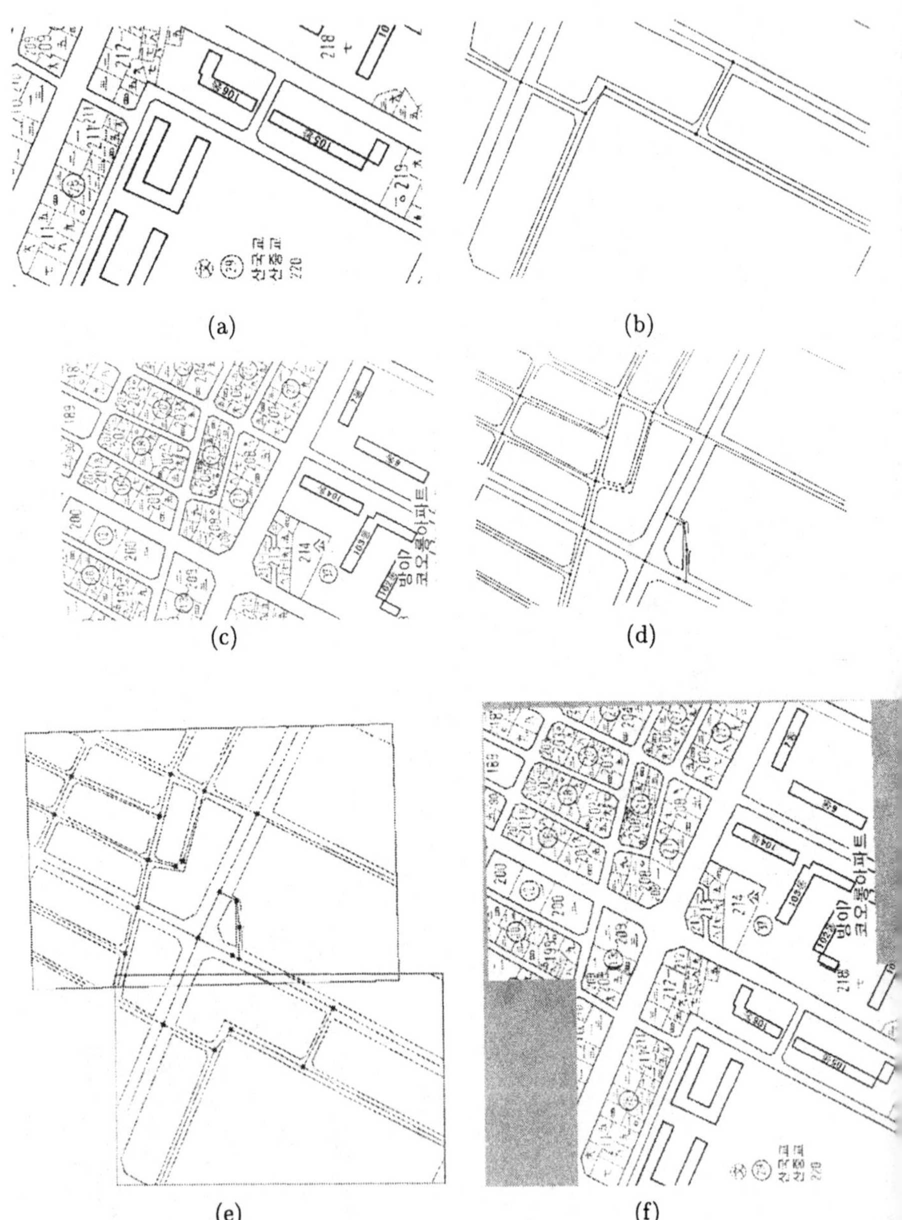

(a) (b)

(c) (d)

(e) (f)

Fig. 7. Examples of the experiment : Problem 2

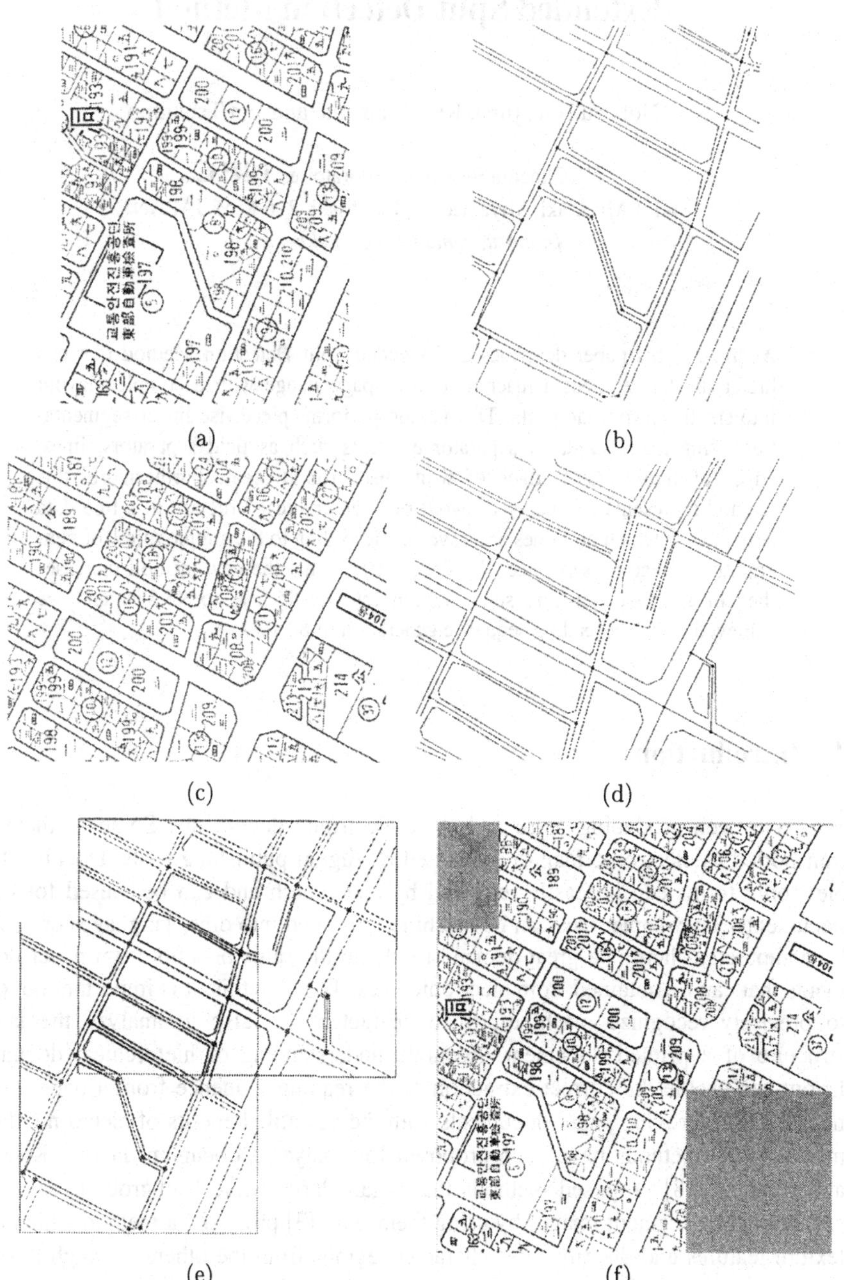

Fig. 8. Examples of the experiment : Problem 3

Document Layout and Reading Sequence Analysis by Extended Split Detection Method

Noboru Nakajima, Keiji Yamada, and Jun Tsukumo

C&C media Research Laboratories, NEC.
4-1-1 Miyazaki, Miyamae-ku, Kawasaki, 216-8555 JAPAN
{noboru, yamada}@ccm.cl.nec.co.jp

Abstract. This paper describes an Extended Split Detection Method that can hierarchically segment a machine-printed page image with a complex layout into smaller layout elements. The method performs piecewise-linear segmentation using many kinds of separator elements such as field separators, lines, edges of figures, and edges of white background areas. Furthermore, this method represents an analyzed layout of a hierarchical structure in a tree data structure, in which all nodes are traversed according to the simple rules for generating the reading sequence. We demonstrated that the new method increases the correct character line segmentation rate by 15.5%, to 95.5%, and we achieved a correct reading sequence generation of 88.1%.

1 Introduction

We have been producing more and more electronic documents. Some of them are transported as electronic mail or generated by digital publishing tools. Documents in electronic forms can be easily retrieved by text search and can be reused for other documents. They sometimes can be machine-translated into other languages or spoken by computers. There is a great demand to obtain the same benefits from paper documents that can be obtained from electronic ones. To solve this, it is important not only to precisely recognize machine-printed characters but also to analyze the layout structure of a printed document. Accurate understanding of hierarchical document layout can enable the correct extraction of the reading sequence from a paper document and can provide paper documents with the versatile benefits of electronic documents. Many methods have been proposed for analyzing document layout. Kise [2] and Okamoto [8] proposed methods that regard large white background regions as separators and segment images by using them. Jain [3] proposed a method which uses texture features and discriminates character regions from the others. Though most of the proposed methods aim at exact extraction of complicated layout components such as character lines and figures, the reading sequence of the document cannot be reproduced from only a set of layout components, but must be manually edited with great effort by an operator.

In order to address this problem, it is essential not only to segment a document image into layout components, but also to extract a hierarchical structure of the layout objects [1]. Tsuji [4] proposed a method named the split detection method, which hierarchically segments an image based on pixel projection patterns and reproduces a hierarchical layout structure according to the recursive segmentation of the layout objects. However, this method cannot segment intricate layout objects because it divides layout objects by a straight line in every segmentation.

We propose a method which expands on the split detection method. It uses piecewise-linear segmentation as well as straight-line segmentation and can analyze a complicated layout structure in order to reproduce a hierarchical layout structure which is represented as a layout tree. Reading sequence analysis from the extracted hierarchical layout structure is also described.

2 Split Detection Method

The split detection method segments a document image (from a page to layout objects such as columns, blocks, and character lines) into subregions in the recursive segmentation manner [4,9]. The recursive segmentation process generates a tree that represents the hierarchical layout structure of segmented layout objects.

The Split Detection Method calculates the possibility of a split which divides a region into subregions and determines the directions and locations of splits by using rules based on both periodicity $\overline{\tau}$ and separability measurement η (cf. Fig. 2) [4].

Periodicity $\overline{\tau}$ is defined as the average of distances between neighboring peaks in a projection pattern. Separability measurement η is obtained from the Fisher ratio when a partial projection pattern including two neighboring peaks is regarded as a probability distribution.

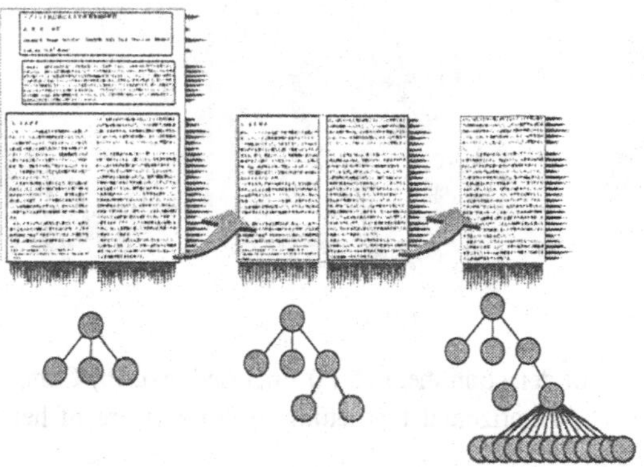

Fig. 1. Layout analysis by hierarchical segmentation.

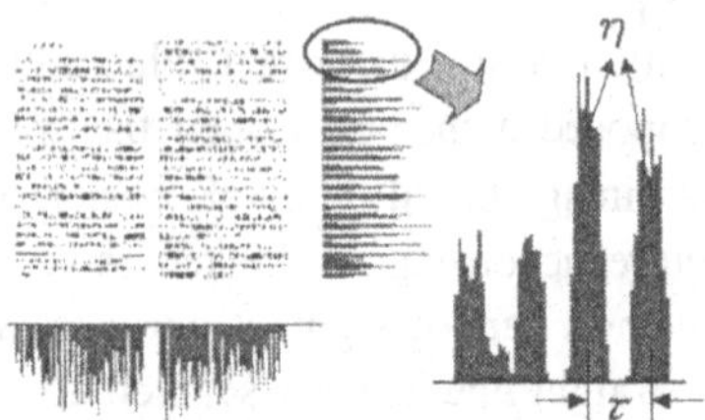

Fig. 2. Segmentation on projection pattern.

The separability measure of a gap between two neighboring peaks in the projection pattern represents the likelihood of the gap being a split in the layout object. As shown in Fig. 2, when periodicity $\overline{\tau}$ is observed in the projection pattern along the vertical axis, the periodicity $\overline{\tau}$ is used to detect split candidates with vertical orientation. This is based on the rule that a white gap between blocks must be wider than the gaps between character lines. In the example in Fig. 2, the gap in the projection pattern along the horizontal axis was detected as a split, because the gap was wider than the periodicity of the projection pattern along the vertical axis.

In order to detect splits, this method estimates character sizes and the widths of gaps between characters, character lines, and blocks. Therefore this method is robust against these variations. Because this method recursively detects splits from a whole document page to subregions, it can easily extract the hierarchical layout structure of the document page. This is accomplished under the condition that the document is arranged according to the ordinary typesetting rules such as, the width of the inter-block gap > the width of the inter-character-line gap > the width of the inter-character gap.

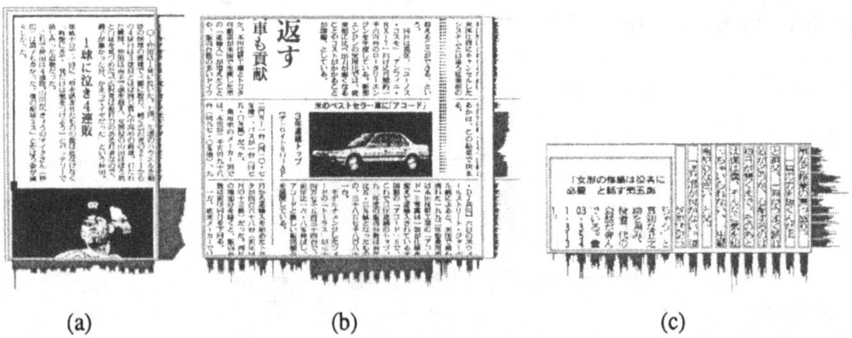

Fig. 3. Errors in the split detection method. (a) Enclosed text. (b) Complex block arrangement (mixture of vertical and horizontal typesetting). (c) Mixture of heterogeneous text (non-rectangular text areas).

But because gaps in projection patterns are used to detect split candidates, when the region is enclosed by field separators as shown in Fig. 3 (a), the gap which corresponds to the correct split is not detected and the correct split is therefore missed. Furthermore, where heterogeneous layout objects are as intricate as those shown in

Fig. 3 (b) and Fig. 3 (c), incorrect segmentation results are obtained because periodicity or separability measurement can not be correctly estimated from the projection patterns.

3 Extended Split Detection Method

3.1 Concept and Outline of the proposed method

The proposed method uses several kinds of separator elements as well as splits, which are used in the split detection method. They are field separators, edges of layout objects, large white background regions, and so on. The conventional split detection method has only to select the widest split from the segmenting region recursively in order to extract the hierarchical layout structure from a document image. However, when many separator elements are used for the segmentation of a document, they generate many possible segmented subregions in terms of combinations of separator elements. In order to extract the correct hierarchical layout structure from the document image, we have to select the most important separator elements from a segmenting region and segment this region into subregions. However, the kind of separator elements that should be selected depends on the kinds of segmenting regions and segmented subregions. For example, we should use the periodicity of character lines in order to segment a text block into character lines. However, we don't use the periodicity of the blocks but use field separators and large white regions as keys to segregate a title and text blocks from a document page.

To solve these requirements, we propose the new document layout analysis method described below (cf. Fig. 4.). The details of the processes used in the method are described after section 3.2.

Step 1 Separator element detection
Objects are detected in this step, such as (1) field separators, (2) large white background regions, (3) figures, tables, and photograph regions, and (4) the borders of the segmenting regions. All of them as well as splits which are extracted by using the split detection method are called separator elements.

Step 2 Subregion candidate generation
Suppose that a region in a document is segmented into subregions. Initially, a region is the whole document image. The process generates subregion candidates enclosed by a set of separator elements.

Step 3 Segmentation rule selection
The subregion candidates are classified into columns, blocks, character lines, etc., according to the feature values which are extracted from them. The class of the region

in the segmentation is already known because it was obtained during the previous segmentation. Then the segmentation rules and their parameter values are selected depending on the class of the region and the classes of subregion candidates. Furthermore, the conventional split detection method is applied to subregion candidates and generated splits are stored as a kind of separator element.

Step 4 Separator element verification

This process compares feature values extracted from subregion candidates and separator elements that have parameter values with the selected segmentation rules in order to verify the subregions and separator elements. If separator elements are accepted, the subregions divided by the separator elements are registered under that node in the tree of the hierarchical layout structure, which indicates the region in the segmentation. If the registered subregions are not character lines, each of the subregions is regarded as a region for segmentation and processes in ***Step* 2, 3, and 4** are recursively executed.

Step 5 Reading sequence analysis

All over the hierarchical layout structure, nodes which have the same parent node are sorted based on their positions and character line directions included in the regions corresponding to the individual nodes.

We describe the process in each step in detail below.

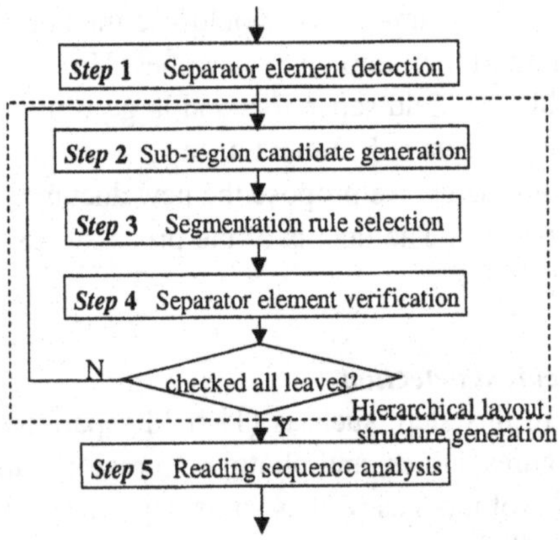

Fig. 4. Processing flow of Extended Split Detection Method.

3.2 Separator element detection *(Step 1)*

Separator elements are extracted in the split and merge manner [5-7] from an input image. First, connected components are extracted from the reduced image with four times lower resolution than the original. As found in the example shown in Fig. 5 (a), some characters are combined together. Almost all pixels in the photograph area belong to a component.

Then, a feature vector is extracted from the part of the original image inside the bounding rectangle area which corresponds to each connected component in the reduced image. It is made up of a black pixel density, an area, a line density, etc. The feature vectors of the connected components are classified into a photograph class, a field separator class, a character class, and so on. Every class has its reference vector and the decision function was designed based on the Mahalanobis distance in the feature domain. Roughly speaking, a photograph class has a large black-pixel-density. A character class has a small black-pixel-density and a relatively large line density as well as a small width or a small height because its features are extracted from the original image with fine resolution. Here, an initial tree data structure is constructed; the root node which indicates the whole document image and all the connected components are registered with their classes as child nodes of the root node.

Next, we detect separator elements using connected components with feature vectors.

Large white regions are extracted using the same method Okamoto [3] proposed. The white rectangles in Fig. 5 (b) indicate these regions. They become a kind of separator element.

Field separators of straight lines are easily detected as combinations of very thin connected components. Dotted lines and decorated field separators have periodic patterns which include small connected components of equal size. The edges of block areas such as photographs, tables, and figures are also determined as kinds of separator elements.

Examples of detected separator elements are indicated by the bold boxes in Fig. 5 (b).

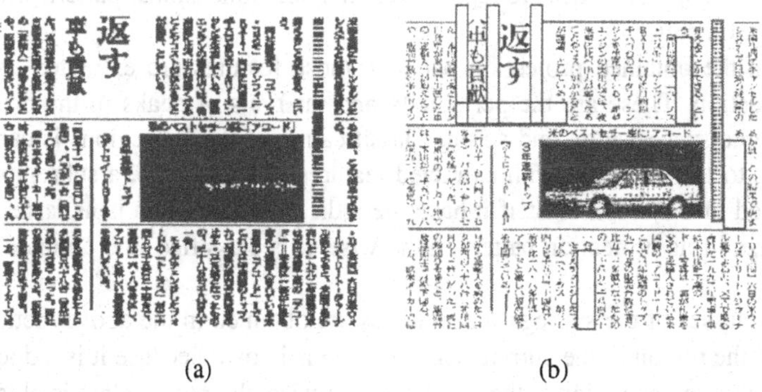

Fig. 5. Separator element detection. (a) Low resolution image (reduced image). (b) Separator element detection result.

3.3 Hierarchical layout structure generation *(Steps 2-4)*

After extracting separator elements the process can extract a hierarchical structure from a document image and represent it in a tree data structure. In order to hierarchically divide a document image, we have to adaptively select the best region borders at each level of the hierarchy. The conventional split detection method selects the widest white straight gap as the best split. However, we increased the number of kinds of separator elements and extended straight splits to the piecewise linear borders of regions. Therefore, in order to select the most important separator elements, the process has to change segmentation rules according to both the classes of the segmenting regions and the classes of the segmented subregions. By estimating the classes of regions before and after segmentation, the proposed method can select segmentation rules and their parameter values that adapt to the classes of the regions.

(1) subregion candidate generation *(Step 2)*
Every separator element is extended in its lengthwise direction until it meets other objects. Extended separator elements are traced in the region before segmentation, and partial regions which are enclosed by separator elements are detected as subregion candidates.

(2) subregion segmentation rule selection *(Step 3)*
Detected subregion candidates are classified into region classes; for example, a character line class, a line segment class, a block class, an undefined region class, a region of blocks class, and a region of an undefined region and blocks class.

First, separator elements are removed from the subregion candidate. Pixel values in the subregion candidate are projected onto the horizontal axis and the vertical axis. Accumulated pixel values are represented in a one-dimensional pattern which is called a projection pattern.

From the obtained projection patterns, those features are extracted for subregion classification. These are the periodicity and intervals of peaks in the projection pattern, white space width, and so on. Classification of the subregions is carried out according to the rule base with extracted features. For example, a subregion should be classified into a block class if it has a periodicity whose pitch is as large as the character size in its projection pattern. Otherwise, it is classified into an undefined region class.

The classes of the subregion candidates are obtained in the above method. And the class of the region in the current segmentation is known because it is a document page class if this segmentation is the first one; otherwise, the region class is obtained during the upper-level segmentation.

(3) separator element verification (*Step* 4)
Region features and separator features are used to verify the segmentation concerning a region and its subregions. Region features are described above as periodicity of each

projection pattern and so on. Separator features consist of a length, a width, a direction, and so on.

The region features and the separator features are examined according to the rule selected based on the region classes. For example, if width of separator elements are wider than the period of the projection pattern of each subregion, the subregions are designated as blocks and the separator elements are designated as spaces between the blocks.

If the segmentation is determined, the child nodes which indicate the subregions are generated under the parent node which indicates the region before segmentation in the hierarchical layout structure. And the connected components belonging to each subregion are moved to the descendant nodes of the child nodes.

An example of a hierarchical layout structure extraction is shown in Fig. 6.

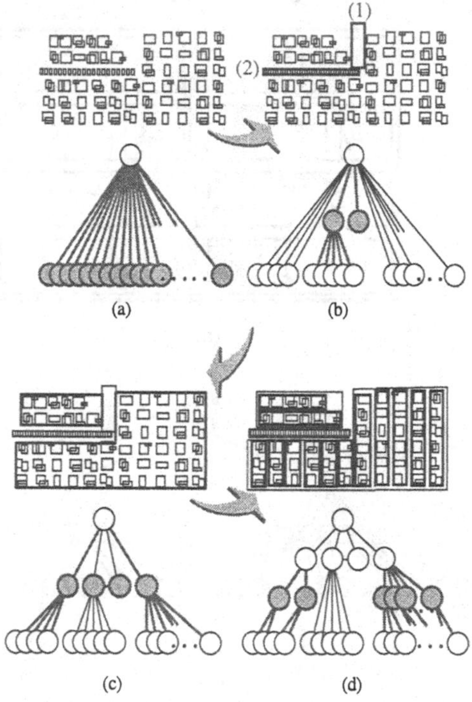

Fig. 6. Process example for the extended split detection method.

Rectangles in the upper part of Fig. 6 (a) show the minimum bounding rectangles of the connected components. The lower part of Fig. 6 (a) is a tree which represents an initial tree of a hierarchical layout structure. Leaf nodes that corresponds to connected components are directly connected to the root node that correspond to a page image.

Then the separator element is detected. The bold line (1) in Fig. 4 (b) indicates a large white region, and (2) indicates a dotted line. Both are extracted as separator elements. At this time, the two separator elements are registered in the tree as nodes. The node of the dotted line has many child nodes which indicate dots. The node of the white region has no child node.

After tracing adjacent separator elements, regions enclosed by the separator elements are extracted as subregion candidates (cf. Fig. 6 (c)). Leaf nodes under the node of the region in the current segmentation are connected to one of the new nodes according to their positions.

The segmentation process enables intricate regions to be correctly segmented. It is applied to each subregion recursively and the hierarchical layout structure is generated from the whole page image (cf. Fig. 6 (d)).

3.4 Reading sequence analysis *(Step 5)*

Once a hierarchical layout structure is extracted, the reading sequence analysis is carried out by sorting nodes in the generated layout tree.

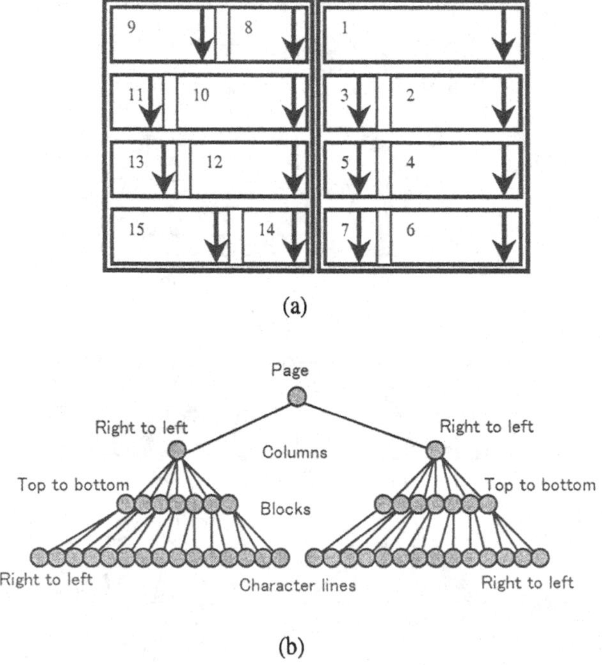

Fig. 7. Reading sequence analysis. (a) Reading sequence (rectangle: block, number: reading sequence, arrow: character line direction). (b) Tree data for hierarchical layout structure.

For the case where child nodes belong to the character line class whose direction is vertical and their parent node is in the block class, character lines are sorted from right to left depending on their position.

For the case where child nodes belong to the character line class whose direction is horizontal and their parent node is in the block class, character lines are sorted in descending order from top to bottom.

When either the parent node is not in the block class or child nodes are not in the character line class, if leaf nodes under the child nodes are in the character line class with vertical orientation then the child nodes are sorted from right to left and then from top to bottom. If the leaf nodes are in the character line class with horizontal orientation, the child nodes are sorted from left to right and from top to bottom. This operation is applied to every set which consists of a parent node and its child nodes and obtains a geometrically adequate reading sequence.

Field separators of straight lines are easily detected as combinations of very narrow connected components. Dotted lines and decorated field separators have periodic patterns which include small connected components of equal size. The edges of block areas such as photographs, tables, and figures are also determined as kinds of separator elements.

Examples of detected separator elements are indicated by the bold boxes in Fig. 5 (b).

4 Experiment

We examined the effectiveness of the proposed method using twenty-four newspaper images. The images were printed in multi-column and complex layouts and they include figures, photographs, and tables with texts.

Tested images included 2770 character lines, of which 2646 were extracted correctly. Therefore, the recall ratio was 95.5%. Furthermore, 15 character lines were extracted from figure regions and noises by mistake. This means that the precision ratio was 99.4%. 68 out of 71 photograph regions (95.8%) were extracted correctly. 2442 character lines (88.1%) were correctly sorted in the reading sequence. Here, the regions such as figures, captions of figures, and boxed articles were excluded from the examination of reading sequence generation because the reading order of these regions was ambiguous.

Examples of the layout analysis results are shown in Fig. 8. In Fig. 8 (a), text regions located at the center and left-bottom position were extracted correctly. The reading sequence was also obtained correctly. In the left-bottom part of Fig. 8 (b), a region of horizontal character lines broke into a region of vertical character lines, but the blocks were segmented correctly.

Over-segmentations were observed in the block where all the horizontal character lines accidentally had white spaces in the same horizontal position. The block was incorrectly segmented into the two parts. There were also under-segmentation errors because of the separator element detection failure.

Figure 9 is an example of a document in which the reading sequence is difficult to analyze. Because a figure and a title broke into the text block, the two character lines have the possibility to follow on the end of the second character line in the right-top block, as shown by the two arrows in Fig. 9. Linguistic information is required to solve this problem.

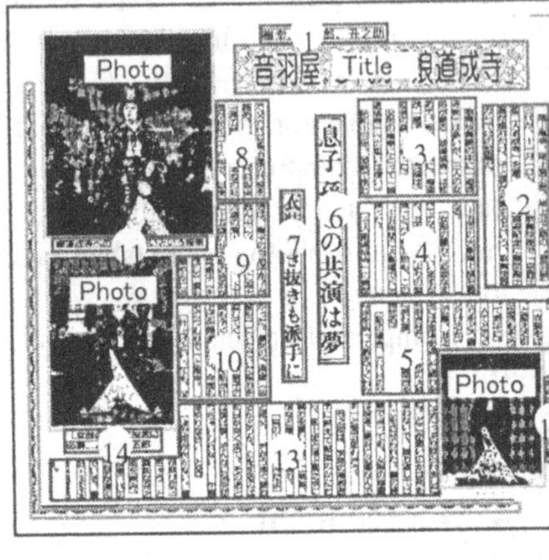

(a) (b)

Fig. 8. Layout analysis results of the proposed method (The numbers in the figures indicate the reading sequences.)

Fig. 9. An example of reading sequence analysis error.

5 Conclusion

We proposed a document layout analysis method which can hierarchically segment a document image into regions not only by using straight lines but also by using piecewise-linear borders. This enables intricate regions to be segmented. Furthermore, this method can generate a reading sequence of segmented blocks from the extracted hierarchical layout structure. Experiments using newspaper images demonstrated the accuracy of the proposed method. Without using character recognition, 95.5% of the character lines were correctly extracted which was a 15.5% increase compared to the conventional method. The precision ratio was 99.4%. Without character recognition, 88.1% of character lines were correctly sorted in the reading sequence.

We will improve the recall and precision of the document layout analysis method by using character recognition and linguistic processing.

Acknowledgments

The authors would like to thank their colleagues in the Pattern Analysis technology group of C&C Media Research Labs, NEC Corporation for their helpful discussions. We would also like to thank Mr. Toshiyuki Tanaka of NEC Information Systems Corporation for constructing the experimental programs.

References

1. Y. Y. Tang, S. W. Lee, and C. Y. Suen, "Automatic Document Processing: a Survey", *Pattern Recognition*, Vol. 29, No. 12, pp. 1931-1952, 1996.
2. A. K. Jain and Y. Zhong, "Page Segmentation Using Texture Analysis", *Pattern Recognition*, Vol. 29, No. 5, pp. 743-770, 1997.
3. M. Okamoto and M. Takahashi, "A Hybrid Page Segmentation Method", *Proc. ICDAR*, pp. 743-748, 1993.
4. Y. Tsuji, "Document Image Analysis for Generating Syntactic Structure Description", *Proc. ICPR*, pp. 744-747, 1988.
5. A. K. Jain and Bin Yu, "Page Segmentation Using Document Model", *Proc. ICDAR*, pp. 34-38. 1997.
6. K. Etemad, D. Doeman, and R. Challappa, "Multi-scale Segmentation of Unstructured Document Pages Using Soft Decision Integration", *Pattern Recognition*, Vol. 30, No. 9, pp. 1505-1519, 1997.
7. Y. Ishitani, Document Layout Analysis Based on Emergent Computation, *Proc. ICDAR*, pp. 45-50, 1997.
8. K. Kise, O. Yanagida, and S. Takamatsu, "Page Segmentation Based on Thinning of Background", *Proc. ICPR*, pp. 788-792, 1996.
9. J. Liu, Y. Y. Tang, Q. He, and C. Y. Suen, "Adaptive document segmentation and geometric relation labeling: algorithm and experimental results", *Proc. ICPR*, pp. 763-767, 1996.

Chinese Handwritten Character Segmentation in Form Documents

Jiun-Lin Chen, Chi-Hong Wu and Hsi-Jian Lee

Department of Computer Science and Information Engineering
National Chiao Tung University,
Hsinchu, Taiwan 30050

Abstract. This paper presents a projection based method for segmenting handwritten Chinese characters in form documents with known structures. In the preprocessing phase, a noise removal method is proposed that preserves stroke connections and character edge points. In the character segmentation phase, the projection profile analysis method is used to segment a text line image into projection blocks. In addition, projection blocks are classified into one of four types: mark, half-word, single-word, and two-word. Large blocks are then split and small blocks are merged. In addition, an OCR system is adopted to eliminate errors resulting from the inappropriate merging of Chinese numerical characters with other characters. As for 1319 Chinese characters are tested during our experiments, the correct segmentation rates of 92.34% and 91.76% are obtained with and without the OCR module.

Keywords: Noise removal, Projection profile analysis, Form document processing, Character segmentation, Optical character recognition.

1. Introduction

Organizations receive many form documents daily, and processing these form documents requires much human effort. Automatic form document processing systems can reduce the human effort involved and increase efficiency. A typical automatic document processing system typically consists of six modules: preprocessing, document layout analysis, character segmentation, feature extraction, character recognition, and content understanding [5].

Character segmentation has long been a critical topic in document analysis. The performance of a character segmentation process significantly affects recognition results of an OCR (optical character recognition) system. A typical form document normally consists of three components: form frames, label fields, and data fields. In this paper, we present a projection based character segmentation algorithm for extracting handwritten characters from input form data fields. The form structures are assumed here to be known, i.e., form frames and label fields with printed characters have been extracted.

Although many systems have been proposed for recognizing printed documents [1] [2] [3] [4], only a few were designed for recognizing handwritten documents. The difficulties of the segmentation of handwritten Chinese characters include the following: (1) skewed and curved text lines, (2) different sizes of characters mixed in a text line, and (3) ill-separated characters. Figure 1 presents several examples which are difficult for character segment.

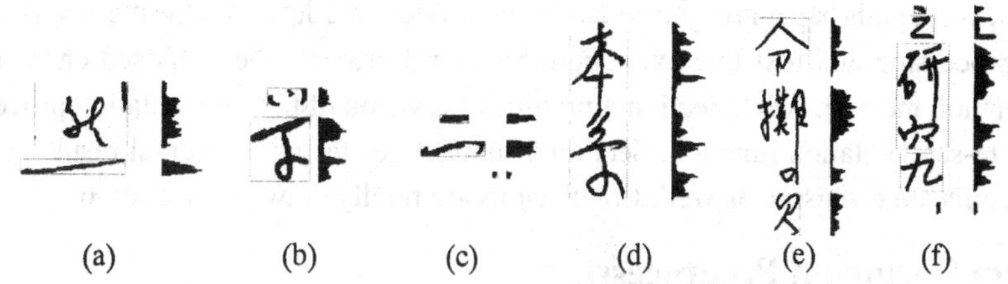

(a) (b) (c) (d) (e) (f)

Fig. 1 Sample charactres which are difficult for character segment.

Three strategies have been proposed for character segmentation [6]: dissection, recognition-based segmentation, and holistic methods. Among the methods proposed for character extraction, Lu [7] presented an overview of machine printed character segmentation. The investigation described various methods for segmenting machine printed characters. Seni and Choen [8] proposed an external word segmentation method for separating lines of unconstrained handwritten texts into words. Chiang and Yu [9] presented an iterative character segmentation method for irregularly formatted Chinese documents. In their method, they estimated parameters using an iterative merging algorithm. Lecolinet and Moreau [10] proposed an approach adopting characters pre-recognition, which detects connected components of single, connected, or broken characters. Lu and Shridhar [11] surveyed literature related to character segmentation for handwritten words.

Projection profile analysis and connected component analysis are two widely used dissection methods. By considering the speed and complexity, we adopt the projection profile analysis method for segmenting handwritten characters. The proposed system consists of four phases: preprocessing, document layout analysis and text line extraction, character segmentation, and post-editing.

In the preprocessing phase, we perform the Niblack [12] binarization operation and remove noises in the image. Data fields are then extracted according to the input form structure. In the character segmentation phase, either the horizontal or the vertical projection operation is performed according to the form structures of the extracted data fields. Next, the parameters are estimated for classifying projection blocks into different categories. The splitting and merging operations are then performed on blocks which are too large and blocks which are too small to satisfy the defined constraints. After all data fields are processed, users can examine the segmentation results through a graphical user interface. If any mis-segmentation has occurred, the users can modify the segmentation results through the user interface.

This study makes the following assumptions. (1) The data fields of input form structures are defined with respect to registration points. (2) The structures of all the form documents to be processed are known in advance. (3) Each data field contains only one text line. Situations in which more than one text line appears in a data field, are left for future research.

The rest of this paper is organized as follows. Section 2 describes the methods used for preprocessing and text line extraction. Section 3 presents the proposed character segmentation method. Next, Section 4 provides a revision of the segmentation process and the re-segmentation function. Section 5 summerizes the experimental results, and those results are discussed as well. Conclusions are finally drawn in Section 6.

2. Form Document Preprocessing

2.1 Form Image Binarization

We use the adaptive method proposed by Niblack [12] to binarize input documents. The mean and standard deviation of an $n \times n$ window ($n = 5$ in our experiments) centered on pixel i in an image are initially computed, denoting them as $mean_i$ and $stddev_i$ respectively. A threshold T for this window is then calculated according to the formula: $T = k \times mean_i + stddev_i$, where k is 0.02. If the gray level of the pixel is greater than the threshold T, the pixel is set to white. Otherwise, the pixel is set to black. This operation is executed on every pixel in the gray scale image. Figure 2 illustrates the differences between the global thresholding and adaptive methods.

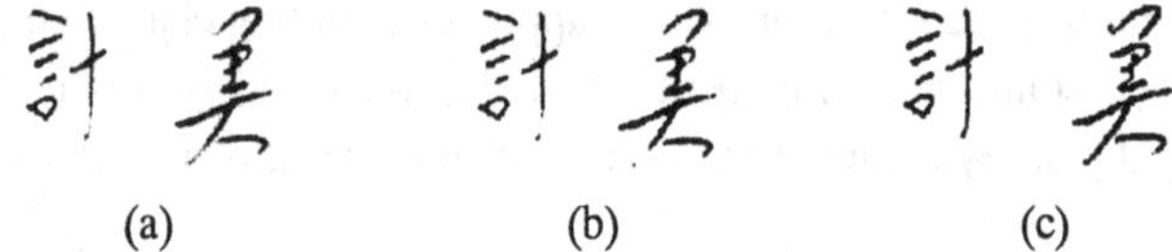

(a) (b) (c)

Fig. 2. Binarization results. (a) Original images. (b) Global thresholding results. (c) Niblack results.

2.2 Noise Removal

Mask filtering and small connected component removal are two commonly used noise removal methods. Mask filtering checks the black pixels count in an $n \times n$ window and removes the black pixels if the count is smaller than a given threshold. Mask filtering is limited in that image edge points are frequently deleted.

To eliminate the drawbacks of mask filtering, we present a novel noise removal operation. The whole image is scanned from top to bottom, and left to right. For each black pixel in the binarized image, we check the pixels in a 3×3 window around it. If none of the 8-neighbors of the target pixel are black, we mark the target pixel as an isolated noise and remove it. If more than one of the 8-neighboring pixels are black, the following operations are performed in a 5×5 window.

(1) For each black pixel, P, if there are fewer than six black pixels in the 8-neighborhood of P and these black pixels have no black 8-neighbors in the outer ring, the black pixels in the central 3×3 window are denoted as noise and then removed. Figure 3 provides an illustrative example.

(2) For a black 8-neighbor, nb_8, of P which has a black 8-neighbor in the outer ring, we make nb_8 as the center of a side of a new 5×5 window as illustrated in Fig. 3.

If the black pixel count is smaller than 1/3 of the pixels in the new 5 × 5 window, then P is considered to be noise and is removed.

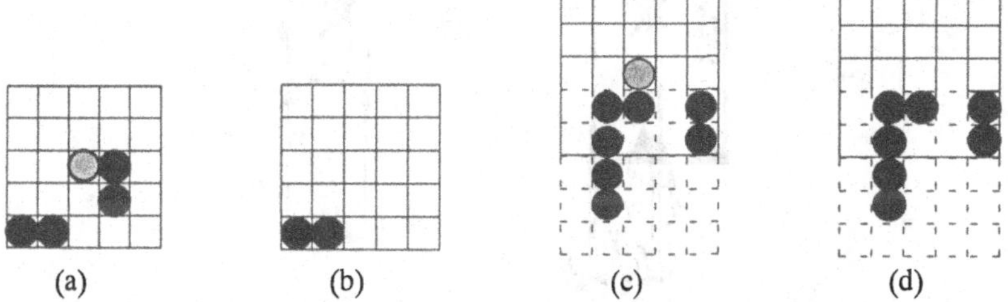

Fig. 3. The 5×5 window used for noise removal. (a) (c) Sample noise. (b) (d) Th noise removal results.

2.3 Text Line Extraction

To extract text lines from an input form document, we initially apply the method of Chen and Lee [13] to obtain the document structure. According to the coordinates of the registered corner point, $P_c = (x_c, y_c)$, and the relative coordinates of data fields $\{(x_{i_l}, y_{i_t}), (x_{i_r}, y_{i_b}) \mid i = 0, ..., n\}$ from the extracted form structure as shown in Fig. 4, the absolute coordinates of each data field can be obtained as follows:

$$P_{i_{l-t}} = P_c + P_{i_{l-t}} = (x_c, y_c) + (x_{i_l}, y_{i_t}),$$
$$p_{i_{r-b}} = P_c + P_{i_{r-b}} = (x_c, y_c) + (x_{i_r}, y_{i_b}).$$

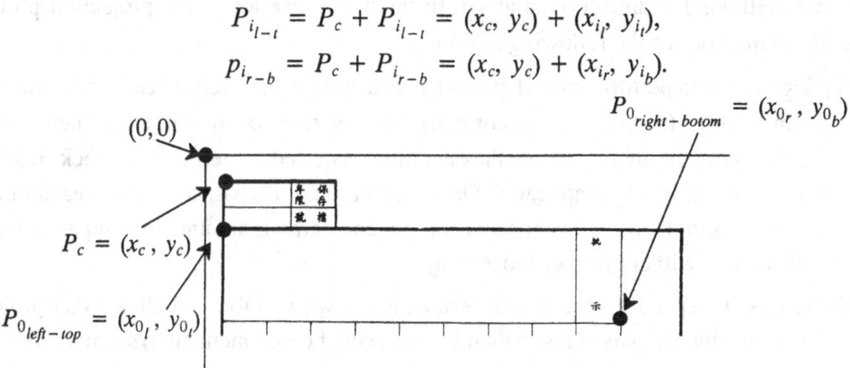

Fig. 4. The form structure and data field coordinates.

The text lines can then be extracted according to the absolute coordinates of the data fields. Next, the projection profiles of the data fields are analyzed to remove the field lines. Figure 5 presents an example of detecting left and right boundaries on a vertical text line. The positions of left and right field lines can be detected at the peaks of the projection profile and are denoted as f_l and f_r. The closest valley points are then found at both sides of each field line and denoted as v_{l_l}, v_{l_r}, .v_{r_l} and v_{r_r}. If the projection value at v_{l_r} is 0, which indicates a gap, we locate the left boundary of the text line at v_{l_r}. Otherwise, the text data touch f_l, and we locate the left boundary of the text line at v_{l_l}. If the projection value at v_{r_l} is 0, which indicates a gap, we locate the right boundary of the text line at v_{r_l}. Otherwise, the text data touch f_r, and we locate the right bound-

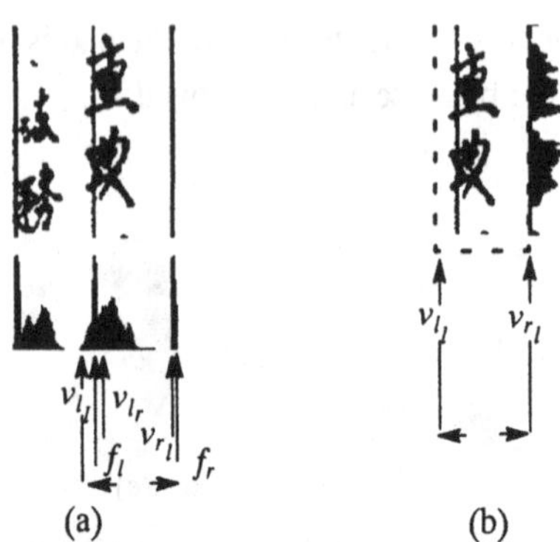

Fig. 5. (a) Locating left and right boundaries in vertical text lines extraction. (b) The extracted text line from (a).

ary of the text line at v_{r_r}. The top and bottom boundaries of the text line can be detected by a similar algorithm.

3. Chinese Handwritten Character Segmentation

Projection profile analysis and connected component analysis are two conventional methods for dissection strategy. In this paper, we adopt the projection profile analysis method for the following reasons:

(1) Segmentation performance. If characters in a text line are well spaced, both methods can separate these characters correctly. However, the connected component method generates more blocks and the operations required to merge these blocks together are much more complicated. On the other hand, if characters touch each other, both the projection and connected component methods are unable to separate these characters without further processing.

(2) Processing speed. Experimental results, as shown in Table 1, indicate that projection profile analysis is faster than the connected component analysis method.

3.1 Character Segmentation Using Projection Profile Analysis

Since the structures of input form documents are known in advance, the writing direction in each data field is known before performing the projection operation. Text lines are then segmented by performing vertical and horizontal projection on horizontal and vertical text lines, respectively. While the following discussion is limited to character segmentation of vertical text lines, a similar procedure can segment horizontal text lines.

The input text lines are segmented at those positions where the projection values are smaller than a given threshold, $T_{projection}$. The bounding rectangles for each segmented area are then detected to obtain projection blocks. The threshold value, $T_{projection}$, is estimated as follows:

$$T_{projection} = w_{f_l} + w_{f_r},$$

$$\text{where } w_{f_l} = \begin{cases} v_{l_r} - f_l & \text{if characters touch the left form line.} \\ 0 & \text{otherwise.} \end{cases}$$

$$w_{f_r} = \begin{cases} v_{r_l} - f_r & \text{if characters touch the right form line.} \\ 0 & \text{otherwise.} \end{cases}$$

Table 1. Computation time of connected component analysis and projection profile analysis methods.

Image size / Method	Connected component analysis		Projection profile analysis (milli–seconds)
	Time (milli–seconds)	Number of components	
121 x 1948	874.670	237	41.363
142 x 2251	780.081	178	58.267
136 x 2002	309.138	43	34.027
2550 x 3162	30037.625	885	574.450

3.2 Projection Block Feature Extraction

For each detected projection block, the following features are extracted as illustrated in Fig. 6.

(1) Block width (W_i) : The width of a projection block.

(2) Block height (H_i) : The height of a projection block.

(3) Block gap (G_{ij}) : The vertical or horizontal distance between projection blocks i and j in horizontal or vertical text lines respectively.

(4) Block aspect ratio ($\frac{W_i}{H_i}$): The ratio of block width to block height.

(5) Density ($\frac{B_i}{W_i \times H_i}$): The ratio of the number of black pixels to the area of a projection block.

Since the aspect ratio of most handwritten Chinese characters is nearly 1, another two related features can be derived, i.e. average character width ($avgC_W$) and average character height ($avgC_H$).

- The average block width in a text line:

$$avgB_W = \sum_{i=1}^{N} w_i/N, \text{ where } N \text{ is the number of projection blocks.}$$

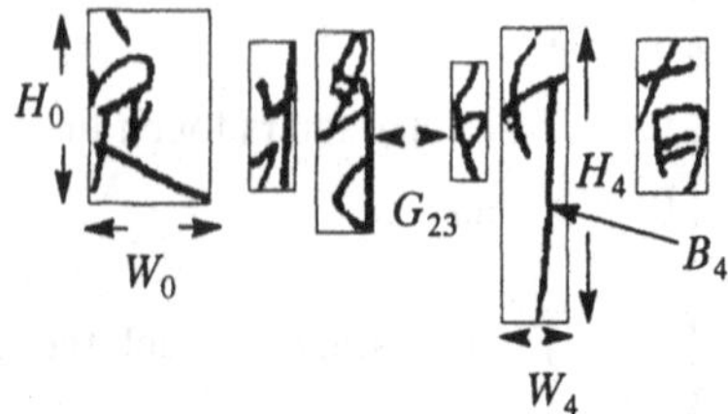

Fig. 6. Projection block features in a horizontal text line.

- The average character width of a vertical text line is obtained from the projection blocks whose widths are larger than $avgB_w$, since smaller blocks are caused by noise and partial characters in a text line.

$$avgC_W = \sum_{i=1}^{M} w_i/M, \ \forall\, W_i > avgB_w,$$

where M is the number of blocks whose widths are larger than $avgB_w$.

- The average character height of a vertical text line is calculated from those projection blocks whose heights are close to $avgC_W$.

$$avgC_H = \sum_{i=1}^{K} h_i/K, \ \forall\, h_i \in \{h_i \mid \frac{h_i}{avgC_W} \approx 1, i = 1...K\}.$$

If several characters in the text line touch one another, a large and unreasonable value for $avgC_H$ will be obtained. Under such circumstances, we set $avgC_H$ equal to $.avgC_W$

According to the above features, projection blocks can be classified into four categories: mark, half-word, single-word, and two-word as follows.

- Mark: The height of a projection block in a vertical text line is smaller than $T_{mark} \times avgC_H$, where $T_{mark} = 0.3$. Figure 7 shows ten projection blocks classified as marks.

Fig. 7. Projection blocks classified as marks (denoted by *). (a) (b) (c) Examples form vertical text lines. (c) (d) Examples from horizontal text lines.

- Half-word: Projection blocks of vertical text lines satisfy

  $$T_{mark} \times avgC_H < H_i < T_{half-word} \times avgC_H, \text{ where } T_{half-word} = 0.7.$$

  Figure 8 (a) presents some half-word projection blocks.

- Single word: Projection blocks of vertical text lines satisfy

  $$T_{half-word} \times avgC_H < H_i < T_{two-word} \times avgC_H, \text{ where } T_{two-word} = 1.5.$$

- Two-word: If the height of a projection block in a vertical text line is greater than $T_{two-word} \times avgC_H$, the block is classified as a two-word block. Figure 8 (b) depicts two examples of two-word projection blocks.

Fig. 8. (a) Half-word projection blocks. (b) Two-word projection blocks.

After classifying all blocks of a text line, we estimate two other features: average inter-character gap (*avgInterG*) and average intra-character gap (*avgIntraG*), according to the category and spatial information of all projection blocks.

(1) Average inter-character gap (*avgInterG*) : The average distance between characters.

$$avgInterG = \frac{\sum G_{ij}}{M},\ G_{ij} = B_{j_{top}} - B_{i_{bottom}},\ \text{or}$$
$$G_{ij} = B_{j_{left}} - B_{i_{right}}\ \forall B_i \in \{half\text{-}word,\ single\text{-}word,\ two\text{-}word\}.$$

(2) Average intra-character gap (*avgIntraG*): The average distance between small projection blocks that may be single Chinese characters.

$$avgIntraG = \frac{\sum G_{ij}}{N},\ G_{ij} = B_{j_{top}} - B_{i_{bottom}},\ \text{or}\ G_{ij} = B_{j_{left}} - B_{i_{right}},$$
$$\text{and}\ G_{ij} < avgIntraG,\ \forall B_i \in \{mark,\ half\text{-}word,\ single\text{-}word\}.$$

Figure 9 summerizes the distances between different categories of projection blocks used herein to estimate intra-character and inter-character gaps.

	Mark	Half-word	Single-word	Two-word
Mark	●	●	●	
Half-word	●	✓ ●	✓ ●	
Single-word	●	✓ ●	✓	
Two-word			✓	✓

● Distances used to estimate average intra-character gaps.
✓ Distances used to estimate average inter-character gaps.

Fig. 9. The consideration of distances between different categories of projection blocks for estimating average intra-character and inter-character gaps.

3.3 Splitting Large Projection Blocks

The two-word projection blocks may contain more than one character, and such blocks must be split. To locate the appropriate cut position for splitting, we search the possible cut area defined as follows.

$$(B_{i_{top}} + avgC_H \times T_{upper\text{-}bound},\ B_{i_{top}} + avgC_H \times T_{lower\text{-}bound}),$$
$$\text{where } T_{upper\text{-}bound} = 0.5 \text{ and } T_{lower\text{-}bound} = 1.5.$$

The cut position is located inside the possible cut area according to the following criteria. (1) The projection value and the number of crossing strokes at the cut position must be a minimum in the possible cut area. (2) The heights of the split blocks must be as close as possible to the average block height, $avgB_H$.

An example of the possible cut area and the located cut position is illustrated in Fig. 10. Examples of split results are shown in Fig. 11.

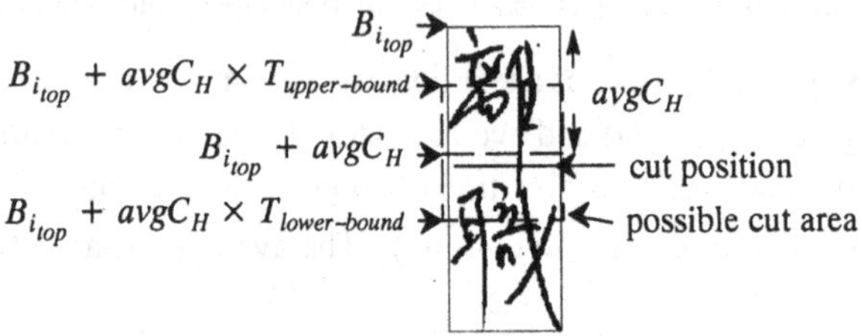

Fig. 10. The possible cut area and the located cut position for a two-word block.

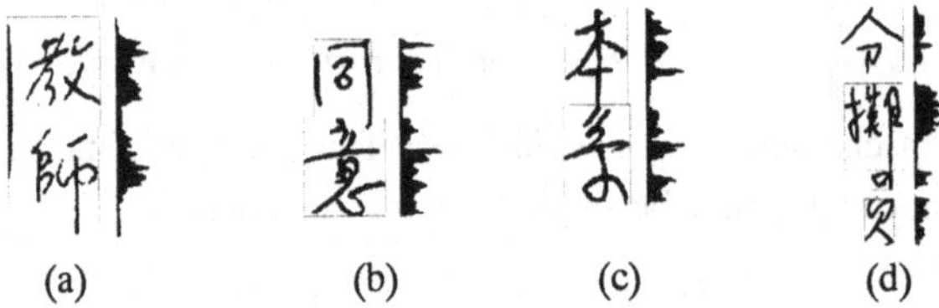

Fig. 11. Examples of split two-word projection blocks.

3.4 Merging Small Projection Blocks

As general known, a handwritten character may be segmented into more than one projection block, accounting for why these blocks must be merged together to extract correct characters. Herein, a two phase process is applied to merge mark blocks, half-word blocks and single-word blocks.

Phase One: Merging Mark Blocks and Single-word Blocks. Mark projection blocks which satisfy one of the following criteria, are classified as punctuation marks.

- The inter-character distances between a given block and its neighboring blocks are all greater than the average inter-character gap, *avgInterG*.
- The block id located at the down-right direction of its predecessor block.

A mark projection block is considered as a primitive stroke and should be merged with its successor block by applying the following heuristic rules.

- The width of the mark block is smaller than the width of its successor block.
- The overlapping length in the horizontal direction, of the mark block and its successor block, is larger than a predefined threshold value.

- The distance between the mark block and its successor block is smaller than the average intra-character gap, *avgIntraG*.
- The height of the merged result is close to the average character height, $avgC_H$.

Figure 12 presents examples of merged results. A merging probability is also provided for each merge operation. These probability values can be used in the manual post-editing (Section 4.2). The merging possibility is formally defined below.

$$PM_{i,i+1} = \begin{cases} 1 - \dfrac{G_{i,i+1}}{avgInterG}, & \text{if } avgInterG > G_{i,i+1} \\ 0.1, & \text{otherwise} \end{cases}$$

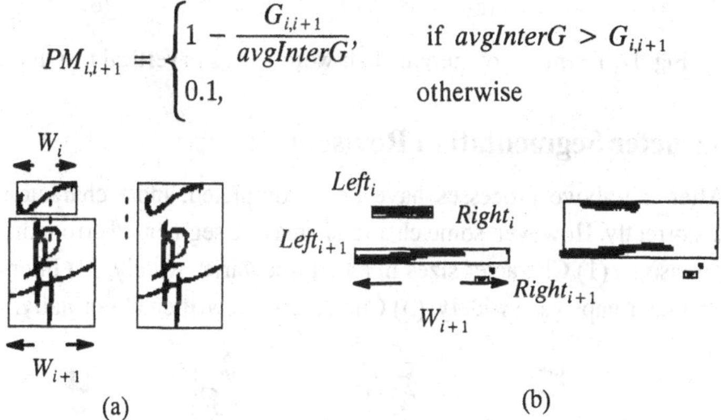

Fig. 12. Examples of merging mark blocks as primitive strokes in vertical text lines.

The single-word projection block is merged with its successor block if the distance between them is smaller than *avgInterG*, and the height of the merged result is close to $avgC_H$. Figure 13 depicts two examples. The merge probability is defined as:

$$PS_{i,i+1} = \begin{cases} 1 - \dfrac{G_{i,i+1}}{avgIntraG} - \left(\left(\dfrac{avgC_H}{H_i + G_{i,i+1} + H_{i+1}}\right) - 1\right), \\ \qquad\qquad \text{if } avgC_H > H_i + G_{i,i+1} + H_{i+1} \\ 1 - \dfrac{G_{i,i+1}}{avgIntraG} - \left(1 - \left(\dfrac{avgC_H}{H_i + G_{i,i+1} + H_{i+1}}\right)\right), \text{ otherwise.} \end{cases}$$

Fig. 13. Two single-word block merged results in vertical text lines.

Phase Two: Merging Half-word Blocks. Before phase two is performed, the values of $avgC_W$, $avgC_H$, *avgInterG*, and *avgIntraG* are re-estimated according to the merged results of phase one. A half-word block is merged with its successor block if the distance between them is smaller than *avgInterG*, and the height of merged result is close to

$avgC_H$. Examples are shown in Fig. 14. The formula for merging probability $PH_{i,i+1}$ is the same as the formula of $PS_{i,i+1}$.

Fig. 14. Examples of merging half-word blocks in vertical text lines.

4. Character Segmentation Revision

After the above processes have been completed, most characters can be segmented correctly. However, some characters may be segmented erroneously for the following reasons. (1) Character sizes in a text line varies widely. (2) Inter-character and intra-character gaps vary widely. (3) Characters are written abnormally.

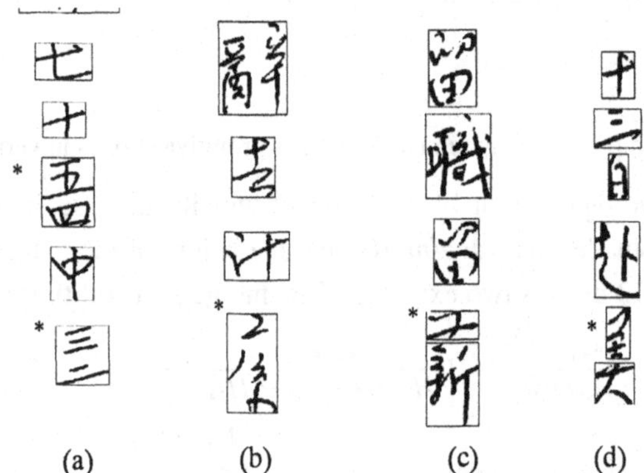

Fig. 15. Examples of incorrect segmentation results (denoted by *). (a) (b) Merging error. (c) (d) Segmentation error.

4.1 Character Segmentation Revision with the OCR Module

In our experiments, we found that consecutive half-word projection blocks are probably individual Chinese characters. In a vertical text line, consecutive half-word blocks may result from the following situations:

(1) The blocks may be "一", "二", "三", "四", "五", "六", "七", "八", "九", or "十" (i.e., Chinese characters for numbers 1-10).

(2) The blocks may be individual characters written smaller than normal characters.

(3) The blocks may actually be parts of characters.

In order to reduce the segmentation errors generated from these ambiguities, we include an OCR module in our segmentation process. The recognition results can be used to improve the segmentation process. However, recognizing every possible projection block is time-consuming and impractical. Thus, the OCR module is designed only for recognizing Chinese numeric characters which introduced most of the segmentation errors in our experiments.

When two consecutive half-word blocks satisfy the merging criteria described in section 3.4, we apply the OCR module to these two blocks for recognition. For a situation in which the OCR module recognizes the half-word block as a Chinese numerical character, the merge operation should be abandoned and this half-word block made into a single character block. Figure 16 illustrates an example.

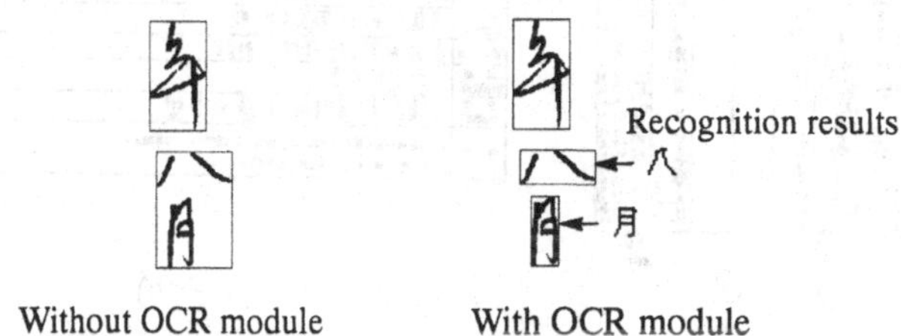

Fig. 16. Segmentation results with and without OCR module.

4.2 Character Segmentation with User Intervention

The proposed system provides a user interface for users to correct some segmentation errors. Users can drag the mouse pointer to merge blocks that are not merged in the above process. To correct erroneously merged blocks, users can double click on the merged blocks, causing the system to separate the blocks at the point of lowest merge probability.

5. Experimental Results and Discussions

The proposed system was implemented in Visual C++ with MFC (Microsoft Foundation Class) on an IBM Pentium90 personal computer. The test sample documents were scanned at a resolution of 300 dpi (dots per inch).

Figure 17 show the segmentation results of vertical and horizontal form documents. Figure 18 presents correctly segmented characters with left-right and top-bottom structured extracted from horizontal and vertical text lines, respectively. Such characters are usually mis-segmented in projection based character segmentation methods.

Herein, we tested a total of nine sample form documents with seventy six text lines and 1319 Chinese characters. Table 2 displays the segmentation rates and processing times obtained without using the OCR module. Table 3 summerizes the results obtained with the OCR module involved. 1206 Chinese characters were correctly extracted without the aid of the OCR module, The correct segmentation rate is 91.43%. With the aid of the OCR module, 1218 Chinese characters were correctly extracted with a correct segmentation rate of 92.34%. The results of the proposed character segmentation method are satisfactory.

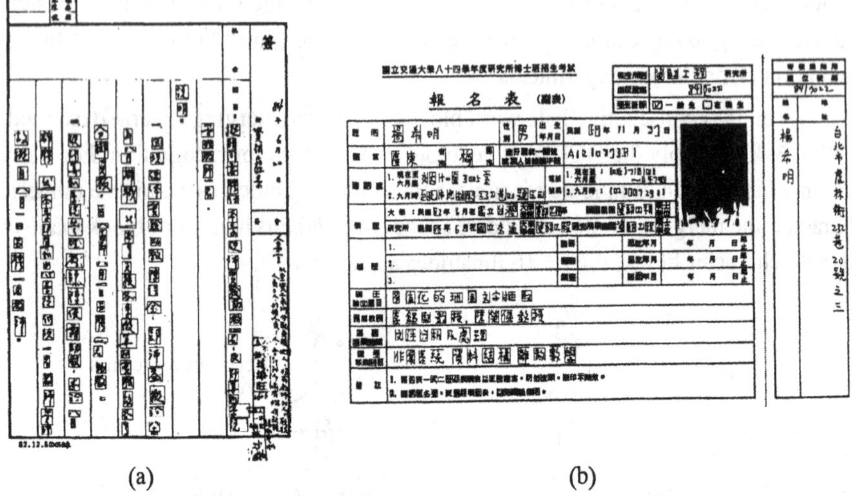

(a) (b)

Fig. 17. Segmentation results. (a) A vertical form document. (b) A horizontal document.

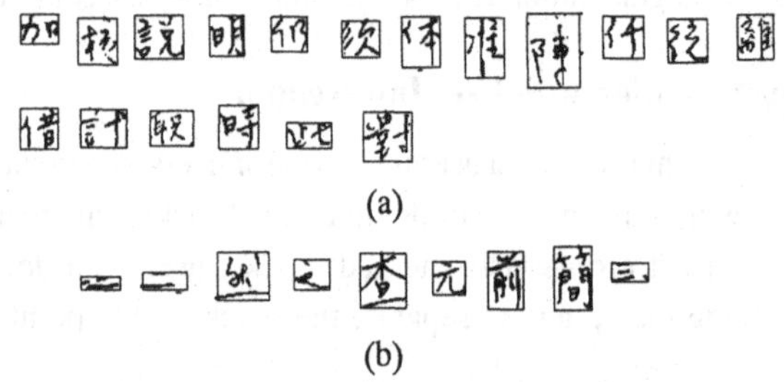

(a)

(b)

Fig. 18. Correct segmented characters. (a) Left-right structured characters from horizontal text lines. (b) Top-bottom structured characters from vertical text lines.

Table 2 Correct segmentation rates and processing times without the OCR module.

	Total words	Correctly segmented words	Correct segmentation rates	Processing time(ms)
Fig. 1	164	157	95.73 %	2831.634
Fig. 2	144	132	91.67 %	2182.325
Fig. 3	118	114	96.61 %	2176.854
Fig. 4	125	121	96.81 %	2543.087
Fig. 5	175	157	89.71 %	2611.529

In our experiments, erroneous segmentation results were due to the following.

(1) The heights of characters in a vertical text line vary widely, as shown in Fig. 19 (a).

(2) Under some circumstances, the cut position with the smallest crossing stroke number and projection value was not the correct split location, as displayed in Fig. 19 (b)

(3) Sparsely written characters, as shown in Fig. 19 (c).

(4) Characters are written too close, as shown in Fig. 19 (d).

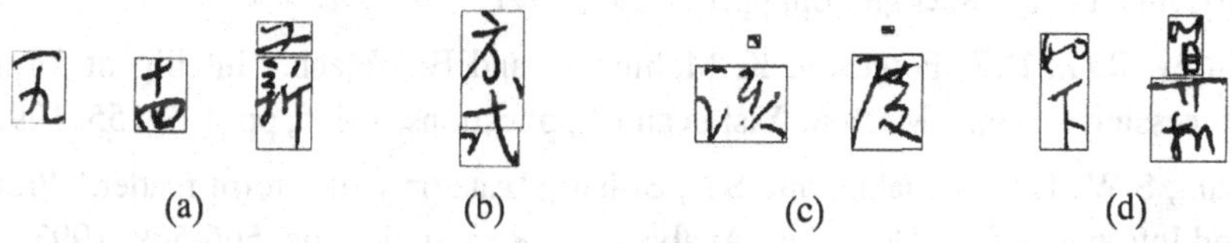

Fig. 19. Examples of erroneously segmented characters.

Table 3 Correct segmentation rate and processing time with the aid of OCR system.

	Total words	Correctly segmented words	Correct segmentation rate	Processing time(ms)
Fig. 1	164	158	96.34 %	4595.960
Fig. 2	144	138	95.93 %	3354.280
Fig. 3	118	115	97.45 %	3782.252
Fig. 4	125	121	96.81 %	2875.377
Fig. 5	175	157	89.71 %	5619.013

6. Conclusions

This paper presents a projection based character segmentation system for separating handwritten Chinese characters in form documents. Handwritten characters vary greatly in style and appearance making it difficult to segment characters accurately in text lines. Our system uses a projection based segmentation method with the aid of an OCR module to achieve better performance. The proposed method can successfully segment characters with left-right or top-bottom structures which cannot be correctly segmented in typical projection based methods. Experimental results demonstrates the validity of our proposed system. The correct segmentation rate is 92.34%. The average process time for segmenting a character is about 29.45ms.

Future research aimed at to enhancing the performance of the proposed system should (1) find more accurate features, (2) segment data fields containing more than one text line, (3) remove form frames from text lines, (4) segment text line characters with editing symbols, and (5) incorporate the system as a module in a complete document analysis system.

References

[1] Srihari, S.N., "Document Image Understanding," Proc. IEEE Computer Society Fall Joint Computer Conf., pp.87-96, 1986.

[2] Wang, D. and S.N. Srihari, "Analysis of Form Images," Proc. 1st Internat. Conf. Document Anal. Recognition, pp.181-191, 1991.

[3] Casey, R.G., D.R. Ferguson, K. Mohiuddin and E. Walach, "Intelligent forms processing system," Machine Vision and Applications, Vol. 5, pp. 143-155, 1992.

[4] Lam, S.W., L. Javanbakht, and S.N. Srihari, "Anatomy of a form reader," Proc. 2nd Intern. Conf. on Document Analysis and Recognition, pp. 506-509, 1993.

[5] L. A. Fletcher and R. Kasturi, "A robust algorithm for text string separation from mixed text/graphic images," IEEE Transactions on Pattern Analysis and Machine Intelligence, Vol. 10, No. 6, pp. 910-918, 1988.

[6] R. G. Casey and E. Lecolinet, "Survey of methods and strategies in character segmentation," IEEE Transaction on Pattern Analysis and Machine Intelligence, Vol. 18, No. 7, pp.690-706, July 1996.

[7] Y. Lu, "Machine printed character segmentation - An overview," Pattern Recognition, Vol. 28, No. 1, pp. 67-80, 1995.

[8] G. Seni and E. Cohen, "External word segmentation of off-line handwritten text lines," Pattern Recognition, Vol. 27, No. 1, pp. 41-52, 1994.

[9] C. C. Chiang and S. S. Yu, "An iterative character segmentation method for irregularly formatted Chinese documents," in Proceedings of the 5th Optical Character Recognition and Document Analysis, Chung Li, Taiwan, 1996, pp. 61-67.

[10] E. Lecolinet and J. V. Moreau, "A new system for automatic segmentation and recognition of unconstrained zip codes," in Proceedings Sixth Scandinavian Conference Image Analysis, Oulu, Finland, June 1989, pp. 585.

[11] Y. Lu and M. Shridhar, "Character segmentation in handwritten words - An overview," Pattern Recognition, Vol. 29, No. 1, 1996, pp. 77-96.

[12] W. Niblack, An Introduction to Digital Image Processing, Prentice Hall, 1986.

[13] J. L. Chen and H. J. Lee, "An efficient algorithm for Form Structure Extraction using Strip Projection," Pattern Recognition, Vol. 31, No. 9, pp. 1353-1368, 1998.

Text Extraction, Enhancement and OCR in Digital Video

Huiping Li[1], David Doermann[1], and Omid Kia[2]

[1] Language and Media Processing Laboratory
Institute for Advanced Computer Studies
University of Maryland
College Park, MD 20742-3275
{huiping,doermann}@cfar.umd.edu
[2] Advanced Network Technologies Division
National Institute of Standards and Technology
Gaithersburg, MD 20899
omid.kia@nist.gov

Abstract. In this paper we address the problem of text extraction, enhancement and recognition in digital video. Compared with optical character recognition (OCR) from document images, text extraction and recognition in digital video presents several new challenges. First, the text in video is often embedded in complex backgrounds, making text extraction and separation difficult. Second, image data contained in video frames is often digitized and/or subsampled at a much lower resolution than is typical for document images. As a result, most commercial OCR software can not recognize text extracted from video. We have implemented a hybrid wavelet/neural network segmenter to extract text regions and use a two stage enhancement scheme prior to recognition. First, we use Shannon interpolation to raise the image resolution, and second we postprocess the block with normal/inverse text classification and adaptive thresholding. Experimental results show that our text extraction scheme can extract both scene text and graphical text robustly and reasonable OCR results are achieved after enhancement.

1 Introduction

The increasing availability of online digital imagery and video has rekindled interest in the problems of how to index multimedia information sources automatically and how to browse and manipulate them efficiently. Text can provide important supplemental index information in video sequences. Examples may include sports scores, product names, scene locations, speaker names, movie credits, program introductions and special announcements. If text can be extracted and recognized robustly, we may, for example, submit queries such as *"Bruce Willis"* and retrieve a list of all movies featuring him, or "stock news" to retrieve relevant financial reports.

Text extraction and recognition from digital video presents several challenges. First, the text is usually embedded in complex backgrounds, making extraction and recognition difficult. Second, the video image is usually digitized or subsampled at an extremely low resolution and as a result, text can not be recognized by most commercial OCR software. For document images, 300 *dpi* is commonplace and normal characters (12 points) occupy an area as large as 40×40 pixels. Video frames are often digitized at 352×240 pixels with text rendered as small as 10×10 pixels, resulting in no output from OCR software, even though text is clearly human readable.

1.1 Related Work

Some work on the extraction of text from road signs [1], license plates [2], library books [3], *WWW* images [4] and isolated video frames [5] has been reported in the literature. The methods can be broadly classified into two types: connected component (*CC*) based and texture based. Scene images and video frames are usually recorded in multivalued (gray-scale or colored) form. For *CC* based approaches, color clustering [6, 7] or binarization [8, 9] are usually used to decompose the multivalued image into several elementary images in which all the pixels share the same color or intensity value. Connected components are then extracted from each decomposed image and heuristic restrictions on component size, number of aligned components and line orientation are used to identify text lines. The second approach is texture-based and uses well-known texture analysis methods such as Gabor filtering [10], Gaussian filtering [11] or spatial variance [12] to locate text regions. In [10], Jain describes a method of separating text and image areas based on a group of multichannel Gabor filters.

Previous work on text enhancement has focused primarily on binary document images with black pixels representing text and white pixels representing background. Hobby presents a method to enhance degraded document images via bitmap clustering and averaging for better display quality and recognition accuracy [13]. OCR accuracy is improved from 6% to 38% for documents with varying quality. Liang [14] addresses the problem of document image restoration using morphological filters and achieves nearly 80% OCR accuracy for subtractive and additive noise images.

Work on text recognition in scene images and digital video is reported in [5], [11], [15] and [16]. Wu and Manmatha describe a text extraction and recognition system and achieve 84% correct OCR rates based only on "*OCRable*" text [11]. Lienhart describes a text recognition system in digital video and achieves a recognition result of nearly 80% [5]. Shim and Dorai present a text extraction system in video sequences. The output of the system is OCR-ready bitmaps but text recognition problem is not addressed [15]. Zhou and Lopresti describe their work on text extraction and recognition from *WWW* images [4, 16]. None of these systems, however, perform text enhancement and all rely on the text having "substantial" resolution.

Our goal is to develop an algorithm to detect both scene text and graphical text in video and to use text enhancement to achieve reasonable OCR accuracy. We use a hybrid wavelet/neural network segmenter to detect text regions.

After text detection, Shannon interpolation is used to increase the image resolution. Postprocessing including normal/inverse text classification and adaptive thresholding are applied to generate OCRable text.

The rest of the paper is organized as follows. In Section 2 we address our text detection scheme in detail. Text enhancement is described in Section 3 and postprocessing is described in Section 4. Experimental results are presented in Section 5 and finally a brief discussion is given in Section 6.

2 Text Detection

Text in digital video is typically overlayed on complex backgrounds. As a result, methods based on connected component analysis usually fail since the text often touches graphical objects after binarization or color segmentation. Figure 1a shows a typical video frame and Figure 1b is the binarized version using an ideal threshold. The binarized image shows connectedness between character components and the background.

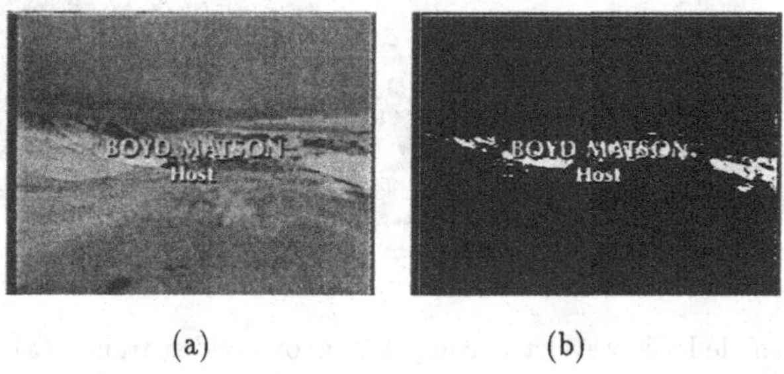

Fig. 1. (a) A video frame, (b) binarization by manually picking up an ideal threshold.

Our approach uses a small window (typically 16×16) to scan the image and classify each window text or non-text. Two important issues we need to consider are the feature extraction and the choice of classifier.

There are types of classifiers which are commonly used. The first is the traditional classifier such as linear discriminant analysis (LDA), maximum likelihood, k-nearest neighbors. The other is the neural network based classifier. In video frames, natural scenes like the leaves of a tree or grass in a field have textures similar to text. As a result, text and nontext often overlap in the feature space. Since the text and nontext are not linearly separable, a neural network classifier's adaptive learning offers an attractive and computationally efficient alternative for classification.

Our feature extraction scheme is based on the observation that text regions typically have different texture properties than the surrounding areas. This texture has similar frequency and orientation information, making wavelets a reasonable candidate for representation. The feature extraction and selection scheme is described in the next section.

2.1 Feature Extraction and Selection

Analysis of scale space provides a method of identifying the spatial frequency content in local regions within the image. We use wavelets to decompose the image because they provide successive approximations to the image by down-sampling and have the ability to detect edges during the high-pass filtering. The low-pass filter creates successive approximations to the image while the detailed signal provides a feature-rich representation of textual content [17]. This is easily seen in the image decomposition shown in Figure 2 where the text region shows high activity in the three high-frequency subbands (HL, LH, HH). As a result of their local nature, only wavelets which are located on or near the edge yield large wavelet coefficients, making text regions detectable in the high frequency subbands.

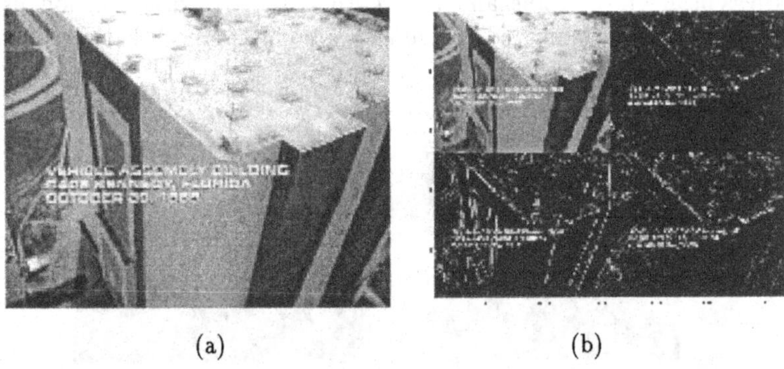

(a) (b)

Fig. 2. The single-level wavelet decomposition of a video frame: (a) Original image, (b) The first level decomposed images.

We use the mean and the second and third-order central moments as features. For an $N \times N$ subblock I we calculate the mean (m), the second-order (μ_2) and third-order (μ_3) central moments as:

$$\begin{aligned} M(I) &= \frac{1}{N^2} \sum_{i=0}^{N-1} \sum_{j=0}^{N-1} I(i,j) \\ \mu_2(I) &= \frac{1}{N^2} \sum_{i=0}^{N-1} \sum_{j=0}^{N-1} (I(i,j) - M(I))^2 \\ \mu_3(I) &= \frac{1}{N^2} \sum_{i=0}^{N-1} \sum_{j=0}^{N-1} (I(i,j) - M(I))^3 \end{aligned} \tag{1}$$

All of features are computed on the decomposed subband images. Since the original window size is 16×16, the maximum decomposition level we could choose is four, with only one pixel left for each subband image in the fourth level. Therefore, the features described in Equation 1 are calculated only in the subblocks of the first three levels. There are 36 features corresponding to each

16×16 window. We conduct feature saliency analysis to reduce feature set since a larger feature set requires more training samples and time.

We collected 1000 text blocks and 1000 nontext blocks and split them training and testing sets. Each feature was trained on the training set and then applied to classify the testing data. We use the Bayes error rate P_e to analyze the saliency of features since it determines whether or not the feature will yield adequate separation between the classes. In most practical cases, the Bayes error rate is estimated using a finite set of labeled samples from the various classes. This is typically done by estimating a posteriori probability of each class for each sample, then assigning each sample to the class with the MAP (maximum a posteriori) probability. The percentage of samples misclassified by applying the MAP decision rule to the posteriori estimates is taken as an estimate of the Bayes error rate. Finally, eight features which have the lowest Bayes error rate are selected from original 36 features and are fed to the neural network.

2.2 Training the Neural Network

After selecting the features, we train the neural network. The neural network consists of 8 input, 12 hidden and 1 output node. Although it is easy to get representative samples of text, it is more difficult to get representative samples of non-text since non-text spans a vast space. To handle this problem we use a *bootstrap* method recommended by Sung and Poggio [18] to train the neural network. The idea is that the training samples are collected in part during training rather than before training:

1. Create an initial set of training samples which includes a complete set of text samples and a partial set of non-text samples.
2. Train the network on these samples.
3. Run the system on a video frame which contains no text and add image blocks which the network incorrectly classifies as text to the non-text sample set.
4. Repeat Step 2 and 3 until the accuracy converges.

2.3 Classification

After training, we use the neural network to classify each block as text or nontext. We can view the output of the neural network as a mapping function which maps each feature set into a real value between 0 and 1. Figure 3a shows the distribution of the neural network outputs. A threshold of 0.5 is a reasonable choice to indicate whether the window contains text or not.

In order to compare the performance of different classifiers, we used LDA [19] to conduct the classification on the same data. Suppose we have C classes with class *means* M_i, $i = 1, 2, ...C$. Then the within-class scatter matrix S_w and between-class scatter matrix S_b can be defined as

$$S_w = \sum_{i=1}^{C} \sum_{j=1}^{N_i} (X_{ij} - M_i)(X_{ij} - M_i)^T$$
$$S_b = \sum_{i=1}^{C} (M_i - M)(M_i - M)^T \tag{2}$$

where X_{ij} is the jth sample vector in class i, N_i is the number of samples in class i and M is the grand *mean* of all sample vectors. The projection matrix P is chosen to maximize $\frac{det(S_b)}{det(S_w)}$. It has been shown that the ratio is maximized when the columns of P are the eigenvectors of $T = S_w^{-1} S_b$ associated with the largest eigenvalues. In our case P consists of one eigenvector corresponding to the largest eigenvalue of T since the first eigenvalue $(4.8317e-04)$ is much bigger than the second largest one (4.5114e-18). Correspondingly, each 16×16 window is mapped to one value:

$$Y = P^T X \tag{3}$$

Figure 3a is the neural network result and 3b is the *LDA* result. In both cases the solid line represents text and the dash line represents nontext. We can see the data in Figure 3a is more easily separable than in 3b, which suggests the neural network has a better performance than *LDA*.

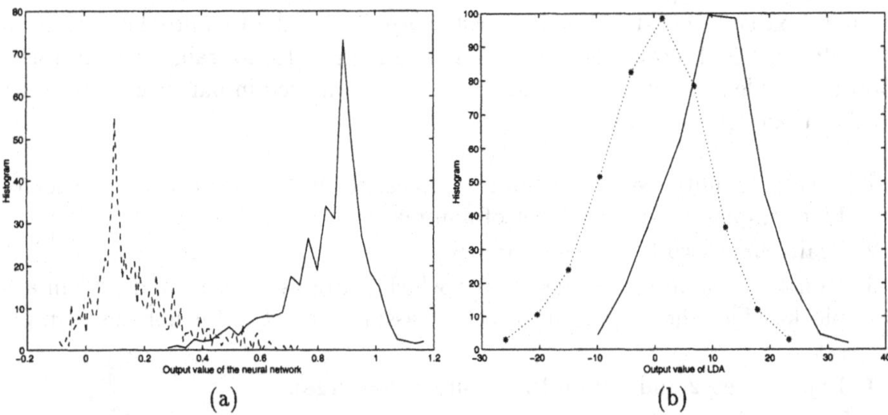

Fig. 3. The comparison of the output distribution when we use trained neural network and LDA for the testing text and nontext blocks. In both cases the solid line represents text and the dash line represents nontext. (a) The distribution of neural network output, (b) The distribution of *LDA* output.

2.4 Text Detection

After training the neural network, we use a 16×16 window to scan the video frame to classify each window as text or nontext. The larger the window step, the fewer the number of windows to be processed but the less refined the result. Considering the trade-off between the precision and speed, we move the window 4 pixels at a time.

If a single window is classified as text, all the pixels in this window are labeled as text. Those pixels which are not covered by any text window are labeled as nontext. The result of classification is a label map of the original image. Figure 4(a) is a video frame and Figure 4(b) is the classified label map corresponding to Figure 4(a). Figure 4(c) shows the extracted text regions. We can see all of the text is labeled correctly, but there are some small isolated areas which are incorrectly labeled as text. We use size constraints between blocks to filter out these areas. The bounding box of the text area is generated by a connected component analysis of the text windows. Figure 4(d) is the result after we filter out the non-text areas and generate the bounding box.

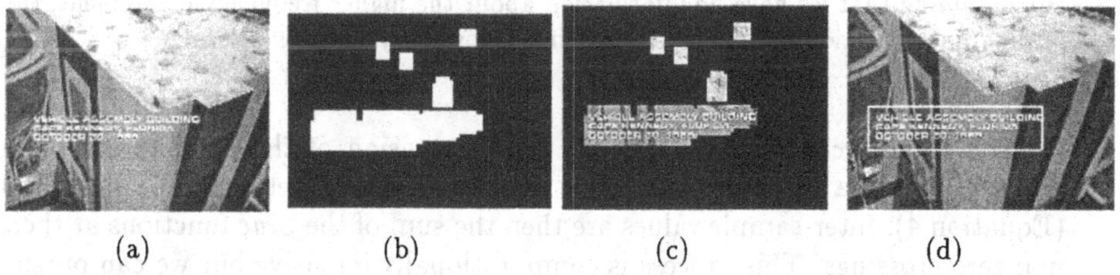

Fig. 4. (a) Original frame, (b) The classified label map, (c) The segmented text area corresponding to (b), (d) The segmented text area after postprocessing and bounding box generation.

3 Text Resolution Enhancement

Video images are limited in spatial resolution. In typical document images, 300 *dpi* is common with characters occupying an area as large as 40×40 pixels. In *MPEG-1* each frame is digitized and subsampled to 352×240 pixels with text rendered as small as 10×10 pixels. Text in this resolution is readable by humans but may not be sufficient for computers to recognize. Image resolution enhancement is necessary to improve the OCR results.

In digital video, a lowpass filter is often applied to filter the high resolution image before subsampling in order to eliminate aliasing. Suppose the original high resolution image is I_0 and the available low resolution image is I. We can model I as the image obtained from lowpass filtering a high resolution image I_0 followed by downsampling (Figure 5a). Since the high frequency information has been lost, it is impossible to recover the original image I_0 from I. If we assume that no information about the high frequency components is available, the optimal interpolation scheme which yields the least mean squared error is upsampling the image I followed by passing the resulting image through a lowpass filter (Figure 5b). It is easy to show that the resulting image I' has the same frequency content as I'_0.

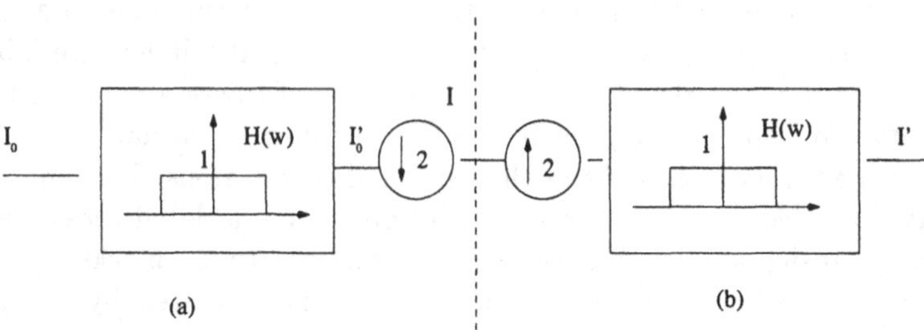

Fig. 5. Problem models. (a) Model the available low resolution image I as the image obtained from lowpass filtering a higher resolution image I_0 followed by downsampling. (b) Assuming that we have no information about the higher frequency component, the optimal interpolation scheme is upsampling followed by lowpass filtering.

The scheme can be implemented as an extension of the Nyquist sampling theorem where a sampled image is a weighted sum of delayed *Sinc* functions (Equation 4). Inter-sample values are then the sum of the *Sinc* functions at their non-zero crossings. This process is computationally intensive but we can pursue a frequency-based approach. The dual of the weighted *Sinc* functions can be performed by Fast Fourier Transforms (FFT) and matrix masking. We increase the resolution of our images by copying each pixel to neighboring pixels in the amount of the desired increase in resolution. We then take the two dimensional FFT. The resulting matrix is then multiplied by a mask matrix which zeros in the high frequency components. The number of low frequency components that are preserved is equal to the size of the original image. This in effect is a low pass filter where high frequency components introduced by copying pixels to neighboring pixels are removed. An inverse two dimensional FFT renders the image in the higher resolution. Figure 6b shows the result of the increase in resolution of Figure 6a by a factor of four. This task does not require a lot of processing and can be easily encoded in hardware.

$$i(X,Y) = \sum_{x=1}^{N}\sum_{y=1}^{M} i(x,y) sinc(X-x, Y-y), \text{ for } X \in \Re(1,N) \text{ and } Y \in \Re(1,M) \tag{4}$$

4 Postprocessing

4.1 Identification of Inverse Text

The classification of normal text and inverse text is necessary since typical OCR software can only handle binary images with black pixels representing text and

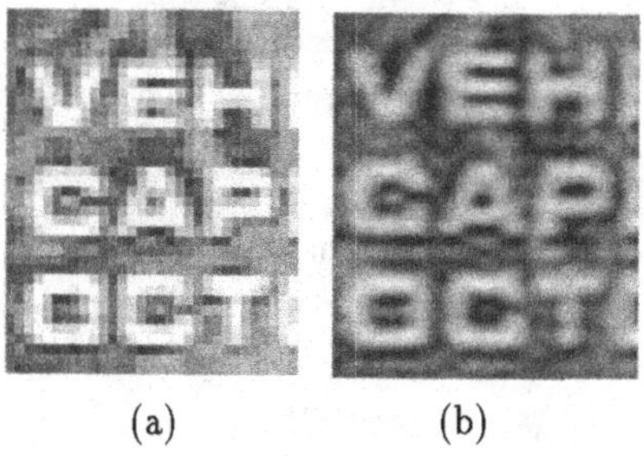

Fig. 6. (a) Anti-aliased image showing blurred edges, (b) Zoomed image by Shannon's interpolation.

white pixels representing background. The scheme we use is simple: First, we calculate the global thresholding value **Th**. The background is typically defined as the maximum part of the histogram of the image, so we can make our decision by comparing the threshold **Th** and the background value **Bg** which corresponds to the maximum part of the histogram. Specifically, if we find **Th** > **Bg**, then it is normal text, otherwise, it is inverse text.

4.2 Adaptive Thresholding

Due to the large variations in font size and contrast with the background, adaptive thresholding techniques are usually required to binarize text blocks. We use modified Niblack's adaptive thresholding method [20] to threshold text images. The basic idea of Niblack's method is to vary a threshold over the image, based on the local mean m and local standard deviation d computed in a small neighborhood of each pixel. A threshold for each pixel is computed from $T = d + k * s$, where k is a user defined parameter. The result of this method is not good for background containing light textures.

We incorporate a simple classification scheme into Niblack's algorithm to improve both the binarization result and speed. Considering that text usually has significant contrast with the background and therefore has a larger standard deviation d than background areas, we can set all pixels in a window as background if the standard deviation $d < th$. We collected over 600 text blocks to determine the proper value for th. As a result, both the binarization result and speed are improved (Figure 7).

5 Experimental Results

5.1 Evaluation of Text Detection

We collected two sets of data for experiments. The first set of data included 500 key frames selected automatically from *MPEG* video using key frame detection algorithm [21]. The second data set included 75 frames selected manually from

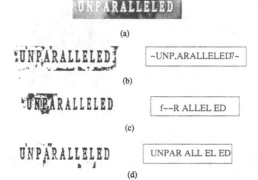

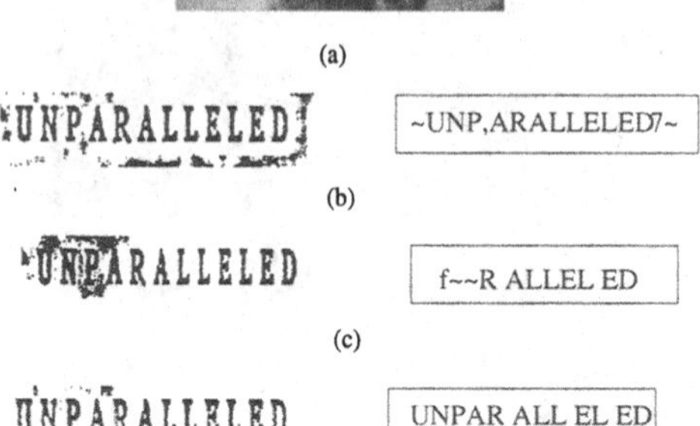

Fig. 7. (a) A gray-scale text block, (b) Global Thresholding and OCR result, (c) Niblack's method and OCR result, (d) Our method and OCR result.

cable TV by using *miro VIDEO DC30 plus* video capture board. The samples include both scene text and graphic text with multiple font sizes.

The detection procedure requires about 1 second on a *Sun Workstation Ultra 1* to process a 352×240 frame with unoptimized code. Classification (including feature extraction) takes 0.5 second; postprocessing and image input and output take another 0.5 second.

Evaluation of Text Event Detection Text event detection checks if a video frame contains text or not and is useful in video indexing and retrieval as well as video classification. We output 1 if a frame contains text and 0 if the frame does not contain text. In 500 video frames, 151 of them contain text and the remaining 349 frames do not contain text (Table 1).

	text	nontext
text (151)	133 (88%)	18(12%)
nontext (349)	81 (23%)	268 (77%)

Table 1. The confusion matrix for text event detection

We use two metrics (*precision* and *recall*) commonly used in information retrieval (IR) to evaluate text event detection:

$$\begin{aligned} precision &= \frac{\text{correctly detected text frames}}{\text{totally returned text frames}} \\ recall &= \frac{\text{correctly detected text frames}}{\text{total text frames in data set}} \end{aligned} \quad (5)$$

Therefore, the *recall* is $\frac{133}{151} = 88\%$ and the *precision* is $\frac{133}{133+81} = 62\%$. *Precision* is relatively low in part because the number of non-text frames is more than that of text frames.

Evaluation of Text Block Detection The second data set is used to evaluate the extraction of text blocks. A text block may contain one or more text lines which are close to each other. There are a total of 153 text blocks in the 75 frames. 142 (93%) of them were correctly detected by our algorithm (Figure 8) and 11 (7%) of them were missed. Errors occur primarily because of low resolution or small text block size. On the other hand, 14 non-text blocks are misclassified as text blocks. Further training, domain-specific training, or attempting OCR will overcome these problems.

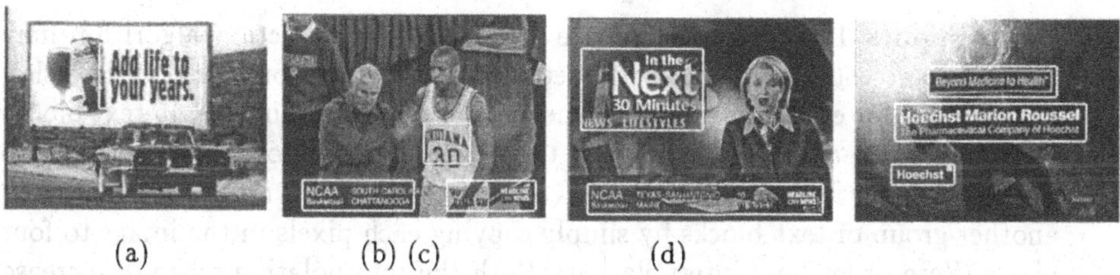

(a) (b) (c) (d)

Fig. 8. Correct results. (a) Reverse text with large font size, (b) Text with low resolution (bottom) and scene text (text on T-shirt of athlete), (c) Text with different font sizes, (d) Text with different font styles.

5.2 Evaluation of Text Enhancement

In this section we describe the experimental setup for enhancement based on OCR. It should be noted that we do not intend to implement our OCR system since there exists many commercial OCR packages. The OCR software we used in our experiment is Xerox TextBridge Pro98. After binarization of text image, we manually feed the image to TextBridge Pro98 for recognition.

Evaluation Metrics The evaluation software we use for OCR is *ope* provided by the University of Washington [22]. *Ope* performs string matching between the ground truth data and the recognized data by counting the amount of character substitutions, insertions, and deletions. The outputs of *ope* have the following parameters:

T : character number of ground truth;
O : character number from OCR output;
R : correctly recognized character number;
D : number of deletion operation;
I : number of insertion operation ;
S : number of substitution operation;

We use the following metrics to evaluate the OCR results:

- *Accuracy* (or *Recall*). Accuracy can be defined as the ratio of correctly recognized character number **R** to character number of ground truth **T** ($accuracy = \frac{R}{T}$).
- *Precision.* Precision is defined as the ratio of correctly recognized character number **R** to character number from OCR output **O** ($Precision = \frac{R}{O}$).
- *Cost.* Cost is defined as the weighted sum of number of deletion (**D**), insertion (**I**) and substitution (**S**) ($cost = D+I+S$). Here we suppose each operation has the same weight.

Experiments In order to eliminate the effect text detection algorithm may introduce, we collected 45 correctly detected text blocks from our text detection experiments for enhancement experiments. We generated another 45 text blocks by Shannon interpolation to magnify the image in the factor of two. In order to observe how our interpolation scheme can improve the OCR results, we generated another group of text blocks by simply copying each pixels in the image to four pixels (Zero order hold interpolation). Both the interpolation schemes increase the resolution by a factor of two. The same text separation scheme mentioned above is applied to all the original text blocks and the interpolated text blocks.

	No Enhancement	Zero order hold Interpolation	Shannon Interpolation
# of Total Blocks	45	45	45
# of Blocks Having OCR Output	13(29%)	36(80%)	45(100%)
# of Ground Truth Characters (T)	1452	1452	1452
# of OCR Output Symbols (O)	308	1032	1341
# of Matched Symbols (R)	188	489	970
# of Deletion Operation (D)	1164	651	241
# of Insertion Operation (I)	20	231	111
# of Substitution Operation (S)	100	312	269
Accuracy $\frac{R}{T}$	13%	34%	66.8%
Precision $\frac{R}{O}$	61%	47%	72%
Cost $D+I+S$	1284	1194	621

Table 2. The Performance evaluation of OCR result with no enhancement, zero order hold and Shannon interpolation (interpolation factor is 2).

As shown in Table 2, only 13(29%) text blocks have OCR output before enhancement, but a significant improvement is achieved even with Zero order hold interpolation (36(80%)). All 45 text blocks have OCR output for Shannon interpolation. The difference here tells us the resolution of most text blocks is beyond the machine recognition capability if no resolution enhancement is performed.

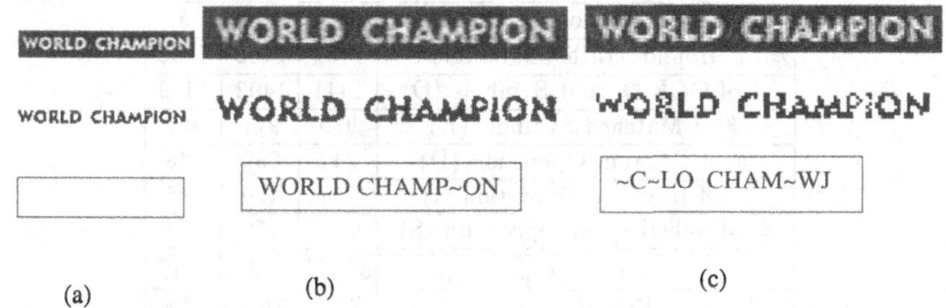

Fig. 9. Comparison of OCR results. (a) No enhancement, (b) Zero order hold interpolation, (c) Shannon interpolation.

There are a total of 1452 characters in the 45 text blocks. Before enhancement, only 188(13%) are correctly OCRed. This is insufficient for any successful indexing operation. For Zero order hold interpolation, the OCR accuracy rate rises to 34% and we observe 66.8% correct rate for Shannon interpolation. We also can see Shannon interpolation has the best precision (72%). The precision of no interpolation is better than Zero order hold interpolation because there are few character outputs in the case of no interpolation. The *Cost* of Shannon interpolation is much smaller than Zero order hold interpolation or no interpolation. Figure 9 shows an example of these three cases. We can see there is no OCR output for original image (Figure 9a), and although Zero order hold interpolation has OCR output, there are considerable recognition errors (Figure 9b). Figure 9c shows the recognition result for Shannon interpolation.

In order to investigate the relation between the interpolation factor and OCR accuracy, we interpolate the image by factor of 4 and 8, respectively for Shannon interpolation. The output of *ope* is shown in Table 3. We can see an increase in image resolution does not necessarily improve OCR accuracy. OCR accuracy at factor 4 is slightly better than that at factor 2. However, the performance begins to decrease at factor 8. Note that the average character sizes are 40×40 for interpolated image at factor 4, which corresponds to 300 *dpi* in typical document images. Consequently, character sizes at factor 2 and 8 correspond to 200 *dpi* and 600 *dpi* respectively. To most commercial OCR software, documents scanned with 300 *dpi* achieve the best OCR results [23].

Although these results are far from perfect, we do not discriminate whether text blocks are OCRable or not (Figure 10). It is very encouraging that we observed over 500% improvement.

6 Discussion and Conclusions

We have presented a hybrid wavelet/neural network method to detect both graphical and scene text in digital video and a text enhancement scheme to improve OCR accuracy in digital video. The text detection algorithm can detect 93% of text blocks. An overall 67% OCR accuracy rate is achieved after enhancement compared with only 13% accuracy rate with no enhancement.

Interpolation Factor	2	4	8
# of Ground Truth Characters (T)	1452	1452	1452
# of OCR Output Symbols (O)	1341	1402	1336
# of Matched Symbols (R)	970	977	892
# of Deletion Operation (D)	241	239	248
# of Insertion Operation (I)	111	120	105
# of Substitution Operation (S)	269	250	279
Accuracy $\frac{R}{T}$	66.8%	67.3%	61.4%
Precision $\frac{R}{O}$	72%	70%	67%
Cost $D+I+S$	621	609	632

Table 3. The Performance evaluation of OCR results with different interpolation factors

Fig. 10. Even with enhancement, there is still no OCR output due to poor image quality.

The experiments on text recognition raise several interesting challenges in text-based indexing of digital video. First, we expect to find missing or incorrectly segmented characters and only partial OCR results. As a result, exact matches between words will not always be possible. *Approximate word matching* instead of *exact word matching* is a possible aid. Second, text in digital video is usually very terse and may lack semantic breadth. *Wordnet* can be used to extend semantic connections. Our next goal is to build a text-based indexing system in digital video database.

References

1. G. Piccioli, E. De Micheli, P. Parodi, and M. Campani. Robust method for road sign detection and recognition. *Image and Vision Computing*, 14:209–254, 1996.
2. S.K. Kim, D.W. Kim, and H.J. Kim. A recognition of vehicle license plate using a genetic algorithm based segmentation. In *Proceedings of ICIP*, pages 661–664, 1996.
3. T. Gotoh, T. Toriu, S. Sasaki, and M. Yoshida. A flexible vision-based algorithm for a book sorting system. *IEEE Trans. PAMI*, 10:393–399, 1988.
4. J. Zhou, D. Lopresti, and T. Tasdizen. Finding text in color images. In *Proceedings of SPIE, Document Recognition V*, pages 130–140, 1998.
5. R. Lienhart and F. Stuber. Automatic text recognition in digital videos. In *Proceedings of ACM Multimedia*, pages 11–20, 1996.
6. A.K. Jain and B. Yu. Automatic text location in images and video frames. In *Proceedings of ICPR*, pages 1497–1499, 1998.

7. Hae-Kwang Kim. Efficient automatic text location method and content-based indexing and structuring of video database. *Journal of Visual Communication and Image Representation*, 7:336–344, 1996.
8. C-M. Lee and A. Kankanhalli. Automatic extraction of characters in complex scene images. *International Journal of Pattern Rocgnition and Artificial Intelligence*, 9:67–82, 1995.
9. J. Ohya, A. Shio, and S. Akamatsu. Recognizing characters in scene images. *IEEE Trans. PAMI*, 16:214 - 220, 1994.
10. A.K. Jain and S. Bhattacharjee. Text segmentation using Gabor filters for automatic document processing. *Machine Vision and Applications*, 5:169 - 184, 1992.
11. V. Wu, R. Manmatha, and E.M. Riseman. Automatic text detection and recognition. pages 707–712. 5 1997.
12. Y. Zhong, K. Karu, and A.K. Jain. Locating text in complex color images. *Pattern Recognition*, 28:1523–1236, 1995.
13. John D. Hobby and Tin K. Ho. Enhancing degraded document images via bitmap clustering and averaging. In *ICDAR'97: Fourth International Conference on Document Analysis and Recogntion*, pages 394–400, August 1997.
14. J. Liang and R.M. Haralick. Document image restoration using binary morphological filters. In *SPIE Vol. 2660*, 1996.
15. J. Shim, C. Dorai, and R. Bolle. Automatic text extraction from video for content-based annotation and retrieval. In *Proceedings of ICPR*, pages 618–620, 1998.
16. J. Zhou and D. Lopresti. Ocr for world wide web images. In *Proceedings of SPIE, Document Recognition IV*, pages 58–66, 1997.
17. S. G. Mallat. A theory for multiresolution signal decomposition: The wavelet representation. *IEEE Trans. PAMI*, 11:674–693, 1989.
18. K. Sung and T. Poggio. Example-based learning for view-based human face detection. Technical report, MIT, A.I. Memo 1521, CBCL Paper 112, 1994.
19. K. Fukunaga. *Introduction to Statistical Pattern Recognition.* Academic Press, New York, 1990.
20. Niblack W. In *An introduction to image processing*, pages 115–116, Englewood Cliffs, N.J.:Prentice Hall, 1986.
21. V. Kobla, D.S. Doermann, and K.I. Lin. Archiving, indexing, and retrieval of video in the compressed domain. In *Proc. of the SPIE Conference on Multimedia Storage and Archiving Systems*, volume 2916, pages 78–89, 1996.
22. S. Chen. OCR performance evaluation software – user's manual. In *The University of Washington Database.*
23. T. Kanungo, G. A. Marton, and O. Bulbul. Omnipage vs. sakhr: Paired model evaluation of two arabic ocr products. In *Proc. of the SPIE Conference on Document Recognition and Retrieval (VI)*, volume 3651, 1999.

Lecture Notes in Computer Science

For information about Vols. 1–1610
please contact your bookseller or Springer-Verlag

Vol. 1611: I. Imam, Y. Kodratoff, A. El-Dessouki, M. Ali (Eds.), Multiple Approaches to Intelligent Systems. Proceedings, 1999. XIX, 899 pages. 1999. (Subseries LNAI).

Vol. 1612: R. Bergmann, S. Breen, M. Göker, M. Manago, S. Wess, Developing Industrial Case-Based Reasoning Applications. XX, 188 pages. 1999. (Subseries LNAI).

Vol. 1613: A. Kuba, M. Šámal, A. Todd-Pokropek (Eds.), Information Processing in Medical Imaging. Proceedings, 1999. XVII, 508 pages. 1999.

Vol. 1614: D.P. Huijsmans, A.W.M. Smeulders (Eds.), Visual Information and Information Systems. Proceedings, 1999. XVII, 827 pages. 1999.

Vol. 1615: C. Polychronopoulos, K. Joe, A. Fukuda, S. Tomita (Eds.), High Performance Computing. Proceedings, 1999. XIV, 408 pages. 1999.

Vol. 1616: P. Cointe (Ed.), Meta-Level Architectures and Reflection. Proceedings, 1999. XI, 273 pages. 1999.

Vol. 1617: N.V. Murray (Ed.), Automated Reasoning with Analytic Tableaux and Related Methods. Proceedings, 1999. X, 325 pages. 1999. (Subseries LNAI).

Vol. 1618: J. Bézivin, P.-A. Muller (Eds.), The Unified Modeling Language. Proceedings, 1998. IX, 443 pages. 1999.

Vol. 1619: M.T. Goodrich, C.C. McGeoch (Eds.), Algorithm Engineering and Experimentation. Proceedings, 1999. VIII, 349 pages. 1999.

Vol. 1620: W. Horn, Y. Shahar, G. Lindberg, S. Andreassen, J. Wyatt (Eds.), Artificial Intelligence in Medicine. Proceedings, 1999. XIII, 454 pages. 1999. (Subseries LNAI).

Vol. 1621: D. Fensel, R. Studer (Eds.), Knowledge Acquisition Modeling and Management. Proceedings, 1999. XI, 404 pages. 1999. (Subseries LNAI).

Vol. 1622: M. González Harbour, J.A. de la Puente (Eds.), Reliable Software Technologies – Ada-Europe'99. Proceedings, 1999. XIII, 451 pages. 1999.

Vol. 1623: T. Reinartz, Focusing Solutions for Data Mining. XV, 309 pages. 1999. (Subseries LNAI).

Vol. 1625: B. Reusch (Ed.), Computational Intelligence. Proceedings, 1999. XIV, 710 pages. 1999.

Vol. 1626: M. Jarke, A. Oberweis (Eds.), Advanced Information Systems Engineering. Proceedings, 1999. XIV, 478 pages. 1999.

Vol. 1627: T. Asano, H. Imai, D.T. Lee, S.-i. Nakano, T. Tokuyama (Eds.), Computing and Combinatorics. Proceedings, 1999. XIV, 494 pages. 1999.

Col. 1628: R. Guerraoui (Ed.), ECOOP'99 - Object-Oriented Programming. Proceedings, 1999. XIII, 529 pages. 1999.

Vol. 1629: H. Leopold, N. García (Eds.), Multimedia Applications, Services and Techniques - ECMAST'99. Proceedings, 1999. XV, 574 pages. 1999.

Vol. 1631: P. Narendran, M. Rusinowitch (Eds.), Rewriting Techniques and Applications. Proceedings, 1999. XI, 397 pages. 1999.

Vol. 1632: H. Ganzinger (Ed.), Automated Deduction – Cade-16. Proceedings, 1999. XIV, 429 pages. 1999. (Subseries LNAI).

Vol. 1633: N. Halbwachs, D. Peled (Eds.), Computer Aided Verification. Proceedings, 1999. XII, 506 pages. 1999.

Vol. 1634: S. Džeroski, P. Flach (Eds.), Inductive Logic Programming. Proceedings, 1999. VIII, 303 pages. 1999. (Subseries LNAI).

Vol. 1636: L. Knudsen (Ed.), Fast Software Encryption. Proceedings, 1999. VIII, 317 pages. 1999.

Vol. 1637: J.P. Walser, Integer Optimization by Local Search. XIX, 137 pages. 1999. (Subseries LNAI).

Vol. 1638: A. Hunter, S. Parsons (Eds.), Symbolic and Quantitative Approaches to Reasoning and Uncertainty. Proceedings, 1999. IX, 397 pages. 1999. (Subseries LNAI).

Vol. 1639: S. Donatelli, J. Kleijn (Eds.), Application and Theory of Petri Nets 1999. Proceedings, 1999. VIII, 425 pages. 1999.

Vol. 1640: W. Tepfenhart, W. Cyre (Eds.), Conceptual Structures: Standards and Practices. Proceedings, 1999. XII, 515 pages. 1999. (Subseries LNAI).

Vol. 1641: D. Hutter, W. Stephan, P. Traverso, M. Ullmann (Eds.), Applied Formal Methods – FM-Trends 98. Proceedings, 1998. XI, 377 pages. 1999.

Vol. 1642: D.J. Hand, J.N. Kok, M.R. Berthold (Eds.), Advances in Intelligent Data Analysis. Proceedings, 1999. XII, 538 pages. 1999.

Vol. 1643: J. Nešetřil (Ed.), Algorithms – ESA '99. Proceedings, 1999. XII, 552 pages. 1999.

Vol. 1644: J. Wiedermann, P. van Emde Boas, M. Nielsen (Eds.), Automata, Languages, and Programming. Proceedings, 1999. XIV, 720 pages. 1999.

Vol. 1645: M. Crochemore, M. Paterson (Eds.), Combinatorial Pattern Matching. Proceedings, 1999. VIII, 295 pages. 1999.

Vol. 1647: F.J. Garijo, M. Boman (Eds.), Multi-Agent System Engineering. Proceedings, 1999. X, 233 pages. 1999. (Subseries LNAI).

Vol. 1648: M. Franklin (Ed.), Financial Cryptography. Proceedings, 1999. VIII, 269 pages. 1999.

Vol. 1649: R.Y. Pinter, S. Tsur (Eds.), Next Generation Information Technologies and Systems. Proceedings, 1999. IX, 327 pages. 1999.

Vol. 1650: K.-D. Althoff, R. Bergmann, L.K. Branting (Eds.), Case-Based Reasoning Research and Development. Proceedings, 1999. XII, 598 pages. 1999. (Subseries LNAI).

Vol. 1651: R.H. Güting, D. Papadias, F. Lochovsky (Eds.), Advances in Spatial Databases. Proceedings, 1999. XI, 371 pages. 1999.

Vol. 1652: M. Klusch, O.M. Shehory, G. Weiss (Eds.), Cooperative Information Agents III. Proceedings, 1999. XI, 404 pages. 1999. (Subseries LNAI).

Vol. 1653: S. Covaci (Ed.), Active Networks. Proceedings, 1999. XIII, 346 pages. 1999.

Vol. 1654: E.R. Hancock, M. Pelillo (Eds.), Energy Minimization Methods in Computer Vision and Pattern Recognition. Proceedings, 1999. IX, 331 pages. 1999.

Vol. 1655: S.-W. Lee, Y. Nakano (Eds.), Document Analysis Systems: Theory and Practice. Proceedings, 1998. XI, 377 pages. 1999.

Vol. 1656: S. Chatterjee, J.F. Prins, L. Carter, J. Ferrante, Z. Li, D. Sehr, P.-C. Yew (Eds.), Languages and Compilers for Parallel Computing. Proceedings, 1998. XI, 384 pages. 1999.

Vol. 1661: C. Freksa, D.M. Mark (Eds.), Spatial Information Theory. Proceedings, 1999. XIII, 477 pages. 1999.

Vol. 1662: V. Malyshkin (Ed.), Parallel Computing Technologies. Proceedings, 1999. XIX, 510 pages. 1999.

Vol. 1663: F. Dehne, A. Gupta. J.-R. Sack, R. Tamassia (Eds.), Algorithms and Data Structures. Proceedings, 1999. IX, 366 pages. 1999.

Vol. 1664: J.C.M. Baeten, S. Mauw (Eds.), CONCUR'99. Concurrency Theory. Proceedings, 1999. XI, 573 pages. 1999.

Vol. 1666: M. Wiener (Ed.), Advances in Cryptology – CRYPTO '99. Proceedings, 1999. XII, 639 pages. 1999.

Vol. 1667: J. Hlavička, E. Maehle, A. Pataricza (Eds.), Dependable Computing – EDCC-3. Proceedings, 1999. XVIII, 455 pages. 1999.

Vol. 1668: J.S. Vitter, C.D. Zaroliagis (Eds.), Algorithm Engineering. Proceedings, 1999. VIII, 361 pages. 1999.

Vol. 1671: D. Hochbaum, K. Jansen, J.D.P. Rolim, A. Sinclair (Eds.), Randomization, Approximation, and Combinatorial Optimization. Proceedings, 1999. IX, 289 pages. 1999.

Vol. 1672: M. Kutylowski, L. Pacholski, T. Wierzbicki (Eds.), Mathematical Foundations of Computer Science 1999. Proceedings, 1999. XII, 455 pages. 1999.

Vol. 1673: P. Lysaght, J. Irvine, R. Hartenstein (Eds.), Field Programmable Logic and Applications. Proceedings, 1999. XI, 541 pages. 1999.

Vol. 1674: D. Floreano, J.-D. Nicoud, F. Mondada (Eds.), Advances in Artificial Life. Proceedings, 1999. XVI, 737 pages. 1999. (Subseries LNAI).

Vol. 1675: J. Estublier (Ed.), System Configuration Management. Proceedings, 1999. VIII, 255 pages. 1999.

Vol. 1976: M. Mohania, A M. Tjoa (Eds.), Data Warehousing and Knowledge Discovery. Proceedings, 1999. XII, 400 pages. 1999.

Vol. 1677: T. Bench-Capon, G. Soda, A M. Tjoa (Eds.), Database and Expert Systems Applications. Proceedings, 1999. XVIII, 1105 pages. 1999.

Vol. 1678: M.H. Böhlen, C.S. Jensen, M.O. Scholl (Eds.), Spatio-Temporal Database Management. Proceedings, 1999. X, 243 pages. 1999.

Vol. 1679: C. Taylor, A. Colchester (Eds.), Medical Image Computing and Computer-Assisted Intervention – MICCAI'99. Proceedings, 1999. XXI, 1240 pages. 1999.

Vol. 1680: D. Dams, R. Gerth, S. Leue, M. Massink (Eds.), Theoretical and Practical Aspects of SPIN Model Checking. Proceedings, 1999. X, 277 pages. 1999.

Vol. 1682: M. Nielsen, P. Johansen, O.F. Olsen, J. Weickert (Eds.), Scale-Space Theories in Computer Vision. Proceedings, 1999. XII, 532 pages. 1999.

Vol. 1684: G. Ciobanu, G. Păun (Eds.), Fundamentals of Computation Theory. Proceedings, 1999. XI, 570 pages. 1999.

Vol. 1685: P. Amestoy, P. Berger, M. Daydé, I. Duff, V. Frayssé, L. Giraud, D. Ruiz (Eds.), Euro-Par'99. Parallel Processing. Proceedings, 1999. XXXII, 1503 pages. 1999.

Vol. 1687: O. Nierstrasz, M. Lemoine (Eds.), Software Engineering – ESEC/FSE '99. Proceedings, 1999. XII, 529 pages. 1999.

Vol. 1688: P. Bouquet, L. Serafini, P. Brézillon, M. Benerecetti, F. Castellani (Eds.), Modeling and Using Context. Proceedings, 1999. XII, 528 pages. 1999. (Subseries LNAI).

Vol. 1689: F. Solina, A. Leonardis (Eds.), Computer Analysis of Images and Patterns. Proceedings, 1999. XIV, 650 pages. 1999.

Vol. 1690: Y. Bertot, G. Dowek, A. Hirschowitz, C. Paulin, L. Théry (Eds.), Theorem Proving in Higher Order Logics. Proceedings, 1999. VIII, 359 pages. 1999.

Vol. 1691: J. Eder, I. Rozman, T. Welzer (Eds.), Advances in Databases and Information Systems. Proceedings, 1999. XIII, 383 pages. 1999.

Vol. 1692: V. Matoušek, P. Mautner, J. Ocelíková, P. Sojka (Eds.), Text, Speech and Dialogue. Proceedings, 1999. XI, 396 pages. 1999. (Subseries LNAI).

Vol. 1693: P. Jayanti (Ed.), Distributed Computing. Proceedings, 1999. X, 357 pages. 1999.

Vol. 1694: A. Cortesi, G. Filé (Eds.), Static Analysis. Proceedings, 1999. VIII, 357 pages. 1999.

Vol. 1698: M. Felici, K. Kanoun, A. Pasquini (Eds.), Computer Safety, Reliability and Security. Proceedings, 1999. XVIII, 482 pages. 1999.

Vol. 1699: S. Albayrak (Ed.), Intelligent Agents for Telecommunication Applications. Proceedings, 1999. IX, 191 pages. 1999. (Subseries LNAI).

Vol. 1701: W. Burgard, T. Christaller, A.B. Cremers (Eds.), KI-99: Advances in Artificial Intelligence. Proceedings, 1999. XI, 311 pages. 1999. (Subseries LNAI).

Vol. 1702: G. Nadathur (Ed.), Principles and Practice of Declarative Programming. Proceedings, 1999. X, 434 pages. 1999.

Vol. 1704: Jan M. Żytkow, J. Rauch (Eds.), Principles of Data Mining and Knowledge Discovery. Proceedings, 1999. XIV, 593 pages. 1999. (Subseries LNAI).

Vol. 1705: H. Ganzinger, D. McAllester, A. Voronkov (Eds.), Logic for Programming and Automated Reasoning. Proceedings, 1999. XII, 397 pages. 1999. (Subseries LNAI).